2015
BLACKBOOK
PRICE GUIDE TO
UNITED STATES
PAPER
MONEY

THE OFFICIAL®

2015
BLACKBOOK
PRICE GUIDE TO
UNITED STATES
PAPER
MONEY

FORTY-SEVENTH EDITION

BY MARC HUDGEONS, N.L.G.
& TOM HUDGEONS, Jr.
& TOM HUDGEONS, Sr.

HOUSE OF COLLECTIBLES

Random House Reference • New York

Copyright © 2014 by Random House LLC

All rights reserved. Published in the United States by House of Collectibles, an imprint of Random House LLC, New York, a Penguin Random House Company and in Canada by Random House of Canada Limited, Toronto.

House of Collectibles and colophon are registered trademarks of Random House LLC

RANDOM HOUSE is a registered trademark of Random House, LLC.

Please address inquiries about electronic licensing of any products for use on a network, in software, or on CD-ROM to the Subsidiary Rights Department, Random House Audio Publishing Group, fax 212-572-6003.

This book is available for special discounts for bulk purchases for sales promotions or premiums. Special editions, including personalized covers, excerpts of existing books, and corporate imprints, can be created in large quantities for special needs. For more information, write to Random House LLC, Special Markets/Premium Sales, 1745 Broadway, MD 3–1, New York, NY 10019 or e-mail specialmarkets@randomhouse.com.

Visit the Random House Web site:
www.randomhouse.com

ISBN: 978-0-375-72356-8

ISSN: 0195-3540

Printed in the United States of America

10 9 8 7 6 5 4 3 2 1

Forty-Seventh Edition: June 2014

CONTENTS

OFFICIAL BOARD OF CONTRIBUTORS

We would like to thank the following contributors for sharing their professional expertise and experiences in the field of United States Paper Money with our readers.

Scott Barman for his article "Using Technology to Enhance Your Collecting Experience". Scott is a collector and author of the Coin Collectors Blog (coinsblog.ws). He is also President of the Montgomery County Coin Club (montgomerycoinclub. org) and President of the Maryland State Numismatic Society (mdstatenumisassn.org). After more than 30 years in the computer and information security industry, Scott recently started Having-Fun Collectibles to serve collectors in multiple markets.

Doris A. & Frederick J. Bart of Executive Currency in Roseville, MI for their article "Error or Freak Notes".

Doris A. Bart is the co-author of chapters on paper money errors which appear in major guidebooks such as Paper Money of the United States (Friedberg), Standard Catalog of United States Paper Money (Cuhaj) and others. She attends every major paper money convention, where she regularly provides auction representation for her clients. Her ability to guide clients to a fair market value and bid for several clients in the same sale is respected industry-wide.

Frederick J. Bart joined the ANA in 1973 foreshadowing a lifelong involvement in coins and currency. After a decade of performing reconstructive surgery, Fred returned to his first love, Bart, Inc. (the parent corporation of Executive Currency). Frederick J. Bart is the author of *United States Paper Money Errors,* currently in its 3rd edition. He has appeared on CNN, NBC and been quoted in USA today.

PUBLISHER'S NOTE

The Official® Blackbook Price Guide to United States Paper Money is designed as a reference aid for collectors, dealers, and the general public. Its purpose is to provide historical and collecting data, as well as current values. Prices are as accurate as possible at the time of going to press, but no guarantee is made. We are not dealers; persons wishing to buy or sell paper money, or have it appraised, are advised to consult collector magazines or the telephone directory for addresses of dealers. We are not responsible for typographical errors.

NOTE TO READERS

All advertisements appearing in this book have been accepted in good faith, but the publisher assumes no responsibility in any transactions that occur between readers and advertisers.

THE OFFICIAL

2015
BLACKBOOK
PRICE GUIDE TO
UNITED STATES
PAPER
MONEY

Market Review
By Bruce Roland Hagen

The more things change, the more they stay the same, and that can be said with the collectible paper money market during calendar 2013 and the prior two years. However, one caveat should be added. 2013 saw some stunningly high auction realizations or private treaty sales of high-ticket Federal large notes into the seven figures. This seemingly created a theoretical valley between the rest of the market and these thermometer exploding million dollar notes. Stack's Bowers Galleries privately placed a $1000 Marcy Silver Certificate (Friedberg 346e) for $2,600,000 in May; a record price for a United States Currency note. In auctions, a few notes broke the seven-figure mark which, of course, was a dream state less than ten years ago. The good news is that when those elite echelon of collectors, limited to a handful, are striving for the trophy notes, there are plenty of desirable notes to acquire for collections in all price ranges.

Much of the trading done these days is over the internet or privately. However, shows still have relevance for the trade and advanced collectors to gather and participate in major auctions. Like always, Memphis and the ANA were both strong trading events in most areas and with few surprises. At Memphis, collectible Federal type notes continue their way back and are in strong demand. At the ANA, all genres of American currency fetched strong prices with several collections new to the fraternity offered. Overall, the enthusiasm at auctions and across internet sales continued for superior items. The significant large format auctions like FUN, Memphis and the ANA Paper Money session were the best attended as logic and tradition dictate. Internet-Only sales and auction catalogue sections are often excellent places for collectors to obtain items for their collections because many dealers have cut down on show travel due the hassles of travel and expense.

Large Size Notes: (1861-1923 series) Large Size was often hotly contested in the auctions of 2013, just like in 2012, and particularly the most popular types. The demand for high grade

"PPQ" and "EPQ" notes is very apparent. Both the FUN and ANA auctions saw significant attention with name collections new to the market. Fresh and vibrant Very Fine and Extremely Fine notes always stay in vogue, as well as the glorious high-end notes that are the "real deal." However, "off quality" Uncirculated notes will sell for less than a high-end, handsome About Uncirculated of the same type.

Small Size Notes: (1928-present) This is an easier area for many collectors and aspiring paper money enthusiasts due to the several handbooks available to use, auction records on the internet, and the fact that we still use this size currency. The Legal Tenders, Silver Certificates, and World War II Emergency issues therefore have some cache to them because of their unusual nature at reasonable prices. Many Small Size notes in Gem condition are impossible to find. If discovered, they might cost a fraction of an EF Educational $5. Federal Reserve notes certified in high grade, often sleeper rarities depending on denomination, date and district, could become very popular over time. There is a high end, as well, with $10,000 notes always in vogue as well other high denominations such as choice Gold Certificates. Like Large Size, high grade "PPQ" notes are always well sought after.

National Bank Notes: (1865-1929) Nationals were once all the rage with several high-end collectors often slugging it out for the same "Trophy" note several years back. Now the world is different and we have five-figure obsolete banknotes more in vogue. In the past few years, some of these expensive Nationals have come back to the auction arena at a fraction of prior cost as a volatile, sometimes thin market for a particular location or type came into play. Like it's always been, if five people collect a small state, all hell breaks loose at an auction. However, some big states have just two collectors; sometimes one. Choice and rare National type notes, though, are a different story. Exceptional Original Series notes and Brown Backs never seem to go out of style and only grow in popularity. Like 2012, 2013 saw this demand increase in fact. Name collections garner great participation, especially when conducted at an appropriate convention.

Fractionals: (1862-1876) Fractional Currency continues its moderate pace with some very high grade slabs selling for record prices. Traditionalists are wary, of course, as the true rarities and specialty notes are still undervalued. Choice notes, though, are hard to find. The 150th Civil War anniversaries might very well make these more collected from the circulated end. The new Reed reference on Civil War Postage Envelopes should increase interest there, but there were no elite Encased Postage stamp auctions like in 2012.

Error Notes: The market appears to still be pretty active for several reasons. The supply of the truly unusual is tight and the neat notes are fascinating. Most errors are small size. Large size errors, when offered, bring strong money and great collections desire double denomination notes, even if they have no other errors. After trending flatly like small size in 2010, they have re-emerged again in the past few years with some aggressive prices.

Obsolete Notes: (1782-1900) Obsolete banknotes may have receded slightly from their 2010-2011 high benchmarks, especially notes eclipsing five figures, but prices are still high for good notes. The March Stack's Bowers auction saw some discovery color proofs bring record prices. A broad, but perhaps overwhelming Rhode Island proof collection saw staggering results over estimate when most naysayers felt too many were being sold at one time. Several of these notes broke five figures. So-called "Commercial Proof" notes (more than five known), once from the ABN Company sales, were still mixed and now represent a tremendous opportunity again. Some proofs that have auction records of nearly or over a $1,000 can now be found at a fraction for the patient newcomer and it reaps benefits to view and pay accordingly for these premium examples. Also, the opportunity to form meaningful collections still exists for collectors in the $15-$200 price ranges as many of these notes have also weakened. These notes are often quite interesting for their price levels. We always recommend issued notes over remainder notes if at all possible. The rarest Mormon notes continue in popularity, but it did not take an Einstein to notice many Kirtland notes in auction and not meeting reserves. Other Western notes are harder to gauge as the expectations of auction sellers and buyers often didn't meet, resulting in an unsold auction item. The supply of quality obsoletes has always been low, the new influx of collectors has driven prices up, of course.

Colonial and Continental Currency: (1690-1800) With some exceptions, these often lack color, dynamic vignettes and panache to immediately appeal to Large Size type collectors. However, much potential is untapped here for the visionary and historically minded. The genre was hotly contested during the landmark Boyd/Ford auctions as Boyd was the definitive collection ever auctioned to this time; the elite notes are closely held to this day by specialists who waited decades to bid upon them. Their historic texture is the fabric which dresses our nation and part of the foundation of our freedoms. The Eric P. Newman reference on the discipline is right up in the pantheon of all American numismatic literature with the last, fifth edition, boasting color images. Interestingly, now that coins from the Eric

P. Newman Numismatic Education Society (or EPNNES) are being auctioned after nine decades of collecting, there is anticipation when and if paper money from EPNNES will begin to be offered for sale. Fresh notes from this cabinet will only stimulate growth of this area. The strongest demand in 2013 was for high-grade Continental and Colonial notes, now listed and priced in Friedberg at the front of the volume, in the $100-$1500 range, preferably certified, with extremely heavy demand for Continental Currency. These issues are Federal related and a complete set (102 notes) can be accomplished with some work and time. The entire series is ripe with opportunity since the supply of desirable notes is rather limited. Required is some study and persistence to obtain excellent value. The Friedberg listings and prices make the series much more accessible.

Depression Scrip, Warrants, Bounties and Bills of Exchange: (Colonial era to 1933) This is a boundless region of collecting opportunities with few books to guide, but perfect for the inquisitively natured. Western Americana drafts and bills from the Gold Rush era sometimes share history with Territorial gold coins. The colonial era has much fiscal paper that has been under-collected, yet offers many fascinating items such as items engraved by Paul Revere. This is a difficult area to invest for investment sake, but many items fit in well with all the traditional areas of paper money collecting and truly are best for collectors.

Military Payment Certificates: (1947-1973) Collected by world note collectors and in the United States. They are "Green Sheet" listed and a complete set is attainable. Many of them, for the price, offer distinctive vignettes and modernist style. The rarity minded look for the replacement serial numbers. One time, few knew what they were until books leveled the playing field and the internet answered most questions.

Related Fiscal Paper: Other items to collect with American paper money include checks and stock certificates. Shares and bonds from the hoards should be considered a separate entity. However, the Federal loan certificates and Liberty Bonds from World War I are not only collectible, they remain in demand, and the supply is lower than collectors realize. Down the road they might even be listed in the Friedberg catalogue. Share Certificates printed by banknote engraving firms prior to 1865 are often an excellent value as they are mostly larger format, have multiple vignettes and most have only a few known. They can sell for a fraction of similarly styled obsolete banknotes from the era.

Like 2011 and 2012, optimism for paper money collecting should continue strongly this year as serious and beginning collectors look for collecting enjoyment as a distraction from our serious world, while finding an excellent hedge for disposable income in this extremely low-interest rate economy. Those taking stock market profits will drive some of the prices higher and faster in some areas rather than others. We always recommend studying what you are buying for genuine value and not necessarily buying what everyone else is at the same time. Look for what might be undervalued and most interesting to you.

PUBLICATIONS

Get a global perspective on paper money collecting from *The Bank Note Reporter*. This monthly tabloid is devoted entirely to U.S. and world paper money, notes, checks, and all related fiscal paper. Find current prices for national and international bank notes, plus an active buy/sell marketplace. *12 monthly issues are $24.98*.

The *Numismatic News* delivers weekly news and information on coin and paper money collecting with exclusive reports from the hobby's only full-time Washington Bureau. Accurate retail/wholesale value guide, current events, and up-to-date calendar make this the most comprehensive numismatic forum available. *52 weekly issues are $29.99*.

For more information, please contact:

Krause Publications
700 East State Street
Iola, WI 54990-0001
Phone 715-445-2214
Subscription Services
1-800-258-0929
www.krausebooks.com

CURRENT TECHNOLOGY TRENDS FOR COIN AND PAPER MONEY COLLECTORS

By Tom Bilotta
Carlisle Development Corporation

The trend toward computing platforms other than the traditional desktop PC has continued to accelerate. Tablet computers such as the iPad and its Windows-based competitors have exploded in use and are now commonly used for functions previously performed on traditional PCs. Microsoft has now entered this market with the new Surface tablet and Windows 8 RT. Smartphones and e-book readers also continue to become more useful and will play an increased role in collector applications. In 2014, the Android platform also gained significant market share.

The year 2014 has seen the emergence of some applications (apps) for numismatists on the iPhone and iPad. These apps go beyond the functionality of simple browsers accessing Web content to fully functional mobile applications. Initial applications have focused on educational information such as coin identification and grading. Also some applications to educate young numismatists have appeared in the app store; 2015 should bring continued growth in numismatic offerings on mobile platforms.

COIN COLLECTING IN RETIREMENT

The demographics of coin collectors continue to show a long-term trend toward older coin collectors. Currently, the average age of serious coin collectors is probably in excess of 55. Collectors nearing or in retirement have specific needs regarding their coin collections. Paramount in their minds is planning for eventual disposition of their collection in a manner that benefits their family. They also face different challenges in order to continue to enjoy the pursuit of coin collecting, sometimes with reduced funding and/or the need to begin to liquidate some portions of the collection. A new website (www.coincollectinginretirement.com) addresses many of the issues faced by such collectors.

Bullion Valuation and Analysis

Over the past several years, the volatility of spot bullion prices has sparked collector interest in understanding the bullion value of their collection. Collectors of gold and silver coins have experience with the complex relationship between bullion and numismatic values. Often numismatic premiums diminish as bullion values rise. This has increased the importance of understanding the bullion value in your collection as well as its impact on the overall value of your collection and projected cost to purchase new items.

Portable Computing

Portable computing has much to offer, especially when supported by access to your data via the Internet. For collectors, use of portable devices is in its infancy. Most available collector-oriented applications are primarily Internet browsers, often enhanced to present content optimally on the mobile device. There are very few numismatic software applications available on these devices that go beyond viewing Web content.

One of the challenges of mobile computing particular to the coin collecting market is the basic demographic. The average age of coin collectors is quite high, and many collectors suffer from eyesight limitations. On home PCs this can be addressed by very affordable, large-screen monitors. Small mobile devices tend to use small fonts to allow maximum content. In the future, flexible, expandable screens may help address this issue.

Cloud Computing

The real benefits of mobile devices for collectors will be realized when user data may be maintained in the cloud and accessed anywhere. In such an environment, a collector could maintain his collection on his PC at home and access it from his cell phone or tablet while attending a show or traveling by airplane. The collector's ability to work with his collection would not be limited to time spent at home. Synchronization of data would be automatic. It is expected that during 2015, cloud computing will find its way into core applications intended to assist collectors in working with their collections.

Cloud Computing—Security

There are a number of issues to be resolved before these benefits are attainable. One of the major ones is security. There are daily reports of security breaches on the Internet. These affect governments, major financial institutions, and corporations and individuals alike. The willingness of collectors to place their sensitive collection data in the cloud will depend on their confidence in the security of their data. It is clear that today we do not understand enough about Internet security to build truly robust and impenetrable defenses. Even major institutions such as the Defense Department are "hacked."

Cloud Computing—Applications Availability

Another issue is the development of collector applications software intended to exploit mobile computing. Such software has to present the capabilities of robust PC-based collectibles software optimized for the smaller viewing area and touch interface of the mobile device. These applications must also perform well in the more limited resource environments available on mobile devices.

The smaller screen areas of mobile devices make it more difficult to present a large amount of information on one screen as well as manipulate it for analytical purposes. Mobile devices currently address this by allowing the user to employ virtual pages that are larger than the device and that can be accessed by simple hand motions.

Cloud Computing—Standards

Several major corporations are setting up resources for cloud computing; these include Apple, Google, and Microsoft. It remains to be seen how these environments will interact. Ideally for the user, data would be seamlessly shared between these environments. A user on a Windows-based PC at home should be able to access data without regard to the specifics of the servers on which it is maintained. The same user should be able to access the same data on an iPhone at a remote location.

Cloud Computing—Reliability Of Access

Early users of cloud computing have experienced significant periods during which their data was not accessible. This unreliability will be an impediment to widespread dependence on the cloud. Cloud infrastructure must approach the uptime of other utilities such as your telephone and electric power, which are expected to be up and running very close to 100% of the time. This will require substantial buildup of infrastructure that is not commonly employed for Internet computing currently. Redundant data centers and communications paths will be required throughout the entire network.

Choosing the Right Portable Device for You

The choice of a portable device is a personal one and is driven by your typical usage, physical limitations, and other considerations. Many users will employ multiple portable devices for different purposes. Many coin collectors are older and would have difficulty with the small screen size and keys on an e-reader or smartphone and would be better served by a traditional laptop or tablet computer. If you find an affordable e-reader or tablet computer which provides adequate viewing quality for you, it will likely be a very convenient choice for all sorts of internet activity associated with your collecting pursuits.

The Internet

As in recent years, Internet activity by collectors continues to grow. The trend toward cloud computing is one of the newest growth areas of Internet activity.

COIN COLLECTING SOFTWARE

Coin collecting software that runs on your own computer avoids the problems of Internet catalogs and provides you with rich functionality to work with your collection.

Collectors who adopt computer inventory programs increase their enjoyment of collecting, provide the needed documentation to protect their collection, gain insight into the value of their collection, and better prepare their families to deal with their collection if the need arises.

In order to exploit the power that computers bring to collecting, the collector must acquire a base level of knowledge sufficient to harness this capability in a safe and productive manner. The remainder of this article will focus on some of the more important points of using numismatic inventory software.

Coin & Paper Money Inventory Software

One of the first applications of a computer is to organize a collection. This activity requires cataloging what you have, deciding how it will be grouped, and determining what kind of reports you will need. Reports will assist you in defining your collecting objectives, tracking value, and assuring that your collection is adequately protected and insured.

Organizing Your Collection With Coin & Paper Money Inventory Software

Collectors of coins and currency fall into several categories. There is the serious coin collector who enjoys the hobby and pursues personally defined collecting objectives. Accumulators retain many of the coins that they receive in normal commerce and build up large quantities of unsorted coins. Investors use coin collecting to build portfolios intended to produce profits. Inheritors receive a coin collection or accumulation from their families and must decide how they will handle a potentially valuable asset.

All of these collectors have a common need to catalog their items and understand their value. Most collectors also have accumulated many items with a very wide range of values.

A modern inventory program can adapt to meet the needs of all types of users from novice collectors to experienced experts. It will incorporate a comprehensive database of coin and/or paper money to assist users in identifying and defining their collections as well as a flexible set of functionality to enable them to organize their collections in a manner consistent with their collection methodology.

Most collectors will want to organize their collections into several groupings. The collector will want to create collections that mirror their physical collection. For example, someone with coin albums of common series such as Mercury dimes, statehood quarters, or Buffalo nickels will want to have software albums organized in similar fashion. Other coins might be grouped into coins for sale, duplicates, partial collections for other family members, or any other categorization that suits the collector.

Using Your Time Wisely

When using computer software to catalog a coin or paper money collection it is important to use it in a manner consistent with your purposes and that will enhance your enjoyment. You should spend your time, therefore, working with the portions of your collection in which you have the most interest or where the primary financial value exists.

For example, if you are collecting a complete set of Mercury dimes, you may wish to scan an image of each individual piece so that you can print picture catalogs of your collection. For these coins, you might choose to enter in complete information including purchase price, source, certification information, origin, etc. For this type of grouping you will also likely want to include coins that you don't have that are required to complete your collection, enabling you to generate want lists. This will also assist you in identifying the cost to complete your collection and planning your approach.

For large quantities of relatively inexpensive items or coins worth only bullion content and where you have no particular collecting interest, you might choose to only enter a single line item and not bother to take the time to list each coin individually. For example, if you have several hundred silver Washington quarters in circulated condition from the 1950s and 1960s you might enter a single line item 225 Washington Quarters with a date range and average value. In this way, large accumulations can be tracked with minimum effort and your attention can be focused on your real collecting interests. Your coin inventory program should adapt to all of these possible approaches to organizing your collection.

Evaluating Coin & Paper Money Inventory Software

The quality of the software that you purchase will greatly impact the success of your efforts.

One of the most important parts of a coin inventory program is the database. The database contains standard information about coins and paper money and saves the user from having to type this information manually. The greater the amount of information in the standard database, the easier the task of data entry. A modern coin collecting program at a minimum should include coin type, date, mint mark, denomination, and variety. Comprehensive programs, such as those made by Carlisle Development Corporation, also include such information as designer/engraver, coinage metal, size, weight, edge, and mintage. The organization of the database should reflect commonly used groupings and thereby provide users with guidance in organizing their collections.

Some inventory programs include current market values. It is important that these are updated frequently and produced by reliable sources. Coin values should evolve to include areas of high market interest. For example, over the past year, the market interest in high grade recent coin issues has become very high. It is also important to allow the user the ability to extend the database to include items that are not listed. These may be specialized varieties, private mint products, or other coin-related collectibles.

Ability to share data with other programs and people is also very important. Most computerized collectors are connected to the Internet and will want to share some information with other collectors and dealers. The ability to export listings in common text readable formats for transmission over the Internet or for input into a word processor or spreadsheet is of great value in buying and selling coins and paper money.

Carlisle Development's inventory software, Collector's Assistant, provides a comprehensive database of all coins ever minted by the United States Mint. This includes all type coins by date and mint mark, bullion coins, sets, old and new commemoratives. Recent additions to the database are the 50 states circulating quarters and the new Sacagawea Dollar. Coin values are licensed from Coin World, Inc., an industry leader in providing coin valuations. Quarterly updates are available by subscription, allowing collectors to maintain trends of their values. Carlisle Development's Currency Collector's Assistant has a complete database based on *Friedberg's Paper Money of the United States,* 19th Edition. This database includes all U.S. paper money, including Confederate notes and Encased postage stamps. A relationship with CDN, publisher of the *Greensheet,* makes value information available to the paper money collector in electronic format.

For collectors of ancient coins, Carlisle offers an add-on database containing color images of several hundred ancient coins and a specialized interface containing data-entry fields appropriate for ancient coins. For example, the date field can handle and sort mixed AD/BC dates and has long fields for obverse and reverse inscriptions. The most recent additions to Carlisle Development's databases include the Euro Coin Database and World Currency Database.

Report Generation

Once you have entered your coin collection into an inventory program, the most important function will become its ability to generate a wide array of reports and/or exports for informational purposes.

You will probably want to have a detailed listing, identifying items, their value, and where they are stored for insurance purposes. You will want to generate partial lists of your collections for sales and trading. You may want to generate labels to aide in identifying your coins. You may want to look at your collection in different ways, such as sorted by value or metal content or collection completeness.

One common need of coin collectors is the printing of inserts for 2" flips. Once coins have been cataloged, computer software can allow you to produce customized flip inserts in a standard format of your own design.

Report generation is the subset of an inventory program that produces the listings that you view on the screen, print on paper, or export to other computer applications. Its flexibility will greatly impact its utility. For example, you may want to generate two listings of coins that you have for sale, one that includes your cost and target price (your copy) and one that does not include this information for general distribution to prospective buyers.

At various times, you will probably want to be able to list any subset of the information fields, filter based on a wide array of parameters, and sort using different criteria.

As mentioned at the beginning of this article, report generation may be used to output PDF files which may be viewed using a portable device such as an e-book reader.

Other Functionality You Should Expect From Your Inventory Software

Inventory software should be able to store all of the information in which a collector is interested. Specific fields will vary based on collector interest and purpose. Some will require detailed certification and descriptive information, others comprehensive purchase and sales history. Some collectors will want to have comprehensive recording of storage location and insurance information. Modern programs provide sufficient information fields to meet all of these needs.

Backup and restore functionality should allow users to easily protect the data they have meticulously entered. History charting enables the user to track the changes in value of a part of a collection over time.

Good software must be easy to use and supported by context-sensitive help that provides users with detailed instructions in a "how-to" format on all of the basic functions that they will wish to perform.

Availability Of Timely Updates

Once you have taken the time to catalog your collection in a computer program, you will want to preserve your investment by having access to database updates incorporating information on new coin releases as well as changes in value. Your supplier of inventory software should have a timely program for availability of annual database and value updates.

Educational Software For Collectors

Adding significantly to your enjoyment of collections are electronic information sources that exploit the power of the computer to present you with high-quality information in an easily accessible format. These programs can provide comprehensive knowledge of all aspects of coin collecting, detailed information on grading coins, and specialized information such as collecting coin varieties.

COIN GRADING

Most coin collectors will want to be able to grade their coins, at least to an approximate grade. This enables them to have an understanding of value as well as identify coins that might be appropriate for certification. Coin grading skill is built up through time and experience.

The Grading Assistant offered by Carlisle Development is based on the official *Grading Guide of the American Numismatic Association,* now published by Whitman Publishing. It enables the user to view side-by-side images of their own coins along with various grades from the ANA grading set. These images are supported by detailed descriptions of the wear points for each grade. Using software such as the Grading Assistant, users can develop their skill in grading coins and establish approximate grades for their collections.

VARIETY COLLECTING

The collecting of coin varieties is an exciting area of the hobby currently experiencing some growth. Varieties are the result of differences in the minting process or dies that produce design differences and/or errors. These include such effects as doubling of some of features or letters, extra pieces of metal on the coin surface, and die breaks. Variety collecting requires the collector to identify subtle differences in coin designs.

The Morgan dollar series is one of the most commonly collected and is categorized by many varieties. Carlisle Development offers a *Top 100 Morgan Dollar* CD, based on the book written by Michael Fey and Jeff Oxman. This work provides pictures, identification information, and values for the most sought after and valuable Morgan dollar varieties. It provides a spectacular set of high-quality pictures to assist you in identifying these coins and also the full text and information provided in this work.

Bullion Analysis

The increase in bullion prices has made understanding of bullion value much more important and significantly impacts the cost of acquiring new items. Carlisle Development offers the Bullion Analyzer to assist collectors in understanding bullion values and their impact on your collecting pursuits.

Mobile Applications for Numismatists

During 2013, Carlisle Development introduced its flagship Collector's Assistant in the Apple app store. Collector's Assistant Mobile allows users to view and edit their collection data on iPhones and iPads, and share it with their PCs if desired. This joins Carlisle's existing two apps, the Coin Identification/Mint Mark Locator and Top 100 Morgan Varieties. Both tools are available at the Apple app store (visit www.carlisledevelopment .com/mobileapps.html for a link to the app store). The Coin Identification/Mint Mark Locator assists a collector in identifying U.S. coin types and also locating the mint mark. It covers all coins from 1793–present and includes basic numismatic data. The Top 100 Morgan Varieties provides high-resolution images and supporting numismatic data to assist collectors in identifying more valuable Morgan dollar varieties.

GENERAL EDUCATIONAL WORKS ON COLLECTING

There is much to learn about coin collecting, whether it is technical knowledge such as grading and authentication or practical knowledge such as buying and selling coins, attending trade shows, or participating in auctions. Educational computer software offers advantages over printed works in that the contents may be searched and indexed allowing the user to rapidly retrieve valuable information.

Carlisle Development offers the *Coin Collector's Survival Manual, Sixth Edition*, an interactive edition of the work by Scott Travers. This work provides a set of information that every collector of coins should have. The entire contents of this book are provided in a searchable, interactive format. This allows the user to easily locate information based on word searching, topics, illustrations, bookmarks, a table of contents, or index. The most recent edition of this work, released in 2008, contains the contents of *How to Make Money in Coins Right Now*, covering such topics as cracking-out coins for upgrade and premium coins. In addition to the contents of the book, a set of high-quality grading images has been included for such topics as identifying MS-63, MS-65, MS-67 coins and toning. An interactive grading calculator brings to life the grading methods described in the book.

WELL-DESIGNED COMPUTER SOFTWARE WILL ADD TO YOUR ENJOYMENT OF COLLECTING

Carlisle Development Corporation publishes the most comprehensive line of collector software available, especially regarding coins and paper money.

Central to Carlisle's product line is the Collector's Assistant, the most advanced and comprehensive collection software available. It is sold in a variety of configurations to serve collectors of over thirty collectible types from autographs to toys. Most extensive is support for coins and paper money. The Collector's Assistant family includes:

- United States Coin Database—complete listings of all U.S. coinage from 1793 to the present. The 50 State quarter program and the Presidents Dollar program are recent additions. This also includes Colonial and Hawaiian coinage.

- World Coin Database—A listing of over 5,000 coin types from over forty-five countries, which may be extended by the user. Also includes comprehensive listings of Canada, Australia, Euro coinage, and world bullion gold and silver coins.

- Ancient Coin Database—includes several thousand listings of Byzantine, Judaic, Roman, and Greek coinage along with several hundred images. Data entry screens are optimized for ancient coin collectors and include long fields for inscriptions and preloaded choice lists of rulers, ancient denominations, towns, mints, and others.

- United States Currency Database—A complete listing of all United States currency based on *Friedberg's 18th Edition, Paper Money of the United States.* This also includes 120 high-quality color images of early U.S. currency.

To learn more about Carlisle Development's product line, visit our website at www.carlisledevelopment.com. You will find current product information and may also place orders. You can reach us by e-mail at support@carlisledevelopment.com or by phone at 800-219-0257.

USING TECHNOLOGY TO ENHANCE YOUR COLLECTING EXPERIENCE

By Scott Barman

When I started collecting coins in the early 1970s, it was still possible to find silver coins and other older coins in pocket change. In fact, it was after being paid several Indian Head cents for delivering newspapers that I became interested in collecting coins. After gathering coins from collecting payments for delivering newspapers, I started to look through my father's pocket change looking for coins to insert into my folders.

Collecting today has advanced far beyond the way I started. To find out more about those Indian Head cents I bought a reference book. To buy or sell coins, I had to travel to a dealer. While there is nothing wrong with dealers, I did not have one in my neighborhood and that made it a difficult proposition. Today, collectors can go online and use their favorite search engine to find information about the coin they found or the coin someone wants to sell them.

Prior to the arrival of the World Wide Web, those of us with access to what was then called the ARPAnet could access simple email lists and a bulletin board–like system called Usenet. Usenet was a distributed messaging system similar to today's online forums except that the articles were distributed to each computer with access. When it was conceived in 1979, computing power and the architecture of the Internet made it easier to distribute the articles in bulk, sometimes overnight, rather than accessing them across the network as we do today.

Among the first technology breakthroughs that helped collectors were the invention of the simple database and spreadsheet programs. Collectors would use these programs to create databases and spreadsheets to track their collection. These would become the basis for inventory programs that would see their popularity rise in the late part of the last century.

Newcomers to the technologies of the Internet and mobile computing might look at these beginnings as ancient times, but it set the tone for the future of adding technology to enhance the collecting experience. The first breakthrough in expanding the information available was the invention of the World Wide Web.

Sir Tim Berners-Lee and Belgian computer scientist Robert Cailliau, while working at CERN, the European Organization for Nuclear Research, invented the concept of the Web. Using the power of technology offered by the Internet, the Web has brought a new way of delivering information from those who have it to those who want it. In numismatics, it allowed people to build sites that not only deliver information, but also enhance the ways for collectors to communicate with each other.

The initial impact of the Web was the ability for collectors to buy and sell coins anywhere in the country and then around the world. First, the online auction site eBay made it easy to bring buyers and sellers together from the comfort of a computer. Dealers, seeing the successes of collectors shopping on eBay joined the online auction site and then began developing their own online presences to sell directly to collectors.

In the computing industry we look at the growth in the capability of technology in terms of "Moore's Law." Named for Intel Corporation co-founder Gordon E. Moore, Moore's Law says that the capabilities of technology double every two years. While Moore was talking about the growth of the microprocessors that are the brains behind the computers, there has been a growth in the capabilities of the computers that make them wonderful tools to enhance your collecting experience.

Online Price Guides

The perpetual question from collectors, investors, and those with passing interest is "What does the coin cost?" While paper books are wonderful references and can be more convenient than electronic alternatives, books have the problem of being static from one year to another. To answer the collecting public's desire for more information, one of the first online services for collectors has been online price guides.

Price guides are as varied as their publishers. Some publishers offer their price guides for the retail market available for free while long-time publishers of price guides provide paid online services for their data. Which is best for you depends on your collecting goals.

News and Blogs

Finding numismatic news and information used to be limited to the weekly and monthly publications sent to us via the postal service. Collectors were tied to publishing schedules, causing news to travel slowly. With the ease of producing a well-designed website and hiring writers to look for stories that would be of interest to collectors, there are now websites dedicated to delivering numismatic community news.

While there are many sources, sites that are dedicated to providing frequent updates to news that would of interest to numismatists, collectors, and those with a passing interest are as follows:

- Coin Collecting News (coincollectingnews.org)
- Coin Update (coinupdate.com)
- Coin News (coinnews.net)
- Coin Week (coinweek.com)

These sites provide various ways for readers to keep up to date with new articles. Some offer a daily email notice while others offer RSS (Rich Site Summary or Really Simple Syndication) feeds. An RSS feed is a special file accessed from the Web that will tell you when new information is available.

As RSS feeds proliferate and their function has expanded, web browsers have been either dropping support for reading RSS feeds (like Apple's Safari) or have not added enhancements (Microsoft's Internet Explorer and Mozilla Firefox), making it difficult to keep up with the news. Two good stand-alone replacements to use at your computer are SharpReader for Windows (sharpreader.net) and NetNewsWire for the Mac (netnewswireapp.com). Both programs have won many industry awards.

Last year, the popular Google shut down its Reader service that provided Web-based access to subscribe to RSS feeds. Reader also had the advantage of being a central repository that allowed other programs to repackage the feeds so the user could read them in more friendly formats. Since the shutdown of the Reader service, there have been others that have stepped into the void. Here is a sample of services that you can choose from:

Web-Only Resources

- AOL Reader (reader.aol.com) is a Web-based service that was started shortly before Google announced the end of the Reader service. It has gained a following for having a plain, no-nonsense but solid working interface that has satisfied some of the people who have switched to the service.

- The Old Reader (theoldreader.com) is a Web-based service that looks and acts like Google's old Reader service. The author of the service makes it clear that this was not an accident.

Web and Mobile Apps

- Feedly (feedly.com) is a Web-based service that is nearly a drop-in replacement for Reader. Feedly has its own apps for iOS devices (iPhone and iPad), Android, and Kindle Fire but interfaces with many other apps to use its data. See www.feedly.com/apps.html for the list of apps that can read Feedly saved feeds.

- FeedBin (feedbin.me) is a paid service that also has support for many mobile apps. The advantage of using a paid service over a free service is that the paid service comes with support and without advertisements.

- NetVibes (netvibes.com) is an all-inclusive dashboard to manage your Web-based reading. It is free for users but has paid accounts for businesses to monitor trends on the Web. Being a paid service, NetVibes also creates its own "apps" that help cultivate news and information from the Internet and deliver it to your NetVibes account.

- Reeder 2 (reederapp.com) is a no-frills reading app for iOS (iPhone and iPad) that integrates with other services. Reeder started as an iOS interface with Google Reader but had to evolve when Reader was discontinued. Reeder is a paid app with a different version for the iPhone and iPad.

Mash-Up Services

Mash-up services combine information from multiple resources to provide a single interface as if it came from a single resource. Mash-up services are usually free to the user but rely on advertising for revenues.

- Digg Reader (digg.com/reader) is a new service from the long-time mash-up system Digg. Digg's new Reader app and service will allow users to create their own mash-ups from selected news feeds rather than create mash-ups on what you read, which is what the Digg service does.

- Flipboard (flipboard.com) is a popular service that turns your interests into an electronic magazine. Users can create their own virtual magazine based on who they follow on Twitter, from RSS feeds, or from various channels that are managed by Flipboard or one of their partners. Flipboard is available for iOS, Android, Windows Phone, and BlackBerry.

This does not mean you have to give up your subscription to the magazines that you have been reading for many years. Rather, you can supplement your collecting news reading at their websites:

- *COINage* (coinagemag.com)

- *Coin World* (coinworld.com), whose current edition can be read online (see the "Digital Edition" section on the website to register for a free account).

- *Coin World neXt* (weekly.coinworld.com) is a weekly electronic publication that focuses on one area of numismatics that strives to bring unique information not available from other sources.

- Krause Publication's Numismaster (numismaster.com), which includes articles from *Numismatic News, World Coin News, Coins,* and *Bank Note Reporter*. In 2014, Krause began to expand online delivery by adding email-only editions to subscribers.

Aside from many specialty websites (you can use a search engine to find information on just about any numismatic topic), there are bloggers dedicated to writing and discussing numismatic information. A blog, which is derived from the term "web log," is the writing of someone with information or an opinion based on the blog's subject manner.

The difference between a blog and a news-based website is that the blog writer, also called a blogger, is not limited to reporting the news. Some bloggers will analyze the news or other issues that affect the numismatic community. Bloggers provide another view into the news, collecting, the numismatic community, and the hobby that adds to the richness of the online information.

Mobile Computing

While there have been ways to carry the Internet in your pocket since the late 1990s, the release of the Apple iPhone and the software that runs the phone (iOS) paved the way for creating a new vehicle to view data on the go. With the addition of the Android system and now the new Windows Mobile phones, tablets, and other mobile devices, the possibilities are endless.

The basic use for a smart mobile phone is to use the built-in browser to explore information on the Web. While many websites may not be enhanced for a mobile display, the browsers have the ability to zoom in to the page so it can be read on the smaller screen. Sites that provide an enhanced display for mobile devices may not provide a lot of information in that format, but it is packaged for the collector on the go.

Two examples of mobile-enhanced websites you may want to bookmark are for the top two grading services: Numismatic Guarantee Corporation (NGC @ m.ngccoin.com) and the Professional Coin Grading Service (PCGS @ m.pcgs.com). Both sites will allow you to enter label information from their holders to help you determine whether the coin is genuine or otherwise. NGC also has the NGC Coin Explorer to give you more information about coins, and PCGS offers the ability to track your grading order. Having access to both websites helps when attending coin shows.

A key area of mobile computing is apps. Apps, short for applications, are programs designed to run on the mobile device that are capable of doing more than what can be done on a website. App markets are a new industry that was pioneered by Apple for its iPhone, iPod Touch, and iPad devices. Google has introduced Google Play for the Android market and Microsoft opened the Windows Store (windows.microsoft.com/en-us/windows-8/apps) for desktop, tablet, and phones running Windows 8.

Since apps are new, there are not many good apps for collectors. Most of the currently available apps that can be found are for Apple's devices. Starter lists of apps are as follows:

- Coin World (iPad)—Brings *Coin World* magazine and its website to the iPad. Included is the "Making the Grade" section with pictures of coins in various state of preservation to help you grade your coins.

- CoinFlation (iPhone, iPod Touch, Android)—the mobile companion to coinflation.com. Find out what the metal values of your coins are worth based on the most up-to-date spot prices.

- Eyenote (iPhone, iPod Touch)—this free iOS application from the U.S. Bureau of Engraving and Printing is designed to allow the visually impaired to identify U.S. paper currency. The app limits the identification to Series 1996 and later currency.

- Money Reader (iPhone, iPod Touch)—this app was created to help the visually impaired use their mobile phones to identify paper currency. Not only does this work for U.S. small size currency, but for many currencies around the world, including the euro, British pound, Canadian dollar, and Australian dollar. You can find out more about Money Reader and other apps for the visually impaired at looktel.com.

- NGC Coin Details (iPhone)—Brings the NGC mobile website to your phone as an app offering more options, including the ability to scan label bar codes to look up information about a coin in an NGC holder.

- Numis (iPhone, iPod Touch, Android)—this is the official app to read *The Numismatist*, the monthly journal of the American Numismatic Association. ANA membership is required.

- Numis HD (iPad) — the official iPad app to read *The Numismatist*, the monthly journal of the American Numismatic Association. ANA membership is required.

- Photograde (iPhone, iPod Touch, iPad, Android)—Brings all of the images from PCGS Photograde Online (pcgs.com/photograde) to your mobile device. Since the detailed images that would be used to help you examine your coins are very big, it will save download time, and you can save money by transmitting the images only once to your device.

As the use of mobile devices grows and the collector community talks about its needs, more apps will be developed to satisfy the market.

E-books

Amazon.com, probably the most successful electronic commerce (e-commerce) website, pioneered this era of electronic books (e-books) with the invention of the Kindle. Amazon designed the Kindle so that it would use a standard that it controlled so that you can gain access to the books and information sold on Amazon.com. The Kindle family of e-book readers was the first of the current era of tablets and has been successful in moving the publishing industry to make books available for users of e-readers.

Electronic books are the future of publishing, which can be seen by the phenomenal increase in e-book sales in the last few years. People of all ages are now turning to e-books to enable them to carry libraries with them when they are on the go. Schools and colleges are now turning to e-books to allow students to purchase the most current information they need to support their learning.

As more publishers are providing access to their titles electronically, e-books are key to providing the next generation of collectors, numismatists, and researchers with information in a manner that suits their lives.

E-books are not limited to current editions. There are a number of out-of-print books online that can be downloaded legally without cost. These are books whose copyright has expired and that have been scanned either through Google's book project (books.google. com) or the Internet Archive Books project (archive.org/details/ text).

There are a lot of gems hidden in the archives. One of those gems is *Domestic and Foreign Coins Manufactured by the Mints of the United States 1792-1965*. Produced by the U.S. Mint and printed by the Government Printing Office, this book has the statistics about every coin manufactured by the Mint from the information published in annual reports. It is a great history reference into the Mint.

Another advantage of e-book readers is that if you find something interesting that is in Portable Document Format (PDF), it can be saved on the e-book reader to be used as a reference. If you find an article on a website, you can have it available on your e-reader to read later. If you can create a PDF copy of a webpage, that can also be saved to read later on your e-reader.

Although each of the devices has its own online bookstore where you can buy e-books, Amazon and Barnes & Noble have apps that run on many devices that will read books bought at their stores. The Kindle app can run on your computer as well as your iOS, Android, BlackBerry, and Widows phones and tablets. If you buy most of your books from Amazon.com, then a Kindle is the best choice, but the Kindle is very restrictive on the number of devices on which you can read the book.

Family readers can benefit from the Nook by Barnes & Noble, where several household members can share an account. The Barnes & Noble Nook app can allow readers to read books bought at bn.com to be read on iPhones, iPads, Android devices, and Windows phones and tablets. These options make the best e-reader a matter of personal preference without limiting access to the best electronic reading experience.

Social Media

It has taken a while for the numismatic community to begin to embrace social media. Some say that the demographic that uses social media tends to be younger than the average collector. While that may be true, there is a growing online community using social media to talk about collecting. Three of the most well-known social media services are Facebook, Twitter, and Pinterest.

Facebook (facebook.com) was not the inventor of social media on the Web, but it has been the most successful because of its ability to adapt to new services. Facebook has made it easy for people of all ages to be social online. Not many collectors have embraced Facebook or they have reserved their Facebook activities to maintaining relationships with friends, relatives, and colleagues. Facebook's very public issues with privacy may have collectors thinking about their use of Facebook and restricting what they share.

Twitter (twitter.com) is called a micro-blogging service. A Twitter message can be no longer than 140 characters in length, making brevity a necessity. Twitter is good for short comments and sending links to interesting information to your followers. Similar to making "friends" on Facebook, on Twitter you follow a user's messages, called Tweets. Bloggers use Twitter to announce when content is available. Others use Twitter to point to interesting articles for their followers to read.

Some people can get confused by Twitter's fast pace. The thing to remember about Twitter is that it is a snapshot in time. If you are not reading Twitter during the workday, do not worry. Much of the information will be available in the media or should not be much of a concern. Pick interesting people to follow and you might want to consider looking back on their timeline to see if they had anything interesting to say.

Pinterest (pinterest.com) is the new social media service that calls itself a "Virtual Pinboard." Think of Pinterest as the Twitter for pictures. While you can post pointers to images on Twitter, Pinterest is all about pictures. One of the best things about the numismatic community that is growing on Pinterest is the ability to find interesting pictures around the Web and post them to Pinterest. The Pinterest mobile apps will also allow you to take pictures with your mobile device and upload them to a board you set up for others to see. All three services have mobile apps for both the Apple and Android devices.

Additionally, those interested in creating online photo albums and photo journals can look into photo blogging services like Yahoo's Flickr (flickr.com), Photobucket (photobucket.com), and Google's Picasa (picasa.google.com). All three have apps for the Apple devices, while only Photobucket and Picasa have apps for Android. Users of Apple iOS devices can use iCloud to share pictures of their collection.

Buying and Selling Online

Although eBay opened the online world to coin buying and selling, it is not the only place for a collector to search for coins. Dealers the world over have embraced online selling and have created e-commerce websites to sell to more people than those in their local area. Their embracing the Web and e-commerce also provides the collector with a wide variety of purchasing options and a way to expand their collections from the comfort of their computers.

A primary option for purchasing current collectibles would be from the manufacturer. For United States coins, that would be the U.S. Mint (usmint.gov). The U.S. Mint will always offer the latest collectibles and continue to offer some from years past as long as it has the inventory to do so. Most coins must be sold in the year that they are minted, so plan your purchases accordingly or plan to buy your collectible on the secondary market.

The U.S. Mint is not the only mint that sells to the public online. Coins from the Royal Canadian Mint (mint.ca), Royal Mint (royalmint.com), Perth Mint (perthmint.com.au), New Zealand Mint (nzmint

.com), and many others can be purchased directly from the source. There are dealers who represent these mints in the United States that offer online ordering with domestic shipping, thus saving costs and customs hassles.

Auctions

Auctions are the oldest type of marketplace, dating back over 2,500 years, with some auction houses in Europe having been in business since the 18th century. As with most businesses, online and mobile technologies have made it easier to participate in auctions from anywhere in the world.

The excitement behind online auctions goes beyond eBay. Traditional auction houses are now moving auctions online as active platforms rather than just as an entry point for absentee bids to floor auctions. Some hold exclusively online auctions while others have found ways to do live bidding online to extend the auction floor to anywhere in the world.

The auction business has seen the growth of a few types of businesses, ranging from ones that fully embrace technology to those that use it as an extension of their traditional business models. Large auction houses like Heritage Auctions (ha.com) have fully embraced the technology and offer exclusively online auctions along with their live auctions that open with pre-bidding online. Heritage has invested a lot into its site, which includes an extensive auction archive with full catalog details and information that makes it a numismatic resource on top of the auctions. Heritage has won awards for Web-based services.

Another evolution in the auction business is the transformation from the telephone to exclusively Web-based, online bidding. One of the first in that transition was Teletrade (teletrade.com), which used to be telephone bidding but now is exclusively online. Others, like David Lawrence Rare Coins (davidlawrence.com), have followed using the exclusively online auction model to make it easier for sellers to consign to the auction and bidders to purchase nice collectibles. As a result, other auction companies have expanded their online auction services, making it easier to consign and participate in auctions regardless of where they are being held.

Some dealers have found that sponsoring online auctions can profitably help them sell inventory and reach a clientele beyond their hometowns. Using the services from companies like Proxibid (proxibid.com) and Live Auctioneers (liveauctioneers.com) to host their auction and provide transaction support, dealers can take the consignments they obtain locally and offer them to a broader audience to help sellers get the best price for their items.

For the collectors bidding on these auctions, technology gives them access to numismatic items that they would normally not see because of not being able to attend an auction.

Looking Into the Future

The first stop on looking into the future is with education. With the number of colleges moving toward online education, there is a lot of software that can support extending education beyond the classroom. Organizations that have education as part of their missions, like the ANA, can expand their education mission to including people online. Classes can be held exclusively online or in conjunction with events like their Summer Seminar or their national conventions.

Next look into the future would be to use the multimedia capabilities that are available to expand education to create virtual clubs. Virtual clubs can be formed around a collecting interest and have international participation from members. Imagine forming a club for enthusiasts of silver bullion coins with members from Canada, Europe, and Asia.

Other technologies could be cataloging coins by just taking a picture, voice-activated searching for coin information, and possibly coin grading using your mobile phone. The possibilities are endless!

Your Security Online

When looking at the tools to use to enhance your collecting experience, remember that scammers and other criminals are using the same tools in their activities. Although the technology is helpful, it is not mature enough to trust to keep you safe. Rather than hope that technology will be safe, there are a few guidelines that you should follow to ensure your safety and security:

1. Make sure your software is up to date. Whether you have an Apple or Windows computer, you should learn how the make sure to update the software on those devices. Updating your software means more than updating the operating system (Windows, OS X, Android, or iOS), it also means updating the apps so that their bugs cannot be used against you. This includes your browser, which is probably the most used program on your computer.

2. Run an anti-virus and anti-malware program. Malware is "malicious software" that would do harm to your computer. This attack would install malware on your system through your browser. Some service providers offer a free download of an anti-virus program. Take advantage of that offer! If you want a good basic anti-virus program try the AVG Anti-Virus

Free Edition (free.avg.com). It is not as full featured as others, but it provides good protection.

3. Once you install your anti-virus program, make sure you keep it up to date! Keeping it up to date means that you download the information about new attacks from the manufacturers of the anti-virus program. Threats are constantly changing and you need to keep up to date. If you are using old information, it is like leaving holes in your defenses for the attackers to get through. Make sure the software is updated. Also, pay for the yearly service to keep it updated. Think of it as an insurance policy for your critical data!

4. Desktop and laptop computer systems now come with built-in protections that you should learn how to turn on. If you do not have a relative or friend who can help you, electronic stores provide services to help teach you and set up these features. It is worth spending the time and money for these services to protect your computer from being attacked.

5. Think about what you are doing before you click that link. If you receive a random link in email even from someone you know, contact that person to make sure they sent the link and are not victims of a cyber-attack. If you receive a link in a text message saying that your bank needs for you to verify your account, do not click the link but call your bank and ask if it is a legitimate request—likely it is not.

6. If you do not know what it is, do not investigate; just delete or ignore the message. Email with attachments, links in tweets, and online forum posts can contain links to sites that are ready to infect your system. If there is any doubt, just throw it out!

7. Know how to tell when a site is legitimate by looking at the visual cues. Does the website's address (URL) look right? If you are supposed to be at your bank's website, is there anything else other than the bank's address? Sometimes scammers in another country will make their addresses look like your bank's address (e.g., yourbank.com.cn, providing your bank is not in China). Remember, the number one and lower-case "l" (letter el) look similar and so does an upper case "O" and zero.

8. Just because there is a lock on your browser does not mean the website is secured. It means that the communications between your browser and the server are secured. The same rules for checking the visual cues (above) apply. If there are any errors when trying to begin what you think is a secure session, you should not trust the connection; instead, contact the company you are trying to do business with. Also, look for the clues for sites that are using enhanced security. When you connect to a website that is using the enhanced security, you should see a green lock or other sig-

nal that says that your browser confirmed the site you are connected to uses the enhanced security standards and can be trusted.

9. Although Wi-Fi hotspots are convenient, they are also convenient to the scammer. Most Wi-Fi hotspots are not secure and anyone can connect. If you do not have to enter a password to access the Wi-Fi hotspot, it is the network equivalent of standing on a street corner and broadcasting your personal information for anyone to hear. Using a direct connection, such as the cellular data connection on your mobile device, is safer than using an unsecured Wi-Fi hotspot.

10. Speaking of Wi-Fi, if you have a wireless network at home you should learn how to properly set it up or get help. Even security professionals who do this for a living often find setting up Wi-Fi networks difficult so do not be afraid of asking for help!

11. Protect your personal information. Understand the information you are being asked to provide and give only what is needed to complete the transaction. For example, there is no reason for anyone to require your social security number for any online transaction. Only fill out the required fields in checkout forms. If there are any questions, find the site's privacy policy and make sure you understand how your personal information will be stored and used.

12. Only use safe payment options like credit cards or a third-party proxy like PayPal (paypal.com). Credit cards are the safest option because the issuers will help if something goes wrong such as a product not being delivered or someone using your card without your permission. Never send cash through the mail or use a money-wiring service, because you do not have any recourse if something should go wrong.

Regardless of what you do, keep a record of your online transactions. You should save as much information as possible until the transaction is completed and you are satisfied that everything is in order. Save online receipts by saving the web receipt to a file or keep a printed copy. Save copies of email and write down all telephone call information during the transaction. Keep this information and verify the transaction on your credit card statement as soon as it arrives. Also, make sure there are not any unauthorized charges. If there are any problems or questions, call the financial institution that issued the credit card immediately.

If you want to learn more about staying safe online, the National Cyber Security Alliance (NCSA) maintains a website (staysafeonline.org) with a lot of good information. NCSA is a consortium of major technology vendors and the U.S. Department of Homeland Security that works hard to keep that site up to date with the latest information. It also sponsors Cyber Security Awareness Month every October to remind everyone that while there is a lot of good in cyberspace you do have to be careful.

Scott Barman is a collector and author of the Coin Collectors Blog (coinsblog.ws). He is also President of the Montgomery County Coin Club (montgomerycoinclub.org) and President of the Maryland State Numismatic Society (mdstatenumisassn.org). After more than thirty years in the computer and information security industry, Scott recently started Having-Fun Collectibles to serve collectors in more markets than just numismatics because collecting should be fun. When not out searching for different and interesting collectibles he can be found with his wife and two puggles while they check out his pocket change.

PROFESSIONAL CURRENCY DEALERS ASSOCIATION (PCDA)

SPECIALISTS IN CURRENCY, STOCKS & BONDS, FISCAL DOCUMENTS, AND RELATED PAPER ITEMS

The PCDA was founded in 1985 and counts among its members over 100 of the world's leading specialists in currency, stocks and bonds, fiscal documents, and related paper items. Among its goals are promoting, stimulating and advancing the profession of dealing in paper currency and related materials; advancing the study of paper money; and promoting honest and ethical commerce between its dealers and the public.

Would you like to learn more about collecting paper money? The PCDA publishes a series of informative, illustrated booklets about different speciality areas of the hobby. Information about these publications can be found in our Membership Directory, available by contacting the Secretary. PCDA also hosts an annual convention where you can meet dealers offering United States, foreign and ancient coins, as well as its traditional base of foreign and United States Paper Money. Visit our website for dates and location.

PCDA aims to make people aware of the joys of collecting, and the knowledge that can be acquired through participation and study. The camaraderie that is also experienced can be looked upon simply as an added fringe benefit!

General Information and Correspondence

James A. Simek
PCDA Secretary
P.O. Box 7157
Westchester, IL 60154
(630) 889-8207
e-mail: nge3@comcast.net
www.pcdaonline.com

PCDA Publication

David A. Berg
PCDA
P.O. Box 348
Portersville, PA 16051

THE SOCIETY OF PAPER MONEY COLLECTORS (SPMC)

The Society of Paper Money Collectors (SPMC) invites you to become a member of our organization. SPMC was founded in 1961 with the following objectives: (1) Encourage the collecting and study of all paper money and financial documents; (2) Provide collectors the opportunity to meet and enjoy fraternal relations with their fellow collectors; (3) Furnish information and knowledge about paper money; (4) Encourage research about paper money and financial documents and publish the resulting information; (5) Promote legislation favorable to collectors; (6) Advance the prestige of the hobby of numismatics; (7) Promote rational and consistent classification of exhibits, and ENCOURAGE participation by our members; (8) Encourage realistic and consistent market valuations.

Paper Money, SPMC's bimonthly journal now in its 36th year, has repeatedly been selected by the ANA as the Best Specialty Publication in numismatics; the Numismatic Literary Guild has also selected Paper Money for first-place recognition. Virtually every article in every issue is written by an SPMC member, who receives no monetary compensation. SPMC coordinates and judges the exhibits at the largest all-paper show every year. SPMC co-sponsors many large all-paper shows held in the U.S. each year.

Information about membership may be obtained by visiting their website at www.spmc.org or contacting them by email at benny_bolin@spmc.org.

PCDA MEMBERSHIP DIRECTORY

Michael Accavallo
Centurial Collectibles
P.O. Box 669
Coram, NY 11727
(516) 457-6573
Web Site:
 www.centurialcollectibles.com
E-mail: centurycoll@aol.com

United States Large Size Type Notes
United States Small Size
 Type Notes
United States National Bank Notes
United States Fractional Currency
Obsolete Notes
Fancy and Low Serial Number Notes
Collections
Star Notes

Rick Allard
Cashmans Currency
3453 Green Pine Place
Simi Valley, CA 93065
(805) 579-0339
Cellular: (805) 279-1641
FAX: (805) 579-0339
Web Site: www.buyoldmoney.com
E-mail:
 cashmanscurrency@aol.com

United States Large Size Type Notes
United States Small Size Gold
 Certificates
Error Notes
Fancy and Low Serial Number Notes
Serial #1 National Bank Notes and
 All Original Series Notes
Collections
Auction Sale Bidder
 Representation

Robert Azpiazu
First City Currency & Collectables,
 Inc.
P.O. Drawer 1629
St. Augustine, FL 32085
(904) 794-0784
Web Site: www.fstctycurr.com
E-mail: fstctycu@bellsouth.net

United States Small Size Type Notes
Star Notes
Error Notes
Fancy and Low Serial Number Notes
$1 FRN Blocks and District Sets
Estate Appraisals
Want List Service
Third Party Graded Key Star Notes

Stephen Barber
S & P Collectibles
P.O. Box 51416
Colorado Springs, CO 80949
(719) 480-2054
E-mail: barbersp77@msn.com

United States Large Size Type Notes
United States Small Size
 Type Notes
United States Fractional Currency
World Banknotes
U.S. Coins

Doris Bart
Bart, Inc.
P.O. Box 2
Roseville, MI 48066
(586) 979-3400
Web Site:
 www.ExecutiveCurrency.com

E-mail: doris@ExecutiveCurrency
.com

Auction Sale Bidder Representation
Rare United States Small Size Notes
United States Large Size
  Type Notes
Error Notes
Autographed Notes

Frederick J. Bart
Bart, Inc.
P.O. Box 2
Roseville, MI 48066
(586) 979-3400
Web Site:
  www.ExecutiveCurrency.com
E-mail:
  bart@ExecutiveCurrency.com

Error Notes
Serial #1 National Bank Notes
Uncut Sheets
Rare Small Size Notes Large Size
  Type Notes
Auction Representation

Keith S. Bauman
TNA Associates
P.O. Box 250027
Franklin, MI 48025-0027
Cellular: (248) 762-6654
E-mail: TNAksbauman@earthlink.net

United States Large and Small Size
  Type Notes
Fractional Currency
Colonial and Continental
World Paper Money
Numismatic Ephemera
Expo and Political Convention
  Tickets
Numismatic Art Work

David A. Berg
P.O. Box 348
Portersville, PA 16051
(724) 452-4586
E-mail: davbergltd@aol.com

Error Notes
United States Fractional Currency
United States Large Size
  Type Notes
United States National Bank Notes
United States Small Size
  Type Notes

Sammy B. Berk
Harlan J. Berk, Ltd.
31 N. Clark Street
Chicago, IL 60602
(312) 609-0016
FAX: (312) 609-1305
Web Site: www.hjbltd.com
E-mail: sammy@hjbltd.com

United States Currency
Antique Maps

Carl Bombara
P.O. Box 524
New York, NY 10116
(212) 989-9108
E-mail: CBcurrency@aol.com

United States Large Size Type Notes
United States Small Size
  Type Notes
United States National Bank Notes
Error Notes
Mail Order Sales
Auction Representation
Want Lists Serviced

C "Bo" Borich
Pacific Numismatics
P.O. Box 268
Santa Cruz, CA 95061
(831) 475-9198
FAX: (831) 475-9128
E-mail: pacnumis@live.com

United States National Bank Notes
  Especially Western States and
  Territories
United States Large Size
  Type Notes
United States Small Size
  Type Notes

Q. David Bowers
Stack's Bowers Galleries
P.O. Box 1804
Wolfeboro, NH 03894
Toll Free: (866) 811-1804
FAX: (603) 569-3875
Web Site: www.stacksbowers.com
E-mail: qdbarchive@metrocast.net

Auction Services for American
  Colonial, Obsolete, Confederate,

Federal and Related Paper Money
of all Eras
Personal Research Interest in New
Hampshire Paper Money, all Eras
Celebrating More Than Half
a Century in Professional
Numismatics, Since 1953
Past President Professional
Numismatists Guild (1977-1979)
Past President American Numismatic
Association (1983-1985)
Award-Winning Columnist for Paper
Money Magazine

Jason W. Bradford
PCGS Currency
P.O. Box 10470
Peoria, IL 61612
(309) 222-8200
Toll Free: (888) 691-PCGS (691-
7247)
Web Site: www.pcgscurrency.com
E-mail: jbradford@pcgscurrency.com

Grading & Authentication of: United
States Large & Small Size
Currency, Fractional Currency,
National Bank Notes, Confederate,
Obsoletes, MPC and World Bank
Notes

Jeff Brueggeman
Action Currency
711 Signal Mtn. Road, #197
Chattanooga, TN 37405
(423) 432-8184
Web Site: www.actioncurrency.com

United States Large Size Type Notes
United States Small Size
Type Notes

Mary Counts Burleson
Whitman Publishing, LLC
3101 Clairmont Road, Suite C
Atlanta, GA 30329
(404) 235-5317
Toll Free: (800) 852-2626
FAX: (404) 214-4398
Web Site: www.whitman.com and
www.whitmanexpo.com
E-mail: mary.counts@whitman.com

Philatelic and Numismatic
Publications & Supplies
Whitman Expos in Baltimore,
Maryland

Jhon E. Cash
Jhon E. Cash Currency and
Collectibles
2804 Woodlake Court
Highland Village, TX 75077
(214) 769-9930
Web Site: www.jhonecash.com
E-mail: jhon@jhonecash.com

United States Large Size Type Notes
United States Small Size
Type Notes
Gold Certificates
$5,000 & $10,000 Bills

Michael Hans Chou
IAsure Champion
Room 907, Silvercord Tower Two
30 Canton Road, TST
Kowloon
HONG KONG
852-2150-5744
FAX: 852-3007-4311
Web Site: www.cghka.com
E-mail: championhka@gmail.com

Chinese Currency
Asian Currency
World Paper Money

Brad Ciociola
Stack's Bowers Galleries
P.O. Box 1474
Fuquay Varina, NC 27526
(919) 650-9418
E-mail:
bciociola@stacksbowers.com

United States Large Size Type Notes
United States Small Size
Type Notes
United States National Bank Notes
Confederate Notes
Obsolete Notes

Arthur D. Cohen
Penfield Note Exchange
P.O. Box 311
Penfield, NY 14526-0311
(585) 377-4677
E-mail: adcohen@frontiernet.net

World Paper Money
Mail Order Price Lists
Custom Labels for Currency Holders,
Flips and Slabs

Terry Coyle
Alex Perakis Coins & Currency, Inc.
P.O. Box 246
Lima, PA 19037
(610) 627-1212
FAX: (610) 891-1466
Web Site: www.perakiscurrency.com
E-mail: apcc1@msn.com

United States National Bank Notes
United States Large Size
  Type Notes
United States Small Size
  Type Notes

Edward A. Dauer
4850 West Oakland Park Blvd.
Suite 145
Fort Lauderdale, FL 33313
(954) 739-0978
FAX: (954) 739-2587
Web Site:
  www.amhistoryuscurrency.com
E-mail: EasyDog5@aol.com

All United States Currency
British Commonwealth Banknotes,
  especially Canada, Australia, New
  Zealand and Great Britain

Alex Delatola
APD Currency Corp.
P.O. Box 577
Pittstown, NJ 08867
(908) 479-1899
FAX: (908) 479-1661
Web Site: www.apdcurrency.com
E-mail: alex@apdcurrency.com

United States Large Size
  Type Notes
United States Small Size Type Note
  Specialist: Silver Certificates,
  United States Notes, Federal
  Reserve Notes, Gold Certificates,
  Uncut Sheets and "Blocks of 4,"
  Web Notes, Engraving
  Errors, Packs of Star and
  Block Notes
Canadian Paper Money
World Banknotes

Phil Delia
Delia Coins & Paper Money
P.O. Box 134
Plainfield, VT 05667

(802) 322-5013
E-mail: phildelia@yahoo.com

World Banknotes

John Demaris
P.O. Box 72
Boys Town, NE 68010
(402) 321-0670
E-mail: siramed@aol.com

United States Small Size Type Notes
United States Large Size
  Type Notes
United States National Bank Notes
United States Fractional Currency
Obsolete Sheets
Confederate Notes
Colonial and Continental
Uncut Sheets, Star Notes, Low
  Serial Numbers, and Original Runs
  of All Notes

Thomas M. Denly
Denly's of Boston
10 High Street, Room 1107
Boston, MA 02110
(617) 482-8477
Toll Free: (800) HI DENLY
FAX: (617) 357-8163
Web Site: www.Denlys.com
E-mail: denlys@aol.com

Colonial and Continental Currency
United States Fractional Currency
United States Large Size
  Type Notes
United States Small Size
  Type Notes
Confederate Currency
Obsolete Notes and Scrip
United States National Bank Notes
Canadian Currency
Books and Supplies
Military Payment Certificates
World Paper Money
Auction Sale Bidder Representation
Mail Order Price Lists
Encased Postage
Mylar D™ Currency Holders
United States & Foreign Coins

Michael Findlay
Certified Coins of Canada
P.O. Box 2043
Angus, Ontario L0M 1B0
CANADA

(705) 423-1140
Toll Free: (888) 649-7777
FAX: (705) 423-1069
E-mail: ccdn@bconnex.net

Canadian Banknotes
World Banknotes
Canadian Merchant Scrip
Publisher: Canadian Coin Dealer
  Newsletter

Don Fisher
Currency Unlimited
P.O. Box 481
Decatur, IL 62525
Cellular: (217) 433-2242
Obsolete Notes
United States National Bank Notes
World Paper Money
United States Coins
World Coins

Jim Fitzgerald
Fitzgerald Currency & Coins
P.O. Box 210845
Bedford, TX 76095
(817) 688-6994
E-mail:
  FitzgeraldCurrency@gmail.com

United States National Bank Notes
Confederate Notes
United States Small Size
  Type Notes
United States Large Size
  Type Notes
United States Fractional Currency
Colonial Notes
Obsolete Notes
Fiscal Documents - Focusing Mainly
  on Texas
United States Coins

Kevin Foley
P.O. Box 370650
Milwaukee, WI 53237
(414) 807-0116
FAX: (414) 747-9490
E-mail: kfoley2@wi.rr.com

Numismatic Convention and Show
  Management
United States Large Size
  Type Notes
United States National Bank Notes
United States Small Size
  Type Notes

United States Fractional
  Currency

Dennis Forgue
Harlan J. Berk, Ltd.
31 North Clark Street
Chicago, IL 60602
(312) 609-0016
FAX: (312) 609-1305
Web Site: www.hjbltd.com
E-mail: dennis@hjbltd.com

United States Large Size Type Notes
United States Small Size
  Type Notes
Confederate
Obsolete Notes
United States National Bank Notes
Error Notes
Autographs

Cory Frampton
Mexican Coin Company
P.O. Box 5270
Carefree, AZ 85377
(480) 921-2562
Web Site:
  www.mexicancoincompany.com
E-mail:
  cory@mexicancoincompany.com

Mexican Coins and Paper Money

Pierre Fricke
P.O. Box 1094
Sudbury, MA 01776
(404) 895-0672
Web Site: www.csaquotes.com
E-mail: pfricke@attglobal.net

Confederate and Southern States
  Paper Money
United States Large Size
  Type Notes (Civil War Era)
Early American Copper Coins
Obsolete Notes

Steve Garvin
Honor Coin & Stamp
4001 U.S. 31 South, Suite D
Traverse City, MI 49685
(231) 943-9991
E-mail: office@honor-coin.com

Error Notes
Military Payment Certificates
Michigan Nationals

Robert Giamboi
ASN Currency, LLC
P.O. Box 8494
Pelham, NY 10803
(914) 500-7999
FAX: (914) 738-6194
Web Site: www.asncurrency.com
E-mail: asncurr@aol.com

*United States Small Size
  Currency - 1928 to Date*

Stephen L. Goldsmith
Spink, USA
145 West 57th Street
New York, NY 10019
(212) 262-8400
Web Site: www.spinksmythe.com
E-mail: sgoldsmith@spink.com

*All United States Paper Money
Obsolete Notes
Colonial and Continental
Confederate Notes and Bonds
Stocks, Bonds and Fiscal
  Documents*

Bill Grubb
Olde Mill Currency
P.O. Box 101
Telford, PA 18969
(215) 527-4380
E-mail: grubbwf@msn.com

*United States National Bank Notes
United States Large Size
  Type Notes
United States Small Size
  Type Notes
Financial Stock Certificates
Savings Banks*

Bruce R. Hagen
Stack's Bowers Galleries
123 West 57th Street
New York, NY 10019
(212) 582-2580
Toll Free: (800) 566-2580
FAX: (646) 443-5548
Web Site: www.stacksbowers.com
E-mail: bhagen@stacksbowers.com

*Auction Sales of United States and
  World Coins, Medals and Paper
  Currency
Colonial and Continental Currency
Obsolete Notes and Proofs*

*All United States Federal
  Currency*

Larry Hanks
Hanks & Associates, Inc.
P.O. Box 913
Indian Rocks Beach, FL 33785
(727) 593-1303
E-mail: whanks3700@aol.com

*United States Large Size Type Notes
United States Small Size
  Type Notes
United States National Bank Notes
Rare Paper Money Counseling*

Chad Hawk
Paper Money Guaranty
5501 Communications Pkwy.
Sarasota, FL 34240
(941) 309-1001
Toll Free: (877) 764-5570
FAX: (941) 309-1002
Web Site: www.pmgnotes.com
E-mail: chawk@pmgnotes.com

*Grading & Authentication of:
United States Large & Small Size
  Currency, Fractional Currency,
  National Bank Notes, Confederate
  Currency, Military Payment
  Certificates, World Paper Money,
  Uncut Sheets of Currency,
  Obsolete Currency and Southern
  States Currency*

Ronald F. Hedglin
Sailboat Coins & Currency
P.O. Box 580
Streator, IL 61364-0580
(815) 672-2548
Cellular: (815) 674-2506
FAX: (815) 672-2906 Attn: Ron
E-mail: hedglin@thegreves.com

United States National Currency

Eric C. Helms
6108 N. Oakland Avenue
Indianapolis, IN 46220
(317) 250-3742
E-mail: echelms@aol.com

*Stocks and Bonds
Confederate Currency
United States Coins
Obsolete Notes*

Edward W. Henley
Unlimited Currency
P.O. Box 514
Greenville, IN 47124
Toll Free: (888) 923-7743
Web Site:
  www.unlimitedcurrency.net
E-mail:
  unlimited_currency@yahoo.com

United States Small Size Type Notes
Third Party Graded High Quality
  Notes

Roland Hill
Rare Choice Currency
P.O. Box 3737
North Fort Myers, FL 33918-3737
(239) 731-5885
E-mail: trots@embarqmail.com

United States Large Size Type Notes
United States Small Size Type Notes
United States National Bank Notes
United States Fractional Currency
Obsolete Notes
Colonial and Continental
Confederate
Civil War Photos
Rare Autographs Canadian
Western Americana
Early Railroad
Star Notes
F.R.N. Red Seals
Military Americana
French and Indian War Material
Indian Artifacts

Meredith J. Hilton
Kagin's, Inc.
1550-G Tiburon Blvd., #201
Tiburon, CA 94920
(415) 435-2601
Toll Free: (888) 8 KAGINS
FAX: (415) 435-2601
Web Site: www.kagins.com
E-mail: meredith@kagins.com

United States Large Size Type Notes
United States Small Size
  Type Notes
United States National Currency
United States Fractional Currency
Colonial and Continental
Mormon Currency
Confederate
Military Payment Certificates

Gregg Hoffman
Premier Precious Metals
  Coins & Currency
P.O. Box 28100
Santa Fe, NM 87592-8100
(505) 989-7680
Toll Free: (800) 557-9958
FAX: (505) 989-7685
Web Site:
  www.premierpreciousmetals.com
E-mail: gahoffman2004@yahoo.com

World Paper Money
United States Large Size
  Type Notes
United States Small Size
  Type Notes
Obsolete Notes
United States National Bank Notes
Error Notes
Silver Dollars
Bust Type Silver Dollars
Older Type Coins

Richard M. Hokanson
Richard Hokanson R.C.I.
P.O. Box 940
Southold, NY 11971
(631) 765-6464
FAX: (631) 765-6466
Web Site: www.hokanson-coins.com
E-mail: coins@optonline.com

United States Large Size Type Notes
United States Small Size
  Type Notes
United States National Bank Notes

Richard L. Horst
P.O. Box 49485
Colorado Springs, CO 80949-9485
(719) 593-0761
E-mail: arelaitch9@yahoo.com

Appraisals
Obsolete Notes Confederate
United States Large Size
  Type Notes
Western Checks and Drafts
World Paper Money World and
  Ancient Coins
Fiscal Ephemera

Steve Ivy
Heritage Auctions
3500 Maple Avenue, 17th Floor
Dallas, TX 75219-3938

(214) 528-3500
Toll Free: (800) 872-6467
FAX: (214) 443-8409
Web Site: www.HA.com
E-mail: steve@HA.com

Auction Sales of:
United States Large Size
Type Notes
United States Small Size
Type Notes
United States National Bank Notes
United States Fractional Currency
Error Notes
Colonial and Continental
Confederate
Obsolete Notes

Dustin Johnston
Heritage Auctions
3500 Maple Avenue, 17th Floor
Dallas, TX 75219
(214) 409-1302
Toll Free: (800) 872-6467
Web Site:
www.heritagecurrency.com
E-mail: dustin@ha.com

United States National Bank Notes
Confederate Notes
United States Small Size
Type Notes
United States Large Size
Type Notes
United States Fractional Currency
Colonial Notes
Obsolete Notes
World Paper Money

Harry E. Jones
Harry E. Jones Rare Currency
7379 Pearl Road Cleveland, OH
44130
(440) 234-3330
FAX: (440) 234-3332
E-mail: hjones6671@aol.com

Error Notes
United States Large Size
Type Notes
United States Small Size Type Notes
United States National Bank Notes
Obsolete Notes
Serial #1 Notes
Uncut Sheets

Jeffrey S. Jones
The Small Size Shop
P.O. Box 2007
Westerville, OH 43086
(614) 296-2659
FAX: (614) 899-1557
E-mail: JonesJeffreyS@aol.com

United States Small Size
Type Notes - Especially High
Grade and Rare
Ohio National Bank Notes
Ohio Obsolete Notes

Glen I. Jorde
P.O. Box 48
Devils Lake, ND 58301
and
P.O. Box 15198
Sarasota, FL 34277
Cellular: (701) 230-1148
E-mail: glenjorde@gmail.com

United States Large Size Currency
United States Small Size Currency
United States Fractional Currency
United States National Bank Notes
Confederate Currency
Military Payment Certificates
Uncut Sheets
World Paper Money
Auction Sale Bidder Representation

Donald H. Kagin
Kagin's, Inc.
1550-G Tiburon Blvd., #201
Tiburon, CA 94920
(415) 435-2601
Toll-Free: (888) 8 KAGINS
FAX: (415) 435-1627
E-mail: don@kagins.com

United States Large Size Type Notes
United States Small Size
Type Notes
United States National Currency
United States Fractional Currency
Colonial and Continental
Mormon Currency
Confederate
Military Payment Certificates

Judith Kagin
X-Tremely Fine, Ltd.
Denver, CO
Cellular: (720) 383-2702
E-mail: Kagins70@aol.com

United States Type Notes
United States National Bank Notes
Obsolete Notes

Christine Karstedt
Stack's Bowers Galleries
P.O. Box 1804
Wolfeboro, NH 03894
(603) 569-0823
Toll Free: (866) 811-1804
FAX: (603) 569-3875
Web Site: www.stacksbowers.com
E-mail:
  ckarstedt@stacksbowers.com

United States Large Size Type Notes
United States Small Size
  Type Notes
United States National Bank Notes
Auction Sales

Don C. Kelly
Paper Money Institute
P.O. Box 85
Oxford, OH 45056
(513) 312-4760
Web Site: www.donckelly.com
E-mail: don@donckelly.com

United States Large Size Type Notes
United States Small Size
  Type Notes
Colonial and Continental
Obsolete Notes
United States National Bank Notes
Confederate States
Error Notes
World Bank Notes
Fancy Serial Numbers

David Kelman
Notes - RR - US
115 Beckworth Drive Taylors, SC
  29687
(864) 787-3535
Web Site: www.notes-rr-us.com
E-mail: davidkelman@aol.com or
davidkelman@charter.net

Serial #1 Notes
United States National Bank Notes
Uncut Sheets
United States Large Size Type Notes
United States Small Size Type Notes
Error Notes
Fancy and Low Serial Number Notes

Laura A. Kessler
Pcgs Currency
P.O. Box 10470
Peoria, IL 61612
(309) 222-8200
Toll Free: (888) 691-PCGS (7247)
FAX: (949) 833-7955
Web Site: www.pcgscurrency.com
E-mail: lkessler@pcgscurrency.com

Grading & Authentication of:
United States Large & Small Size
  Currency, Fractional Currency,
  National Bank Notes, Confederate,
  Obsoletes, MPC and World Bank
  Notes

Don Ketterling
Dh Ketterling Consulting
3835-R E. Thousand Oaks Blvd.,
  #136
Westlake Village, CA 91362
(818) 632-2352
FAX: (805) 418-7455
Web Site: www.dhketterling.com
E-mail: dhconsulting@verizon.net

Obsolete Notes
United States Large Size
  Type Notes
United States Small Size
  Type Notes
United States National Bank Notes
General Paper Ephemera

Lyn F. Knight
Lyn Knight Currency Auctions
P.O. Box 7364
Overland Park, KS 66207-0364
(913) 338-3779
FAX: (913) 338-4754
Web Site: www.lynknight.com
E-mail: lyn@lynknight.com

Auction Sales for National
  Conventions
United States Currency
World Paper Money
United States & World Coins
Ephemera
Posters
Postcards

David R. Koble
Mid American Currency
P.O. Box 1282
Bartlesville, OK 74005

(918) 335-0847
Cellular: (918) 914-1496
E-mail: dkoble@cableone.net

United States Large Size Type Notes
United States Small Size
Type Notes
United States National Bank Notes
Auction Representation

Tim Kyzivat
P.O. Box 451
Western Springs, IL 60558
(708) 784-0974
Web Site: www.kyzivatcurrency.com
E-mail:
tkyzivat@kyzivatcurrency.com

United States Large Size Type Notes
United States National Bank Notes
United States Small Size
Type Notes
Confederate Currency
Obsolete Notes
Error Notes
United States Fractional Currency
Fancy and Low Serial Number Notes

George H. LaBarre
George H. LaBarre Galleries, Inc.
P.O. Box 746
Hollis, NH 03049
(603) 882-2411
Toll Free: (800) 717-9529
FAX: (603) 882-4797
Web Site: www.glabarre.com
E-mail: collect@glabarre.com

Obsolete Notes
Colonial and Continental
Military Payment Certificates
Error Notes
Confederate
World Paper Money
Autographs
General Americana

Dr. Frank G. Laiacona
P.O. Box 1512
Mt. Shasta, CA 96067
(530) 859-2814
FAX: (530) 926-9306
Web Site: www.franksdollars.com *or*
www.peacedollars.net
E-mail: cyncadom@juno.com

United States Large Size Type Notes
$500, $1,000, $5,000 and
$10,000 Notes
World Paper Money

Jay Laws
Scotsman Coins
11262 Olive Blvd.
St. Louis, MO 63141
(314) 692-2646
Toll Free: (800) 642-4305
Cellular: (314) 210-4443
FAX: (314) 692-0410
E-mail: jlaws@scoins.com

United States National Bank Notes
United States Large Size
Type Notes
United States Small Size
Type Notes
Confederate Currency
Military Payment Certificates

David Leong
Paper M, LLC
P.O. Box 1388
Seabrook, NH 03874
(216) 338-7723
Web Site: www.paperm.com
E-mail: david@paperm.com

World Paper Money
Stack's Bowers Galleries
Consignment Director

Stuart Levine
P.O. Box 806
Marblehead, MA 01945
(781) 477-0552
FAX: (781) 477-0827
E-mail: stuartlevine@comcast.net

Colonial and Continental Currency

Scott Lindquist
P.O. Box 2175
Minot, ND 58702
(602) 741-3385
Web Site: www.scottlindquist.com
E-mail: slindquist1963@gmail.com
or scott@scottlindquist.com

United States and Canadian
Currency - Large and Small Size
World Paper Money
United States National Bank Notes
Auction Sale Representation

Dana Linett
Early American Numismatics
P.O. Box 675390
Rancho Santa Fe, CA 92067
**Early American History
Auctions, Inc.**
P.O. Box 3507
Rancho Santa Fe, CA 92067
(858) 759-3290
FAX: (858) 759-1439
Web Site: www.earlyamerican.com
E-mail: dana@earlyamerican.com

Colonial and Continental Currency
United States Fractional Currency
United States Large Size
  Type Notes
United States Small Size Type Notes
Confederate
Stocks, Bonds and Fiscal
  Documents
Checks
Books and Supplies
Auction Sales
Mail Order Price Lists
Mail Bid Sales
Encased Postage Stamps
Historic Maps
Rare Autographs

William Litt
**William Litt Rare Coins &
Currency**
P.O. Box 221148
Carmel, CA 93922
(650) 430-2024
Web Site:
  www.WilliamLittCurrency.com
E-mail: BillLitt@aol.com

United States National Bank Notes
United States Large Size
  Type Notes
National Bank Memorabilia

Claire Lobel
Coincraft
44 & 45 Great Russell Street
London WC1B 3LU
ENGLAND
(44) 20 7636 1188
FAX: (44) 20 7323 2860
E-mail: clairelob@aol.com

England, Scotland, Ireland, Channel
  Islands, Isle of Man
General World

John Markis
Trusted Traditions
275 Commercial Blvd., Suite 275
Lauderdale-by-the-Sea, FL 33308
(954) 938-9700
Toll Free: (877) NGC-COINS
FAX: (954) 938-9876
Web Site: www.trustedtraditions.com
E-mail: sales@trustedtraditions.com

Certified Paper Money

Ray Marrello
Antique Currency Llc
10170 W. Tropicana Ave., Suite
  156-386
Las Vegas, NV 89147
(702) 202-0140
Toll Free: (877) 396-5322
Web Site: www.rmcurrency.com
E-mail: RMCurrency@aol.com

United States Large Size Type Notes
United States Small Size
  Type Notes
United States National Bank Notes

David V. Messner
Constellation Numismatic
P.O. Box 209
Akron, PA 17501-0209
(717) 721-9504
Web Site: www.errorcurrency.com

Error Notes
Colonial and Continental
United States Error and Die
  Variety Coins

James W. Miller
Ft. Oglethorpe Rare Coins, LLC
402 Battlefield Parkway, Suite 19
Ft. Oglethorpe, GA 30742
(706) 861-0900
FAX: (706) 861-8555
Cellular: (912) 536-6222
Web Site: ftocoins.com
E-mail: jwmiller11@aol.com

Obsolete Notes
Confederate
Colonial and Continental
United States National Currency
United States Large Size
  Type Notes
United States Small Size
  Type Notes

Barry Minster
P.O. Box 113
Clawson, MI 48017
(248) 227-7421
E-mail: bminc123@gmail.com

United States Large Size Type Notes
United States Small Size
Type Notes
United States Fractional Currency

Michael G. Moczalla
Heritage Auctions
3500 Maple Avenue, 17th Floor
Dallas, TX 75219
(214) 409-1481
Toll Free: (800) 872-6467
Web Site: www.ha.com
E-mail: michaelm@ha.com

United States National Bank Notes
Confederate Notes
United States Small Size
Type Notes
United States Large Size
Type Notes
United States Fractional Currency
Colonial Notes
Obsolete Notes
World Paper Money

Richard Nachbar
Nachbar Rare Coins
P.O. Box 98
Williamsville, NY 14231-0098
(716) 635-9700
Toll Free: (877) 622-4227
FAX: (716) 635-9762
Web Site: www.coinexpert.com
E-mail: nachbar@coinexpert.com

Buyer of Collections and Better
Notes
United States Large Size
Type Notes
United States Rare Coins

John Pack
Stack's Bowers Galleries
P.O. Box 18523
Irvine, CA 92623
(949) 955-1250
FAX: (949) 955-1824
Web Site: www.stacksbowers.com
E-mail: jpack@stacksbowers.com

Auction Consultation for All Types of
Paper Money

Gary Parietti
L.I. Numismatics, Inc.
P.O. Box 42
Bedford Hills, NY 10507-0042
(914) 242-6090
FAX: (914) 242-6091
Web Site: www.linumis.com
E-mail: garyparietti@aol.com

All United States Paper, especially
United States National Bank Notes
Rare Coins
Historical Autographs

Charles C. Parrish
P.O. Box 481
Rosemount, MN 55068
(651) 423-1039
E-mail: chuckparrish@frontiernet.net

United States Large Size Type Notes
United States Small Size
Type Notes
United States National Bank Notes
Obsolete Notes
All Minnesota Currency

Jeffrey R. Paunicka
Insight3
P.O. Box 683
Portage, IN 46368
(574) 315-0238
Toll Free: (800) 949-0361
FAX: (800) 708-6708
Web Site: www.oldbucks.com
E-mail: money@oldbucks.com

United States Fractional Currency
Confederate
United States Large Size
Type Notes
United States Small Size
Type Notes
Colonial and Continental
World Bank Notes (Bahamas,
Canada, Pre-Castro Cuba,
Philippines 1902-49, Bermuda,
Japan)
Encased Postage
Military Payment Certificates

Alex G. Perakis
12941 North Pioneer Way
Oro Valley, AZ 85755

(520) 544-7778
FAX: (520) 544-7779
E-mail: aperakis@dakotacom.net

United States Fractional Currency
United States Large Size
   Type Notes
United States Small Size
   Type Notes
United States National Bank Notes
United States Obsoletes
World Bank Notes

Stephen Perakis
Alex Perakis Coins & Currency,
   Inc.
P.O. Box 246
Lima, PA 19037
(610) 565-1110
FAX: (610) 891-1466
Web Site: www.perakiscurrency.com
E-mail: apcc1@msn.com

United States Large Size Type Notes
United States Small Size
   Type Notes
United States National Bank Notes
United States Fractional Currency

Joe Peruski
Monroe Currency & Coin
P.O. Box 932
Monroe, MI 48161
(734) 777-4285
Web Site: www.monroecurrency.com
E-mail:
   jperuski@monroecurrency.com

Obsolete Notes
United States National Bank Notes
Checks
Civil War Items
United States Bank Notes
World Bank Notes

Moon Phaengsavanh
Paper Money Guaranty
P.O. Box 4755
Sarasota, FL 34230
(941) 309-1001
Web Site: www.pmgnotes.com
E-mail: moon@pmgnotes.com

Grading & Authentication of:
United States Large & Small Size
   Currency, Fractional Currency,
   National Bank Notes, Confederate

Currency, Military Payment
   Certificates, World Paper Money
   and Uncut Sheets of Currency

James Polis
4501 Connecticut Avenue, N W
Suite 306
Washington, DC 20008
(202) 363-6650
FAX: (202) 363-4712
E-mail: jpolis7935@aol.com

Colonial and Continental
United States Fractional Currency
United States Large Size
   Type Notes
United States Small Size
   Type Notes
United States National Bank Notes
Confederate Currency
Auction Sale Bidder Representation

Richard H. Ponterio
Ponterio & Associates, Inc.
1063 McGaw Avenue, Suite 100
Irvine, CA 92614
(949) 253-0916
Toll Free: (800) 458-4646
FAX: (949) 253-4091

World Paper Money
Mexican Paper Money
Auction Sales

Vern Potter
Vern Potter Currency &
   Collectibles
P.O. Box 10040
Torrance, CA 90505-0740
(310) 326-0406
FAX: (310) 326-0406
Web Site: www.vernpotter.com
E-mail: vern@vernpotter.com

Obsolete Notes
Confederate Currency, Bonds and
   Ephemera
United States Fractional Currency
Colonial and Continental
United States Small Size
   Type Notes
United States Large Size Type Notes

Matthew W. Quinn
Stack's Bowers Galleries /
   Ponterio & Assoc.
1063 McGaw Avenue, Suite 100

Irvine, CA 92614
Toll Free: (800) 458-4646
Web Site: www.stacksbowers.com
E-mail: mattq@coins.com

Obsolete Notes
United States Large Size
 Type Notes
United States Small Size
 Type Notes
World Paper Money

Lou Rasera
Southland Coins & Currency
P.O. Box 403
Woodland Hills, CA 91365
(818) 348-5275
Cellular: (818) 388-0099
FAX: (818) 348-5275
E-mail: ljrasera@aol.com

United States Large Size Type Notes
United States Small Size
 Type Notes
United States National Bank Notes
Confederate
Error Notes
Professional Auction Representation

Kent Robertson
U.S. Currency
P.O. Box 779
Charlestown, RI 02813
(404) 229-7184
E-mail: usckr26@yahoo.com

United States Large Size Type Notes
United States Small Size
 Type Notes
United States National Bank Notes
Obsolete Notes
Confederate Notes
Confederate Bonds
Political Memorabilia
Autographs
Auction Sale Bidder Representation

Edward M. Rothberg Emporium
 Coin & Currency
P.O. Box 606
Moorhead, MN 56561
Toll Free: (800) 248-9751 *or* (800)
 342-1994
Cellular: (701) 219-1224

United States Large Size Type Notes
United States Small Size
 Type Notes
United States National Bank Notes
United States Fractional Currency
Colonial and Continental
Errors, Stars and Misc.
Obsolete Notes
Canadian Currency
United States Coins
Giori Test Currency

Costa Roupas
Costa's Coins and Currency
339 N. Milwaukee Avenue
Libertyville, IL 60048
(224) 433-6634
FAX: (224) 513-5917
E-mail: costascurrency@yahoo.com

United States Small Size Type Notes
United States Large Size Type Notes
High Denomination Notes

John N. Rowe III
Southwest Numismatic Corp.
6116 N. Central Expy., Suite 921
Dallas, TX 75206
(214) 826-3036
FAX: (214) 823-1923

United States Large Size Type Notes
United States Small Size Type Notes
Confederate
Obsolete Notes
United States National Bank Notes
Republic of Texas

O.E. "Dusty" Royer
Notes Of Note
34 Lake Charles Drive
 St. Peters, MO 63376
(636) 441-0481
E-mail: dustylB@netscape.net

World Currency
German Notgeld
Military Notes
U.S. Obsolete Notes
World Coins
Propaganda Items (World War II)
Disney Dollars

Gaylen Rust
Rust Rare Coin Co.
252 East 300 South
Salt Lake City, UT 84111

(801) 363-4014
Toll Free: (800) 343-7878
FAX: (801) 364-0929
Web Site: www.rustcoin.com
E-mail: grust@rustcoin.com

Mormon and Related Items
Utah and Intermountain Area Notes

Sergio Sanchez, Jr.
Sergio Sanchez, Jr. Currency
P.O. Box 44-2809
Miami, FL 33144-2809
(305) 264-1101
FAX: (305) 264-1102
Web Site:
  www.sanchezcurrency.com
E-mail:
  sergio@sanchezcurrency.com

United States Large Size
  Type Notes
United States Small Size
  Type Notes

Joe Sande
Joe Sande - Professional
  Numismatist
P.O. Box 318
Nichols, FL 33863-0318
(863) 607-6337
FAX: (863) 607-6337

United States Large Size Type Notes
United States National Bank Notes
United States Small Size
  Type Notes
United States Fractional Currency
Mail Bid Sales
Auction Sale Bidder Representation

Paul James Schupp (Associate
  Member)
Legal Tender Currency
Lake in the Hills, IL 60156
(847) 946-1982
E-mail: joy.schupp@att.net

Currency for the Mid-Range
  Collector

George Schweighofer
Currency Quest
P.O. Box 384
Reynoldsburg, OH 43068
(614) 864-8875
Web Site: www.currencyquest.com

E-mail: currencyquest@aol.com *or*
  info@currencyquest.com

All United States Currency

David F. Seelye
P.O. Box 13117
Prescott, AZ 86304-3117
Cellular: (505) 305-4848
E-mail: davideseelye@gmail.com

World Paper Money
Military Payment Certificates
Allied Military Currency

Donald Severance
P.O. Box 140
Pembroke, NH 03275
(603) 738-7032
E-mail: rd_rarities@yahoo.com

United States Large Size Type Notes
United States Small Size
  Type Notes
United States Fractional Currency
United States National Bank Notes
Obsolete Notes
Military Payment Certificates

Joel Shafer
P.O. Box 170985
Milwaukee, WI 53217
(414) 350-6980
E-mail: grbaypa@aol.com

World Paper Money

Amanda Sheheen
A & O Currency, LLC
P.O. Box 1711
Camden, SC 29021
(803) 432-2435
Web Site: www.aocurrency.com
E-mail: amanda@aocurrency.com

Confederate Notes
Obsolete Notes and Scrip
South Carolina National Bank Notes
Colonial and Continental Currency
United States Fractional Currency
Military Payment Certificates
Books and Supplies
Auction Sale Bidder Representation

Austin M. Sheheen, Jr.
P.O. Box 428
Camden, SC 29020

(803) 432-1424
FAX: (803) 432-1831
E-mail: ams@shgcpa.com

South Carolina Colonial Notes
South Carolina Obsolete Notes
South Carolina National Bank Notes

Micky Shipley
Micky's Currency
P.O. Box 114
Devils Lake, ND 58301
Cellular: (701) 230-0036
E-mail: micky@gondtc.com

United States National Bank Notes
United States Large Size Type Notes
United States Small Size Type Notes

Randy Shipley
Shipley's Currency
709 Jim Town Road
   Mooresburg, TN 37811
(423) 335-6811
FAX: (423) 921-0586
Web Site:
   www.shipleyscurrency.com
E-mail:
   randy@shipleyscurrency.com

Confederate Notes
Southern States Currency
Obsolete Notes and Scrip
Confederate Fiscal Documents

Andrew A. Shiva
205 West 76th Street
New York, NY 10023
(917) 873-8144
Web Site:
   www.nationalcurrencyfoundation
   .org
E-mail: nbncensus@gmail.com

United States National Bank Notes:
   Census, Research, Signing
   Bankers

Hugh Shull
P.O. Box 2522
Lexington, SC 29071
(803) 996-3660
FAX: (803) 996-4885

Confederate Notes
Obsolete Notes and Scrip
South Carolina National Bank Notes

Colonial and Continental Notes
United States Fractional Currency
Stocks, Bonds and Fiscal
   Documents
Mail Order Catalogs
Books and Supplies
Auction Sale Bidder Representation

James A. Simek
Numisgraphic Enterprises
P.O. Box 7157
Westchester, IL 60154
(630) 889-8207
E-mail: nge3@comcast.net

United States National Bank Notes
United States Small Size
   Type Notes
United States Large Size
   Type Notes
Error Notes
Hawaiian Related Material

Jeff Smith
TreasuredStocks.com
1605 Michigan Avenue Horseshoe
   Bend, AR 72512
(870) 670-4255
Web Site: www.treasuredstocks.com
E-mail: jeff@treasuredstocks.com

United States Large Size
   Type Notes
United States Small Size
   Type Notes
Gold Certificates
United States National Bank Notes
United States Fractional Currency
Colonial and Continental
Confederate
Error Notes
Military Payment Certificates
Obsolete Notes
PCGS and PMG Top Population
   Notes
World Paper Money
Disney Dollars

David Steckling
Gold-N-Silver Rarities
1615 First Street South
St. Cloud, MN 56301
(320) 259-0233

Minnesota National Bank Notes
Minnesota Obsolete Notes
Obsolete Notes

United States Large Size
 Type Notes
United States Small Size
 Type Notes

Richard Stelzer
Estate Coin & Jewelry
1650 Main Street
Sarasota, FL 34236
Cellular: (605) 321-1449
Office: (941) 952-0100
Wob Sito:
 www.estate-coin-jewelry-gallerla
 .com
E-mail: rick52447@grnail.com

United States Large Size Type Notes
United States Small Size Type Notes
United States National Bank Notes
United States Fractional Currency
Error Notes
Star / Replacement Notes - U.S.
 and World
Confederate Notes
World Bank Notes
Auction Sale Bidder Representation
Appraisal Services
United States and World Coins
Canadian Coins and Paper Money

Mike Storeim
Michael R. Storeim, Inc.
32135 Castle Court, Suite 100A
Evergreen, CO 80439
(303) 670-3212
Cellular: (303) 903-9932
E-mail: mike@numispro.com

United States Large Size Type Notes
United States National Bank Notes
United States Small Size
 Type Notes

David M. Sundman
Littleton Coin Company, LLC
1309 Mt. Eustis Road
Littleton, NH 03561-3735
(603) 444-5386
FAX: (603) 444-3512
Web Site: www.littletoncoin.com
E-mail: dsundman@littletoncoin.com

Fixed Price Lists and Catalogs to
 Collectors
Always Buying and Selling:
United States Large Size
 Type Notes

United States Small Size
 Type Notes
United States National Bank Notes
United States Fractional Currency
United Statos Coins

David Sweet
Dave's Premier Coins & Currency
Lansing, MI (517) 819-9639
Toll Free: (800) 933-4720
FAX: (517) 351-3466
Web Site: llbertycoinservice.com
E-mail: premiercoin@yahoo.com

Michigan National Bank Notes
Obsolete Notes
General Currency
United States Coins
Collectibles

Allan L. Teal
P.O. Box 429
Chester Heights, PA 19017
(610) 459-5265
FAX: (610) 459-8821 Sundays at
 Store 7:30 AM - 4 PM
Renninger's Antique Market
Adamstown, PA
(717) 336-6622

Pennsylvania National Bank Notes
Delaware National Bank Notes
Confederate
Obsolete Notes
United States Large Size Type Notes
United States National Bank Notes

Anthony Terranova
Anthony Terranova, Inc.
P.O. Box 985, FDR Station
New York, NY 10150
(212) 787-5682
FAX: (212) 787-9323

Early American Paper Money
U.S. Colonial and State Coinage
 Issues
Early U.S. Mint Issues and Rare
 Gold
Historical American Medals
Services to the Trade Only

Bruce Thornton
Paper Money Guaranty
P.O. Box 4755
Sarasota, FL 34230
(941) 309-1001

Web Site: www.pmgnotes.com
E-mail: bthornton@pmgnotes.com

*Grading & Authentication of: United
States Large & Small Size
Currency, Fractional Currency,
National Bank Notes, Confederate
Currency, Military Payment
Certificates, World Paper
Money and Uncut Sheets
of Currency*

Greg Ton
P.O. Box 9
Franklin, TN 37065
(901) 487-5944
Web Site: www.gregtoncurrency.com
E-mail: gton1@aol.com

*Confederate Notes
Southern States Notes
Southern Obsolete Notes
Northern Obsolete Notes
Colonial Notes
Southern Financial Documents
Confederate and Civil War Artifacts*

Peter A. Treglia
Stack's Bowers Galleries
P.O. Box 18523
Irvine, CA 92623
(949) 955-1250, Ext. 250
Cellular: (617) 462-7267
FAX: (949) 955-1824
Web Site: www.StacksBowers.com
E-mail: petert@StacksBowers.com

*United States Large Size
Type Notes
United States Small Size
Type Notes
Error Notes
Fancy Serial Numbers
United States National Bank Notes
Confederate
United States Fractional Currency
World Paper Money
Auction Sale Bidder Representation*

Robert L. Vandevender II
American Paper Connection, Inc.
P.O. Box 1505
Jupiter, FL 33468
(815) 355-0233
Web Site: www
   .americanpaperconnection.com
E-mail: rvpaperman@aol.com

*United States Small Size Type Notes
United States Large Size Type Notes
United States Fractional Currency
United States National Bank Notes*

George K. Warner
P.O. Box 842
Sheridan, WY 82801
(307) 751-3230

*World Paper Money
United States Small Size Type Notes
United States Fractional Currency
Wyoming National Bank Notes*

Harry Warren
Mid-South Coin Co., Inc.
3894 Park Avenue
Memphis, TN 38111
Store: (901) 324-2244
Cellular: (901) 494-2244
FAX: (901) 324-2249
Web Site: www.midsouthcoin.com
E-mail: midsouthcoin@aol.com

*United States Large Size Type Notes
Tennessee National Bank Notes*

Gene Wheeler
**Gene Wheeler Rare Coin &
   Currency**
P.O. Box 747
Seymour, TX 76380
(940) 888-3832
FAX: (940) 888-3807
Web Site: www.gwcoins.com
E-mail: gwcoins@windstream.net

*Texas National Bank Notes
United States Large Size
Type Notes
United States Small Size
Type Notes*

Gary Whitelock
Whitelock Rare Currency
P.O. Box 370392
Reseda, CA 91337-0392
(818) 739-9485
Cellular: (562) 673-0794
E-mail: whiteloc@ktb.net

All United States Currency

William Crutchfield Williams II
Crutchfield's Currency
P.O. Box 3221

Quinlan, TX 75474
(903) 560-0458
Web Site: www.crutchwilliams.com
  and www.csatrainmen.com
E-mail: crutchwilliams@hughes.net

Republic of Texas Currency
Confederate States of America
  Notes
Southern States Currency
Mexican Bancos & Revolutionary
  Paper Money
United States Large Size Type Notes
United States Small Size Type Notes
World Paper Money
United States and Foreign Coins
Colonial and Continental Currency

Scott Winslow
P.O. Box 10240
Bedford, NH 03110
(603) 641-8292
Toll Free: (800) 225-6233
FAX: (603) 641-5583
Web Site: www.scottwinslow.com
E-mail: info@scottwinslow.com

Autographs & Financial History
Stocks, Bonds and Fiscal
  Documents

John Yasuk
Florida Calls
Caribbean Sun Gold
JSG Boggs Market Place
P.O. Box 571084
Miami, FL 33257-1084
(305) 256-7201

Web Site: www.floridacalls.com and
  www.jsgboggsmarketplace.com
E-mail: john@floridacalls.com

Florida Obsolete Currency
Florida State Notes
Artist JSG Boggs Material
United States Large Size Type Notes
United States Small Size Type Notes
United States Small Size Packs
United States Small Size Star Notes
Radars, Repeaters and Fancy Serial
  Numbers
Military Payment Certificates
World Paper Money

William Youngerman
William Youngerman, Inc.
Bank of America Bldg.
150 E. Palmetto Park Road, #101
Boca Raton, FL 33432
(561) 368-7707
(800) 327-5010 (Outside Florida)
(800) 826-9713 (Within Florida)
FAX: (561) 394-6084
Web Site:
  www.williamyoungerman.com
E-mail: bill@youngermans.com

Specialist: United States National
  Bank Notes
Florida National Bank Notes
Florida Obsolete Notes
United States Large Size Type Notes
United States Small Size
  Type Notes
United States Fractional Currency
Confederate

Honorary Life Member

Ronald Horstman
P.O. Box 2999
Leslie, MO 63056
(573) 764-4139 and (573) 764-4206
E-mail: ruderonnie@hotmail.com

St. Louis National Bank Notes
St. Louis Obsolete Notes
St. Louis Checks
St. Louis Merchant and Bank Tokens

BUYING PAPER MONEY

Browsing in coin shops is the usual way in which beginners start buying paper money. Just about every coin dealer—and many stamp dealers—stock paper money to one degree or another, from a single display album with elementary material to vaults filled with literally millions of dollars worth of specimens. Be observant of condition when shopping from dealers' stocks. Get to know the dealer and become familiar with his grading practices. Some dealers will grade a specimen higher than another dealer, but this may be offset by the fact that they charge a lower price.

Bargains. Is it possible to get bargains in buying paper money? To the extent that prices vary somewhat from dealer to dealer, yes. But if you're talking about finding a note worth $100 selling at $50, this is unlikely to happen. The dealers are well aware of market values, and the slight price differences that do occur are merely the result of some dealers being overstocked on certain notes or, possibly, having made a very good "buy" from the public. What may appear to be a bargain will generally prove, on closer examination, to be a specimen in undesirable condition, such as a washed bill on which the color has faded.

Auction sales. Many coin auctions feature selections of paper money, and there are occasional sales (mostly of the postal-bid variety) devoted exclusively to it. There is much to be said for auction buying if you have some experience and know how to read an auction catalog.

Shows and conventions. Paper money is offered for sale at every coin show and exposition. These present excellent opportunities to buy, as the dealers exhibiting at such shows are generally out-of-towners whose stock you would not otherwise have a chance to examine. As many sellers are likely to be offering the same type of material, you have the opportunity to make price and condition comparisons before buying.

COLLECTING DO'S
AND DON'TS

Paper money is not at all difficult to care for, store, and display attractively.

There is not much question that albums are the favorite storage method of nearly all paper money enthusiasts. Many ills to which paper money falls prey result from not being housed in a suitable album, or any album at all. Framing and mounting present some risk, as the item may then be exposed to long periods of direct sunlight, almost sure to cause fading or "bleaching" of its color.

Faded color. There is no known restorative for faded color.

Holes. It is suggested that no effort be undertaken to repair holes, as this will almost certainly result in a further reduction in value.

Missing corners. Missing corners can seldom be restored in a manner that is totally satisfactory. The best that can be done is to secure some paper of approximately the same color and texture, trim a small piece to the proper size, and glue it in place as described below. If a portion of printed matter is missing, this can be hand-drawn, in ink, after restoration. Obviously, this kind of repair is not carried out to "fool" anybody, but simply to give a damaged specimen a less objectionable appearance.

Repairs to paper money. Repair work on damaged or defaced paper money is carried out strictly for cosmetic purposes; to improve its physical appearance. Repairs, even if skillfully executed, will not enhance the value of a specimen, as it will still be classified as defective. Amateurish repair efforts can very possibly make matters worse.

Tears. Tears can be closed by brushing a very small quantity of clear-drying glue to both sides of the tear, placing the note between sheets of waxed kitchen paper, and setting it under a weight to dry. A dictionary of moderate size serves this function well. Allow plenty of drying time and handle gently thereafter.

Wrinkles. Wrinkles, creases, and the like can sometimes be improved by wetting the note (in plain water) and drying it between sheets of waxed paper beneath a reasonably heavy weight—five pounds or more. This should not be done with a modern or recent specimen if there is danger of losing crispness.

SELLING YOUR COLLECTION

Selling to a dealer. All dealers in paper money buy from the public, but not all buy every collection offered to them. Some are specialists and are interested only in collections within their fields of specialization. Some will not purchase (or even examine) collections worth under $100, or $500, or whatever their line of demarcation happens to be. Obviously, a valuable collection containing many hard-to-get notes in VF or UNC condition is easier to interest a dealer in than a beginner-type collection. If a dealer is interested enough to make an offer, this is no guarantee that another dealer would not offer more. In the case of a collection worth $50,000, offers from several dealers might vary by as much as $5,000. This is not an indication that the dealer making the lowest offer is unscrupulous. Dealers will pay as much as the material is worth to them, and one dealer may be overstocked on items that another badly needs. Or one dealer may have customers for certain material that another doesn't. For this reason it makes good sense, if you choose to sell to a dealer, to obtain several offers before accepting any. But should you sell to a dealer at all? The chief advantage is quick payment and reduced risk. The price may not be as high as would be obtained at auction, however, depending on the property's nature and pure luck.

Selling by auction. Auction selling presents uncertainties but at the same time offers the possibility of gaining a much better return than could be had by selling to a dealer. It is no easy matter deciding which route to follow. If your collection is better than average, you may be better advised to sell by auction. This will involve a waiting period of, generally, four to six months between consigning the collection and receiving settlement; over the summer months it may be longer. However, some auctioneers will give a cash advance, usually about 25 percent of the sum they believe the material is worth. In special circumstances a larger advance may be made, or the usual terms and conditions altered. One auctioneer paid $100,000 under a special contract, stipulating that the money was not to be returned regardless of the sale's outcome or even if no sale took place. But this was on a million-dollar collection. Auctioneers' commissions vary. The normal is 20 percent, but some houses take 10 percent from the buyer and 10 percent from the seller. This would appear to work to the seller's advantage, but such a practice may discourage bidding and result in lower sales prices.

Selling to other collectors. Unless the owner is personally acquainted with a large circle of collectors, this will likely involve running ads in periodicals and "playing dealer," which runs into some expense. Unless you offer material at very favorable prices, you are not apt to be as successful with your ads as are the established dealers, who have a reputation and an established clientele.

GLOSSARY

BROKEN BANK NOTE (a.k.a. obsolete note)

Literally, a Broken Bank Note is a note issued by a "broken" bank—a bank that failed and whose obligations could therefore not be redeemed. It may be presumed, by those who recall passing of legislation establishing the Federal Deposit Insurance Corporation, that banks failed only in the financial panic of 1929. During the 19th century, bank failures were common, especially in western and southwestern states. These were generally small organizations set up in frontier towns which suffered either from mismanagement or a sudden decline in the town's fortunes. Some collectors make a specialty of Broken Bank Notes.

DEMAND NOTES

Demand Notes have the distinction of being the first official circulating paper currency of this country, issued in 1861. There are three denominations: $5, $10, and $20, each bearing its own design on front and back. Demand Notes arose out of the coinage shortage brought about by the Civil War. A total of $60,000,000 in Demand Notes was authorized to be printed, amounting to several million individual specimens. Though this was an extraordinary number for the time, it was small compared to modern output, and only a fraction of the total survived. These notes were signed not by any specially designated Treasury Department officers, but a battery of employees, each of whom was given authority to sign and affix his name by hand in a slow assembly-line process, two signatures to each note. Originally the spaces left blank for signatures were marked "Register of the Treasury" and "Treasurer of the United States." As the persons actually signing occupied neither of these offices, they were obliged to perpetually add "for the . . ." to their signatures. In an effort to relieve their tedium, fresh plates were prepared reading "For the Register of the Treasury" and "For the Treasurer of the United States," which required nothing but a signature. This created a rarity status for the earlier specimens, which are now very desirable collectors' items.

ENGRAVING

Engraving is the process by which designs are printed on U.S. paper money. Bank note engraving involves the use of a metal plate, traditionally steel, into which the design is cut with sharp instruments called "burins" or "gravers." Ink is smeared over the surface and allowed to work into the grooves or lines comprising the design. The ink is then cleaned away from raised portions (intended to show blank in the printing). The engraving is pressed against a sheet of moistened paper, and the ink left in these grooves transfers to the paper, resulting in a printed image. When done by modern rotary press, it's a fast-moving process.

FEDERAL RESERVE BANK NOTES

Federal Reserve Bank Notes were issued briefly in 1915 and 1918. Like National Bank Notes, they were secured by bonds or securities placed on deposit by each Federal Reserve Bank with the U.S. government. While issued and redeemable by the member banks of the Federal Reserve system, these notes are secured by—and are obligations of—the government.

FEDERAL RESERVE NOTES

Federal Reserve Notes, the notes in current circulation, were authorized by the Federal Reserve Act of December 23, 1913. Issued under control of the Federal Reserve Board, these notes are released through twelve Federal Reserve Banks in various parts of the country. Originally they were redeemable in gold at the U.S. Treasury or "lawful money" (coins) at a Federal Reserve Bank. In 1934 the option of redemption for gold was removed.

FREAK AND ERROR NOTES

These are bills which, by virtue of error or accident, are in some respect different from normal specimens. See the chapter on Error or Freak Notes.

GOLD CERTIFICATES

When gold coinage became a significant medium of exchange, the government decided to hold aside quantities of it and issue paper notes redeemable by the Treasury Department. The first Gold Certificates for public circulation were released in 1882. The series lasted until the era of small-size currency, ending in 1928. In 1933 all were ordered returned to the Treasury Department for redemption, including those in possession of collectors. A new law in 1964 permitted their ownership by collectors, though they can no longer be redeemed for gold.

LARGE SIZE CURRENCY

Large Size currency is the term generally used to refer to U.S. notes issued up to 1929, which were somewhat larger in size than those printed subsequently. The increased size permitted more elaborate design, which seldom fails to endear Large Size currency to beginners. Some of the earlier examples (especially of the 1870s, 1880s, and 1890s) are works of art. Though economic considerations were mainly responsible for the switch to a reduced size, there is no doubt that today's notes are far more convenient to handle and carry. Large Size notes are sometimes referred to as "bedsheet notes."

NATIONAL BANK NOTES

This is the largest group of notes available to the collector. They were issued from 1863 to 1929 and present collecting potential that can only be termed vast. More than 14,000 banks issued notes, in all parts of the country. While the approach to collecting them is usually regional, sets and series can also be built up, virtually without end. The National Banking Act was instituted in 1863, during the Civil War, to permit chartered banks to issue and circulate their own currency. Printing was done at the U.S. Government Printing Office and the designs were all alike, differing only in names of the banks, state seals, bank signatures, and the bank's charter number. Each charter bank was limited to issuing currency up to 90 percent of the value of bonds that it kept on deposit with the government. Charters remained in force for twenty years and could be renewed for an additional twenty years. National Bank Notes circulated in the same fashion as conventional currency and, thanks to the bond-deposit system, gained public confidence. The financial panic of 1929, which brought ruin or near-ruin to many banks, put an end to National Bank Notes.

NATIONAL GOLD BANK NOTES

These notes were issued exclusively by California banks during the 1870s under the same terms as ordinary National Bank Notes, their values backed by bonds deposited with the government. Events surrounding their origins form a unique chapter in the history of American economy. Following the discoveries of substantial quantities of gold in California in the late 1840s, that metal soon became the chief medium of local exchange, largely because it was more readily available in that remote region than coinage. Later, when gold coins and tokens began to circulate heavily in California, banks became so swamped with them that they petitioned Washington for authority to issue Gold Notes that could be substituted for the actual coinage. On July 12, 1870, Congress voted favorably on this measure, giving the right to issue such notes to nine banks in California and one in Boston. The Boston bank, Kidder National Gold Bank, appears not to have exercised its right, as no Gold Notes of this institution have been recorded.

The California banks wasted no time in exercising their authority, the result being a series of notes ranging from $5–$500. All were printed on yellow-toned paper so as to be instantly identifiable. The banks issuing these notes were permitted to redeem them in gold coins.

REFUNDING CERTIFICATES

Refunding Certificates, a sort of hybrid between currency and bonds or securities, were issued under a Congressional Act of February 26, 1879. These were notes with a $10 face value which could be spent and exchanged in the fashion of ordinary money but drew interest at the rate of 4 percent per year. The purposes behind Refunding Certificates were several. They were chiefly designed to encourage saving and thereby curb inflation, which even at that time was becoming a problem. Also, they provided a safe means of saving for persons who distrusted banks (safe so long as the certificates were not lost or stolen), and, probably more important, were readily obtainable in areas of the country not well served by banks. In 1907 the interest was halted. Their redemption value today, with interest, is $21.30.

SERIAL NUMBER

The serial number is the control number placed on all U.S. paper bills, appearing below left-center and above right-center. No two bills in the same series bear repetitive serial numbers. The use of serial numbers is not only an aid in counting and sorting bills as printed, but a deterrent to counterfeiting.

SIGNATURES

The inclusion of signatures of Treasury Department officials on our paper bills, a practice as old as our currency (1861), began as a mark of authorization and as a foil to counterfeiters. The belief was that the handwriting would be more difficult to copy than an engraved design. Persons whose signatures appear on notes did not always occupy the same office. From 1862 to 1923, the two signers were the Treasurer and the Register (or Registrar as it appears in old writings) of the Treasury. Subsequently, the Treasurer and the Secretary of the Treasury were represented. These signatures are of great importance to collectors, as some notes are relatively common with certain combinations of signatures and others are rare. A "series" collection is not considered complete until one obtains every existing combination, even though the specimens may be in other respects identical.

SILVER CERTIFICATES

Silver Certificates were authorized in 1878. America's economy was booming at that time, and the demand for silver coinage in day-to-day business transactions outdistanced the supply. Silver Certificates were not intended to replace coinage but to create a convenient medium of exchange, whereby the government held specific quantities of Silver Dollars (later bullion) and agreed to redeem the notes or certificates against them. In 1934 the Treasury Department ceased redemption of these notes in Silver Dollars, and on June 24, 1968, redemption in all forms was ended. The notes are still, however, legal tender at their face value. When printing of Silver Certificates was discontinued, a flurry of speculation arose and many persons began hoarding them. This was done not only in hope of eventual redemption for bullion but in the belief that such notes would become valuable to collectors. Though Silver Certificates are popular with hobbyists, they have not increased sufficiently in price to yield speculators any great profits—especially since many collectors saved specimens in circulated condition.

STAR NOTES

United States Notes, Silver Certificates, and Gold Certificates sometimes have a star or asterisk in place of the letter in front of the serial number. Federal Reserve Notes and Federal Reserve Bank Notes have it at the end of the serial number. These notes are known as "Star Notes."

When a note is mutilated or otherwise unfit for issue, it must be replaced. To replace it with a note of the same serial numbers would be impractical, and Star Notes are therefore substituted. Other than having their own special serial number and a star, these notes are the same as the others. On United States Notes and Silver Certificates, the star is substituted for the prefix letter; on Federal Reserve Notes, for the suffix letter. All defective notes are accounted for and destroyed by burning them in an incinerator.

Large stars after the serial number on the 1869 Series of United States Notes, and 1890 and 1891 Treasury Notes, do not signify replacement notes as are known in later and present-day Star Notes.

Serial numbers on early Large Size Notes were preceded by a letter and were ended by various odd characters or symbols. These characters are not known to have any significance, except to show that the number was terminated, and prevented any elimination or addition of digits. The suffix characters were replaced by alphabet letters on later issues of notes.

TREASURY OR COIN NOTES

Treasury Notes were authorized by Congress in 1890. Their official title was Coin Notes, as they could be redeemed for silver or gold coins. The series did not prove popular and was discontinued after the issue of 1891.

TREASURY SEAL

The Treasury Seal is the official emblem of the U.S. Treasury Department, which has appeared on all our currency since 1862. It is missing only from the early Demand Notes, issued in 1861, and some Fractional Currency. Two versions have been employed, distinguished readily by the fact that one (the original) bears a Latin inscription, while the current Treasury Seal is in English. The basic motif is the same, a badge displaying scales and a key. The original Seal, somewhat more decorative, was in use until 1968.

UNITED STATES NOTES

Also known as Legal Tender Notes, this substantial and ambitious series followed Demand Notes and constitutes the second earliest variety of U.S. paper currency. There are five distinct issues, running from 1862 to 1923. Though United States Notes are all "Large Size" and their designs not very similar to those in present use, they show in their successive stages the evolutionary advance from this nation's first efforts at paper money to its currency of today. The first issue is dated March 10, 1862. Denominations are $1, $2, $5, $10, $20, $50, $100, $500, $1,000, $5,000, and $10,000. Individuals portrayed included not only presidents but other government officials: Salmon P. Chase (Lincoln's Secretary of the Treasury), Daniel Webster, and Lewis and Clark. Some of the reverse designs are masterpieces of geometrical linework. A number of rarities are to be found among Legal Tender Notes, but in general the lower denominations can be collected without great expense.

WILDCAT NOTES

Wildcat Notes are the notes that were issued by so-called "wildcat banks" in the era of State Bank Notes before the Civil War. Numerous banks sprang up around the middle part of the 19th century, mostly in the west and southwest, operated by persons of questionable integrity. Some never had capital backing and were instituted purely as a front for confidence swindles. After issuing notes, the bank shut down, its directors disappeared, and owners of the notes were left with worthless paper. As news traveled slowly in those days, the same persons could move from town to town and work the scheme repeatedly. Notes issued by these banks, or any banks that became insolvent, are also called Broken Bank Notes. Apparently the origin of the term "wildcat" derives from public sentiment of the time, which held that owners of such banks had no greater trustworthiness than a wild animal. "Wildcat" may also refer to the rapid movement of swindling bank officials from one locality to another.

DEPARTMENT OF THE TREASURY, BUREAU OF ENGRAVING AND PRINTING

Reprinted with permission of the Department of the Treasury, Bureau of Printing and Engraving, Washington, D.C.

BUREAU FACTS

- Since October 1, 1877, all U.S. paper currency has been printed by the Bureau of Engraving and Printing, which began as a six-person operation using steam-powered presses in the Department of the Treasury's basement.
- Now 1,900 Bureau employees occupy 25 acres of floor space in two Washington, D.C. buildings flanking 14th Street. Currency and stamps are designed, engraved, and printed 24 hours a day, 5 days a week on 23 high-speed presses. An additional 600 Bureau employees are at the Western Currency Facility in Fort Worth, Texas, where currency is printed 24 hours a day, 5 days a week on 12 high-speed presses.
- In Fiscal Year 1999, at a cost of 4.5 cents each, the Bureau of Engraving and Printing produced for the Federal Reserve System a record 11.3 billion notes worth approximately $142 billion. Ninety-five percent will replace unfit notes, and five percent will support economic growth. At any one time, $200 million in notes may be in production.
- Of total production, notes currently produced are the $1 (48% of production time), $2 (1%), $5 (9%), $10 (11%), $20 (19%), $50 (5%), and $100 (7%).
- The Bureau also prints White House invitations and some 500 engraved items, such as visa counterfoils, naturalization documents, commissions, and certificates for almost 75 federal departments and agencies.

TOURS

BEP Public Tour Contact Information
Bureau of Engraving and Printing
14th and C Streets, S.W.
Washington, DC 20228
Telephone: 1.866.874.2330 (toll-free), 202.874.2330 (local)
School Group Tours Fax: 202.874.6331
Congressional Tours Fax: 202.874.0968

VISITORS' CENTER

- At the Visitors' Center, history, production, and counterfeit exhibits showcase interesting information about U.S. currency.
- Many unique items can be purchased at the sales counter. Items include uncut currency sheets of 32, 16, 8, or 4 $1, $2, and $5 notes; a premium portfolio containing a new series 1996 $20 note with a low serial number and one of the last previous series $20 notes; a deluxe single note in the series 1996 with a low serial number; $150 worth of shredded currency in plastic bags that are sold for $1.50; engraved collectors' prints; souvenir cards; and Department of the Interior Duck Stamps.
- If you are planning a trip to Washington, please call our information number at 1.866.874.2330 (toll-free) for updated information or program changes.

MAIL ORDER SALES

The Bureau of Engraving and Printing (BEP) is experiencing extended delays in the delivery of incoming mail. At this moment, it is unknown when timely mail deliveries will resume. In order to get timely delivery of numismatic products, it is recommended that customers order by telephone, fax, or Internet.

- For telephone orders, call toll free at 1-800-456-3408.
- For fax orders, call toll free at 1-888-891-7585.
- For Internet orders, the BEP Web site is bep.treas.gov/

INTERNET

The Bureau's **Internet address** is *www.bep.treas.gov/*. We also offer an **interactive website** at www.moneyfactory.gov/.

THE FEDERAL
RESERVE BANKS

Reprinted with permission of the Department of the Treasury, Bureau of Printing and Engraving, Washington, D.C.

The Federal Reserve System is divided into twelve Federal Reserve districts, in each of which is a Federal Reserve Bank. There are also twenty-four branches. Each district is designated by a number and the corresponding letter of the alphabet. The district numbers, the cities in which the twelve banks are located, and the letter symbols are:

1-A—Boston	5-E—Richmond	9-I—Minneapolis
2-B—New York	6-F—Atlanta	10-J—Kansas City
3-C—Philadelphia	7-G—Chicago	11-K—Dallas
4-D—Cleveland	8-H—St. Louis	12-L—San Francisco

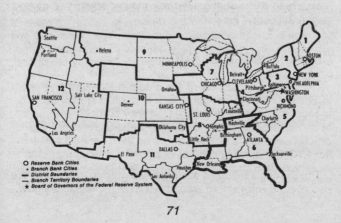

○ Reserve Bank Cities
• Branch Bank Cities
— District Boundaries
--- Branch Territory Boundaries
★ Board of Governors of the Federal Reserve System

FEDERAL RESERVE SYSTEM

The Federal Reserve System was created by the Federal Reserve Act, which was passed by Congress in 1913, in order to provide a safer and more flexible banking and monetary system. For approximately 100 years before the creation of the Federal Reserve, periodic financial panics had led to failures of a large number of banks, with associated business bankruptcies and general economic contractions. Following the studies of the National Monetary Commission, established by Congress a year after the particularly severe panic of 1907, several proposals were put forward for the creation of an institution designed to counter such financial disruptions. Following considerable debate, the Federal Reserve System was established. Its original purposes were to give the country an elastic currency, provide facilities for discounting commercial credits, and improve the supervision of the banking system.

ECONOMIC STABILITY AND GROWTH

From the inception of the Federal Reserve System, it was clear that these original purposes were aspects of broader national economic and financial objectives. Over the years, stability and growth of the economy, a high level of employment, stability in the purchasing power of the dollar, and a reasonable balance in transactions with foreign countries have come to be recognized as primary objectives of governmental economic policy.

CURRENCY CIRCULATION

An important function of the Federal Reserve System is to ensure that the economy has enough currency and coin to meet the public's demand. Currency and coin are put into or retired from circulation by the Federal Reserve Banks, which use depository institutions as the channel of distribution. When banks and other depository institutions need to replenish their supply of currency and coin—for example, when the public's need for cash increases around holiday shopping periods—depository institutions order the cash from the Federal Reserve Bank or Branch in their area, and the face value of that cash is charged to their accounts at the Federal Reserve. When the public's need for currency and coin declines, depository institutions return excess cash to the Federal Reserve Bank, which in turn credits their accounts.

UNFIT AND COUNTERFEIT NOTES

The Federal Reserve Banks and the U.S. Department of the Treasury share responsibility for maintaining the physical quality of U.S. paper currency in circulation. Each day, millions of dollars of deposits to Reserve Banks by depository institutions are carefully scrutinized. The Reserve Banks are responsible for receiving, verifying, authenticating, and storing currency and shipping it as needed. Currency in good condition is stored for later distribution. Worn or mutilated notes are removed from circulation and destroyed. Counterfeit notes are forwarded to the U.S. Secret Service, an agency of the Treasury Department.

FEDERAL RESERVE NOTES

Virtually all currency in circulation is in the form of Federal Reserve Notes, which are printed by the Bureau of Engraving and Printing of the U.S. Treasury. The Reserve Banks are currently authorized to issue notes in denominations of $1, $2, $5, $10, $20, $50, and $100. Coins are produced by the Treasury's U.S. Mint.

CASH TRANSFERS

Currency and coin are used primarily for small transactions. In the aggregate, such transactions probably account for only a small proportion of the value of all transfers of funds.

32-SUBJECT SHEET LAYOUT

All U.S. currency is now printed with 32 subjects (notes) to a large sheet. The first printing is the greenback. The second printing is the face of the note, in black. This includes the portrait and border, the series year, the check letter and quadrant number, two signatures, and the face plate number. The sheet is then cut in half vertically for the third printing. This includes the black Federal Reserve seal, the four Federal Reserve district numbers, the green Treasury seal, and two green serial numbers.

The 32-subject sheet is divided into four quarters called quadrants for numbering and other controls. Each quadrant has its own numbering sequence for the eight notes, with serial numbers advancing by 20,000 to the next note. The quadrant number and check letter in the upper left section indicate the first, second, third, or fourth quadrant and the position of the note in the quadrant. In the lower right corner the position letter is shown again with a plate number. On the back of the note the same small number in the lower right is the back plate number.

	FIRST QUADRANT				THIRD QUADRANT		
A1			E1		A3		E3
A00000001A	A100	A00080001A	E100	A00320001A	A100	A00400001A	E100
B1			F1		B3		F3
A00020001A	B100	A00100001A	F100	A00340001A	B100	A00420001A	F100
C1			G1		C3		G3
A00040001A	C100	A00120001A	G100	A00360001A	C100	A00440001A	G100
D1			H1		D3		H3
A00060001A	D100	A00140001A	H100	A00380001A	D100	A004600001A	H100
A2			E2		A4		E4
A00160001A	A100	A00240001A	E100	A00480001A	A100	A005600001A	E100
B2			F2		B4		F4
A00180001A	B100	A00260001A	F100	A00500001A	B100	A00580001A	F100
C2			G2		C4		G4
A00200001A	C100	A00280001A	G100	A0050001A	C100	A00600001A	G100
D2			H2		D4		H4
A00220001A	D100	A00300001A	H100	A00540001A	D100	A00620001A	H100
	SECOND QUADRANT				FOURTH QUADRANT		

NUMBERING SYSTEM

The system of numbering paper money must be adequate to accommodate a large volume of notes. For security and accountability purposes, no two notes of any one class, denomination, and series may have the same serial number. The two serial numbers on each note have a full complement of eight digits and an alphabetical prefix and suffix letter. When necessary, ciphers are used at the left of the number to make a total of eight digits.

Whenever a numbering sequence is initiated for United States Notes or Silver Certificates, the first note is numbered A 00 000 001 A; the second A 00 000 002 A; the hundredth A 00 000 100 A; the thousandth A 00 001 000 A; and so on through A 99 999 999 A. The suffix letter A will remain the same until a total of twenty-five groups, or "blocks," of 99 999 999 notes are numbered, each group having a different prefix letter of the alphabet from A to Z. The letter "O" is omitted, either as a prefix or as a suffix, because of its similarity to zero. The 100 000 000th note in each group will be a Star Note, since eight digits are the maximum in the mechanical operation of numbering machines.

At this point, the suffix letter changes to B for the next twenty-five groups of 99 999 999 notes, and proceeds in the same manner as the suffix letter A. A total of 62,500,000,000 notes could be numbered before a duplication of serial numbers would occur. However, it has never been required to number that many notes of any one class, denomination, and series.

The Federal Reserve Notes printed for the twelve districts are numbered in the same progression as United States Notes and Silver Certificates, except that a specific alphabetical letter identifies a specific Federal Reserve district. The letter identifying each district is used as a prefix letter at the beginning of the serial numbers on all Federal Reserve Notes and does not change. Only the suffix letter changes in the serial numbers on Federal Reserve currency.

PORTRAITS AND BACK DESIGN ON SMALL SIZE NOTES

DENOMINATION	PORTRAIT	BACK DESIGN
$1	Washington	Great Seal of the United States
$2	Jefferson	Monticello
$5	Lincoln	Lincoln Memorial
$10	Hamilton	United States Treasury
$20	Jackson	The White House
$50	Grant	United States Capitol
$100	Franklin	Independence Hall
$500	McKinley	Five Hundred
$1000	Cleveland	One Thousand
$5000	Madison	Five Thousand
$10,000	Chase	Ten Thousand
$100,000	Wilson	One Hundred Thousand

DATING U.S. CURRENCY

Unlike coins, the date is not changed each year on U.S. currency.

The date appearing on all notes, large or small, is that of the year in which the design was first approved or issued. For instance, Large Size $1 United States Notes of the Series 1880 were issued with the same date until the new Series 1917 was issued. There was no further date change until the Series 1923.

The same rule applies to Small Size Notes. However, in this case a letter is added after the date to designate or indicate a minor change in the main design or probably a change in one or both of the signatures. For example: the $1 Silver Certificate of 1935 was changed to 1935-A because of a change in the size of the tiny plate numbers appearing in the lower right corners of the face and back of the note. It was changed again from 1935-A to 1935-B in 1945 when the signatures of Julian/Morganthau were changed to Julian/Vinson. Subsequent changes in signatures continued in the 1935 Series to the year 1963 when the signatures of Smith/Dillon terminated the issue with the Series 1935-H. Therefore, these notes were issued for twenty-eight years bearing the date 1935.

THE TREASURY SEAL

FORMER DESIGN:
The former design had the Latin inscription *Thesaur. Amer. Septent. Sigil.,* which has several translations. It was the Seal of the North American Treasury.

NEW DESIGN:
This new design drops the Latin and states THE DEPARTMENT OF THE TREASURY, 1789. First used on the $100 Note of the Series 1966.

GRADES AND CONDITIONS OF PAPER MONEY

CONDITION

The physical condition of a note or bill plays an important role in determining its value. There are many notes that have no premium value beyond face value in ordinary condition but are valuable or moderately valuable when uncirculated. Even in the case of scarce early specimens, the price given for an Average example is generally much less than that commanded by Fine or Very Fine condition.

Defects encountered in paper money include:

Creases, folds, wrinkles. Generally the characteristic that distinguishes uncirculated notes from those that almost—but not quite—qualify for such designation is a barely noticeable crease running approximately down the center vertically, resulting from the note being folded for insertion into a wallet or billfold. It may be possible, through manipulation or storage beneath a heavy weight, to remove evidence of the crease; but the knowledge that it once existed cannot be obliterated.

Discoloration. Discoloration is not as easy to recognize as most defects, but it must be classed as one. A distinction should be made between notes printed from underinked rollers and those which originally were normally colored but became "washed out." Sometimes washing is indeed the cause; a well-intentioned collector will bathe a note, attempting to clean it, with the result that its color is no longer strong. This should not happen if warm water is used, without strong cleanser. Atmospheric conditions may play some part in discoloration.

Foxing. Fox spots may sometimes be observed on old notes, especially those of the pre-1890 era, just as on old paper in general. They seem more common to foreign currency than American, but their presence on our notes is certainly not rare. These are tiny brownish-red dots, caused by an infestation of lice attacking the paper fibers.

Holes. Holes are more likely to be encountered in early paper money than specimens of recent origin. In early years it was customary for Federal Reserve Banks to use wire clips in making up bundles of notes for distribution to banking organizations, and these clips or staples often pierced the bills. Another common occurrence years ago was the practice of shop clerks and cashiers in general to impale notes upon holders consisting of nails mounted on stands.

Missing pieces. Missing pieces is a highly undesirable defect which, except in the case of rare specimens, renders the item valueless to collectors. Even if only a blank unprinted corner is torn away, this is called a missing-piece note and hardly anyone will give it a second glance.

Stains. Notes sometimes become stained with ink or other liquids. If the specimen is commonplace and easily obtainable in Very Fine or Uncirculated condition, it will be worthless with any kind of stain. In a note of moderate value, its price will be hurt to a greater or lesser degree depending on the stain's intensity, size, nature, and the area it touches. A stain in an outer margin or at a corner is not so objectionable as one occurring at the center or across a signature or serial number. Ink stains, because of their strong color, are generally deemed the worst, but bad staining can also be caused by oil, crayon, "magic marker," and food substances. Pencil markings, which frequently are found on bank notes, will yield to ordinary erasing with a piece of soft "artgum" worked gently over the surface and brushed away with an artist's camel-hair brush. Most other stains cannot be so easily removed. With ink there is no hope, as any caustic sufficiently strong to remove the ink will also injure the printing and possibly eat through the paper as well. Oil stains can sometimes be lightened, though not removed, by sprinkling the note on both sides (even if the stain shows only on one) with talcum powder or other absorbent powder, placing it between sheets of waxed kitchen paper, and leaving it beneath a heavy weight for several days in a room where the humidity is not unduly high.

Tears. Tears in notes are very common defects, which may be minute or run nearly the whole length of the bill. As a rule the paper on which American currency is printed is fairly rugged and will not tear as readily as most ordinary paper, but given careless or hurried handling anything is possible. An old worn note is more apt to tear in handling than a new one. Repaired tears are more common in the world of paper money collecting than may be generally supposed. A clean tear—one which does not involve loss of surface—can be patched so as to become virtually unnoticed, unless examined against a light or through a strong magnifying glass. X-ray examination will reveal repairs when all else fails.

CONDITION GRADES

The following condition standards have been used throughout this book and, with slight variations depending upon individual interpretation, are generally current in the trade.

Uncirculated—UNC. A specimen that for all appearances has not been handled or passed through general circulation; a crisp fresh note in "bank" condition. There may be minor blemishes, such as a finger smudge or pinhole, but if these are in any respect severe the condition merits description as "Almost Uncirculated." There is not much satisfaction to be taken in a note fresh and crisp that has gaping holes and fingerprints. Obviously, an 1870 Uncirculated note should not be expected to match a 1970 in appearance or feel.

*Uncirculated—*Unc. An uncirculated "Star Note."

Almost Uncirculated—A.U. In the case of modern or semi-modern notes, this is generally taken to mean a specimen that shows no evidence of having passed through general circulation but, because of some detraction, fails to measure up to a rating of Uncirculated. The problem may be finger smudges, counting crinkles, a light crease, a fold along one or more of the corners, or pinholes. But if more than one of these impairments is present, the item would surely not deserve a classification of Almost Uncirculated.

Extremely Fine—X.F. A note exhibiting little evidence of wear from handling, but not so perfect or near-perfect as to qualify for a rating of Uncirculated or Almost Uncirculated. On a used note issued before 1900 there may be clear evidence of circulation, but no disfiguring marks.

Very Fine—V.F. A Very Fine note has experienced some circulation but escaped without "being mangled." It is still clean and crisp, and its creases are not offensive.

Fine—F. Here the scale begins sliding down. It is obvious that, being the fifth in rank of condition grades, Fine notes are quite a good deal removed from Uncirculated. They have been handed around pretty thoroughly and suffered the normal consequences, but still are without serious blemishes such as tears, missing corners, serious stains, or holes.

Very Good—V.G. A well-circulated note bearing evidence of much folding, creasing, and wrinkling. It may possibly be lightly stained, smudged, or pin punctured, but major defects—such as a torn-off corner—would drop it into an even lower category.

Good—G. Heavily circulated, worn notes that are possibly stained or scribbled on, edges could be frayed or "dog-eared." There may be holes larger than pin punctures, but not on the central portion of design. This is the lowest grade of condition acceptable to a collector, and only when nothing better is available. Unless very rare, such specimens are considered space-fillers only.

Average Buying Prices—A.B.P. The Average Buying Prices given here are the approximate sums paid by retail dealers for specimens in Good condition. As selling prices vary, so do buying prices, and, in fact, they usually vary a bit more.

RECORD KEEPING

For your convenience, we suggest you use the following record-keeping system to note condition of your paper money in the checklist box:

☒ FAIR	☒ VERY GOOD	☐ VERY FINE	☒ ALMOST UNC
☒ GOOD	☐ FINE	☒ EXTREMELY FINE	■ UNCIRCULATED

ABOUT THE PRICES
IN THIS BOOK

Prices are compiled from offerings made by dealers and from auction sale results. In all cases (except for the Average Buying Price) the prices are retail selling prices. While prices are current at the time of publication, the market can be influenced by buying or selling trends, causing prices to change. All prices, except in the case of seldom-offered rarities, are averages, calculated from numerous sales. The actual prices charged by any individual currency dealer may be slightly higher or lower than those indicated in this book. In any given sale various factors play a role, such as whether the seller is overstocked on notes of that type.

HOW TO USE THIS BOOK

The Official Blackbook Price Guide to United States Paper Money provides a convenient reference to prices of all standard U.S. currency, old and new, as well as many unusual issues.

Notes are divided into section by denomination. Within each section can be found the various series of notes for that denomination. The series are arranged chronologically and will vary slightly from section to section, as some notes were issued in one series and not in another. An index page is provided at the beginning of each section.

To familiarize yourself with the various currency terms, the following illustration might be helpful:

To price a note correctly, it is necessary that it be accurately identified and graded. The illustrations will aid in identification, and a grading guide has been provided. In the case of some notes, particularly very old ones, the value depends upon minor details. In all such cases these details have been clearly noted.

Listings include the following information:

Date. This is the "series date," as it appears on the note, and may bear no relation whatsoever to the year in which the note was actually issued. The date of actual issue is not of importance to collectors. If the series date on the note carries a suffix letter, such as 1935A, it will be so indicated in the listing.

Seal. The color of the Treasury Seal will be noted, along with other information if relevant. The following abbreviations are also used: Sm.—small, Lg.—large; w/r—with rays; w/s—with scallops.

Signatures. All U.S. notes carry two signatures, and the names of each signer are given for every note listed. If different signature combinations exist for your note, be sure you refer to the correct signature combination. The listings will show you whether there is just one set of signatures for that note or more than one.

Type. In a small minority of cases, notes were issued in more than one type. For example, a slight change was made in the paper or printing. All recorded types are identified in the listings.

Issuing Bank. This information is provided for Federal Reserve Notes and Federal Reserve Bank Notes only. Check the Federal Reserve seal on your note to identify the issuing bank. In some instances there is a difference in value depending on where the note originated. Space prevents us from listing the numerous local banks issuing National Bank Notes.

A.B.P. The first price column is the A.B.P. or Average Buying Price. This is the approximate sum being paid by dealers for a specimen in the lowest listed grade of condition. The lowest listed grade of condition is the column next to the A.B.P. If the next column is headed "Good," the A.B.P. is for a specimen in Good condition. In all cases the A.B.P. includes the face value of the note. This is an important consideration insofar as U.S. notes, regardless of their age or physical condition, can still be spent as legal tender.

Current Selling Prices. The current selling prices are given in two or three different grades of condition, as indicated at the top of each price column. Different groups of notes are priced in different condition grades, owing to market availability. Some are virtually unobtainable in Uncirculated condition, so it would be pointless to give such a price. Others are of no premium value in less than V.F., hence V.F. is the lowest grade shown.

ONE DOLLAR NOTES

ORDER OF ISSUE

ONE DOLLAR NOTES (1862) UNITED STATES NOTES
(ALSO KNOWN AS LEGAL TENDER NOTES)
(Large Size)

Face Design: Portrait of Salmon Portland Chase
(1808–73), Secretary of the Treasury under Lincoln, red
Treasury Seal, signatures of Chittenden and Spinner, lower
right.

Back Design: Large circle center with legal tender obligation.

SERIES	SIGNATURES	SEAL	A.B.P.	GOOD	V. FINE	UNC.
1862	Chittenden-Spinner					
☐Type I, National Bank Note, American Bank						
Note without monogram		Red	225.00	400.00	1025.00	2800.00
☐Type II, National Bank Note, American Bank						
Note with monogram ABNCO		Red	105.00	185.00	700.00	2500.00
☐Type III, National Bank Note, National Bank						
Note without monogram		Red	105.00	185.00	800.00	2400.00
☐Type IV, National Bank Note, National Bank						
Note with monogram ABNCO		Red	120.00	210.00	750.00	2400.00

ONE DOLLAR NOTES (1869) UNITED STATES NOTES
(ALSO KNOWN AS LEGAL TENDER NOTES)
(Large Size)

Face Design: Portrait of President Washington in the center, large red seal to the right. Scene of Columbus in sight of land to left; also called "Rainbow Note" because of the many colors used in printing. Black ink for main design, red seal and serial numbers, green background for the serial number, green shading in upper-half and blue tint in paper left of portrait to deter counterfeiting.

Back Design: Green, ONE DOLLAR and ONE over "1" center, letters U.S. interwoven to left. Legal tender obligation to right of center.

SERIES	SIGNATURES	SEAL	A.B.P.	GOOD	V. FINE	UNC.
☐1869	Allison-Spinner	Red	120.00	200.00	850.00	3500.00
☐1869	Allison-Spinner Water Mark Paper		360.00	600.00	2000.00	3650.00

ONE DOLLAR NOTES (1874–1917)
UNITED STATES NOTES
(ALSO KNOWN AS LEGAL TENDER NOTES)
(Large Size)

Back Design: Large green "X" with UNITED STATES OF AMERICA in the center. Legal tender obligation and counterfeiting warning to right.

Face Design: No blue or green shading and tinting.

SERIES	SIGNATURES	SEAL	A.B.P.	GOOD	V. FINE	UNC.
☐1874	Allison-Spinner	Sm. Red	48.00	95.00	425.00	1800.00
☐1875	Allison-New	Sm. Red	48.00	95.00	425.00	1450.00
☐1875	Same Series A	Sm. Red	210.00	350.00	1100.00	3250.00
☐1875	Same Series B	Sm. Red	210.00	350.00	1100.00	3250.00
☐1875	Same Series C	Sm. Red	210.00	350.00	1400.00	3500.00
☐1875	Same Series D	Sm. Red	270.00	450.00	1200.00	3400.00
☐1875	Same Series E	Sm. Red	387.00	645.00	1400.00	3500.00
☐1875	Allison-Wyman	Sm. Red	48.00	95.00	375.00	1400.00
☐1878	Allison-Gilfillan	Sm. Red	51.00	95.00	375.00	1400.00
☐1878	Allison-Gilfillan Water Marked Paper		72.00	120.00	525.00	1850.00
☐1880	Scofield-Gilfillan	Lg. Brown	60.00	110.00	450.00	1250.00
☐1880	Bruce-Gilfillan	Lg. Brown	60.00	110.00	450.00	1250.00
☐1880	Bruce-Wyman	Lg. Brown	60.00	110.00	450.00	1200.00
☐1880	Rosecrans-Huston	Lg. Red	153.00	255.00	1100.00	RARE
☐1880	Rosecrans-Huston	Lg. Brown	120.00	200.00	1100.00	4500.00
☐1880	Rosecrans-Nebeker	Lg. Brown	120.00	200.00	1100.00	4600.00
☐1880	Rosecrans-Nebeker	Sm. Red	60.00	100.00	300.00	1200.00
☐1880	Tillman-Morgan	Sm. Red	60.00	100.00	300.00	1200.00
☐1917	Tehee-Burke	Sm. Red	45.00	75.00	125.00	400.00

Sm.—Small Seal, Lg.—Large Seal

*This note with signatures of Burke and Elliott is an error issue. The regular procedure was to have the signature of the Register of the Treasury on the left, and that of the Treasurer to the right. The signatures were transposed in this instance.

SERIES	SIGNATURES	SEAL	A.B.P.	GOOD	V. FINE	UNC.
☐1917	Elliott-Burke	Sm. Red	36.00	60.00	175.00	400.00
☐1917	Burke-Elliott*	Sm. Red	69.00	115.00	530.00	1650.00
☐1917	Elliott-White	Sm. Red	42.00	70.00	200.00	550.00
☐1917	Speelman-White	Sm. Red	42.00	70.00	175.00	450.00

ONE DOLLAR NOTES (1923) UNITED STATES NOTES
(ALSO KNOWN AS LEGAL TENDER NOTES)
(Large Size)

Face Design: Portrait of President Washington in center. Red seal to left, red "1" to the right, red serial numbers.

Back Design: UNITED STATES OF AMERICA and ONE DOLLAR in center. Figures "1" to right and left. This was the last issue of Large Size ONE DOLLAR United States Notes. The last series of Large Size Notes was kept in use until 1929 when the first issue of Small Size Notes was released.

SERIES	SIGNATURES	SEAL	A.B.P.	GOOD	V. FINE	UNC.
☐1923	Speelman-White	Red	45.00	75.00	250.00	850.00

ONE DOLLAR NOTES (1928) UNITED STATES NOTES
(ALSO KNOWN AS LEGAL TENDER NOTES)
(Small Size)

Face Design: Red seal to left—red serial numbers, large ONE to right. This is the only issue of the $1 United States Note, Small Size. At the present time only the $100 United States Note is current.

Back Design: Large ONE in center with ONE DOLLAR overprint, back printed in green.

					★SERIES
SIGNATURES	**SEAL**	**A.B.P.**	**GOOD**	**V. FINE**	**UNC.**	**★UNC.**
☐1928 Woods-Woodin	Red	36.00	65.00	325.00	550.00	RARE

*Star Notes: Damaged or unsatisfactory notes were replaced at the Bureau of Engraving with new notes bearing a star (★) in place of the first letter and preceding the serial no. Example: *12345678A

ONE DOLLAR NOTES (1863–1875)
NATIONAL BANK NOTES
FIRST CHARTER PERIOD (Large Size)

Face Design: Name of National Bank top center, maidens at altar below.

Back Design: Landing of Pilgrims center, State Seal of state issuing bank to left, eagle and flag.

SERIES	SIGNATURES	SEAL	A.B.P.	GOOD	V. FINE	UNC.
☐ Original*	Colby-Spinner	Red w/r	135.00	220.00	1320.00	3800.00
☐ Original*	Jeffries-Spinner	Red w/r	350.00	590.00	1600.00	5500.00
☐ Original*	Allison-Spinner	Red w/r	165.00	275.00	1350.00	3800.00
☐ 1875	Allison-New	Red w/s	165.00	275.00	1350.00	3800.00
☐ 1875	Allison-Wyman	Red w/s	165.00	275.00	1350.00	3800.00
☐ 1875	Allison-Gilfillan	Red w/s	165.00	275.00	1350.00	3800.00
☐ 1875	Scofield-Gilfillan	Red w/s	165.00	275.00	1350.00	3800.00

w/r—with Rays, w/s—with Scallops
*Early notes of the First Charter Period did not have the series imprinted on them. They are known by the date on the bill which was usually the date of charter or organization, or as the Original Series. These notes had a seal with rays or small notches. In 1875 the series was imprinted in red, and the seal was changed to have scallops around the border. The charter number was added to later issues of notes of the original series and to all notes of the 1875 series.

ONE DOLLAR NOTES (1886) SILVER CERTIFICATES
(Large Size)

SERIES	SIGNATURES	SEAL	A.B.P.	GOOD	V. FINE	UNC.
☐1886	Rosecrans-Jordan	Sm. Red	110.00	185.00	625.00	2200.00
☐1886	Rosecrans-Hyatt	Sm. Red	110.00	185.00	625.00	2200.00
☐1886	Rosecrans-Hyatt	Lg. Red	110.00	185.00	625.00	2400.00
☐1886	Rosecrans-Huston	Lg. Red	110.00	185.00	625.00	2400.00
☐1886	Rosecrans-Huston	Lg. Brown	110.00	185.00	625.00	2100.00
☐1886	Rosecrans-Nebeker	Lg. Brown	110.00	185.00	625.00	2100.00
☐1886	Rosecrans-Nebeker	Sm. Red	110.00	185.00	625.00	2200.00

ONE DOLLAR NOTES (1891) SILVER CERTIFICATES
(Large Size)
Back Design
Face Design:
Same as 1886
note.

SERIES	SIGNATURES	SEAL	A.B.P.	GOOD	V. FINE	UNC.
☐1891	Rosecrans-Nebeker	Sm. Red	105.00	175.00	525.00	1500.00
☐1891	Tillman-Morgan	Sm. Red	105.00	175.00	600.00	1500.00

ONE DOLLAR NOTES (1896) SILVER CERTIFICATES
(Large Size)

Face Design: History instructing youth. To the right, panoramic view of the Capitol and Washington Monument. Constitution on tablet, names of famous Americans on top and side borders.

Back Design: Portrait of Martha Washington to left and President Washington to right with large numeral "1" in center.

There is a story that when this note was issued people objected to it because they said No. "1" (ONE) shouldn't stand between George and Martha Washington. The set consists of $1, $2, and $5 denominations. They all have very beautiful engravings, and they are truly the most beautiful notes ever issued by our government. They were first released in 1896 and replaced by a new issue in 1899. They were short-lived because of objections to the unclad female on the $5 Note.

SERIES	SIGNATURES	SEAL	A.B.P.	GOOD	V. FINE	UNC.
☐1896	Tillman-Morgan	Red	220.00	365.00	1280.00	3375.00
☐1896	Bruce-Roberts	Red	220.00	365.00	1280.00	3375.00

ONE DOLLAR NOTES (1899) SILVER CERTIFICATES
(Large Size)

Face Design: Eagle on flag and Capitol background over
portraits of Presidents Lincoln and Grant.

Back Design

SERIES	SIGNATURES	SEAL	A.B.P.	GOOD	V. FINE	UNC.
	SERIES OF 1899 (above upper right serial number)					
☐1899	Lyons-Roberts	Blue	42.00	75.00	150.00	700.00
	SERIES OF 1899 (below upper right serial number)					
☐1899	Lyons-Roberts	Blue	30.00	50.00	235.00	625.00
☐1899	Lyons-Treat	Blue	30.00	50.00	235.00	625.00
☐1899	Vernon-Treat	Blue	40.00	65.00	235.00	625.00
☐1899	Vernon-McClung	Blue	40.00	65.00	235.00	625.00
	SERIES OF 1899 (vertical to right of blue seal)					
☐1899	Napier-McClung	Blue	35.00	55.00	135.00	575.00
☐1899	Napier-Thompson	Blue	48.00	80.00	350.00	1500.00
☐1899	Parker-Burke	Blue	42.00	75.00	160.00	550.00
☐1899	Teehee-Burke	Blue	42.00	75.00	160.00	550.00
☐1899	Elliott-Burke	Blue	42.00	75.00	160.00	550.00
☐1899	Elliott-White	Blue	42.00	75.00	160.00	550.00

SERIES	SIGNATURES	SEAL	A.B.P.	GOOD	V. FINE	UNC.
☐1899	Speelman-White	Blue	30.00	50.00	165.00	450.00

ONE DOLLAR NOTES (1923) SILVER CERTIFICATES
(Large Size)

Face Design: Portrait of President Washington in center, blue seal left, blue 1 DOLLAR right, blue numbers.

Back Design: Same as 1923 note.

SERIES	SIGNATURES	SEAL	A.B.P.	GOOD	V. FINE	UNC.
☐1923	Speelman-White	Blue	24.00	40.00	85.00	200.00
☐1923	Woods-White	Blue	24.00	40.00	110.00	200.00
☐1923	Woods-Tate	Blue	36.00	60.00	510.00	1050.00

ONE DOLLAR NOTES (1928) SILVER CERTIFICATES
(Small Size)

Face Design: Portrait of President Washington, blue seal to
the left, ONE to right, blue seal and numbers. ONE SILVER DOL-
LAR under portrait.
Back Design

First issue of Series 1928. U.S. paper money was reduced
in 1928 from the old Large Size to the size presently in use.
This was mostly an economy measure. Unlike Large Size
Notes, the Small Notes have a letter designation after the
date to denote a minor change in design or change of one
or both signatures.

SERIES	SIGNATURES	SEAL	A.B.P.	GOOD	V. FINE	UNC.	★UNC.
☐ 1928	Tate-Mellon	Blue	12.00	20.00	45.00	150.00	735.00
☐ 1928A	Woods-Mellon	Blue	12.00	20.00	45.00	150.00	650.00
☐ 1928B	Woods-Mills	Blue	12.00	20.00	45.00	150.00	1750.00
☐ 1928C	Woods-Woodin	Blue	42.00	70.00	300.00	775.00	RARE
☐ 1928D	Julian-Woodin	Blue	30.00	50.00	100.00	475.00	RARE
☐ 1928E	Julian-Morgenthau	Blue	120.00	200.00	650.00	2400.00	RARE

ONE DOLLAR NOTES (1934) SILVER CERTIFICATES
(Small Size)

Face Design: Portrait of President Washington, blue "1" to
left. ONE and blue seal to right. ONE DOLLAR IN SILVER under
portrait.
Back Design: Same as 1928 note.

SERIES	SIGNATURES	SEAL	A.B.P.	GOOD	V. FINE	UNC.	★UNC.
☐1934	Julian-Morgenthau	Blue	12.00	20.00	35.00	180.00	2070.00

ONE DOLLAR NOTES (1935) SILVER CERTIFICATES
(Small Size)

Face Design: Portrait of President Washington in center.
Gray "1" to left, blue seal right, and blue numbers. ONE DOL-
LAR IN SILVER under portrait.

The following notes are without IN GOD WE TRUST on back.

SERIES	SIGNATURES	SEAL	A.B.P.	GOOD	V. FINE	UNC.	★UNC.
☐1935	Julian-Morgenthau	Blue	6.00	10.00	25.00	80.00	675.00
☐1935A	Julian-Morgenthau	Blue	6.00	10.00	25.00	50.00	200.00
☐1935A	Julian-Morgenthau	Brown	6.00	10.00	40.00	185.00	2000.00

This note was a special issue for use in war zones in the Pacific area during
World War II. Brown serial numbers and HAWAII stamped on front and back.

ONE DOLLAR NOTES (1935) SILVER CERTIFICATES
(Small Size)

SERIES SIGNATURES	SEAL	A.B.P.	GOOD	V. FINE	UNC.	★UNC.
☐ 1935A Julian-Morgenthau	Yellow	12.00	20.00	50.00	200.00	2750.00

The above note was a special issue for use in war zones in the North African and European areas during World War II. Blue serial numbers and yellow seal.

☐ 1935A Julian-Morgenthau	Blue	20.00	35.00	145.00	435.00	RARE

Red "R" between the Treasury Seal and signature of Morgenthau. This was an experimental issue to test wearing qualities of differently treated paper.

☐ 1935A Julian-Morgenthau	Blue	25.00	50.00	90.00	425.00	RARE

Above note with red "S" between Treasury Seal and signature of Morgenthau. Experimental issue "R" was for regular paper, "S" for special paper.

☐ 1935B Julian-Vinson	Blue	3.60	6.00	12.00	30.00	350.00
☐ 1935C Julian-Snyder	Blue	2.50	4.00	10.00	20.00	115.00
☐ 1935D Clark-Snyder	Blue	2.50	4.00	10.00	20.00	90.00

Wide design on back. This and all notes of 1935 prior to this have the wide design. See Fig I.

☐ 1935D Clark-Snyder	Blue	2.00	3.00	6.00	18.00	75.00

Narrow design on back. This and all $1 Notes following have narrow design. See Fig. II.

Figure I

Figure II

ONE DOLLAR NOTES (1935) SILVER CERTIFICATES
(Small Size)

SERIES	SIGNATURES	SEAL	A.B.P.	GOOD	V. FINE	UNC.	★UNC.
☐1935E Priest-Humphrey		Blue	1.00	3.00	8.00	25.00	60.00
☐1935F Priest-Anderson		Blue	1.80	3.00	8.00	25.00	60.00
☐1935G Smith-Dillon		Blue	1.80	3.00	8.00	20.00	60.00

IN GOD WE TRUST added. All notes following have the motto.

☐1935G Smith-Dillon	Blue	3.00	5.00	15.00	65.00	350.00
☐1935H Granahan-Dillon	Blue	2.10	3.50	8.00	20.00	80.00

ONE DOLLAR NOTES (1957) SILVER CERTIFICATES
(Small Size)

The following three notes are the last issue of the $1 Silver Certificates. The reason for the change in series from 1935H to 1957 was due to printing improvements. The 1935 Series, up until the issue of Clark and Snyder, was printed in sheets of twelve subjects to a sheet. During the term of Clark and Snyder notes were printed eighteen subjects to a sheet. Starting with Series 1957, new high-speed rotary presses were installed and notes were printed thirty-two subjects to a sheet.

SERIES	SIGNATURES	SEAL	A.B.P.	GOOD	V. FINE	UNC.	★UNC.
☐1957 Priest-Anderson		Blue	1.50	2.00	5.00	12.00	35.00
☐1957A Smith-Dillon		Blue	1.50	2.00	5.00	12.00	25.00
☐1957B Granahan-Dillon		Blue	1.50	2.00	5.00	12.00	20.00

The redemption of Silver Certificates by the U.S. Treasury Department ended on June 24, 1968. These notes are now worth only their face value, plus the numismatic value to collectors. Notes in used condition are not regarded as collectors' items.

ONE DOLLAR NOTES (1890)
TREASURY OR COIN NOTES

(Large Size)

Face Design: Portrait of Stanton, Secretary of War during the Civil War.

Back Design: Green large ornate ONE. Entire back is beautifully engraved.

SERIES	SIGNATURES	SEAL	A.B.P.	GOOD	V. FINE	UNC.
☐1890	Rosecrans-Huston	Brown	120.00	210.00	1150.00	3850.00
☐1890	Rosecrans-Nebeker	Brown	120.00	210.00	1150.00	3850.00
☐1890	Rosecrans-Nebeker	Red	120.00	210.00	1150.00	3850.00

ONE DOLLAR NOTES (1891)
TREASURY OR COIN NOTES

(Large Size)

Face Design: Is similar to 1890 note.

Back Design: More unengraved area, numerous ONES and "1"s.

SERIES	SIGNATURES	SEAL	A.B.P.	GOOD	V. FINE	UNC.
☐1891	Rosecrans-Nebeker	Red	100.00	175.00	325.00	1785.00
☐1891	Tillman-Morgan	Red	100.00	175.00	325.00	1700.00
☐1891	Bruce-Roberts	Red	100.00	175.00	325.00	1700.00

ONE DOLLAR NOTES (1918)
FEDERAL RESERVE BANK NOTES
(Large Size)

Face Design: Portrait of President Washington, signature to left of center. Bank and city center, blue seal to right. Signatures of government officials above. Signatures of bank officials below. Federal Reserve district letter and numbers in four corners.

Back Design: Flying eagle and flag in center. All are Series 1918 and have blue seals and blue numbers.

BANK	GOV'T SIGNATURES	BANK SIGNATURES	A.B.P.	GOOD	V. FINE	UNC.
☐ Boston	Teehee-Burke	Bullen-Morss				
			60.00	125.00	200.00	450.00
☐ Boston	Teehee-Burke	Willet-Morss				
			60.00	125.00	200.00	675.00
☐ Boston	Elliot-Burke	Willet-Morss				
			60.00	125.00	200.00	450.00

BANK	GOV'T SIGNATURES	BANK SIGNATURES	A.B.P.	GOOD	V. FINE	UNC.
☐ New York	Teehee-Burke	Sailer-Strong	36.00	60.00	225.00	425.00
☐ New York	Toohoo-Burke	Hendricks-Strong	36.00	60.00	225.00	425.00
☐ New York	Elliott-Burke	Hendricks-Strong	36.00	60.00	225.00	425.00
☐ Philadelphia	Teehee-Burke	Hardt-Passmore	36.00	60.00	175.00	425.00
☐ Philadelphia	Teehee-Burke	Dyer-Passmore	36.00	60.00	175.00	425.00
☐ Philadelphia	Elliott-Burke	Dyer-Passmore	45.00	75.00	325.00	1000.00
☐ Philadelphia	Elliott-Burke	Dyer-Norris	35.00	50.00	170.00	475.00
☐ Cleveland	Teehee-Burke	Baxter-Fancher	36.00	60.00	170.00	475.00
☐ Cleveland	Teehee-Burke	Davis-Fancher	36.00	60.00	175.00	475.00
☐ Cleveland	Elliott-Burke	Davis-Fancher	36.00	60.00	175.00	475.00
☐ Richmond	Teehee-Burke	Keesee-Seay	36.00	60.00	175.00	475.00
☐ Richmond	Elliott-Burke	Keesee-Seay	36.00	60.00	175.00	475.00
☐ Atlanta	Teehee-Burke	Pike-McCord	36.00	60.00	175.00	475.00
☐ Atlanta	Teehee-Burke	Bell-McCord	42.00	70.00	350.00	1100.00
☐ Atlanta	Teehee-Burke	Bell-Wellborn	42.00	70.00	325.00	925.00
☐ Atlanta	Elliott-Burke	Bell-Wellborn	33.00	55.00	155.00	480.00
☐ Chicago	Teehee-Burke	McCloud-McDougal	36.00	60.00	175.00	480.00
☐ Chicago	Teehee-Burke	Cramer-McDougal	36.00	60.00	175.00	480.00
☐ Chicago	Elliott-Burke	Cramer-McDougal	36.00	60.00	175.00	480.00
☐ St. Louis	Teehee-Burke	Attebery-Wells	36.00	60.00	175.00	480.00
☐ St. Louis	Teehee-Burke	Attebery-Biggs	42.00	70.00	310.00	950.00

BANK	GOV'T SIGNATURES	BANK SIGNATURES	A.B.P.	GOOD	V. FINE	UNC.
☐ St. Louis	Elliott-Burke	Attebery-Biggs	45.00	75.00	320.00	950.00
☐ St. Louis	Elliott-Burke	White-Biggs	45.00	75.00	165.00	375.00
☐ Minneapolis	Teehee-Burke	Cook-Wold	45.00	75.00	165.00	375.00
☐ Minneapolis	Teehee-Burke	Cook-Young	128.00	230.00	575.00	1400.00
☐ Minneapolis	Elliott-Burke	Cook-Young	45.00	75.00	175.00	500.00
☐ Kansas City	Teehee-Burke	Anderson-Miller	45.00	75.00	175.00	500.00
☐ Kansas City	Elliott-Burke	Anderson-Miller	45.00	75.00	175.00	500.00
☐ Kansas City	Elliott-Burke	Helm-Miller	45.00	75.00	175.00	500.00
☐ Dallas	Teehee-Burke	Talley-VanZandt	45.00	75.00	175.00	500.00
☐ Dallas	Elliott-Burke	Talley-VanZandt	36.00	60.00	200.00	500.00
☐ Dallas	Elliott-Burke	Lawder-VanZandt	33.00	60.00	200.00	400.00
☐ San Francisco	Teehee-Burke	Clerk-Lynch	33.00	60.00	200.00	400.00
☐ San Francisco	Teehee-Burke	Clerk-Calkins	60.00	100.00	260.00	725.00
☐ San Francisco	Elliott-Burke	Clerk-Calkins	39.00	75.00	200.00	535.00
☐ San Francisco	Elliott-Burke	Ambrose-Calkins	39.00	75.00	200.00	400.00

ONE DOLLAR NOTES (1963)
FEDERAL RESERVE NOTES

(Small Size)

Face Design: Portrait of President Washington in center, black Federal Reserve seal with city and district letter to left, green Treasury Seal to right. Green serial numbers, Federal Reserve numbers in four corners.

Back Design: Same as all $1 Notes from 1935.

SERIES OF 1963, GRANAHAN-DILLON, GREEN SEAL

DISTRICT	A.B.P.	UNC.	★UNC.	DISTRICT	A.B.P.	UNC.	★UNC.
☐1A Boston	3.60	6.25	10.00	☐7G Chicago	3.60	6.25	12.50
☐2B New York	3.60	6.25	8.50	☐8H St. Louis	3.60	6.25	12.50
☐3C Philadelphia	3.60	6.25	9.25	☐9I Minneapolis	3.60	6.25	15.50
☐4D Cleveland	3.60	6.25	9.25	☐10J Kansas City	3.60	6.25	12.50
☐5E Richmond	3.60	6.25	8.50	☐11K Dallas	3.60	6.25	12.50
☐6F Atlanta	3.60	6.25	8.50	☐12L San Francisco	3.60	6.25	15.50
District Sets (12 notes)		100.00					

The Dallas note of this series, with the letter "K" in the black seal and the number "11" in the four corners, does not have any more significance or value than any other notes with their respective district letter and corresponding number.

A false rumor was circulated several years ago that the "K" was for Kennedy, the "11" was for November (the month in which he was assassinated), and that the note was issued by the Dallas Bank to commemorate the occasion. The entire story is apocryphal.

This note is in no way associated with the late President Kennedy. The notes were authorized by the Act of June 4, 1963. This was five months before Kennedy was assassinated. The Federal Reserve district for Dallas is K-11.

SERIES OF 1963A, GRANAHAN-FOWLER, GREEN SEAL

DISTRICT	A.B.P.	UNC.	★UNC.	DISTRICT	A.B.P.	UNC.	★UNC.
☐1A Boston	3.00	5.25	10.50	☐7G Chicago	3.00	5.25	12.00
☐2B New York	3.00	5.25	10.50	☐8H St. Louis	3.00	5.25	12.00
☐3C Philadelphia	3.00	5.25	10.50	☐9I Minneapolis	3.00	5.25	12.00
☐4D Cleveland	3.00	5.25	10.50	☐10J Kansas City	3.00	5.25	12.00
☐5E Richmond	3.00	5.25	10.50	☐11K Dallas	3.00	5.25	12.00
☐6F Atlanta	3.00	5.25	10.50	☐12L San Francisco	3.00	5.25	10.50
District Sets (12 notes)	100.00						

ONE DOLLAR NOTES (1963-B) FEDERAL RESERVE (WITH SIGNATURE OF JOSEPH W. BARR)
(Small Size)

Joseph W. Barr served as Secretary of the Treasury from December 20, 1968, to January 20, 1969, filling the unexpired term of Henry H. Fowler. His signature appears on the $1 Federal Reserve Notes of the Series of 1963-B only.

During the one-month term of Joseph W. Barr, about 471 million notes were printed with his signature. These notes were for the following Federal Reserve Banks.

	REGULAR NUMBERS	A.B.P.	UNC.	★UNC.
☐2B New York	123,040,000	3.60	6.75	22.75
☐5E Richmond	93,600,000	3.60	6.75	22.75
☐7G Chicago	91,040,000	3.60	6.75	22.75
☐10J Kansas City	44,800,000	3.60	6.75	22.75
☐12L San Francisco	106,400,000	3.60	6.75	22.75
District Sets (5 notes)				85.00

ONE DOLLAR NOTES (1969)
FEDERAL RESERVE NOTES
(WORDING IN GREEN, TREASURY SEAL CHANGED FROM LATIN TO ENGLISH)

FORMER DESIGN:
The former design had the Latin inscription: *"Thesaur. Amer. Septent. Sigil.,"* which has several translations. It was the Seal of the North American Treasury.

NEW DESIGN:
This new design drops the Latin and states *"The Department of The Treasury, 1789."* First used on the $100 Note of the Series 1966.

ONE DOLLAR NOTES (1969)
FEDERAL RESERVE NOTES

(Small Size)

SERIES OF 1969, SIGNATURES OF ELSTON-KENNEDY, GREEN SEAL

BANK	A.B.P.	V.FINE	UNC.	★UNC.	BANK	A.B.P.	V.FINE	UNC.	★UNC.
☐ Boston	—	1.25	6.50	10.75	☐ Chicago	—	1.50	6.50	10.75
☐ New York	—	1.25	6.50	10.75	☐ St. Louis	—	1.50	6.50	10.75
☐ Philadelphia	—	1.25	6.50	10.75	☐ Minneapolis	—	1.50	6.50	10.75
☐ Cleveland	—	1.25	6.50	10.75	☐ Kansas City	—	1.50	6.50	10.75
☐ Richmond	—	1.25	6.50	10.75	☐ Dallas	—	1.50	6.50	10.75
☐ Atlanta	—	1.25	6.50	10.75	☐ San Francisco	—	1.50	6.50	10.75

SERIES OF 1969A, SIGNATURES OF KABIS-KENNEDY, GREEN SEAL

BANK	A.B.P.	V.FINE	UNC.	★UNC.	BANK	A.B.P.	V.FINE	UNC.	★UNC.
☐ Boston	—	1.25	5.75	10.75	☐ Chicago	—	1.25	5.75	10.75
☐ New York	—	1.25	5.75	10.75	☐ St. Louis	—	1.25	5.75	10.75
☐ Philadelphia	—	1.25	5.75	10.75	☐ Minneapolis	—	1.25	5.75	10.75
☐ Cleveland	—	1.25	5.75	10.75	☐ Kansas City	—	1.25	5.75	10.75
☐ Richmond	—	1.25	5.75	10.75	☐ Dallas	—	1.25	5.75	10.75
☐ Atlanta	—	1.25	5.75	10.75	☐ San Francisco	—	1.25	5.75	10.75

SERIES OF 1969B, SIGNATURES OF KABIS-CONNALLY, GREEN SEAL

BANK	A.B.P.	V.FINE	UNC.	★UNC.	BANK	A.B.P.	V.FINE	UNC.	★UNC.
☐ Boston	—	1.25	6.50	10.75	☐ Chicago	—	1.25	6.50	10.75
☐ New York	—	1.25	6.50	10.75	☐ St. Louis	—	1.25	6.50	10.75
☐ Philadelphia—		1.25	6.50	10.75	☐ Minneapolis	—	1.25	6.50	10.75
☐ Cleveland	—	1.25	6.50	10.75	☐ Kansas City	—	1.25	6.50	10.75
☐ Richmond	—	1.25	6.50	10.75	☐ Dallas	—	1.25	6.50	10.75
☐ Atlanta	—	1.25	6.50	10.75	☐ San Francisco—		1.25	6.50	10.75

SERIES OF 1969C, SIGNATURES OF BANUELOS-CONNALLY, GREEN SEAL

BANK	A.B.P.	V.FINE	UNC.	★UNC.	BANK	A.B.P.	V.FINE	UNC.	★UNC.
☐ New York	—	1.25	6.25	—	☐ Chicago	—	1.25	6.25	42.00
☐ Cleveland	—	1.25	6.25	42.00	☐ St. Louis	—	1.25	6.25	42.00
☐ Richmond	—	1.25	6.25	45.00	☐ Minneapolis	—	1.25	6.25	42.00
☐ Atlanta	—	1.25	6.25	42.00	☐ Kansas City	—	1.25	6.25	42.00
					☐ Dallas	—	1.25	6.25	42.00
					☐ San Francisco—		1.25	6.25	42.00

SERIES OF 1969D, SIGNATURES OF BANUELOS-SHULTZ, GREEN SEAL

BANK	A.B.P.	V.FINE	UNC.	★UNC.	BANK	A.B.P.	V.FINE	UNC.	★UNC.
☐ Boston	—	1.25	6.50	14.00	☐ Chicago	—	1.25	6.50	14.00
☐ New York	—	1.25	6.50	14.00	☐ St. Louis	—	1.25	6.50	14.00
☐ Philadelphia—		1.25	6.50	14.00	☐ Minneapolis	—	1.25	6.50	14.00
☐ Cleveland	—	1.25	6.50	14.00	☐ Kansas City	—	1.25	6.50	14.00
☐ Richmond	—	1.25	6.50	14.00	☐ Dallas	—	1.25	6.50	14.00
☐ Atlanta	—	1.25	6.50	14.00	☐ San Francisco—		1.25	6.50	14.00

SERIES OF 1974, SIGNATURES OF NEFF-SIMON, GREEN SEAL

BANK	A.B.P.	V.FINE	UNC.	★UNC.	BANK	A.B.P.	V.FINE	UNC.	★UNC.
☐ Boston	—	1.25	5.00	10.00	☐ Chicago	—	1.25	5.00	7.75
☐ New York	—	1.25	5.00	8.50	☐ St. Louis	—	1.25	5.00	7.75
☐ Philadelphia—		1.25	5.00	8.50	☐ Minneapolis	—	1.25	5.00	42.00
☐ Cleveland	—	1.25	5.00	20.00	☐ Kansas City	—	1.25	5.00	7.75
☐ Richmond	—	1.25	5.00	8.50	☐ Dallas	—	1.25	5.00	10.00
☐ Atlanta	—	1.25	5.00	6.00	☐ San Francisco—		1.25	5.00	7.75

SERIES OF 1977, SIGNATURES OF MORTON-BLUMENTHAL, GREEN SEAL

BANK	A.B.P.	V.FINE	UNC.	★UNC.	BANK	A.B.P.	V.FINE	UNC.	★UNC.
☐ Boston	—	1.25	6.75	11.75	☐ Chicago	—	1.25	6.75	11.75
☐ New York	—	1.25	6.75	11.75	☐ St. Louis	—	1.25	6.75	11.75
☐ Philadelphia—		1.25	6.75	11.75	☐ Minneapolis	—	1.25	6.75	11.75
☐ Cleveland	—	1.25	6.75	11.75	☐ Kansas City	—	1.25	6.75	11.75
☐ Richmond	—	1.25	6.75	11.75	☐ Dallas	—	1.25	6.75	11.75
☐ Atlanta	—	1.25	6.75	11.75	☐ San Francisco—		1.25	6.75	11.75

SERIES OF 1977A, SIGNATURES OF MORTON-MILLER, GREEN SEAL

BANK	A.B.P.	V.FINE	UNC.	★UNC.	BANK	A.B.P.	V.FINE	UNC.	★UNC.
☐ Boston	—	1.10	6.75	9.75	☐ Chicago	—	1.10	6.75	9.75
☐ New York	—	1.10	6.75	9.75	☐ St. Louis	—	1.10	6.75	9.75
☐ Philadelphia	—	1.10	6.75	9.75	☐ Minneapolis	—	1.10	8.75	25.00
☐ Cleveland	—	1.10	6.75	9.75	☐ Kansas City	—	1.10	6.75	9.75
☐ Richmond	—	1.10	6.75	9.75	☐ Dallas	—	1.10	6.75	9.75
☐ Atlanta	—	1.10	6.75	9.75	☐ San Francisco	—	1.10	6.75	9.75

SERIES OF 1981, SIGNATURES OF BUCHANAN-REGAN, GREEN SEAL

BANK	A.B.P.	V.FINE	UNC.	★UNC.	BANK	A.B.P.	V.FINE	UNC.	★UNC.
☐ Boston	—	1.10	6.75	14.75	☐ Chicago	—	1.10	6.75	14.75
☐ New York	—	1.10	6.75	14.75	☐ St. Louis	—	1.10	6.75	15.00
☐ Philadelphia	—	1.10	6.75	50.00	☐ Minneapolis	—	1.10	6.75	15.00
☐ Cleveland	—	1.10	6.75	14.75	☐ Kansas City	—	1.10	6.75	14.75
☐ Richmond	—	1.10	6.75	14.75	☐ Dallas	—	1.10	6.75	15.00
☐ Atlanta	—	1.10	6.75	14.75	☐ San Francisco	—	1.10	6.75	14.75

SERIES OF 1981A, SIGNATURES OF ORTEGA-REGAN, GREEN SEAL

BANK	A.B.P.	V.FINE	UNC.	★UNC.	BANK	A.B.P.	V.FINE	UNC.	★UNC.
☐ Boston	—	1.10	6.75	16.50	☐ Chicago	—	1.10	6.75	16.50
☐ New York	—	1.10	6.75	16.50	☐ St.Louis	—	1.10	6.75	16.50
☐ Philadelphia	—	1.10	6.75	16.50	☐ Minneapolis	—	1.10	6.75	16.50
☐ Cleveland	—	1.10	6.75	16.50	☐ Kansas City	—	1.10	6.75	16.50
☐ Richmond	—	1.10	6.75	16.50	☐ Dallas	—	1.10	6.75	1100.00
☐ Atlanta	—	1.10	6.75	16.50	☐ San Francisco	—	1.10	6.75	16.50

SERIES OF 1981A or 1985 (REVERSE #129 LEFT), SIGNATURES OF ORTEGA-REGAN, GREEN SEAL

BANK	A.B.P.	V.FINE	UNC.	★UNC.	BANK	A.B.P.	V.FINE	UNC.	★UNC.
☐ Boston	15.00	25.00	60.00	—	☐ Chicago	15.00	25.00	60.00	—
☐ New York	15.00	25.00	60.00	—	☐ St. Louis	15.00	25.00	60.00	—
☐ Philadelphia	15.00	25.00	60.00	—	☐ Minneapolis	15.00	25.00	60.00	—
☐ Cleveland	15.00	25.00	60.00	—	☐ Kansas City	15.00	25.00	60.00	—
☐ Richmond	15.00	25.00	60.00	—	☐ Dallas	15.00	25.00	60.00	—
☐ Atlanta	15.00	25.00	60.00	—	☐ San Francisco	15.00	25.00	60.00	—

SERIES OF 1985, SIGNATURES OF ORTEGA-BAKER, GREEN SEAL

★Notes not issued for all banks

BANK	A.B.P.	V.FINE	UNC.	★UNC.	BANK	A.B.P.	V.FINE	UNC.	★UNC.
☐ Boston	—	1.10	6.00	—	☐ Chicago	—	1.10	6.00	12.50
☐ New York	—	1.10	6.00	—	☐ St. Louis	—	1.10	6.00	12.50
☐ Philadelphia	—	1.10	6.00	—	☐ Minneapolis	—	1.10	6.00	12.50
☐ Cleveland	—	1.10	6.00	—	☐ Kansas City	—	1.10	6.00	12.50
☐ Richmond	—	1.10	6.00	12.75	☐ Dallas	—	1.10	6.00	12.50
☐ Atlanta	—	1.10	6.00	—	☐ San Francisco	—	1.10	6.00	12.50

SERIES OF 1985 (REVERSE #129 LEFT), SIGNATURES OF ORTEGA-BAKER, GREEN SEAL

BANK	A.B.P.	V.FINE	UNC.	★UNC.	BANK	A.B.P.	V.FINE	UNC.	★UNC.
☐ Boston	15.00	25.00	42.00	—	☐ Chicago	15.00	25.00	42.00	—
☐ New York	15.00	25.00	42.00	—	☐ St. Louis	15.00	25.00	42.00	—
☐ Philadelphia	15.00	25.00	42.00	—	☐ Minneapolis	15.00	25.00	42.00	—
☐ Cleveland	15.00	25.00	42.00	—	☐ Kansas City	15.00	25.00	42.00	—
☐ Richmond	15.00	25.00	42.00	—	☐ Dallas	15.00	25.00	42.00	—

SERIES OF 1988, SIGNATURES OF ORTEGA-BRADY, GREEN SEAL

★Notes not issued for all banks

BANK	A.B.P.	V.FINE	UNC.	★UNC.	BANK	A.B.P.	V.FINE	UNC.	★UNC.
☐ Boston	—	1.15	6.50	12.50	☐ Chicago	—	1.15	6.50	—
☐ New York	—	1.15	6.50	12.50	☐ St. Louis	—	1.15	6.50	—
☐ Philadelphia	—	1.15	6.50	—	☐ Minneapolis	—	1.15	6.50	—
☐ Cleveland	—	1.15	6.50	—	☐ Kansas City	—	1.15	6.50	12.50
☐ Richmond	—	1.15	6.50	12.50	☐ Dallas	—	1.15	6.50	12.50
☐ Atlanta	—	1.15	6.50	12.50	☐ San Francisco	—	1.15	6.50	12.50

SERIES OF 1988A, SIGNATURES OF VILLALPANDO-BRADY, GREEN SEAL

★Notes not issued for all banks

BANK	A.B.P.	V.FINE	UNC.	★UNC.	BANK	A.B.P.	V.FINE	UNC.	★UNC.
☐ Boston	—	1.15	4.50	—	☐ Chicago	—	1.15	4.50	14.75
☐ New York	—	1.15	4.50	14.25	☐ St. Louis	—	1.15	4.50	14.75
☐ Philadelphia	—	1.15	4.50	—	☐ Minneapolis	—	1.15	4.50	14.75
☐ Cleveland	—	1.15	4.50	14.25	☐ Kansas City	—	1.15	4.50	—
☐ Richmond	—	1.15	4.50	14.25	☐ Dallas	—	1.15	4.50	14.75
☐ Atlanta	—	1.15	4.50	14.25	☐ San Francisco	—	1.15	4.50	14.75

SERIES OF 1993, SIGNATURES OF WITHROW-BENTSEN, GREEN SEAL

★Notes not issued for all banks

BANK	A.B.P.	V.FINE	UNC.	★UNC.	BANK	A.B.P.	V.FINE	UNC.	★UNC.
☐ Boston	—	1.15	2.25	—	☐ Chicago	—	1.15	2.25	5.75
☐ New York	—	1.15	2.25	5.75	☐ St. Louis	—	1.15	2.25	—
☐ Philadelphia	—	1.15	2.25	225.00	☐ Minneapolis	—	1.15	160.00	—
☐ Cleveland	—	1.15	2.25	—	☐ Dallas	—	1.15	2.25	5.75
☐ Richmond	—	1.15	2.25	—	☐ San Francisco	—	1.15	2.25	—
☐ Atlanta	—	1.15	2.25	5.75					

SERIES OF 1995, SIGNATURES OF WITHROW-RUBIN, GREEN SEAL

★Notes not issued for all banks

BANK	A.B.P.	V.FINE	UNC.	★UNC.	BANK	A.B.P.	V.FINE	UNC.	★UNC.
☐ Boston	—	1.15	2.65	7.50	☐ Chicago	—	1.15	2.65	7.50
☐ New York	—	1.15	2.65	7.50	☐ St. Louis	—	1.15	2.65	—
☐ Philadelphia	—	1.15	2.65	7.50	☐ Minneapolis	—	1.15	2.65	7.50
☐ Cleveland	—	1.15	2.65	7.50	☐ Kansas City	—	1.15	2.65	7.50
☐ Richmond	—	1.15	2.65	7.50	☐ Dallas	—	1.15	2.65	25.00
☐ Atlanta	—	1.15	2.65	7.50	☐ San Francisco	—	1.15	2.65	7.50

TWO DOLLAR NOTES

TWO DOLLAR NOTES (1862) UNITED STATES NOTES
(ALSO KNOWN AS LEGAL TENDER NOTES)
(Large Size)

Face Design: Portrait of Alexander Hamilton (1754–1804), cloverleaf "2"s in upper corners, medallion with "II" in lower left, medallion with "1, 2, 3" right of portrait.

Back Design: "2" in each corner, with "2" motif repeated in scallop circles around obligation; back is printed green.

SERIES	SIGNATURES	SEAL	A.B.P.	GOOD	V. FINE	UNC.
☐ 1862	Chittenden-Spinner					
	Type I, American Banknote Company vertical					
	in left border	Red	150.00	275.00	1700.00	3850.00
☐ 1862	Chittenden-Spinner					
	Type II, National Banknote Company vertical					
	in left border	Red	150.00	275.00	1700.00	3850.00

TWO DOLLAR NOTES (1869) UNITED STATES NOTES
(ALSO KNOWN AS LEGAL TENDER NOTES)
(Large Size)

Face Design: Portrait of President Jefferson to left, Capitol in center, large red seal to right.

Back Design: Roman "II" left, arabic "2" center, TWO right. This is the companion note to the $1 "Rainbow Note."

SERIES	SIGNATURES	SEAL	A.B.P.	GOOD	V. FINE	UNC.
☐1869	Allison-Spinner	Red	200.00	350.00	1200.00	RARE
☐1869	Allison-Spinner	Water Mark Paper	255.00	450.00	2000.00	RARE

TWO DOLLAR NOTES (1874) UNITED STATES NOTES
(ALSO KNOWN AS LEGAL TENDER NOTES)
(Large Size)

Face Design: Portrait of President Jefferson; same as 1869 note.

Back Design: Completely revised.

SERIES	SIGNATURES	SEAL	A.B.P.	GOOD	V. FINE	UNC.
☐1874	Allison-Spinner	Red	120.00	200.00	1000.00	2800.00
☐1875	Allison-New	Red	120.00	200.00	1200.00	3000.00
☐Series A	Allison-New	Red	210.00	375.00	3200.00	RARE
☐Series B	Allison-New	Red	210.00	375.00	3200.00	RARE
☐1875	Allison-Wyman	Red	120.00	200.00	850.00	2400.00
☐1878	Allison-Gilfillan	Red	105.00	175.00	850.00	2400.00
☐1878	Scofield-Gilfillan	Red	840.00	1400.00	RARE	RARE
☐1880	Scofield-Gilfillan	Brown	75.00	135.00	350.00	1500.00
☐1880	Bruce-Gilfillan	Brown	75.00	135.00	375.00	1200.00
☐1880	Bruce-Wyman	Brown	75.00	135.00	375.00	1500.00
☐1880	Rosecrans-Huston	Red	405.00	675.00	2000.00	RARE
☐1880	Rosecrans-Huston	Brown	835.00	1375.00	RARE	RARE
☐1880	Rosecrans-Nebeker	Red	90.00	175.00	650.00	2200.00
☐1880	Tillman-Morgan	Red	60.00	125.00	350.00	900.00

SERIES	SIGNATURES	SEAL	A.B.P.	GOOD	V. FINE	UNC.
☐1917	Teehee-Burke	Red	30.00	50.00	225.00	425.00
☐1917	Elliott-Burke	Red	30.00	50.00	225.00	425.00
☐1917	Elliott-Burke (error)	Red	66.00	110.00	400.00	1250.00
☐1917	Elliott-White	Red	30.00	50.00	225.00	425.00
☐1917	Speelman-White	Red	30.00	50.00	225.00	425.00

TWO DOLLAR NOTES (1928) UNITED STATES NOTES (ALSO KNOWN AS LEGAL TENDER NOTES)

(Small Size)

Face Design: Portrait of President Jefferson, red seal left, TWO right, red serial numbers.

Back Design: Jefferson Home—Monticello.

SERIES	SIGNATURES	SEAL	A.B.P.	GOOD	V. FINE	UNC.	★UNC.
☐1928	Tate-Mellon	Red	7.20	12.00	50.00	225.00	1200.00
☐1928A	Woods-Mellon	Red	12.00	20.00	75.00	475.00	RARE
☐1928B	Woods-Mills	Red	39.00	65.00	225.00	1500.00	RARE
☐1928C	Julian-Morgenthau	Red	7.20	12.00	25.00	225.00	3000.00
☐1928D	Julian-Morgenthau	Red	4.20	7.00	25.00	100.00	625.00
☐1928E	Julian-Vinson	Red	6.00	10.00	25.00	150.00	RARE
☐1928F	Julian-Snyder	Red	4.80	8.00	25.00	100.00	750.00
☐1928G	Clark-Snyder	Red	4.80	8.00	25.00	100.00	750.00

TWO DOLLAR NOTES (1953) UNITED STATES NOTES (ALSO KNOWN AS LEGAL TENDER NOTES)

(Small Size)

Face Design: Portrait of President Jefferson, gray "2" to left, red seal to right over TWO.

Back Design: Same as 1928 note.

SERIES	SIGNATURES	SEAL	A.B.P.	GOOD	V. FINE	UNC.	★UNC.
☐1953	Priest-Humphrey	Red	3.00	4.00	8.00	30.00	75.00
☐1953A	Priest-Anderson	Red	3.00	4.00	8.00	30.00	100.00
☐1953B	Smith-Dillon	Red	3.00	4.00	8.00	28.00	100.00
☐1953C	Granahan-Dillon	Red	3.00	4.00	8.00	28.00	110.00

Back Design: IN GOD WE TRUST on back.

Face Design: Same as previous note.

SERIES	SIGNATURES	SEAL	A.B.P.	GOOD	V. FINE	UNC.	★UNC.
☐1963	Granahan-Dillon	Red	3.00	4.00	8.00	20.00	65.00
☐1963A	Granahan-Fowler	Red	3.00	4.00	8.00	28.00	70.00

Production of $2 United States Notes was discontinued on August 10, 1966.

TWO DOLLAR NOTES (1875) NATIONAL BANK NOTES
FIRST CHARTER PERIOD (Large Size)

Face Design: This note is known as the "Lazy Two Note"
due to the unusual "lying down" shape of the "2" shown on
the face. Liberty with flag and red seal.

Back Design: Sir Walter Raleigh in England, 1585, exhibiting corn and smoking tobacco from America, State Seal,
and eagle.

SERIES	SIGNATURES	SEAL	A.B.P.	GOOD	V. FINE	UNC.
☐Original	Colby-Spinner	Red	630.00	1075.00	4125.00	RARE
☐Original	Jeffries-Spinner	Red	630.00	1075.00	3800.00	RARE
☐Original	Allison-Spinner	Red	630.00	1075.00	4125.00	RARE
☐1875	Allison-New	Red	630.00	1075.00	4125.00	RARE
☐1875	Allison-Wyman	Red	630.00	1075.00	4125.00	RARE
☐1875	Allison-Gilfillan	Red	630.00	1075.00	4125.00	RARE
☐1875	Scofield-Gilfillan	Red	630.00	1075.00	4125.00	RARE

TWO DOLLAR NOTES (1886) SILVER CERTIFICATES
(Large Size)

Face Design: General Hancock portrait left. Treasury Seal
to the right of center.

Back Design: "2" left and right, very ornate engraving,
obligation in center of note. Note is printed in green.

SERIES	SIGNATURES	SEAL	A.B.P.	GOOD	V. FINE	UNC.
☐1886	Rosecrans-Jordan	Red	144.00	250.00	1275.00	3650.00
☐1886	Rosecrans-Hyatt	Sm.Red	144.00	250.00	1275.00	3650.00
☐1886	Rosecrans-Hyatt	Lg.Red	144.00	250.00	1275.00	3650.00
☐1886	Rosecrans-Huston	Red	144.00	250.00	1275.00	3650.00
☐1886	Rosecrans-Huston	Brown	144.00	250.00	1275.00	3650.00

TWO DOLLAR NOTES (1891) SILVER CERTIFICATES
(Large Size)

Face Design: Portrait of William Windom, Secretary of the Treasury 1881–84 and 1889–91, red seal right.

Back Design: "2" left and right, scalloped design center with obligation, printed in green.

SERIES	SIGNATURES	SEAL	A.B.P.	GOOD	V. FINE	UNC.
☐1891	Rosecrans-Nebeker	Red	150.00	265.00	1200.00	4200.00
☐1091	Tillman-Morgan	Red	150.00	265.00	1200.00	4200.00

TWO DOLLAR NOTES (1896) SILVER CERTIFICATES
(Large Size)

Face Design: Science presenting Steam and Electricity to Industry and Commerce.

Back Design: Portraits of Robert Fulton and Samuel F.B. Morse.

This is the second note of the popular Educational Series.

SERIES	SIGNATURES	SEAL	A.B.P.	GOOD	V. FINE	UNC.
☐1896	Tillman-Morgan	Red	180.00	325.00	1850.00	RARE
☐1896	Bruce-Roberts	Red	180.00	325.00	1850.00	RARE

TWO DOLLAR NOTES (1899) SILVER CERTIFICATES
(Large Size)

Face Design: Portrait of President Washington between figures of Trade and Agriculture, blue "2" left, blue seal right.

Back Design

SERIES	SIGNATURES	SEAL	A.B.P.	GOOD	V. FINE	UNC.
☐1899	Lyons-Roberts	Blue	90.00	150.00	400.00	1850.00
☐1899	Lyons-Treat	Blue	90.00	150.00	400.00	1850.00
☐1899	Vernon-Treat	Blue	90.00	150.00	400.00	1850.00
☐1899	Vernon-McClung	Blue	90.00	150.00	400.00	1850.00
☐1899	Napier-McClung	Blue	90.00	150.00	400.00	1850.00
☐1899	Napier-Thompson	Blue	90.00	150.00	450.00	4000.00
☐1899	Parker-Burke	Blue	90.00	150.00	400.00	1850.00
☐1899	Teehee-Burke	Blue	90.00	150.00	400.00	1850.00
☐1899	Elliott-Burke	Blue	90.00	150.00	400.00	1850.00
☐1899	Speelman-White	Blue	90.00	150.00	400.00	1850.00

TWO DOLLAR NOTES (1890–1891)
TREASURY OR COIN NOTES

(Large Size)

Face Design: Portrait of General James McPherson.

Back Design: Large TWO center, over obligation. Large "2" on engraved background right. Intricate engraving, printed green.

SERIES	SIGNATURES	SEAL	A.B.P.	GOOD	V. FINE	UNC.
☐1890	Rosecrans-Huston	Brown	270.00	450.00	3250.00	RARE
☐1890	Rosecrans-Nebeker	Brown	270.00	450.00	3250.00	RARE
☐1890	Rosecrans-Nebeker	Red	270.00	450.00	3250.00	RARE

TWO DOLLAR NOTES (1890–1891)
TREASURY OR COIN NOTES

(Large Size)   **NOTE NO. 30**

Face Design: Similar to 1890–1891 note.
Back Design: Revised.

SERIES	SIGNATURES	SEAL	A.B.P.	GOOD	V. FINE	UNC.
☐1891	Rosecrans-Nebeker	Red	120.00	200.00	850.00	3500.00
☐1891	Tillman-Morgan	Red	120.00	200.00	850.00	3500.00
☐1891	Bruce-Roberts	Red	120.00	200.00	850.00	3500.00

TWO DOLLAR NOTES (1918)
FEDERAL RESERVE BANK NOTES
(Large Size)

Face Design: Portrait of President Jefferson to left, name of bank in center, blue seal to the right, blue numbers, Federal Reserve district letter and number in four corners.

Back Design: American battleship of World War I.

TWO DOLLAR NOTES (1918)
FEDERAL RESERVE BANK NOTES
(Large Size)

BANK	GOV'T SIGNATURES	BANK SIGNATURES	A.B.P.	GOOD	V. FINE	UNC.
☐ Boston	Teehee-Burke	Bullen-Morss				
			150.00	250.00	700.00	2675.00
☐ Boston	Teehee-Burke	Willet-Morss				
			150.00	250.00	700.00	2675.00
☐ Boston	Elliot-Burke	Willet-Morss				
			150.00	250.00	700.00	2675.00
☐ New York	Teehee-Burke	Sailer-Strong				
			150.00	250.00	700.00	2675.00
☐ New York	Teehee-Burke	Hendricks-Strong				
			150.00	250.00	700.00	2675.00
☐ New York	Elliott-Burke	Hendricks-Strong				
			150.00	250.00	700.00	2675.00
☐ Philadelphia	Teehee-Burke	Hardt-Passmore				
			150.00	250.00	700.00	2675.00
☐ Philadelphia	Teehee-Burke	Dyer-Passmore				
			150.00	250.00	700.00	2800.00
☐ Philadelphia	Elliott-Burke	Dyer-Passmore				
			150.00	250.00	1200.00	3500.00
☐ Philadelphia	Elliott-Burke	Dyer-Norris				
			150.00	250.00	700.00	2675.00
☐ Cleveland	Teehee-Burke	Baxter-Francher				
			150.00	250.00	700.00	2675.00
☐ Cleveland	Teehee-Burke	Davis-Francher				
			150.00	250.00	700.00	2675.00
☐ Cleveland	Elliott-Burke	Davis-Francher				
			150.00	250.00	700.00	2675.00
☐ Richmond	Teehee-Burke	Keesee-Seay				
			150.00	250.00	700.00	2675.00
☐ Richmond	Elliott-Burke	Keesee-Seay				
			150.00	250.00	700.00	2675.00
☐ Atlanta	Teehee-Burke	Pike-McCord				
			150.00	250.00	700.00	2450.00
☐ Atlanta	Teehee-Burke	Bell-McCord				
			150.00	250.00	1400.00	3250.00
☐ Atlanta	Elliott-Burke	Bell-Wellborn				
			150.00	250.00	1200.00	3250.00
☐ Chicago	Teehee-Burke	McCloud-McDougal				
			150.00	250.00	675.00	2200.00

BANK	GOV'T SIGNATURES	BANK SIGNATURES	A.B.P.	GOOD	V. FINE	UNC.
☐ Chicago	Teehee-Burke	Cramer-McDougal				
			150.00	255.00	650.00	2450.00
☐ Chicago	Elliott-Burke	Cramer-McDougal				
			150.00	255.00	725.00	2450.00
☐ St. Louis	Teehee-Burke	Attebery-Wells				
			150.00	255.00	725.00	2450.00
☐ St. Louis	Teehee-Burke	Attebery-Biggs				
			150.00	255.00	925.00	3250.00
☐ St. Louis	Elliott-Burke	Attebery-Biggs				
			150.00	255.00	925.00	3250.00
☐ St. Louis	Elliott-Burke	White-Biggs				
			150.00	255.00	925.00	3250.00
☐ Minneapolis	Teehee-Burke	Cook-Wold				
			150.00	255.00	675.00	2450.00
☐ Minneapolis	Elliott-Burke	Cook-Young				
			150.00	255.00	775.00	2275.00
☐ Kansas City	Teehee-Burke	Anderson-Miller				
			150.00	255.00	675.00	2200.00
☐ Kansas City	Elliott-Burke	Helm-Miller				
			150.00	255.00	675.00	2200.00
☐ Dallas	Teehee-Burke	Talley-VanZandt				
			150.00	255.00	800.00	2450.00
☐ Dallas	Elliott-Burke	Talley-VanZandt				
			150.00	255.00	800.00	2450.00
☐ San Francisco	Teehee-Burke	Clerk-Lynch				
			150.00	255.00	725.00	2450.00
☐ San Francisco	Elliott-Burke	Clerk-Calkins				
			150.00	255.00	725.00	2450.00
☐ San Francisco	Elliott-Burke	Ambrose-Calkins				
			150.00	255.00	725.00	2450.00

TWO DOLLAR NOTES (1976)
FEDERAL RESERVE NOTES
(Small Size)

Face Design: Portrait of President Jefferson.

Back Design: Signing of the Declaration of Independence.

SERIES OF 1976, NEFF-SIMON, GREEN SEAL

DISTRICT	A.B.P.	UNC.	★UNC.	DISTRICT	A.B.P.	UNC.	★UNC.
☐1A Boston	—	7.00	25.00	☐7G Chicago	—	9.50	90.00
☐2B New York	—	7.00	25.00	☐8H St. Louis	—	6.00	20.00
☐3C Philadelphia	—	7.00	25.00	☐9I Minneapolis	—	14.00	250.00
☐4D Cleveland	—	7.00	30.00	☐10J Kansas City	—	30.00	315.00
☐5E Richmond	—	7.00	40.00	☐11K Dallas	—	12.00	36.75
☐6F Atlanta	—	7.00	25.00	☐12L San Francisco	—	12.00	36.75

SERIES OF 1995, GREEN SEAL

DISTRICT	A.B.P.	★UNC.
☐6F Atlanta	—	20.00

FIVE DOLLAR NOTES

ORDER OF ISSUE

FIVE DOLLAR NOTES (1861) DEMAND NOTES
(Large Size)

Face Design: Left, Statue of America by Crawford atop United States Capitol. Center, numeral "5" in green. Right, portrait of Alexander Hamilton, statesman, first Secretary of the Treasury.

Back Design: Numerous small "5"s in ovals. This note has no Treasury Seal. The signatures are those of Treasury Department employees who signed for officials.

CITY	A.B.P.	GOOD	V. GOOD
☐Boston (I)	1920.00	3200.00	4850.00
☐New York (I)	1920.00	3200.00	4850.00
☐Philadelphia (I)	1920.00	3200.00	4850.00
☐Cincinnati (I)	—	RARE	RARE
☐St. Louis (I)	—	RARE	RARE
☐Boston (II)	600.00	1150.00	2450.00
☐New York (II)	600.00	1150.00	2450.00
☐Philadelphia (II)	600.00	1150.00	2225.00
☐Cincinnati (II)	—	RARE	RARE
☐St. Louis (II)	—	RARE	RARE

FIVE DOLLAR NOTES (1875–1907)
UNITED STATES NOTES
(ALSO KNOWN AS LEGAL TENDER NOTES)
(Large Size)

Back Design: First Obligation

Back Design: Second Obligation

SERIES	SIGNATURES	SEAL	A.B.P.	GOOD	V. FINE	UNC.
☐1862	Crittenden-Spinner*	Red	144.00	240.00	1150.00	2475.00
☐1862	Crittenden-Spinner**	Red	144.00	240.00	1150.00	2475.00
☐1863	Crittenden-Spinner**	Red	144.00	240.00	1150.00	2475.00

*First Obligation
**Second Obligation

FIVE DOLLAR NOTES (1869) UNITED STATES NOTES (ALSO KNOWN AS LEGAL TENDER NOTES)

(Large Size)

Face Design: Portrait of President Jackson on left. Pioneer and family in center.

Back Design: Color, green. This is a companion note to the $1 and $2 Notes of 1869 "Rainbow Notes."

SERIES	SIGNATURES	SEAL	A.B.P.	GOOD	V. FINE	UNC.
☐1869	Allison-Spinner	Red	84.00	140.00	775.00	2000.00
☐1869	Allison-Spinner Water Marked Paper	105.00	175.00	1475.00	3000.00

FIVE DOLLAR NOTES (1875–1907)
UNITED STATES NOTES
(ALSO KNOWN AS LEGAL TENDER NOTES)
(Large Size)

Back Design: Revised.
Face Design: Similar to 1869 note.

SERIES	SIGNATURES	SEAL	A.B.P.	GOOD	V. FINE	UNC.
☐1875	Allison-New	Red	72.00	130.00	450.00	1875.00
☐1875A	Allison-New	Red	96.00	160.00	535.00	2250.00
☐1875B	Allison-New	Red	100.00	175.00	525.00	1325.00
☐1875	Allison-Wyman	Red	100.00	175.00	525.00	1680.00
☐1878	Allison-Gilfillan	Red	100.00	175.00	450.00	1680.00
☐1880	Scofield-Gilfillan	Brown	435.00	725.00	3525.00	RARE
☐1880	Bruce-Gilfillan	Brown	120.00	200.00	875.00	2750.00
☐1880	Bruce-Wyman	Brown	95.00	125.00	450.00	2450.00
☐1880	Bruce-Wyman	Red	90.00	150.00	500.00	2250.00
☐1880	Rosecrans-Jordan	Red	85.00	130.00	470.00	1680.00
☐1880	Rosecrans-Hyatt	Red	450.00	750.00	3500.00	RARE
☐1880	Rosecrans-Huston	Red	135.00	225.00	700.00	2250.00
☐1880	Rosecrans-Huston	Brown	135.00	225.00	700.00	2415.00
☐1880	Rosecrans-Nebeker	Brown	135.00	225.00	750.00	2000.00
☐1880	Rosecrans-Nebeker	Red	80.00	130.00	320.00	1680.00
☐1880	Tillman-Morgan	Red	80.00	130.00	285.00	1680.00
☐1880	Bruce-Roberts	Red	80.00	130.00	250.00	1680.00
☐1880	Lyons-Roberts	Red	63.00	105.00	940.00	2350.00
☐1907	Vernon-Treat	Red	48.00	80.00	300.00	1375.00
☐1907	Vernon-McClung	Red	48.00	80.00	315.00	1275.00
☐1907	Napier-McClung	Red	36.00	60.00	250.00	970.00
☐1907	Napier-Thompson	Red	80.00	130.00	425.00	1200.00
☐1907	Parker-Burke	Red	45.00	75.00	300.00	1070.00
☐1907	Teehee-Burke	Red	45.00	75.00	300.00	1070.00
☐1907	Elliott-Burke	Red	45.00	75.00	250.00	945.00

SERIES	SIGNATURES	SEAL	A.B.P.	GOOD	V. FINE	UNC.
☐1907	Elliott-White	Red	45.00	75.00	315.00	775.00
☐1907	Speelman-White	Red	48.00	80.00	225.00	625.00
☐1907	Woods-White	Red	45.00	75.00	325.00	750.00

FIVE DOLLAR NOTES (1928) UNITED STATES NOTES (ALSO KNOWN AS LEGAL TENDER NOTES)

(Small Size)

Face Design: Portrait of President Lincoln center. Red seal to left, red serial numbers.

Back Design: Lincoln Memorial in Washington, D.C.

SERIES	SIGNATURES	SEAL	A.B.P	GOOD	V. FINE	UNC.	★UNC.
☐1928	Woods-Mellon	Red	9.00	15.00	20.00	165.00	2550.00
☐1928A	Woods-Mills	Red	9.00	15.00	26.00	200.00	RARE
☐1928B	Julian-Morgenthau	Red	9.00	15.00	22.00	100.00	1650.00
☐1928C	Julian-Morgenthau	Red	9.00	15.00	22.00	100.00	870.00
☐1928D	Julian-Vinson	Red	9.00	15.00	40.00	550.00	3500.00
☐1928E	Julian-Snyder	Red	9.00	15.00	22.00	100.00	1175.00
☐1928F	Clark-Snyder	Red	9.00	15.00	22.00	125.00	875.00

FIVE DOLLAR NOTES (1953–1963)
UNITED STATES NOTES
(Small Size)

Face Design: Similar to previous note. Portrait of President Lincoln center. Red seal is moved to the right, red numbers.
Back Design: Similar to 1928 note.

SERIES	SIGNATURES	SEAL	A.B.P.	GOOD	V. FINE	UNC.	★UNC.
☐1953	Priest-Humphrey	Red	6.00	10.00	15.00	85.00	350.00
☐1953A	Priest-Anderson	Red	6.00	10.00	16.00	75.00	260.00
☐1953B	Smith-Dillon	Red	6.00	10.00	15.00	55.00	250.00
☐1953C	Granahan-Dillon	Red	7.20	12.00	18.00	80.00	450.00

FIVE DOLLAR NOTES (1953–1963)
UNITED STATES NOTES
(ALSO KNOWN AS LEGAL TENDER NOTES)
(Small Size)

Back Design: The following notes have IN GOD WE TRUST on the back.
Face Design: Similar to 1953–1963 note.

SERIES	SIGNATURES	SEAL	A.B.P.	GOOD	V. FINE	UNC.	★UNC.
☐1963	Granahan-Dillon	Red	7.20	12.00	20.00	50.00	150.00

Production of $5 United States Notes ended in 1967.

FIVE DOLLAR NOTES (1863–1875)
NATIONAL BANK NOTES
FIRST CHARTER PERIOD (Large Size)

Face Design: The Columbus Note. The face shows Columbus in sight of land and Columbus with an Indian princess.

Back Design: Christopher Columbus landing at San Salvador, 1492. Also the State Seal left, and American eagle right.

SERIES	SIGNATURES	SEAL	A.B.P.	GOOD	V. FINE	UNC.
☐Original	Chittenden-Spinner	Red	360.00	625.00	1650.00	RARE
☐Original	Colby-Spinner	Red	360.00	625.00	1650.00	RARE
☐Original	Jeffries-Spinner	Red	720.00	1200.00	4000.00	RARE
☐Original	Allison-Spinner	Red	360.00	625.00	1850.00	RARE
☐1875	Allison-New	Red	360.00	625.00	1850.00	RARE
☐1875	Allison-Wyman	Red	360.00	625.00	1850.00	RARE
☐1875	Allison-Gilfillan	Red	360.00	625.00	1850.00	RARE
☐1875	Scofield-Gilfillan	Red	360.00	625.00	1850.00	RARE
☐1875	Bruce-Gilfillan	Red	360.00	625.00	1850.00	RARE
☐1875	Bruce-Wyman	Red	360.00	625.00	1850.00	RARE
☐1875	Bruce-Jordan	Red	—	EXTREMELY RARE		
☐1875	Rosecrans-Huston	Red	360.00	625.00	1650.00	RARE
☐1875	Rosecrans-Jordan	Red	360.00	625.00	1650.00	RARE

FIVE DOLLAR NOTES (1882) NATIONAL BANK NOTES
SECOND CHARTER PERIOD (Large Size)

First Issue (Brown seal and brown backs.)
Face Design: Portrait of President Garfield left. Name of bank
and city center, brown seal to right. Brown charter number.

Back Design: Brown border design similar to previous note.
Center oval now has the bank's charter number in green.
The top signatures are those of the Treasury officials.
Bottom signatures, usually handwritten or probably rubber-
stamped, are bank officials.

SERIES	SIGNATURES	SEAL	A.B.P.	GOOD	V. FINE	UNC.
☐1882	Bruce-Gilfillan	Brown	185.00	325.00	850.00	3450.00
☐1882	Bruce-Wyman	Brown	185.00	325.00	850.00	3450.00
☐1882	Bruce-Jordan	Brown	185.00	325.00	850.00	3450.00
☐1882	Rosecrans-Jordan	Brown	185.00	325.00	850.00	3450.00
☐1882	Rosecrans-Hyatt	Brown	185.00	325.00	850.00	3450.00
☐1882	Rosecrans-Huston	Brown	185.00	325.00	850.00	3450.00
☐1882	Rosecrans-Nebeker	Brown	185.00	325.00	825.00	3450.00
☐1882	Rosecrans-Morgan	Brown	185.00	325.00	900.00	3500.00
☐1882	Tillman-Morgan	Brown	185.00	325.00	850.00	3450.00
☐1882	Tillman-Roberts	Brown	185.00	325.00	850.00	3450.00
☐1882	Bruce-Roberts	Brown	185.00	325.00	850.00	3450.00
☐1882	Lyons-Roberts	Brown	185.00	325.00	850.00	3450.00
☐1882	Lyons-Treat		(Unknown in any collection)			
☐1882	Vernon-Treat	Brown	185.00	325.00	825.00	3500.00

FIVE DOLLAR NOTES (1882) NATIONAL BANK NOTES
SECOND CHARTER PERIOD, Second Issue (Large Size)

Face Design: Similar to preceding portrait of President Garfield.

Back Design: Back is now green with date "1882–1908" in center.

SERIES	SIGNATURES	SEAL	A.B.P.	GOOD	V. FINE	UNC.
☐1882	Rosecrans-Huston	Blue	150.00	260.00	1275.00	2650.00
☐1882	Rosecrans-Nebeker	Blue	150.00	260.00	1275.00	2650.00
☐1882	Rosecrans-Morgan	Blue	150.00	260.00	1275.00	2650.00
☐1882	Tillman-Morgan	Blue	150.00	260.00	1275.00	2650.00
☐1882	Tillman-Roberts	Blue	150.00	260.00	1275.00	2650.00
☐1882	Bruce-Roberts	Blue	150.00	260.00	1275.00	2650.00
☐1882	Lyons-Roberts	Blue	150.00	260.00	1275.00	2650.00
☐1882	Vernon-Treat	Blue	150.00	260.00	1275.00	2650.00
☐1882	Vernon-McClung	Blue				RARE
☐1882	Napier-McClung	Blue	180.00	315.00	1450.00	3600.00

FIVE DOLLAR NOTES (1882) NATIONAL BANK NOTES
SECOND CHARTER PERIOD, Third Issue (Large Size)

Face Design: Same as 1882 note. Blue seal.

Back Design: Similar to 1882 Second Issue note. FIVE DOLLARS replaces "1882–1908."

SERIES	SIGNATURES	SEAL	A.B.P.	GOOD	V. FINE	UNC.
☐1882	Tillman-Morgan	Blue	180.00	300.00	900.00	3650.00
☐1882	Tillman-Roberts	Blue	240.00	400.00	1000.00	3650.00
☐1882	Bruce-Roberts	Blue	180.00	300.00	900.00	3650.00
☐1882	Lyons-Roberts	Blue	180.00	300.00	900.00	4000.00
☐1882	Vernon-Treat	Blue	180.00	300.00	900.00	3650.00
☐1882	Napier-McClung	Blue	180.00	300.00	900.00	3650.00
☐1882	Teehee-Burke	Blue	—	EXTREMELY RARE		

FIVE DOLLAR NOTES (1902) NATIONAL BANK NOTES
THIRD CHARTER PERIOD (Large Size)

First Issue (Red seal and charter numbers.)
Face Design: Portrait of President Harrison left, name of
bank and city center, Treasury Seal to right, red seal and
charter number.

Back Design: Landing of Pilgrims.

SERIES	SIGNATURES	SEAL	A.B.P.	GOOD	V. FINE	UNC.
☐1902	Lyons-Roberts	Red	182.00	300.00	850.00	RARE
☐1902	Lyons-Treat	Red	182.00	300.00	850.00	RARE
☐1902	Vernon-Treat	Red	182.00	300.00	850.00	RARE

FIVE DOLLAR NOTES (1902) NATIONAL BANK NOTES
THIRD CHARTER PERIOD (Large Size)
SECOND ISSUE

SERIES	SIGNATURES	SEAL	A.B.P.	GOOD	V. FINE	UNC.
☐1902	Lyons-Roberts	Blue	84.00	140.00	525.00	1375.00
☐1902	Lyons-Treat	Blue	84.00	140.00	525.00	1375.00
☐1902	Vernon-Treat	Blue	84.00	140.00	525.00	1375.00
☐1902	Vernon-McClung	Blue	84.00	140.00	525.00	1375.00
☐1902	Napier-McClung	Blue	84.00	140.00	525.00	1375.00
☐1902	Napier-Thompson	Blue	120.00	200.00	525.00	1375.00
☐1902	Napier-Burke	Blue	84.00	140.00	525.00	1375.00
☐1902	Parker-Burke	Blue	84.00	140.00	525.00	1375.00
☐1902	Teehee-Burke	Blue	84.00	140.00	525.00	1375.00

FIVE DOLLAR NOTES (1902) NATIONAL BANK NOTES
THIRD CHARTER PERIOD (Large Size)
Third Issue (Blue seal and numbers.)
The following notes do not have date of "1902–1908" on
the back.

SERIES	SIGNATURES	SEAL	A.B.P.	GOOD	V. FINE	UNC.
☐1902	Lyons-Roberts	Blue	90.00	150.00	325.00	1075.00
☐1902	Lyons-Treat	Blue	90.00	150.00	325.00	1075.00
☐1902	Vernon-Treat	Blue	90.00	150.00	325.00	1075.00
☐1902	Vernon-McClung	Blue	90.00	150.00	325.00	1075.00
☐1902	Napier-McClung	Blue	90.00	150.00	325.00	1075.00
☐1902	Napier-Thompson	Blue	90.00	150.00	325.00	1075.00
☐1902	Napier-Burke	Blue	90.00	150.00	325.00	1075.00
☐1902	Parker-Burke	Blue	90.00	150.00	325.00	1075.00
☐1902	Teehee-Burke	Blue	90.00	150.00	325.00	1075.00
☐1902	Elliott-Burke	Blue	90.00	150.00	325.00	1075.00
☐1902	Elliott-White	Blue	90.00	150.00	325.00	1075.00
☐1902	Speelman-White	Blue	90.00	150.00	325.00	1075.00
☐1902	Woods-White	Blue	90.00	150.00	325.00	1075.00
☐1902	Woods-Tate	Blue	90.00	150.00	325.00	1075.00
☐1902	Jones-Woods	Blue	105.00	175.00	550.00	1375.00

FIVE DOLLAR NOTES (1929) NATIONAL BANK NOTES
(Small Size)

TYPE I

TYPE II

Face Design: Portrait of President Lincoln in center, name of
bank to left, brown seal to the right. Type I—charter number
in black. Type II—similar; charter number added in brown.

Back Design: Lincoln Memorial.

SERIES	SIGNATURES	SEAL	A.B.P.	GOOD	V. FINE	UNC.
☐1929	Type I Jones-Woods	Brown	50.00	50.00	150.00	475.00
☐1929	Type II Jones-Woods	Brown	45.00	75.00	175.00	445.00

FIVE DOLLAR NOTES (1870)
NATIONAL GOLD BANK NOTES

(Large Size)

Face Design: Vignettes of Columbus sighting land. Presentation of an Indian princess. Red seal. Signatures, Allison-Spinner.

Back Design: California State Seal left, gold coins center, American eagle right.

DATE	BANK	CITY	A.B.P.	GOOD	V. GOOD
☐1870 First National Gold Bank		San Francisco	1500.00	2500.00	3700.00
☐1872 National Gold Bank and Trust Co.					
		San Francisco	1500.00	2500.00	3700.00
☐1872 National Gold Bank of D.O. Mills and Co.					
		Sacramento	1500.00	2500.00	3700.00
☐1873 First National Gold Bank		Santa Barbara	1500.00	2500.00	3700.00
☐1873 First National Gold Bank		Stockton	1590.00	2650.00	4300.00
☐1874 Farmers National Gold Bank		San Jose	1590.00	2650.00	4300.00

FIVE DOLLAR NOTES (1886–1891)
SILVER CERTIFICATES

(Large Size)

Face Design: Portrait of President Grant.

Back Design: Five silver dollars.

SERIES	SIGNATURES	SEAL	A.B.P.	GOOD	V. FINE	UNC.
☐1886	Rosecrans-Jordan	Red	175.00	285.00	2700.00	RARE
☐1886	Rosecrans-Hyatt	Sm. Red	175.00	285.00	2700.00	RARE
☐1886	Rosecrans-Hyatt	Lg. Red	175.00	285.00	2700.00	RARE
☐1886	Rosecrans-Huston	Lg. Red	175.00	285.00	2700.00	RARE
☐1886	Rosecrans-Huston	Brown	175.00	285.00	2700.00	RARE
☐1886	Rosecrans-Nebeker	Brown	175.00	285.00	2700.00	RARE
☐1886	Rosecrans-Nebeker	Sm. Red	180.00	300.00	2950.00	RARE

FIVE DOLLAR NOTES (1891) SILVER CERTIFICATES
(Large Size)

Face Design: Similar to previous note.

Back Design: Revised.

SERIES	SIGNATURES	SEAL	A.B.P.	GOOD	V. FINE	UNC.
☐1891	Rosecrans-Nebeker	Red	120.00	200.00	1350.00	4000.00
☐1891	Tillman-Morgan	Red	105.00	175.00	1175.00	3500.00

FIVE DOLLAR NOTES (1896) SILVER CERTIFICATES
(Large Size)

Face Design: Portraits of General Grant and General Sheridan.

Back Design: Five females representing Electricity as the dominant force in the world.

This was the last note of the popular Education Series.

SERIES	SIGNATURES	SEAL	A.B.P.	GOOD	V. FINE	UNC.
☐1896	Tillman-Morgan	Red	250.00	450.00	2650.00	RARE
☐1896	Bruce-Roberts	Red	250.00	450.00	2650.00	RARE
☐1896	Lyons-Roberts	Red	250.00	450.00	2650.00	RARE

FIVE DOLLAR NOTES (1899) SILVER CERTIFICATES
(Large Size)

Face Design: Portrait of Indian chief.

Back Design: Green "V" and "5."

SERIES	SIGNATURES	SEAL	A.B.P.	GOOD	V. FINE	UNC.
☐1899	Lyons-Roberts	Blue	165.00	275.00	950.00	3600.00
☐1899	Lyons-Treat	Blue	165.00	275.00	950.00	3600.00
☐1899	Vernon-Treat	Blue	165.00	275.00	950.00	3600.00
☐1899	Vernon-McClung	Blue	165.00	275.00	950.00	3600.00
☐1899	Napier-McClung	Blue	165.00	275.00	950.00	3600.00
☐1899	Napier-Thompson	Blue	165.00	275.00	1150.00	4000.00
☐1899	Parker-Burke	Blue	165.00	275.00	950.00	3600.00
☐1899	Teehee-Burke	Blue	165.00	275.00	950.00	3600.00
☐1899	Elliott-Burke	Blue	165.00	275.00	950.00	3600.00
☐1899	Elliott-White	Blue	165.00	275.00	950.00	3600.00
☐1899	Speelman-White	Blue	165.00	275.00	950.00	3600.00

FIVE DOLLAR NOTES (1923) SILVER CERTIFICATES
(Large Size)

Face Design: Portrait of President Lincoln In oval, nick-name "Porthole Note," blue seal left, blue "5" right.

Back Design: Obverse of Great Seal of the United States.

SERIES	SIGNATURES	SEAL	A.B.P.	GOOD	V. FINE	UNC.
☐1923	Speelman-White	Blue	240.00	400.00	950.00	3000.00

FIVE DOLLAR NOTES (1934) SILVER CERTIFICATES
(Small Size)

First Issue (Small size of $5 Silver Certificates 1934.)
Face Design: Portrait of President Lincoln, blue "5" to left,
blue seal to right.

Back Design: All Small Size $5 Notes have the same back
design.

SERIES	SIGNATURES	SEAL	A.B.P.	GOOD	V. FINE	UNC.	★UNC.
☐1934	Julian-Morgenthau	Blue	5.40	9.00	15.00	65.00	650.00
☐1934A	Julian-Morgenthau	Blue	6.00	8.00	15.00	52.00	525.00
☐1934A	Julian-Morgenthau	Yellow	21.00	35.00	75.00	350.00	900.00

This note, with yellow Treasury Seal, was a Special Issue
during World War II for military use in combat areas of North
Africa and Europe.

SERIES	SIGNATURES	SEAL	A.B.P.	GOOD	V. FINE	UNC.	★UNC.
☐1934B	Julian-Vinson	Blue	6.00	10.00	25.00	175.00	650.00
☐1934C	Julian-Synder	Blue	6.00	10.00	18.00	50.00	325.00
☐1934D	Clark-Snyder	Blue	6.00	10.00	18.00	50.00	350.00

FIVE DOLLAR NOTES (1953) SILVER CERTIFICATES
(Small Size)

Face Design: The following notes are similar to the previous note. The face design has been revised. Gray "5" replaces blue "5" to left of Lincoln. Blue seal is slightly smaller.

Back Design: Same as previous note.

SERIES	SIGNATURES	SEAL	A.B.P.	GOOD	V. FINE	UNC.	★UNC.
☐1953	Priest-Humphrey	Blue	7.20	12.00	20.00	65.00	85.00
☐1953A	Priest-Anderson	Blue	6.00	10.00	15.00	35.00	65.00
☐1953B	Smith-Dillon	Blue	6.00	10.00	15.00	40.00	RARE

Production of $5 Silver Certificates ended in 1962.

FIVE DOLLAR NOTES (1890) TREASURY OR COIN NOTES
(Large Size)

Face Design: Portrait of General George Henry Thomas (1816–70), the "Rock of Chickamauga."

Back Design:

SERIES	SIGNATURES	SEAL	A.B.P.	GOOD	V. FINE	UNC.
☐1890	Rosecrans-Huston	Brown	150.00	250.00	1600.00	RARE
☐1890	Rosecrans-Nebeker	Brown	150.00	250.00	1850.00	RARE
☐1890	Rosecrans-Nebeker	Red	150.00	250.00	1650.00	RARE

Back Design: Second Issue

SERIES	SIGNATURES	SEAL	A.B.P.	GOOD	V.FINE	UNC.
☐1891	Rosecrans-Nebeker	Red	120.00	200.00	650.00	3050.00
☐1891	Tillman-Morgan	Red	120.00	200.00	650.00	3050.00
☐1891	Bruce-Roberts	Red	120.00	200.00	650.00	3050.00
☐1891	Lyons-Roberts	Red	120.00	200.00	650.00	3050.00

FIVE DOLLAR NOTES (1914)
FEDERAL RESERVE NOTES

(Large Size)

Face Design: Portrait of President Lincoln center, Federal Reserve Seal left, Treasury Seal right.

Back Design: Scene of Columbus in sight of land left, landing of Pilgrims right.

SERIES OF 1914, RED TREASURY SEAL AND RED NUMBERS

SERIES BANK	SIGNATURES	SEAL	A.B.P.	GOOD	V. FINE	UNC.
☐1914 Boston	Burke-McAdoo	Red	105.00	175.00	735.00	2650.00
☐1914 New York	Burke-McAdoo	Red	105.00	175.00	675.00	2650.00
☐1914 Philadelphia	Burke-McAdoo	Red	105.00	175.00	675.00	2650.00
☐1914 Cleveland	Burke-McAdoo	Red	105.00	175.00	675.00	2340.00
☐1914 Richmond	Burke-McAdoo	Red	105.00	175.00	675.00	2800.00
☐1914 Atlanta	Burke-McAdoo	Red	105.00	175.00	675.00	2500.00
☐1914 Chicago	Burke-McAdoo	Red	105.00	175.00	780.00	2750.00
☐1914 St. Louis	Burke-McAdoo	Red	105.00	175.00	675.00	2500.00
☐1914 Minneapolis	Burke-McAdoo	Red	105.00	175.00	680.00	2800.00
☐1914 Kansas City	Burke-McAdoo	Red	105.00	175.00	675.00	2550.00
☐1914 Dallas	Burke-McAdoo	Red	105.00	175.00	700.00	2650.00
☐1914 San Francisco	Burke-McAdoo	Red	105.00	175.00	700.00	2700.00

FIVE DOLLAR NOTES (1914)
FEDERAL RESERVE NOTES

SERIES OF 1914, BLUE TREASURY SEAL AND BLUE NUMBERS

SERIES BANK	SIGNATURES	SEAL	A.B.P.	GOOD	V. FINE	UNC.
☐1914 Boston	Burke-McAdoo	Blue	42.00	70.00	175.00	600.00
☐1914 Boston	Burke-Glass	Blue	42.00	70.00	150.00	475.00
☐1914 Boston	Burke-Huston	Blue	42.00	70.00	175.00	600.00
☐1914 Boston	White-Mellon	Blue	42.00	70.00	175.00	600.00
☐1914 New York	Burke-McAdoo	Blue	42.00	70.00	175.00	600.00
☐1914 New York	Burke-Glass	Blue	42.00	70.00	135.00	600.00
☐1914 New York	Burke-Huston	Blue	42.00	70.00	150.00	490.00
☐1914 New York	White-Mellon	Blue	42.00	70.00	125.00	490.00
☐1914 Philadelphia	Burke-McAdoo	Blue	42.00	70.00	175.00	676.00
☐1914 Philadelphia	Burke-Glass	Blue	42.00	70.00	175.00	675.00
☐1914 Philadelphia	Burke-Huston	Blue	42.00	70.00	150.00	490.00

SERIES BANK	SIGNATURES	SEAL	A.B.P.	GOOD	V. FINE	UNC.
☐1914 Philadelphia	White-Mellon	Blue	24.00	40.00	155.00	470.00
☐1914 Cleveland	Burke-McAdoo	Blue	24.00	40.00	155.00	470.00
☐1914 Cleveland	Burke-Glass	Blue	24.00	40.00	210.00	550.00
☐1914 Cleveland	Burke-Huston	Blue	24.00	40.00	130.00	350.00
☐1914 Cleveland	White-Mellon	Blue	24.00	40.00	140.00	400.00
☐1914 Richmond	Burke-McAdoo	Blue	24.00	40.00	140.00	400.00
☐1914 Richmond	Burke-Glass	Blue	24.00	40.00	200.00	545.00
☐1914 Richmond	Burke-Huston	Blue	24.00	40.00	135.00	475.00
☐1914 Richmond	White-Mellon	Blue	24.00	40.00	145.00	470.00
☐1914 Atlanta	Burke-McAdoo	Blue	24.00	40.00	200.00	525.00
☐1914 Atlanta	Burke-Glass	Blue	24.00	40.00	360.00	825.00
☐1914 Atlanta	Burke-Huston	Blue	24.00	40.00	150.00	375.00
☐1914 Atlanta	White-Mellon	Blue	24.00	40.00	150.00	390.00
☐1914 Chicago	Burke-McAdoo	Blue	24.00	40.00	210.00	550.00
☐1914 Chicago	Burke-Glass	Blue	24.00	40.00	150.00	450.00
☐1914 Chicago	Burke-Huston	Blue	24.00	40.00	150.00	450.00
☐1914 Chicago	White-Mellon	Blue	24.00	40.00	150.00	400.00
☐1914 St. Louis	Burke-McAdoo	Blue	24.00	40.00	140.00	400.00
☐1914 St. Louis	Burke-Glass	Blue	24.00	40.00	140.00	405.00
☐1914 St. Louis	Burke-Huston	Blue	24.00	40.00	155.00	380.00
☐1914 St. Louis	White-Mellon	Blue	24.00	40.00	135.00	380.00
☐1914 Minneapolis	Burke-McAdoo	Blue	24.00	40.00	155.00	450.00
☐1914 Minneapolis	Burke-Glass	Blue	24.00	40.00	200.00	475.00
☐1914 Minneapolis	Burke-Huston	Blue	24.00	40.00	175.00	470.00
☐1914 Minneapolis	White-Mellon	Blue	24.00	40.00	155.00	445.00
☐1914 Kansas City	Burke-McAdoo	Blue	24.00	40.00	150.00	445.00
☐1914 Kansas City	Burke-Glass	Blue	24.00	40.00	165.00	475.00
☐1914 Kansas City	Burke-Huston	Blue	24.00	40.00	135.00	480.00
☐1914 Kansas City	White-Mellon	Blue	24.00	40.00	210.00	380.00
☐1914 Dallas	Burke-McAdoo	Blue	24.00	40.00	210.00	400.00
☐1914 Dallas	Burke-Glass	Blue	24.00	40.00	210.00	465.00
☐1914 Dallas	Burke-Huston	Blue	24.00	40.00	210.00	455.00
☐1914 Dallas	White-Mellon	Blue	24.00	40.00	160.00	390.00
☐1914 San Francisco	Burke-McAdoo	Blue	24.00	40.00	225.00	550.00
☐1914 San Francisco	Burke-Glass	Blue	24.00	40.00	250.00	625.00
☐1914 San Francisco	Burke-Huston	Blue	24.00	40.00	205.00	550.00
☐1914 San Francisco	White-Mellon	Blue	24.00	40.00	160.00	390.00

FIVE DOLLAR NOTES (1928)
FEDERAL RESERVE NOTES

(Small Size)

Face Design: Portrait of President Lincoln center, black Federal Reserve Seal with numeral for district in center. City of issuing bank in seal circle. Green Treasury Seal to right.
Back Design: Similar to 1935 note. Lincoln Memorial in Washington, D.C.

SERIES OF 1928,
SIGNATURES OF TATE AND MELLON, GREEN SEAL

BANK	A.B.P.	GOOD	V.FINE	UNC.	★UNC.	BANK	A.B.P.	GOOD	V.FINE	UNC.	★UNC.
☐ Boston	8.00	14.00	50.00	400.00	1600.00	☐ Chicago	8.40	14.00	40.00	240.00	1500.00
☐ New York	8.00	14.00	38.00	325.00	875.00	☐ St. Louis	8.40	14.00	40.00	240.00	1600.00
☐ Philadelphia	8.00	14.00	38.00	325.00	875.00	☐ Minneapolis	48.00	80.00	125.00	1000.00	3000.00
☐ Cleveland	8.00	14.00	38.00	325.00	1000.00	☐ Kansas City	8.40	14.00	40.00	250.00	1350.00
☐ Richmond	8.00	14.00	38.00	325.00	1275.00	☐ Dallas	8.40	14.00	40.00	360.00	1350.00
☐ Atlanta	8.00	14.00	38.00	325.00	1525.00	☐ San Francisco	8.40	14.00	40.00	500.00	1650.00

SERIES OF 1928A,
SIGNATURES OF WOODS-MELLON, GREEN SEAL

BANK	A.B.P.	GOOD	V.FINE	UNC.	★UNC.	BANK	A.B.P.	GOOD	V.FINE	UNC.	★UNC.
☐ Boston	8.00	15.00	38.00	285.00	1550.00	☐ Chicago	9.00	15.00	38.00	215.00	1250.00
☐ New York	8.00	15.00	38.00	160.00	1050.00	☐ St. Louis	9.00	15.00	38.00	200.00	2700.00
☐ Philadelphia	8.00	15.00	38.00	200.00	1050.00	☐ Minneapolis	9.00	15.00	135.00	1265.00	RARE
☐ Cleveland	8.00	15.00	38.00	200.00	1200.00	☐ Kansas City	9.00	15.00	38.00	350.00	RARE
☐ Richmond	8.00	15.00	38.00	200.00	1200.00	☐ Dallas	21.00	35.00	60.00	425.00	2100.00
☐ Atlanta	8.00	15.00	38.00	385.00	2550.00	☐ San Francisco	9.00	15.00	38.00	350.00	1650.00

SERIES OF 1928B,
SIGNATURES OF WOODS-MELLON, GREEN SEAL

The black Federal Reserve Seal now has a letter for district in place of the numeral.

BANK	A.B.P.	GOOD	V.FINE	UNC.	★UNC.	BANK	A.B.P.	GOOD	V.FINE	UNC.	★UNC.
☐ Boston	7.80	13.00	24.00	135.00	900.00	☐ Chicago	9.00	15.00	24.00	150.00	1000.00
☐ New York	7.80	13.00	24.00	135.00	900.00	☐ St. Louis	9.00	15.00	24.00	150.00	1000.00
☐ Philadelphia	7.80	13.00	24.00	135.00	900.00	☐ Minneapolis	9.00	15.00	24.00	225.00	1300.00
☐ Cleveland	7.80	13.00	24.00	135.00	900.00	☐ Kansas City	9.00	15.00	24.00	150.00	1300.00
☐ Richmond	7.80	13.00	24.00	135.00	900.00	☐ Dallas	9.00	15.00	24.00	175.00	1300.00
☐ Atlanta	7.80	13.00	24.00	135.00	900.00	☐ San Francisco	9.00	15.00	24.00	150.00	1300.00

SERIES OF 1928C,
SIGNATURES OF WOODS-WOODIN, GREEN SEAL

BANK	A.B.P.	GOOD	V.FINE	UNC.	★UNC.
☐ Atlanta	66.00	110.00	600.00	3500.00	RARE

SERIES OF 1928D,
SIGNATURES OF WOODS-MILLS, GREEN SEAL

BANK	A.B.P.	GOOD	V.FINE	UNC.	★UNC.
☐ Atlanta	255.00	425.00	1600.00	RARE	RARE

FIVE DOLLAR NOTES (1934)
FEDERAL RESERVE NOTES
SERIES OF 1934,
JULIAN-MORGENTHAU, GREEN SEAL

"Redeemable in Gold" was removed from obligation over Federal Reserve Seal. Also, the green Treasury Seal on this note is known in a light and dark color. The light seal is worth about 10–20 percent more in most cases.

BANK	A.B.P.	V.FINE	UNC.	★UNC.	BANK	A.B.P.	V.FINE	UNC.	★UNC.
☐ Boston	9.00	15.75	75.00	300.00	☐ St. Louis	10.80	18.00	50.00	250.00
☐ New York	9.00	15.75	60.00	300.00	☐ Minneapolis	13.20	22.00	65.00	250.00
☐ Philadelphia	9.00	15.75	65.00	300.00	☐ Kansas City	10.80	18.00	50.00	250.00
☐ Cleveland	9.00	15.75	60.00	300.00	☐ Dallas	10.80	18.00	85.00	250.00
☐ Richmond	9.00	15.75	80.00	300.00	☐ San Francisco	10.80	18.00	50.00	250.00
☐ Atlanta	9.00	15.75	65.00	300.00	☐ San Francisco*	76.50	130.00	800.00	7000.00
☐ Chicago	9.00	15.75	50.00	300.00					

*This note has brown Treasury Seal and is surprinted HAWAII. For use in Pacific area of operations during World War II.

(Small Size)

Note—1934A (Julian-Morgenthau) Is surprinted HAWAII. It was used in the Pacific area during World War II.

SERIES OF 1934A, JULIAN-MORGENTHAU, GREEN SEAL

BANK	A.B.P.	V.FINE	UNC.	★UNC.	BANK	A.B.P.	V.FINE	UNC.	★UNC.
☐ Boston	9.60	16.00	60.00	370.00	☐ Atlanta	16.20	27.00	80.00	790.00
☐ New York	9.60	16.00	60.00	370.00	☐ Chicago	9.90	16.50	75.00	445.00
☐ Philadelphia	9.60	16.00	60.00	370.00	☐ St. Louis	9.90	16.50	75.00	445.00
☐ Cleveland	9.60	16.00	60.00	550.00	☐ San Francisco	9.90	16.50	75.00	445.00
☐ Richmond	9.60	16.00	60.00	445.00	☐ Hawaii*	50.40	84.00	750.00	RARE

*This note has brown Treasury Seal and is surprinted HAWAII. For use in Pacific area of operations during World War II.
(Small Size)

SERIES OF 1934B, SIGNATURES OF JULIAN-VINSON, GREEN SEAL

BANK	A.B.P.	V.FINE	UNC.	★UNC.	BANK	A.B.P.	V.FINE	UNC.	★UNC.
☐ Boston	12.00	20.00	65.00	625.00	☐ Chicago	16.80	28.00	68.00	650.00
☐ New York	12.00	20.00	65.00	625.00	☐ St. Louis	16.80	28.00	68.00	650.00
☐ Philadelphia	12.00	20.00	65.00	625.00	☐ Minneapolis	16.80	28.00	68.00	650.00
☐ Cleveland	12.00	20.00	65.00	625.00	☐ Kansas City	780.00	1300.00	2600.00	RARE
☐ Richmond	12.00	20.00	65.00	625.00	☐ Dallas			NOT ISSUED	
☐ Atlanta	12.00	20.00	65.00	625.00	☐ San Francisco	16.20	27.00	63.00	575.00

SERIES OF 1934C, SIGNATURES OF JULIAN-SNYDER, GREEN SEAL

BANK	A.B.P.	V.FINE	UNC.	★UNC.	BANK	A.B.P.	V.FINE	UNC.	★UNC.
☐ Boston	10.80	18.00	85.00	890.00	☐ Chicago	10.80	18.00	85.00	750.00
☐ New York	10.80	18.00	85.00	735.00	☐ St. Louis	10.80	18.00	85.00	750.00
☐ Philadelphia	10.80	18.00	85.00	785.00	☐ Minneapolis	10.80	18.00	85.00	1300.00
☐ Cleveland	10.80	18.00	85.00	630.00	☐ Kansas City	10.80	18.00	85.00	850.00
☐ Richmond	10.80	18.00	85.00	735.00	☐ Dallas	19.80	33.00	130.00	1700.00
☐ Atlanta	10.80	18.00	85.00	850.00	☐ San Francisco	10.80	18.00	85.00	850.00

SERIES OF 1934D,
SIGNATURES OF CLARK-SNYDER, GREEN SEAL

BANK	A.B.P.	V.FINE	UNC.	★UNC.	BANK	A.B.P.	V.FINE	UNC.	★UNC.
☐ Boston	10.05	16.75	80.00	785.00	☐ Chicago	7.50	12.50	65.00	680.00
☐ New York	10.05	16.75	70.00	630.00	☐ St. Louis	7.50	12.50	75.00	875.00
☐ Philadelphia	10.05	16.75	75.00	825.00	☐ Minneapolis	7.50	12.50	350.00	1300.00
☐ Cleveland	10.05	16.75	75.00	890.00	☐ Kansas City	12.60	21.00	80.00	900.00
☐ Richmond	10.05	16.75	120.00	825.00	☐ Dallas	12.60	21.00	180.00	900.00
☐ Atlanta	180.00	300.00	800.00	3200.00	☐ San Francisco	12.60	21.00	80.00	875.00

FIVE DOLLAR NOTES (1950)
FEDERAL RESERVE NOTES
BLACK FEDERAL RESERVE SEAL AND
GREEN TREASURY SEALS ARE NOW SMALLER
(Small Size)
SERIES OF 1950, SIGNATURES OF CLARK-SNYDER, GREEN SEAL

BANK	A.B.P.	V.FINE	UNC.	★UNC.	BANK	A.B.P.	V.FINE	UNC.	★UNC.
☐ Boston	10.05	16.75	50.00	525.00	☐ Chicago	9.45	15.75	36.00	550.00
☐ New York	10.05	16.75	36.00	400.00	☐ St. Louis	9.45	15.75	55.00	550.00
☐ Philadelphia	10.05	16.75	36.00	475.00	☐ Minneapolis	9.45	15.75	80.00	825.00
☐ Cleveland	10.05	16.75	35.00	475.00	☐ Kansas City	9.45	15.75	80.00	500.00
☐ Richmond	10.05	16.75	50.00	560.00	☐ Dallas	9.45	15.75	75.00	675.00
☐ Atlanta	10.05	16.75	50.00	560.00	☐ San Francisco	9.45	15.75	55.00	675.00

SERIES OF 1950A, SIGNATURES OF PRIEST-HUMPHREY,
GREEN SEAL

BANK	A.B.P.	V.FINE	UNC.	★UNC.	BANK	A.B.P.	V.FINE	UNC.	★UNC.
☐ Boston	9.90	16.50	28.00	80.00	☐ Chicago	9.45	15.75	32.00	120.00
☐ New York	9.90	16.50	28.00	80.00	☐ St. Louis	9.45	15.75	32.00	175.00
☐ Philadelphia	9.90	16.50	28.00	80.00	☐ Minneapolis	9.45	15.75	32.00	210.00
☐ Cleveland	9.90	16.50	28.00	80.00	☐ Kansas City	9.45	15.75	32.00	125.00
☐ Richmond	9.90	16.50	28.00	85.00	☐ Dallas	9.45	15.75	32.00	175.00
☐ Atlanta	9.90	16.50	28.00	85.00	☐ San Francisco	9.45	15.75	32.00	125.00

SERIES OF 1950B, SIGNATURES OF PRIEST-ANDERSON,
GREEN SEAL

BANK	A.B.P.	V.FINE	UNC.	★UNC.	BANK	A.B.P.	V.FINE	UNC.	★UNC.
☐ Boston	9.90	16.50	30.00	70.00	☐ Chicago	9.30	15.50	30.00	75.00
☐ New York	9.90	16.50	30.00	70.00	☐ St. Louis	9.30	15.50	30.00	75.00
☐ Philadelphia	9.90	16.50	30.00	70.00	☐ Minneapolis	9.30	15.50	30.00	75.00
☐ Cleveland	9.90	16.50	30.00	70.00	☐ Kansas City	9.30	15.50	30.00	75.00
☐ Richmond	9.90	16.50	30.00	70.00	☐ Dallas	9.30	15.50	30.00	75.00
☐ Atlanta	9.90	16.50	30.00	70.00	☐ San Francisco	9.30	15.50	30.00	75.00

SERIES OF 1950C, SIGNATURES OF SMITH-DILLON, GREEN SEAL

BANK	A.B.P.	V.FINE	UNC.	★UNC.	BANK	A.B.P.	V.FINE	UNC.	★UNC.
☐ Boston	5.50	9.00	26.00	125.00	☐ Chicago	5.50	9.00	26.00	78.00
☐ New York	5.50	9.00	26.00	90.00	☐ St. Louis	5.50	9.00	26.00	210.00
☐ Philadelphia	5.50	9.00	26.00	120.00	☐ Minneapolis	5.50	9.00	26.00	255.00
☐ Cleveland	5.50	9.00	26.00	100.00	☐ Kansas City	5.50	9.00	26.00	155.00
☐ Richmond	5.50	9.00	26.00	140.00	☐ Dallas	5.50	9.00	26.00	340.00
☐ Atlanta	5.50	9.00	26.00	100.00	☐ San Francisco	5.50	9.00	26.00	345.00

SERIES OF 1950D, SIGNATURES OF GRANAHAN-DILLON, GREEN SEAL

BANK	A.B.P.	V.FINE	UNC.	★UNC.	BANK	A.B.P.	V.FINE	UNC.	★UNC.
☐ Boston	5.50	9.00	28.00	105.00	☐ Chicago	5.50	9.00	20.00	85.00
☐ New York	5.50	9.00	20.00	85.00	☐ St. Louis	5.50	9.00	28.00	150.00
☐ Philadelphia	5.50	9.00	28.00	110.00	☐ Minneapolis	5.50	9.00	35.00	180.00
☐ Cleveland	5.50	9.00	20.00	110.00	☐ Kansas City	5.50	9.00	25.00	145.00
☐ Richmond	5.50	9.00	26.00	110.00	☐ Dallas	5.50	9.00	26.00	225.00
☐ Atlanta	5.50	9.00	26.00	115.00	☐ San Francisco	5.50	9.00	20.00	140.00

SERIES OF 1950E, SIGNATURES OF GRANAHAN-FOWLER, GREEN SEAL

BANK	A.B.P.	V.FINE	UNC.	★UNC.
☐ Chicago	8.10	13.50	95.00	265.00
☐ New York	8.10	13.50	58.00	115.00
☐ San Francisco	8.10	13.50	78.00	265.00

FIVE DOLLAR NOTES (1963)
FEDERAL RESERVE NOTES
(IN GOD WE TRUST IS ADDED ON BACK)
SERIES OF 1963, SIGNATURES OF GRANAHAN-DILLON, GREEN SEAL

BANK	A.B.P.	V.FINE	UNC.	★UNC.	BANK	A.B.P.	V.FINE	UNC.	★UNC.
☐ Boston	5.50	9.00	27.00	80.00	☐ Chicago	5.50	9.00	22.00	80.00
☐ New York	5.50	9.00	24.00	80.00	☐ St. Louis	5.50	9.00	28.00	95.00
☐ Philadelphia	5.50	9.00	24.00	80.00	☐ Minneapolis	5.50	9.00	28.00	95.00
☐ Cleveland	6.50	9.00	24.00	80.00	☐ Kansas City	5.50	9.00	28.00	95.00
☐ Richmond	5.50	9.00	24.00	80.00	☐ Dallas	5.50	9.00	28.00	95.00
☐ Atlanta	5.50	9.00	24.00	80.00	☐ San Francisco	5.50	9.00	28.00	80.00

SERIES OF 1963A, SIGNATURES OF GRANAHAN-FOWLER, GREEN SEAL

BANK	A.B.P.	V.FINE	UNC.	★UNC.	BANK	A.B.P.	V.FINE	UNC.	★UNC.
☐ Boston	5.50	9.00	22.00	45.00	☐ Chicago	5.50	9.00	22.00	45.00
☐ New York	5.50	9.00	22.00	45.00	☐ St. Louis	5.50	9.00	22.00	45.00
☐ Philadelphia	5.50	9.00	22.00	45.00	☐ Minneapolis	5.50	9.00	22.00	45.00
☐ Cleveland	5.50	9.00	22.00	45.00	☐ Kansas City	5.50	9.00	22.00	45.00
☐ Richmond	5.50	9.00	22.00	45.00	☐ Dallas	5.50	9.00	22.00	45.00
☐ Atlanta	5.50	9.00	22.00	45.00	☐ San Francisco	5.50	9.00	22.00	45.00

FIVE DOLLAR NOTES (1969)
FEDERAL RESERVE NOTES
(WORDING IN GREEN TREASURY SEAL IS CHANGED FROM LATIN TO ENGLISH)

SERIES OF 1969, SIGNATURES OF ELSTON-KENNEDY, GREEN SEAL

BANK	A.B.P.	V.FINE	UNC.	★UNC.	BANK	A.B.P.	V.FINE	UNC.	★UNC.
☐ Boston	5.50	6.50	22.00	45.00	☐ Chicago	5.50	6.50	22.00	45.00
☐ New York	5.50	6.50	22.00	45.00	☐ St. Louis	5.50	6.50	22.00	45.00
☐ Philadelphia	5.50	6.50	22.00	45.00	☐ Minneapolis	5.50	6.50	22.00	45.00
☐ Cleveland	5.50	6.50	22.00	45.00	☐ Kansas City	5.50	6.50	22.00	45.00
☐ Richmond	5.50	6.50	22.00	45.00	☐ Dallas	5.50	6.50	22.00	45.00
☐ Atlanta	5.50	6.50	22.00	45.00	☐ San Francisco	5.50	6.50	22.00	45.00

SERIES OF 1969A, SIGNATURES OF KABIS-CONNALLY, GREEN SEAL

BANK	A.B.P.	V.FINE	UNC.	★UNC.	BANK	A.B.P.	V.FINE	UNC.	★UNC.
☐ Boston	5.50	7.00	36.00	70.00	☐ Chicago	5.50	7.00	36.00	70.00
☐ New York	5.50	7.00	36.00	70.00	☐ St. Louis	5.50	7.00	36.00	70.00
☐ Philadelphia	5.50	7.00	36.00	70.00	☐ Minneapolis	5.50	7.00	36.00	70.00
☐ Cleveland	5.50	7.00	36.00	70.00	☐ Kansas City	5.50	7.00	36.00	70.00
☐ Richmond	5.50	7.00	36.00	70.00	☐ Dallas	5.50	7.00	36.00	70.00
☐ Atlanta	5.50	7.00	36.00	70.00	☐ San Francisco	5.50	7.00	36.00	70.00

SERIES OF 1969B, SIGNATURES OF BANUELOS-CONNALLY, GREEN SEAL

BANK	A.B.P.	V.FINE	UNC.	★UNC.	BANK	A.B.P.	V.FINE	UNC.	★UNC.
☐ Boston	13.50	22.00	80.00	—	☐ Chicago	13.50	22.00	55.00	210.00
☐ New York	13.50	22.00	65.00	155.00	☐ St. Louis	13.50	22.00	95.00	—
☐ Philadelphia	13.50	22.00	65.00	—	☐ Minneapolis	13.50	22.00	95.00	—
☐ Cleveland	13.50	22.00	65.00	—	☐ Kansas City	13.50	22.00	84.00	205.00
☐ Richmond	13.50	22.00	65.00	185.00	☐ Dallas	13.50	22.00	65.00	—
☐ Atlanta	13.50	22.00	65.00	195.00	☐ San Francisco	13.50	22.00	65.00	205.00

SERIES OF 1969C, SIGNATURES OF BANUELOS-SHULTZ, GREEN SEAL

BANK	A.B.P.	V.FINE	UNC.	★UNC.	BANK	A.B.P.	V.FINE	UNC.	★UNC.
☐ Boston	—	6.00	20.00	65.00	☐ Chicago	—	6.00	18.00	
☐ New York	—	6.00	20.00	65.00	☐ St. Louis	—	6.00	18.00	65.00
☐ Philadelphia	—	6.00	20.00	65.00	☐ Minneapolis	—	6.00	18.00	65.00
☐ Cleveland	—	6.00	20.00	65.00	☐ Kansas City	—	6.00	18.00	65.00
☐ Richmond	—	6.00	20.00	65.00	☐ Dallas	—	6.00	18.00	65.00
☐ Atlanta	—	6.00	20.00	65.00	☐ San Francisco	—	6.00	18.00	65.00

FIVE DOLLAR NOTES (1974)
FEDERAL RESERVE NOTES
SERIES OF 1974, SIGNATURES OF NEFF-SIMON, GREEN SEAL

BANK	A.B.P.	V.FINE	UNC.	★UNC.	BANK	A.B.P.	V.FINE	UNC.	★UNC.
☐ Boston	—	6.00	15.00	38.00	☐ Chicago	—	6.00	15.00	38.00
☐ New York	—	6.00	15.00	38.00	☐ St. Louis	—	6.00	15.00	38.00
☐ Philadelphia	—	6.00	15.00	38.00	☐ Minneapolis	—	6.00	15.00	38.00
☐ Cleveland	—	6.00	15.00	38.00	☐ Kansas City	—	6.00	15.00	38.00
☐ Richmond	—	6.00	15.00	38.00	☐ Dallas	—	6.00	15.00	38.00
☐ Atlanta	—	6.00	15.00	38.00	☐ San Francisco	—	6.00	15.00	38.00

FIVE DOLLAR NOTES (1977)
FEDERAL RESERVE NOTES
SERIES OF 1977, SIGNATURES OF MORTON-BLUMENTHAL, GREEN SEAL

★Notes not issued for all banks

BANK	A.B.P.	V.FINE	UNC.	★UNC.	BANK	A.B.P.	V.FINE	UNC.	★UNC.
☐ Boston	—	6.00	15.00	68.00	☐ Chicago	—	6.00	15.00	45.00
☐ New York	—	6.00	15.00	34.50	☐ St. Louis	—	6.00	15.00	63.00
☐ Philadelphia	—	6.00	15.00	45.00	☐ Kansas City	—	6.00	15.00	50.00
☐ Cleveland	—	6.00	15.00	45.00	☐ Dallas	—	6.00	15.00	50.00
☐ Richmond	—	6.00	15.00	45.00	☐ San Francisco	—	6.00	15.00	50.00
☐ Atlanta	—	6.00	15.00	45.00					

SERIES OF 1977A, SIGNATURES OF MORTON-BLUMENTHAL, GREEN SEAL

BANK	A.B.P.	V.FINE	UNC.	★UNC.	BANK	A.B.P.	V.FINE	UNC.	★UNC.
☐ Boston	—	6.00	15.00	80.00	☐ Chicago	—	6.00	15.00	45.00
☐ New York	—	6.00	15.00	40.00	☐ St. Louis	—	6.00	15.00	80.00
☐ Philadelphia	—	6.00	15.00	40.00	☐ Minneapolis	—	6.00	15.00	89.00
☐ Cleveland	—	6.00	15.00	54.00	☐ Kansas City	—	6.00	15.00	68.00
☐ Richmond	—	6.00	15.00	105.00	☐ Dallas	—	6.00	15.00	55.00
☐ Atlanta	—	6.00	15.00	40.00	☐ San Francisco	—	6.00	15.00	40.00

FIVE DOLLAR NOTES (1981)
FEDERAL RESERVE NOTES
SERIES OF 1981, SIGNATURES OF BUCHANAN-REGAN, GREEN SEAL
★Notes not issued for all banks

BANK	A.B.P.	V.FINE	UNC.	★UNC.	BANK	A.B.P.	V.FINE	UNC.	★UNC.
☐ Boston	—	6.00	15.00	—	☐ Chicago	—	6.00	15.00	60.00
☐ New York	—	6.00	15.00	60.00	☐ St. Louis	—	6.00	15.00	60.00
☐ Philadelphia	—	6.00	15.00	60.00	☐ Minneapolis	—	6.00	15.00	60.00
☐ Cleveland	—	6.00	15.00	60.00	☐ Kansas City	—	6.00	15.00	60.00
☐ Richmond	—	6.00	15.00	60.00	☐ Dallas	—	6.00	15.00	60.00
☐ Atlanta	—	6.00	15.00	60.00	☐ San Francisco	—	6.00	15.00	60.00

SERIES OF 1981A, SIGNATURES OF ORTEGA-REGAN, GREEN SEAL
★Notes not issued for all banks

BANK	A.B.P.	V.FINE	UNC.	★UNC.	BANK	A.B.P.	V.FINE	UNC.	★UNC.
☐ Boston	—	10.50	25.00	—	☐ Chicago	—	11.50	25.00	—
☐ New York	—	10.50	25.00	63.00	☐ St. Louis	—	11.50	25.00	—
☐ Philadelphia	—	10.50	25.00	—	☐ Minneapolis	—	11.50	25.00	—
☐ Cleveland	—	10.50	25.00	—	☐ Kansas City	—	11.50	25.00	—
☐ Richmond	—	10.50	25.00	—	☐ Dallas	—	11.50	25.00	—
☐ Atlanta	—	10.50	25.00	—	☐ San Francisco	—	11.50	25.00	85.00

FIVE DOLLAR NOTES (1985)
FEDERAL RESERVE NOTES
SERIES OF 1985, SIGNATURES OF ORTEGA-BAKER, GREEN SEAL
★Notes not issued for all banks

BANK	A.B.P.	V.FINE	UNC.	★UNC.	BANK	A.B.P.	V.FINE	UNC.	★UNC.
☐ Boston	—	6.00	20.00	35.00	☐ Chicago	—	6.00	20.00	35.00
☐ New York	—	6.00	20.00	35.00	☐ St. Louis	—	6.00	20.00	35.00
☐ Philadelphia	—	6.00	20.00	35.00	☐ Minneapolis	—	6.00	20.00	35.00
☐ Cleveland	—	6.00	20.00	35.00	☐ Kansas City	—	6.00	20.00	35.00
☐ Richmond	—	6.00	20.00	35.00	☐ Dallas	—	6.00	20.00	35.00
☐ Atlanta	—	6.00	20.00	35.00	☐ San Francisco	—	6.00	20.00	35.00

FIVE DOLLAR NOTES (1988)
FEDERAL RESERVE NOTES
SERIES OF 1988, SIGNATURES OF ORTEGA-BRADY, GREEN SEAL
★Notes not issued for all banks

BANK	A.B.P.	V.FINE	UNC.	★UNC.	BANK	A.B.P.	V.FINE	UNC.	★UNC.
☐ Boston	—	6.00	16.00	25.00	☐ Chicago	—	6.00	16.00	25.00
☐ New York	—	6.00	16.00	25.00	☐ St. Louis	—	6.00	18.00	25.00
☐ Philadelphia	—	6.00	16.00	25.00	☐ Minneapolis	—	6.00	16.00	25.00
☐ Cleveland	—	6.00	16.00	25.00	☐ Kansas City	—	6.00	16.00	25.00
☐ Richmond	—	6.00	16.00	25.00	☐ Dallas	—	6.00	16.00	25.00
☐ Atlanta	—	6.00	16.00	25.00	☐ San Francisco	—	6.00	16.00	25.00

SERIES OF 1988A, SIGNATURES OF VILLALPANDO-BRADY, GREEN SEAL
★Notes not issued for all banks

BANK	A.B.P.	V.FINE	UNC.	★UNC.	BANK	A.B.P.	V.FINE	UNC.	★UNC.
☐ Boston	—	6.00	15.00	30.00	☐ Chicago	—	6.00	15.00	30.00
☐ New York	—	6.00	15.00	30.00	☐ St. Louis	—	6.00	15.00	30.00
☐ Philadelphia	—	6.00	15.00	30.00	☐ Minneapolis	—	6.00	15.00	30.00
☐ Cleveland	—	6.00	15.00	30.00	☐ Kansas City	—	6.00	15.00	30.00
☐ Richmond	—	6.00	15.00	30.00	☐ Dallas	—	6.00	15.00	30.00
☐ Atlanta	—	6.00	15.00	30.00	☐ San Francisco	—	6.00	15.00	30.00

FIVE DOLLAR NOTES (1993)
FEDERAL RESERVE NOTES
SERIES OF 1993, SIGNATURES OF WITHROW-BENTSEN, GREEN SEAL
★Notes not issued for all banks

BANK	A.B.P.	V.FINE	UNC.	★UNC.	BANK	A.B.P.	V.FINE	UNC.	★UNC.
☐ Boston	—	6.00	15.00	30.00	☐ Chicago	—	6.00	15.00	30.00
☐ New York	—	6.00	15.00	30.00	☐ St. Louis	—	6.00	15.00	30.00
☐ Philadelphia	—	6.00	15.00	30.00	☐ Minneapolis	—	6.00	15.00	30.00
☐ Cleveland	—	6.00	15.00	30.00	☐ Kansas City	—	6.00	15.00	30.00
☐ Richmond	—	6.00	15.00	30.00	☐ Dallas	—	6.00	15.00	30.00
☐ Atlanta	—	6.00	15.00	30.00	☐ San Francisco	—	6.00	15.00	30.00

FIVE DOLLAR NOTES (1995)
FEDERAL RESERVE NOTES
SERIES OF 1995, SIGNATURES OF WITHROW-RUBIN, GREEN SEAL
★Notes not issued for all banks

BANK	A.B.P.	V.FINE	UNC.	★UNC.	BANK	A.B.P.	V.FINE	UNC.	★UNC.
☐ Boston	—	6.00	12.00	25.00	☐ Chicago	—	6.00	12.00	25.00
☐ New York	—	6.00	12.00	25.00	☐ St. Louis	—	6.00	12.00	25.00
☐ Philadelphia	—	6.00	12.00	25.00	☐ Minneapolis	—	6.00	12.00	25.00
☐ Cleveland	—	6.00	12.00	25.00	☐ Kansas City	—	6.00	12.00	25.00
☐ Richmond	—	6.00	12.00	25.00	☐ Dallas	—	6.00	12.00	25.00
☐ Atlanta	—	6.00	12.00	25.00	☐ San Francisco	—	6.00	12.00	25.00

FIVE DOLLAR NOTES (1918)
FEDERAL RESERVE BANK NOTES
(ALL WITH BLUE SEAL AND BLUE SERIAL NUMBERS)
(Large Size)

Face Design: Portrait of President Lincoln with Reserve City in center.
Back Design: Same as 1914 note.

BANK	SERIES	GOV'T SIGNATURES	BANK SIGNATURES	A.B.P.	GOOD	V. FINE	UNC.
☐Boston	1918	Teehee-Burke	Bullen-Morse	81.00	135.00	1550.00	4000.00
☐New York	1918	Teehee-Burke	Hendricks-Strong	81.00	135.00	485.00	2150.00
☐Philadelphia	1918	Teehee-Burke	Hardt-Passmore	81.00	135.00	485.00	2150.00
☐Philadelphia	1918	Teehee-Burke	Dyer-Passmore	81.00	135.00	550.00	2150.00
☐Cleveland	1918	Teehee-Burke	Dyer-Fancher	81.00	135.00	480.00	1950.00
☐Cleveland	1918	Teehee-Burke	Davis-Fancher	81.00	135.00	575.00	1950.00
☐Cleveland	1918	Elliott-Burke	Davis-Fancher	81.00	135.00	575.00	1950.00
☐Atlanta	1915	Teehee-Burke	Bell-Wellborn	81.00	135.00	1500.00	3500.00
☐Atlanta	1915	Teehee-Burke	Pike-McCord	81.00	135.00	480.00	1950.00
☐Atlanta	1918	Teehee-Burke	Pike-McCord	81.00	135.00	575.00	1950.00
☐Atlanta	1918	Teehee-Burke	Bell-Wellborn	81.00	135.00	575.00	2000.00

BANK	SERIES	GOV'T SIGNATURES	BANK SIGNATURES	A.B.P.	BANK GOOD	V. FINE	UNC.
☐ Atlanta	1918	Elliott-Burke	Bell-Wellborn	69.00	115.00	550.00	1580.00
☐ Chicago	1915	Teehee-Burke	McLallen-McDougal	69.00	115.00	400.00	1580.00
☐ Chicago	1918	Teehee-Burke	McCloud-McDougal	69.00	115.00	375.00	1580.00
☐ Chicago	1918	Teehee-Burke	Cramer-McDougal	69.00	115.00	425.00	1600.00
☐ St. Louis	1918	Teehee-Burke	Attebery-Wells	69.00	115.00	400.00	1580.00
☐ St. Louis	1918	Teehee-Burke	Attebery-Biggs	69.00	115.00	575.00	1625.00
☐ St. Louis	1918	Elliott-Burke	White-Biggs	69.00	115.00	575.00	1350.00
☐ Minneapolis	1918	Teehee-Burke	Cook-Wold	69.00	115.00	375.00	1580.00
☐ Kansas City	1915	Teehee-Burke	Anderson-Miller	65.00	110.00	575.00	1530.00
☐ Kansas City	1915	Teehee-Burke	Cross-Miller	65.00	110.00	575.00	1530.00
☐ Kansas City	1915	Teehee-Burke	Helm-Miller	65.00	110.00	1425.00	3000.00
☐ Kansas City	1918	Teehee-Burke	Anderson-Miller	65.00	110.00	400.00	1600.00
☐ Kansas City	1918	Elliott-Burke	Helm-Miller	65.00	110.00	390.00	1600.00
☐ Dallas	1915	Teehee-Burke	Hoopoc-VanZandt	65.00	110.00	575.00	1600.00
☐ Dallas	1915	Teehee-Burke	Talley-VanZandt	65.00	110.00	650.00	1600.00
☐ Dallas	1918	Teehee-Burke	Talley-VanZandt	65.00	110.00	1500.00	3750.00
☐ San Francisco	1915	Teehee-Burke	Clerk-Lynch	65.00	110.00	1200.00	3000.00
☐ San Francisco	1918	Teehee-Burke	Clerk-Lynch	65.00	110.00	1975.00	3800.00

FIVE DOLLAR NOTES (1929)
FEDERAL RESERVE BANK NOTES

(Small Size)
Face Design: Portrait of President Lincoln.
SERIES 1929, BROWN SEAL

BANK & CITY	SIGNATURES	A.B.P.	GOOD	V.FINE	UNC.	*UNC.
☐Boston	Jones-Woods	9.60	16.00	50.00	225.00	3900.00
☐New York	Jones-Woods	9.60	16.00	50.00	225.00	3800.00
☐Philadelphia	Jones-Woods	9.60	16.00	50.00	225.00	3800.00
☐Cleveland	Jones-Woods	9.60	16.00	50.00	225.00	3800.00
☐Atlanta	Jones-Woods	9.60	16.00	50.00	375.00	3750.00
☐Chicago	Jones-Woods	9.60	16.00	50.00	225.00	3800.00
☐St. Louis	Jones-Woods	9.60	16.00	450.00	3200.00	3900.00
☐Minneapolis	Jones-Woods	9.60	16.00	75.00	1150.00	3800.00
☐Kansas City	Jones-Woods	9.60	16.00	45.00	300.00	RARE
☐Dallas	Jones-Woods	9.60	16.00	45.00	225.00	RARE
☐San Francisco	Jones-Woods	150.00	250.00	875.00	—	RARE

TEN DOLLAR NOTES

TEN DOLLAR NOTES (1861) DEMAND NOTES (NO TREASURY SEAL)

(Large Size)

Face Design: Portrait of President Lincoln left, female figure with sword and shield.

Back Design: Ornate designs of TEN.

PAYABLE AT	A.B.P.	GOOD	V. GOOD	FINE
☐Boston (I)	—	—	—	RARE
☐New York (I)	—	—	—	RARE
☐Philadelphia (I)	—	—	—	RARE
☐Cincinnati (I)	—	—	—	RARE
☐St. Louis (I)	—	—	—	RARE
☐Boston (II)	950.00	1250.00	2000.00	4500.00
☐New York (II)	900.00	1500.00	2200.00	4800.00
☐Philadelphia (II)	900.00	1500.00	2200.00	4800.00
☐Cincinnati (II)	—	—	—	RARE
☐St. Louis (II)	—	—	—	RARE

TEN DOLLAR NOTES (1862–1863)
UNITED STATES NOTES
(ALSO KNOWN AS LEGAL TENDER NOTES)
(Large Size)

Back Design
Face Design: Similar to 1861 note.

SERIES	SIGNATURES	SEAL	A.B.P.	GOOD	V.FINE	UNC.
☐1862	Chittenden-Spinner*	Red	270.00	475.00	2000.00	RARE
☐1862	Chittenden-Spinner**	Red	270.00	475.00	2000.00	RARE
☐1863	Chittenden-Spinner**	Red	270.00	475.00	2000.00	RARE

* First Obligation: Similar to 1875–190/ $5 note.
** Second Obligation: Shown above.

TEN DOLLAR NOTES (1869) UNITED STATES NOTES
(Large Size)

Face Design: Portrait of Daniel Webster left, presentation of
Indian princess right. (This note is nicknamed "Jackass Note,"
because the EAGLE between the signatures resembles a don-
key when it is held upside down.)

SERIES	SIGNATURES	SEAL	A.B.P.	GOOD	V.FINE	UNC.
☐1869	Allison-Spinner	Red	240.00	425.00	1250.00	RARE

TEN DOLLAR NOTES (1875–1880)
UNITED STATES NOTES
(Large Size)

Face Design: Similar to 1869 note.

Back Design: Revised.

SERIES	SIGNATURES	SEAL	A.B.P.	GOOD	V.FINE	UNC.
☐1875	Allison-New	Red	—	—	—	RARE
☐Same as above, Series A		Red	150.00	275.00	1250.00	RARE
☐1878	Allison-Gilfillan	Red	150.00	275.00	1400.00	RARE
☐1880	Scofield-Gilfillan	Brown	150.00	275.00	1200.00	2400.00
☐1880	Bruce-Gilfillan	Brown	150.00	275.00	1250.00	3000.00
☐1880	Bruce-Wyman	Brown	150.00	275.00	1250.00	3000.00
☐1880	Bruce-Wyman	Red Plain	150.00	275.00	1250.00	2600.00
☐1880	Rosecrans-Jordan	Red Plain	150.00	275.00	1250.00	3400.00
☐1880	Rosecrans-Hyatt	Red Plain	150.00	275.00	1250.00	3000.00
☐1880	Rosecrans-Hyatt	Red Spikes	150.00	275.00	1250.00	2800.00
☐1880	Rosecrans-Huston	Red Spikes	150.00	275.00	1250.00	2800.00
☐1880	Rosecrans-Huston	Brown	150.00	275.00	1250.00	3200.00
☐1880	Rosecrans-Nebeker	Brown	—	—	—	RARE
☐1880	Rosecrans-Nebeker	Red	255.00	425.00	625.00	2200.00
☐1880	Tillman-Morgan	Red	255.00	425.00	625.00	2200.00

SERIES	SIGNATURES	SEAL	A.B.P.	GOOD	V.FINE	UNC.
☐1880 Bruce-Roberts		Red	150.00	250.00	650.00	2750.00
☐1880 Lyons-Roberts		Red	150.00	250.00	650.00	2750.00

TEN DOLLAR NOTES (1901) UNITED STATES NOTES
(Large Size)

Face Design: American bison (buffalo) center, portrait of Lewis left, portrait of Clark right.

Back Design: Female allegorical figure in arch.

SERIES	SIGNATURES	SEAL	A.B.P.	GOOD	V.FINE	UNC.
☐1901	Lyons-Roberts	Red	255.00	425.00	1250.00	4850.00
☐1901	Lyons-Treat	Red	255.00	425.00	1250.00	4850.00
☐1901	Vernon-Treat	Red	255.00	425.00	1250.00	4850.00
☐1901	Vernon-McClung	Red	255.00	425.00	1250.00	4850.00
☐1901	Napier-McClung	Red	255.00	425.00	1250.00	4850.00
☐1901	Parker-Burke	Red	255.00	425.00	1250.00	4850.00
☐1901	Teehee-Burke	Red	255.00	425.00	1250.00	4850.00
☐1901	Elliott-White	Red	255.00	425.00	1250.00	4850.00
☐1901	Speelman-White	Red	255.00	425.00	1250.00	4850.00

TEN DOLLAR NOTES (1923) UNITED STATES NOTES
(Large Size)

Face Design: Portrait of President Jackson center, red seal left, red "X" to right.

Back Design

SERIES	SIGNATURES	SEAL	A.B.P.	GOOD	V.FINE	UNC.
☐1923	Speelman-White	Red	360.00	600.00	2500.00	RARE

TEN DOLLAR NOTES (1863–1875)
NATIONAL BANK NOTES
FIRST CHARTER PERIOD (Large Size)

Face Design: Benjamin Franklin and kite left, name of bank and city center. Effigy of Liberty and eagle right.

Back Design: Border green, center black. DeSoto on horseback at Mississippi River.

SERIES	SIGNATURES	SEAL	A.B.P.	GOOD	V.FINE	UNC.
☐Original	Chittenden-Spinner	Red	225.00	400.00	2350.00	RARE
☐Original	Colby-Spinner	Red	225.00	400.00	2350.00	RARE
☐Original	Jeffries-Spinner	Red	390.00	650.00	2500.00	RARE
☐Original	Allison-Spinner	Red	225.00	400.00	2350.00	RARE
☐1875	Allison-New	Red	225.00	400.00	2350.00	RARE
☐1875	Allison-Wyman	Red	225.00	400.00	2350.00	RARE
☐1875	Allison-Gilfillan	Red	225.00	400.00	2350.00	RARE
☐1875	Scofield-Gilfillan	Red	225.00	400.00	2350.00	RARE
☐1875	Bruce-Gilfillan	Red	225.00	400.00	2350.00	RARE
☐1875	Bruce-Wyman	Red	225.00	400.00	2350.00	RARE
☐1875	Rosecrans-Huston	Red	225.00	400.00	2350.00	RARE
☐1875	Rosecrans-Nebeker	Red	225.00	400.00	2350.00	RARE

TEN DOLLAR NOTES (1882) NATIONAL BANK NOTES
SECOND CHARTER PERIOD (Large Size)

First Issue (Brown seal and brown backs)
Face Design: Similar to 1863–1875 note.
Back Design: Similar to 1882 $5 note. Border in brown with green Charter Number.

SERIES	SIGNATURES	SEAL	A.B.P.	GOOD	V.FINE	UNC.
☐1882	Bruce-Gilfillan	Brown	195.00	350.00	1275.00	3500.00
☐1882	Bruce-Wyman	Brown	195.00	350.00	1275.00	3500.00
☐1882	Bruce-Jordan	Brown	195.00	350.00	1275.00	3500.00
☐1882	Rosecrans-Jordan	Brown	195.00	350.00	1275.00	3500.00
☐1882	Rosecrans-Hyatt	Brown	195.00	350.00	1275.00	3500.00
☐1882	Rosecrans-Huston	Brown	195.00	350.00	1275.00	3500.00
☐1882	Rosecrans-Nebeker	Brown	195.00	350.00	1275.00	3500.00
☐1882	Rosecrans-Morgan	Brown	195.00	350.00	1275.00	3500.00
☐1882	Tillman-Morgan	Brown	195.00	350.00	1275.00	3500.00
☐1882	Tillman-Roberts	Brown	195.00	350.00	1275.00	3500.00

SERIES	SIGNATURES	SEAL	A.B.P.	GOOD	V.FINE	UNC.
☐1882	Bruce-Roberts	Brown	204.00	340.00	1250.00	3500.00
☐1882	Lyons-Roberts	Brown	204.00	340.00	1250.00	3500.00
☐1882	Lyons-Treat	Brown	204.00	340.00	1400.00	3800.00
☐1882	Vernon-Treat	Brown	204.00	340.00	1400.00	3800.00

Second Issue (Blue seal, green back with date "1882–1908")
Face Design: Similar to 1863–1875 note.
Back Design: Similar to 1882 $5 Second Issue note.
(Large Size)

SERIES	SIGNATURES	SEAL	A.B.P.	GOOD	V.FINE	UNC.
☐1882	Rosecrans-Huston	Blue	195.00	325.00	1375.00	2700.00
☐1882	Rosecrans-Nebeker	Blue	195.00	325.00	1375.00	2700.00
☐1882	Rosecrans-Morgan	Blue	195.00	325.00	1375.00	2880.00
☐1882	Tillman-Morgan	Blue	195.00	325.00	1375.00	2880.00
☐1882	Tillman-Roberts	Blue	195.00	325.00	1375.00	2880.00
☐1882	Bruce-Roberts	Blue	195.00	325.00	1375.00	2880.00
☐1882	Lyons-Roberts	Blue	195.00	325.00	1375.00	2880.00
☐1882	Vernon-Treat	Blue	195.00	325.00	1375.00	2880.00
☐1882	Vernon-McClung	Blue	195.00	325.00	1375.00	2880.00
☐1882	Napier-McClung	Blue	195.00	325.00	1375.00	2880.00

TEN DOLLAR NOTES (1882) NATIONAL BANK NOTES
(Large Size)

Third Issue (Blue seal, green back with value in block letters)
Face Design: Similar to previous notes. (see 1863–1875 note).
Back Design: Similar to 1882 $500 Third Issue note.

SERIES	SIGNATURES	SEAL	A.B.P.	GOOD	V. FINE	UNC.
☐1882	Tillman-Roberts	Blue	270.00	450.00	1675.00	4750.00
☐1882	Lyons-Roberts	Blue	270.00	450.00	1675.00	4750.00
☐1882	Vernon-Treat	Blue	270.00	450.00	1675.00	4750.00
☐1882	Napier-McClung	Blue	270.00	450.00	1675.00	4750.00

These notes may exist with other signatures, but are very rare.

TEN DOLLAR NOTES (1902) NATIONAL BANK NOTES
THIRD CHARTER PERIOD (Large Size)

First Issue (Red seal and red Charter Numbers)
Face Design: Portrait of President McKinley left, name of
bank and city in center.

SERIES	SIGNATURES	SEAL	A.B.P.	GOOD	V.FINE	UNC.
☐1902	Lyons-Roberts	Red	165.00	275.00	1250.00	3200.00
☐1902	Lyons-Treat	Red	165.00	275.00	1250.00	3200.00
☐1902	Vernon-Treat	Red	165.00	275.00	1250.00	3200.00

TEN DOLLAR NOTES (1902) NATIONAL BANK NOTES
THIRD CHARTER PERIOD (Large Size)

Second Issue (Blue seal and numbers, "1902–1908" on the
back)
Face Design: Same as 1882 Third Issue note.
Back Design: Same as 1882 Second Issue note. Date 1902–
1908.

SERIES	SIGNATURES	SEAL	A.B.P.	GOOD	V.FINE	UNC.
☐1902	Lyons-Roberts	Blue	75.00	125.00	325.00	850.00
☐1902	Lyons-Treat	Blue	75.00	125.00	325.00	850.00
☐1902	Vernon-Treat	Blue	75.00	125.00	325.00	850.00
☐1902	Vernon-McClung	Blue	75.00	125.00	325.00	850.00

SERIES	SIGNATURES	SEAL	A.B.P.	GOOD	V.FINE	UNC.
☐1902	Napier-McClung	Blue	75.00	125.00	210.00	1750.00
☐1902	Napier-Thompson	Blue	60.00	100.00	350.00	1650.00
☐1902	Napier-Burke	Blue	60.00	100.00	325.00	850.00
☐1902	Parker-Burke	Blue	60.00	100.00	325.00	850.00
☐1902	Teehee-Burke	Blue	60.00	100.00	325.00	1610.00

Third Issue (Blue seal and numbers, without date on back.)

SERIES	SIGNATURES	SEAL	A.B.P.	GOOD	V.FINE	UNC.
☐1902	Lyons-Roberts	Blue	75.00	125.00	290.00	1125.00
☐1902	Lyons-Treat	Blue	75.00	125.00	290.00	1125.00
☐1902	Vernon-Treat	Blue	75.00	125.00	290.00	1125.00
☐1902	Vernon-McClung	Blue	75.00	125.00	290.00	1125.00
☐1902	Napier-McClung	Blue	75.00	125.00	290.00	1422.00
☐1902	Napier-Thompson	Blue	75.00	125.00	290.00	1125.00
☐1902	Napier-Burke	Blue	75.00	125.00	290.00	1125.00
☐1902	Parker-Burke	Blue	75.00	125.00	290.00	1125.00
☐1902	Teehee-Burke	Blue	75.00	125.00	290.00	1125.00
☐1902	Elliott-Burke	Blue	75.00	125.00	290.00	1125.00
☐1902	Elliott-White	Blue	75.00	125.00	290.00	1125.00
☐1902	Speelman-White	Blue	75.00	125.00	290.00	1125.00
☐1902	Woods-White	Blue	75.00	125.00	290.00	1125.00
☐1902	Woods-Tate	Blue	75.00	125.00	290.00	1125.00
☐1902	Jones-Woods	Blue	84.00	140.00	500.00	2500.00

TEN DOLLAR NOTES (1929) NATIONAL BANK NOTES
(Small Size)

Face Design, Type I: Portrait of Hamilton center, name of bank left, brown seal right, Charter Number black.

Face Design, Type II: Charter Number added in brown.

Back Design: United States Treasury Building.

SERIES SIGNATURES	SEAL	A.B.P.	GOOD	V.FINE	UNC.
☐1929, Type I Jones-Woods	Brown	39.00	65.00	145.00	300.00
☐1929, Type II Jones-Woods	Brown	39.00	65.00	145.00	300.00

TEN DOLLAR NOTES (1870–1875)
NATIONAL GOLD BANK NOTES
(Large Size)

Face Design: Similar to 1863–1875 First Charter Period note.

Back Design: State Seal left, gold coins center, American eagle right.

The following have signatures of Allison-Spinner and a red Treasury Seal.

DATE	BANK	CITY	A.B.P.	GOOD	V. GOOD
☐1870	First National Gold Bank	San Francisco	1200.00	2000.00	RARE
☐1872	National Gold Bank and Trust Co.	San Francisco	1200.00	2000.00	RARE
☐1872	National Gold Bank of D.O. Mills and Co.	Sacramento	1800.00	3000.00	RARE
☐1873	First National Gold Bank	Santa Barbara	1800.00	3000.00	RARE
☐1873	First National Gold Bank	Stockton	1800.00	3000.00	RARE
☐1874	Farmers Nat'l Gold Bank	San Jose	1800.00	3000.00	RARE
☐1874	First National Gold Bank	Petaluma	2100.00	3500.00	RARE
☐1875	First National Gold Bank	Oakland	2100.00	3500.00	RARE

TEN DOLLAR NOTES (1880) SILVER CERTIFICATES
(Large Size)

Face Design: Portrait of Robert Morris left.

Back Design: Printed in black ink, SILVER in large letters.

SERIES	SIGNATURES	SEAL	A.B.P.	GOOD	V.FINE	UNC.
☐1880	Scofield-Gilfillan	Brown	480.00	800.00	4000.00	RARE
☐1880	Bruce-Gilfillan	Brown	480.00	800.00	4000.00	RARE
☐1880	Bruce-Wyman	Brown	480.00	800.00	4000.00	RARE
☐1880	Bruce-Wyman	Red	600.00	1000.00	4500.00	RARE

TEN DOLLAR NOTES (1886) SILVER CERTIFICATES
(Large Size)

SERIES	SIGNATURES	SEAL	A.B.P.	GOOD	V.FINE	UNC.
☐1886	Rosencrans-Jordan	Sm. Red	360.00	600.00	3500.00	RARE
☐1886	Rosecrans-Hyatt	Sm. Red	300.00	500.00	2500.00	RARE
☐1886	Rosecrans-Hyatt	Lg. Red	300.00	500.00	2500.00	RARE
☐1886	Rosecrans-Huston	Lg. Red	300.00	500.00	2500.00	RARE
☐1886	Rosecrans-Huston	Lg. Brown	300.00	500.00	2500.00	RARE
☐1886	Rosecrans-Nebeker	Lg. Brown	300.00	500.00	2500.00	RARE
☐1886	Rosecrans-Nebeker	Sm. Red	360.00	600.00	2800.00	RARE

TEN DOLLAR NOTES (1891–1908)
SILVER CERTIFICATES

(Large Size)

Face Design:
Same as 1886
note.
Back Design

SERIES	SIGNATURES	SEAL	A.B.P.	GOOD	V.FINE	UNC.
☐1891	Rosecrans-Nebeker	Red	135.00	225.00	1620.00	RARE
☐1891	Tillman-Morgan	Red	135.00	225.00	1620.00	RARE
☐1891	Bruce-Roberts	Red	135.00	225.00	1620.00	RARE
☐1891	Lyons-Roberts	Red	135.00	225.00	1620.00	RARE
☐1891	Vernon-Treat	Blue	135.00	225.00	1620.00	RARE
☐1891	Vernon-McClung	Blue	120.00	200.00	1575.00	4500.00
☐1891	Parker-Burke	Blue	120.00	200.00	1575.00	4500.00

TEN DOLLAR NOTES (1933) SILVER CERTIFICATES
(Small Size)

Face Design: Portrait of Alexander Hamilton center. Blue seal to left, blue numbers.

Back Design: Green United States Treasury Building.

SERIES	SIGNATURES	SEAL	A.B.P.	GOOD	V.FINE	UNC.
☐1933	Julian-Woodin	Blue	2100.00	3500.00	—	RARE

TEN DOLLAR NOTES (1934) SILVER CERTIFICATES
(Small Size)

Face Design: Blue "10" to left of portrait, Treasury Seal is now to right.
Back Design: Similar to 1933 issue.

TEN DOLLAR NOTES (1934) SILVER CERTIFICATES
(Small Size)

SERIES	SIGNATURES	SEAL	A.B.P.	GOOD	V.FINE	UNC.	★UNC.
☐1934	Julian-Morgenthau	Blue	15.00	25.00	60.00	235.00	1925.00
☐1934	Julian-Morgenthau*	Yellow	450.00	750.00	4000.00	RARE	RARE
☐1934A	Julian-Morgenthau	Blue	12.00	20.00	60.00	333.00	2385.00
☐1934A	Julian-Morgenthau*	Yellow	15.00	25.00	60.00	333.00	2385.00
☐1934B	Julian-Vinson	Blue	30.00	50.00	300.00	—	RARE
☐1934C	Julian-Snyder	Blue	15.00	25.00	50.00	333.00	2015.00
☐1934D	Clark-Snyder	Blue	15.00	25.00	50.00	333.00	2980.00

* Silver Certificates with a yellow seal were a special issue for use in combat areas of North Africa and Europe during World War II.

TEN DOLLAR NOTES (1953) SILVER CERTIFICATES
(Small Size)

Face Design: Gray "10" to left of portrait. Treasury Seal is smaller.
Back Design: Back similar to previous note.

SERIES	SIGNATURES	SEAL	A.B.P.	GOOD	V.FINE	UNC.	★UNC.
☐1953	Priest-Humphrey	Blue	9.60	16.00	35.00	350.00	1100.00
☐1953A	Priest-Anderson	Blue	12.00	20.00	50.00	375.00	1375.00
☐1953B	Smith-Dillon	Blue	10.80	18.00	40.00	225.00	NONE

Regarding the 1953 note, there were 720,000 issued. This was the last issue of $10 Silver Certificates. These were not issued with IN GOD WE TRUST on the back. Production ended in 1962.

TEN DOLLAR (1879) REFUNDING CERTIFICATES

Face Design: Portrait of Benjamin Franklin.

Back Design: Large TEN, ornate cornucopia border.

SERIES	SIGNATURES	SEAL	A.B.P.	GOOD	V.FINE	UNC.
☐1879	Scofield-Giltfillan					
PAY TO ORDER		Red			VERY RARE	
☐1879	Scofield-Gilfillan					
PAY TO BEARER		Red	900.00	1500.00	2750.00	RARE

TEN DOLLAR NOTES (1907) GOLD CERTIFICATES
(Large Size)

Face Design: Portrait of Hillegas center, yellow x left, yellow seal right, yellow numbers.

Back Design: The backs are a bright yellow color.

SERIES	SIGNATURES	SEAL	A.B.P.	GOOD	V.FINE	UNC.
☐1907	Vernon-Treat	Gold	75.00	125.00	350.00	1575.00
☐1907	Vernon-McClung	Gold	75.00	125.00	350.00	1650.00
☐1907	Napier-McClung (1882)	Gold	75.00	125.00	350.00	1260.00
☐1907	Napier-McClung (1907)	Gold	75.00	125.00	350.00	1800.00
☐1907	Napier-Thompson (1882)	Gold	75.00	125.00	380.00	1800.00
☐1907	Napier-Thompson (1907)	Gold	75.00	125.00	420.00	2100.00
☐1907	Parker-Burke (1882)	Gold	75.00	125.00	375.00	1700.00
☐1907	Teehee-Burke	Gold	75.00	125.00	375.00	1700.00
☐1922	Speelman-White	Gold	75.00	125.00	375.00	1020.00

TEN DOLLAR NOTES (1928) GOLD CERTIFICATES
(Small Size)

Face Design: Portrait of Alexander Hamilton center, yellow seal to left, yellow numbers.

Back Design: Printed in green ink.

SERIES	SIGNATURES	SEAL	A.B.P.	GOOD	V.FINE	UNC.
☐1928	Woods-Mellon	Gold	45.00	75.00	235.00	945.00

TEN DOLLAR NOTES (1890) TREASURY OR COIN NOTES
(Large Size)

Face Design: Portrait of General Philip Sheridan.

Back Design:
Very ornate
large TEN.

SERIES	SIGNATURES	SEAL	A.B.P.	GOOD	V.FINE	UNC.
☐1890	Rosecrans-Huston	Lg. Brown	270.00	450.00	2500.00	RARE
☐1890	Rosecrans-Nebeker	Lg. Brown	270.00	450.00	2500.00	RARE
☐1890	Rosecrans-Nebeker	Sm. Red	270.00	450.00	2500.00	RARE

TEN DOLLAR NOTES (1891) TREASURY OR COIN NOTES
(Large Size)

Face Design:
Same as 1890 note.
Back Design:
Ornate small
TEN.

SERIES	SIGNATURES	SEAL	A.B.P.	GOOD	V.FINE	UNC.
☐1891	Rosecrans-Nebeker	Sm. Red	210.00	350.00	1800.00	4200.00
☐1891	Tillman-Morgan	Sm. Red	210.00	350.00	1800.00	4200.00
☐1891	Bruce-Roberts	Sm. Red	210.00	350.00	1800.00	RARE

TEN DOLLAR NOTES (1914)
FEDERAL RESERVE NOTES
(Large Size)

Face Design: Portrait of President Jackson center, Federal Reserve Seal left, Treasury Seal right.

Back Design: Scenes of farming and industry.

The following have signatures of Burke-McAdoo, red seals and red serial numbers.

SERIES	BANK	SEAL	A.B.P.	GOOD	V.FINE	UNC.
☐1914	Boston	Red	165.00	275.00	1285.00	3600.00
☐1914	New York	Red	165.00	275.00	1200.00	2705.00
☐1914	Philadelphia	Red	165.00	275.00	1200.00	3060.00
☐1914	Cleveland	Red	165.00	275.00	1200.00	3600.00
☐1914	Richmond	Red	165.00	275.00	1200.00	3600.00
☐1914	Atlanta	Red	165.00	275.00	1200.00	3600.00
☐1914	Chicago	Red	165.00	275.00	1200.00	3470.00
☐1914	St. Louis	Red	165.00	275.00	1200.00	3470.00
☐1914	Minneapolis	Red	165.00	275.00	1200.00	3470.00
☐1914	Kansas City	Red	165.00	275.00	1200.00	3600.00
☐1914	Dallas	Red	165.00	275.00	1200.00	3260.00
☐1914	San Francisco	Red	165.00	275.00	1200.00	3600.00

TEN DOLLAR NOTES (1914)
FEDERAL RESERVE NOTES

(Large Size)

BANK	SIGNATURES	SEAL	A.B.P.	V.FINE	UNC.
☐ Boston	Burke-McAdoo	Blue	85.00	145.00	625.00
☐ Boston	Burke-Glass	Blue	141.00	235.00	755.00
☐ Boston	Burke-Huston	Blue	85.00	150.00	625.00
☐ Boston	White-Mellon	Blue	85.00	150.00	625.00
☐ New York	Burke-McAdoo	Blue	70.00	150.00	640.00
☐ New York	Burke-Glass	Blue	90.00	150.00	640.00
☐ New York	Burke-Huston	Blue	90.00	150.00	590.00
☐ New York	White-Mellon	Blue	90.00	150.00	590.00
☐ Philadelphia	Burke-McAdoo	Blue	255.00	475.00	1835.00
☐ Philadelphia	Burke-Glass	Blue	255.00	475.00	1835.00
☐ Philadelphia	Burke-Huston	Blue	90.00	150.00	600.00
☐ Philadelphia	White-Mellon	Blue	90.00	150.00	600.00
☐ Cleveland	Burke-McAdoo	Blue	200.00	335.00	1645.00
☐ Cleveland	Burke-Glass	Blue	243.00	405.00	1675.00
☐ Cleveland	Burke-Huston	Blue	90.00	150.00	565.00
☐ Cleveland	White-Mellon	Blue	90.00	150.00	565.00
☐ Richmond	Burke-McAdoo	Blue	370.00	615.00	1285.00
☐ Richmond	Burke-Glass	Blue	370.00	615.00	1285.00
☐ Richmond	Burke-Huston	Blue	80.00	150.00	685.00
☐ Richmond	White-Mellon	Blue	90.00	150.00	685.00
☐ Atlanta	Burke-McAdoo	Blue	99.00	165.00	680.00
☐ Atlanta	Burke-Glass	Blue	480.00	800.00	2045.00
☐ Atlanta	Burke-Huston	Blue	285.00	475.00	1650.00
☐ Atlanta	White-Mellon	Blue	80.00	150.00	920.00
☐ Chicago	Burke-McAdoo	Blue	80.00	150.00	760.00
☐ Chicago	Burke-Glass	Blue	90.00	150.00	685.00
☐ Chicago	Burke-Huston	Blue	90.00	150.00	575.00
☐ Chicago	White-Mellon	Blue	90.00	150.00	575.00
☐ St. Louis	Burke-McAdoo	Blue	175.00	295.00	1105.00
☐ St. Louis	Burke-Glass	Blue	245.00	405.00	1150.00
☐ St. Louis	Burke-Huston	Blue	90.00	150.00	725.00
☐ St. Louis	White-Mellon	Blue	90.00	150.00	725.00
☐ Minneapolis	Burke-McAdoo	Blue	200.00	335.00	1125.00
☐ Minneapolis	Burke-Glass	Blue	175.00	295.00	1170.00
☐ Minneapolis	Burke-Huston	Blue	175.00	295.00	1170.00
☐ Minneapolis	White-Mellon	Blue	190.00	150.00	825.00
☐ Kansas City	Burke-McAdoo	Blue	190.00	150.00	1310.00
☐ Kansas City	Burke-Glass	Blue	230.00	385.00	1835.00

BANK	SIGNATURES	SEAL	A.B.P.	V.FINE	UNC.
☐Kansas City	Burke-Huston	Blue	90.00	150.00	755.00
☐Kansas City	White-Mellon	Blue	90.00	150.00	755.00
☐Dallas	Burke-McAdoo	Blue	90.00	150.00	660.00
☐Dallas	Burke-Glass	Blue	420.00	700.00	1800.00
☐Dallas	Burke-Huston	Blue	90.00	150.00	1285.00
☐Dallas	White-Mellon	Blue	96.00	160.00	1470.00
☐San Francisco	Burke-McAdoo	Blue	215.00	360.00	1500.00
☐San Francisco	Burke-Glass	Blue	150.00	250.00	1375.00
☐San Francisco	Burke-Huston	Blue	160.00	270.00	1500.00
☐San Francisco	White Mellon	Blue	90.00	150.00	735.00

TEN DOLLAR NOTES (1928–1928A)
FEDERAL RESERVE NOTES

(Small Size)

Face Design: Portrait of Alexander Hamilton center, black Federal Reserve Seal left, with number over green Treasury Seal to the right.

Back Design: United States Treasury Building.

SERIES OF 1928, SIGNATURES OF TATE-MELLON, GREEN SEAL

BANK	A.B.P.	V.FINE	UNC.	★UNC.	BANK	A.B.P.	V.FINE	UNC.	★UNC.
☐ Boston	17.00	46.00	375.00	1550.00	☐ Chicago	24.00	40.00	425.00	1600.00
☐ New York	17.00	36.00	245.00	1150.00	☐ St. Louis	33.00	55.00	225.00	1500.00
☐ Philadelphia	21.00	36.00	200.00	1150.00	☐ Minneapolis	60.00	100.00	425.00	3060.00
☐ Cleveland	21.00	36.00	200.00	1150.00	☐ Kansas City	39.00	65.00	405.00	1500.00

BANK	A.B.P.	V.FINE	UNC.	★UNC.	BANK	A.B.P.	V.FINE	UNC.	★UNC.
□ Richmond	39.00	65.00	300.00	2250.00	□ Dallas	45.00	75.00	400.00	5800.00
□ Atlanta	39.00	65.00	300.00	2250.00	□ San Francisco	45.00	75.00	400.00	5800.00

SERIES OF 1928A,
SIGNATURES OF WOODS-MELLON, GREEN SEAL

BANK	A.B.P.	V.FINE	UNC.	★UNC.	BANK	A.B.P.	V.FINE	UNC.	★UNC.
□ Boston	54.00	90.00	540.00	1635.00	□ Chicago	60.00	100.00	315.00	1635.00
□ New York	54.00	90.00	340.00	1428.00	□ St. Louis	60.00	100.00	315.00	1635.00
□ Philadelphia	54.00	90.00	340.00	1685.00	□ Minneapolis	210.00	350.00	2000.00	5500.00
□ Cleveland	54.00	90.00	250.00	1480.00	□ Kansas City	114.00	190.00	385.00	5500.00
□ Richmond	69.00	115.00	630.00	2195.00	□ Dallas	114.00	190.00	715.00	5500.00
□ Atlanta	54.00	90.00	405.00	1635.00	□ San Francisco	65.00	160.00	450.00	2245.00

TEN DOLLAR NOTES (1928B–1928C)
FEDERAL RESERVE NOTES

(Small Size)

Face Design: Alexander Hamilton; black Federal Reserve Seal left, has letter instead of number.
Back Design: Same as 1928–1928A note.

SERIES OF 1928B,
SIGNATURES OF WOODS-MELLON, GREEN SEAL

BANK	A.B.P.	V.FINE	UNC.	★UNC.	BANK	A.B.P.	V.FINE	UNC.	★UNC.
□ Boston	21.60	36.00	155.00	1024.00	□ Chicago	18.00	30.00	160.00	1020.00
□ New York	15.60	26.00	125.00	1024.00	□ St. Louis	18.00	30.00	160.00	1020.00
□ Philadelphia	21.60	21.60	155.00	1024.00	□ Minneapolis	36.00	60.00	205.00	1020.00
□ Cleveland	21.60	21.60	170.00	1024.00	□ Kansas City	18.00	30.00	155.00	1020.00
□ Richmond	24.00	40.00	175.00	1024.00	□ Dallas	30.00	50.00	210.00	1020.00
□ Atlanta	24.00	40.00	175.00	1024.00	□ San Francisco	27.00	45.00	210.00	1020.00

SERIES OF 1928C,
SIGNATURES OF WOOD-MILLS, GREEN SEAL

BANK	A.B.P.	V.FINE	UNC.
□ New York	80.00	135.00	565.00
□ Cleveland	315.00	525.00	RARE
□ Richmond	1500.00	2500.00	RARE
□ Chicago	95.00	155.00	640.00

TEN DOLLAR NOTES (1934)
FEDERAL RESERVE NOTES
(Small Size)

SERIES OF 1934,
SIGNATURES OF JULIAN-MORGENTHAU, GREEN SEAL

BANK	A.B.P.	V.FINE	UNC.	★UNC.	BANK	A.B.P.	V.FINE	UNC.	★UNC.
☐ Boston	10.00	15.00	55.00	420.00	☐ Chicago	15.00	25.00	75.00	500.00
☐ New York	15.00	25.00	60.00	550.00	☐ St. Louis	15.00	25.00	75.00	550.00
☐ Philadelphia	15.00	25.00	75.00	550.00	☐ Minneapolis	15.00	25.00	75.00	550.00
☐ Cleveland	15.00	25.00	75.00	550.00	☐ Kansas City	15.00	25.00	75.00	550.00
☐ Richmond	15.00	25.00	75.00	550.00	☐ Dallas	15.00	25.00	75.00	550.00
☐ Atlanta	15.00	25.00	75.00	550.00	☐ San Francisco	15.00	25.00	75.00	550.00

The green Treasury Seal on this note is known in a light and dark color. The light seal is worth about 10–20 percent more in most cases. REDEEMABLE IN GOLD removed from obligation over Federal Reserve Seal.

TEN DOLLAR NOTES (1934)
FEDERAL RESERVE NOTES
(Small Size)

SERIES OF 1934A,
SIGNATURES OF JULIAN-MORGENTHAU, GREEN SEAL

BANK	A.B.P.	V.FINE	UNC.	★UNC.	BANK	A.B.P.	V.FINE	UNC.	★UNC.
☐ Boston	12.00	15.00	50.00	375.00	☐ Chicago	12.00	15.00	50.00	375.00
☐ New York	12.00	15.00	50.00	375.00	☐ St. Louis	12.00	15.00	50.00	375.00
☐ Philadelphia	12.00	15.00	50.00	375.00	☐ Minneapolis	12.00	15.00	50.00	375.00
☐ Cleveland	12.00	15.00	50.00	375.00	☐ Kansas City	12.00	15.00	50.00	375.00
☐ Richmond	12.00	15.00	50.00	375.00	☐ Dallas	12.50	20.00	90.00	475.00
☐ Atlanta	12.00	15.00	50.00	375.00	☐ San Francisco	*12.50	20.00	90.00	475.00

* San Francisco, 1934A, with brown seal and overprinted HAWAII on face and back. Special issue for use in combat areas during World War II. Value in V. FINE $100, value in UNC. $1000, value in ★UNC. $10,000.00.

SERIES OF 1934B,
SIGNATURES OF JULIAN-VINSON, GREEN SEAL

BANK	A.B.P.	V.FINE	UNC.	★UNC.	BANK	A.B.P.	V.FINE	UNC.	★UNC.
☐ Boston	16.00	25.00	110.00	675.00	☐ Chicago	15.00	25.00	85.00	675.00
☐ New York	16.00	25.00	60.00	675.00	☐ St. Louis	15.00	25.00	85.00	675.00
☐ Philadelphia	16.00	25.00	60.00	675.00	☐ Minneapolis	15.00	25.00	125.00	2040.00
☐ Cleveland	16.00	25.00	100.00	675.00	☐ Kansas City	15.00	25.00	75.00	675.00
☐ Richmond	16.00	25.00	85.00	675.00	☐ Dallas	15.00	25.00	100.00	1560.00
☐ Atlanta	16.00	25.00	85.00	675.00	☐ San Francisco	15.00	25.00	85.00	675.00

SERIES OF 1934C,
SIGNATURES OF JULIAN-SNYDER, GREEN SEAL

BANK	A.B.P.	V.FINE	UNC.	★UNC.	BANK	A.B.P.	V.FINE	UNC.	★UNC.
☐ Boston	15.00	25.00	75.00	580.00	☐ Chicago	15.00	25.00	85.00	610.00
☐ New York	15.00	25.00	75.00	580.00	☐ St. Louis	15.00	25.00	85.00	610.00
☐ Philadelphia	15.00	25.00	75.00	580.00	☐ Minneapolis	15.00	25.00	85.00	1050.00
☐ Cleveland	15.00	25.00	75.00	580.00	☐ Kansas City	15.00	25.00	85.00	610.00
☐ Richmond	15.00	25.00	75.00	580.00	☐ Dallas	15.00	25.00	72.00	555.00
☐ Atlanta	15.00	25.00	75.00	580.00	☐ San Francisco	15.00	25.00	85.00	610.00

SERIES OF 1934D,
SIGNATURES OF CLARK-SNYDER, GREEN SEAL

BANK	A.B.P.	V.FINE	UNC.	★UNC.	BANK	A.B.P.	V.FINE	UNC.	★UNC.
☐ Boston	15.00	25.00	75.00	610.00	☐ Chicago	15.00	25.00	65.00	610.00
☐ New York	15.00	25.00	75.00	610.00	☐ St. Louis	15.00	25.00	75.00	685.00
☐ Philadelphia	15.00	25.00	75.00	610.00	☐ Minneapolis	15.00	25.00	75.00	1020.00
☐ Cleveland	15.00	25.00	75.00	610.00	☐ Kansas City	15.00	25.00	75.00	1020.00
☐ Richmond	15.00	25.00	75.00	995.00	☐ Dallas	15.00	25.00	75.00	1225.00
☐ Atlanta	15.00	25.00	75.00	605.00	☐ San Francisco	15.00	25.00	75.00	1225.00

TEN DOLLAR NOTES (1950)
FEDERAL RESERVE NOTES
SERIES OF 1950, SIGNATURES OF CLARK-SNYDER, GREEN SEAL

BANK	A.B.P.	V.FINE	UNC.	★UNC.	BANK	A.B.P.	V.FINE	UNC.	★UNC.
☐ Boston	15.00	25.00	110.00	610.00	☐ Chicago	15.00	25.00	110.00	575.00
☐ New York	15.00	25.00	110.00	610.00	☐ St. Louis	15.00	25.00	110.00	575.00
☐ Philadelphia	15.00	25.00	110.00	610.00	☐ Minneapolis	15.00	25.00	110.00	575.00
☐ Cleveland	15.00	25.00	110.00	610.00	☐ Kansas City	15.00	25.00	110.00	575.00
☐ Richmond	15.00	25.00	110.00	610.00	☐ Dallas	15.00	25.00	110.00	575.00
☐ Atlanta	15.00	25.00	110.00	610.00	☐ San Francisco	15.00	25.00	110.00	575.00

(Small Size)

SERIES OF 1950A, SIGNATURES OF PRIEST-HUMPHERY,
GREEN SEAL

BANK	A.B.P.	V.FINE	UNC.	★UNC.	BANK	A.B.P.	V.FINE	UNC.	★UNC.
☐ Boston	18.00	30.00	75.00	250.00	☐ Chicago	18.00	30.00	75.00	450.00
☐ New York	12.00	20.00	75.00	250.00	☐ St. Louis	18.00	30.00	75.00	450.00
☐ Philadelphia	18.00	30.00	75.00	250.00	☐ Minneapolis	18.00	30.00	110.00	500.00
☐ Cleveland	18.00	30.00	75.00	330.00	☐ Kansas City	18.00	30.00	75.00	445.00
☐ Richmond	18.00	30.00	75.00	470.00	☐ Dallas	18.00	30.00	75.00	330.00
☐ Atlanta	18.00	30.00	75.00	330.00	☐ San Francisco	18.00	30.00	75.00	330.00

SERIES OF 1950B, SIGNATURES OF PRIEST-ANDERSON, GREEN SEAL

BANK	A.D.P.	V.FINF	UNC.	★UNC.	BANK	A.B.P.	V.FINE	UNC.	★UNC.
☐ Boston	12.00	20.00	65.00	200.00	☐ Chicago	12.00	20.00	65.00	212.00
☐ New York	12.00	20.00	65.00	200.00	☐ St. Louis	12.00	20.00	65.00	212.00
☐ Philadelphia	12.00	20.00	65.00	200.00	☐ Minneapolis	13.80	23.00	65.00	395.00
☐ Cleveland	12.00	20.00	65.00	200.00	☐ Kansas City	13.80	23.00	65.00	212.00
☐ Richmond	12.00	20.00	65.00	200.00	☐ Dallas	13.80	23.00	65.00	420.00
☐ Atlanta	12.00	20.00	65.00	200.00	☐ San Francisco	12.00	20.00	65.00	200.00

SERIES OF 1950C, SIGNATURES OF SMITH-DILLON, GREEN SEAL

BANK	A.B.P.	V.FINE	UNC.	★UNC.	BANK	A.B.P.	V.FINE	UNC.	★UNC.
☐ Boston	12.00	20.00	60.00	375.00	☐ Chicago	12.00	60.00	70.00	375.00
☐ New York	12.00	20.00	60.00	375.00	☐ St. Louis	12.00	60.00	70.00	375.00
☐ Philadelphia	12.00	20.00	60.00	375.00	☐ Minneapolis	15.00	60.00	100.00	375.00
☐ Cleveland	12.00	20.00	60.00	375.00	☐ Kansas City	15.00	60.00	100.00	375.00
☐ Richmond	12.00	20.00	60.00	375.00	☐ Dallas	15.00	60.00	85.00	375.00
☐ Atlanta	12.00	20.00	60.00	375.00	☐ San Francisco	12.00	60.00	85.00	375.00

SERIES OF 1950D, SIGNATURES OF GRANAHAN-DILLON, GREEN SEAL

BANK	A.B.P.	V.FINE	UNC.	★UNC.	BANK	A.B.P.	V.FINE	UNC.	★UNC.
☐ Boston	15.00	25.00	60.00	275.00	☐ Chicago	21.00	35.00	60.00	275.00
☐ New York	15.00	25.00	60.00	275.00	☐ St. Louis	21.00	35.00	60.00	275.00
☐ Philadelphia	15.00	25.00	60.00	275.00	☐ Minneapolis	21.00	35.00	60.00	275.00
☐ Cleveland	15.00	25.00	60.00	275.00	☐ Kansas City	21.00	35.00	60.00	275.00
☐ Richmond	15.00	25.00	60.00	275.00	☐ Dallas	21.00	35.00	60.00	275.00
☐ Atlanta	15.00	25.00	60.00	275.00	☐ San Francisco	21.00	35.00	60.00	275.00

SERIES OF 1950E, SIGNATURES OF GRANAHAN-FOWLER, GREEN SEAL

BANK	A.B.P.	V.FINE	UNC.	★UNC.	BANK	A.B.P.	V.FINE	UNC.	★UNC.
☐ New York	15.00	25.00	100.00	310.00	☐ Chicago	14.00	25.00	95.00	300.00
					☐ San Francisco	14.00	25.00	150.00	555.00

TEN DOLLAR NOTES (1963)
FEDERAL RESERVE NOTES
(IN GOD WE TRUST IS ADDED ON BACK)
SERIES OF 1963, SIGNATURES OF GRANAHAN-DILLON, GREEN SEAL

BANK	A.B.P.	V.FINE	UNC.	★UNC.	BANK	A.B.P.	V.FINE	UNC.	★UNC.
☐ Boston	—	14.00	65.00	165.00	☐ Chicago	—	14.00	65.00	165.00
☐ New York	—	14.00	65.00	165.00	☐ St. Louis	—	14.00	65.00	165.00
☐ Philadelphia	—	14.00	65.00	165.00	☐ Minneapolis	—	14.00	65.00	165.00
☐ Cleveland	—	14.00	65.00	165.00	☐ Kansas City	—	14.00	65.00	165.00
☐ Richmond	—	14.00	65.00	165.00	☐ Dallas	—	14.00	65.00	165.00
☐ Atlanta	—	14.00	65.00	165.00	☐ San Francisco	—	14.00	65.00	165.00

SERIES OF 1963A, SIGNATURES OF GRANAHAN-FOWLER, GREEN SEAL

BANK	A.B.P.	V.FINE	UNC.	★UNC.	BANK	A.B.P.	V.FINE	UNC.	★UNC.
☐ Boston	—	15.00	50.00	175.00	☐ Chicago	—	15.00	50.00	175.00
☐ New York	—	15.00	50.00	175.00	☐ St. Louis	—	15.00	50.00	175.00
☐ Philadelphia	—	15.00	50.00	175.00	☐ Minneapolis	—	15.00	50.00	175.00
☐ Cleveland	—	15.00	50.00	175.00	☐ Kansas City	—	15.00	50.00	175.00
☐ Richmond	—	15.00	50.00	175.00	☐ Dallas	—	15.00	50.00	175.00
☐ Atlanta	—	15.00	50.00	175.00	☐ San Francisco	—	15.00	50.00	175.00

TEN DOLLAR NOTES (1969)
FEDERAL RESERVE NOTES
(WORDING IN GREEN TREASURY SEAL IS CHANGED FROM LATIN TO ENGLISH)

SERIES OF 1969, SIGNATURES OF ELSTON-KENNEDY, GREEN SEAL

BANK	A.B.P.	V.FINE	UNC.	★UNC.	BANK	A.B.P.	V.FINE	UNC.	★UNC.
☐ Boston	—	14.00	50.00	110.00	☐ Chicago	—	14.00	50.00	110.00
☐ New York	—	14.00	50.00	110.00	☐ St. Louis	—	14.00	50.00	110.00
☐ Philadelphia	—	14.00	50.00	110.00	☐ Minneapolis	—	14.00	50.00	110.00
☐ Cleveland	—	14.00	50.00	110.00	☐ Kansas City	—	14.00	50.00	110.00
☐ Richmond	—	14.00	50.00	110.00	☐ Dallas	—	14.00	50.00	110.00
☐ Atlanta	—	14.00	50.00	110.00	☐ San Francisco	—	14.00	50.00	110.00

SERIES OF 1969A, SIGNATURES OF KABIS-CONNALLY, GREEN SEAL

BANK	A.B.P.	V.FINE	UNC.	★UNC.	BANK	A.B.P.	V.FINE	UNC.	★UNC.
☐ Boston	—	14.00	50.00	100.00	☐ Chicago	—	14.00	50.00	100.00
☐ New York	—	14.00	50.00	100.00	☐ St. Louis	—	14.00	50.00	100.00
☐ Philadelphia	—	14.00	50.00	100.00	☐ Minneapolis	—	14.00	50.00	100.00
☐ Cleveland	—	14.00	50.00	100.00	☐ Kansas City	—	14.00	50.00	100.00
☐ Richmond	—	14.00	50.00	100.00	☐ Dallas	—	14.00	50.00	100.00
☐ Atlanta	—	14.00	50.00	100.00	☐ San Francisco	—	14.00	50.00	100.00

SERIES OF 1969B, SIGNATURES OF BANUELOS-CONNALLY, GREEN SEAL

BANK	A.B.P.	V.FINE	UNC.	★UNC.	BANK	A.B.P.	V.FINE	UNC.	★UNC.
☐ Boston	13.20	22.00	185.00	—	☐ Chicago	13.20	22.00	175.00	380.00
☐ New York	13.20	22.00	185.00	360.00	☐ St. Louis	13.20	22.00	175.00	380.00
☐ Philadelphia	13.20	22.00	185.00	—	☐ Minneapolis	13.20	22.00	175.00	—
☐ Cleveland	13.20	22.00	185.00	—	☐ Kansas City	13.20	22.00	175.00	360.00
☐ Richmond	13.20	22.00	185.00	400.00	☐ Dallas	13.20	22.00	175.00	—
☐ Atlanta	13.20	22.00	185.00	360.00	☐ San Francisco	13.20	22.00	175.00	360.00

SERIES OF 1969C, SIGNATURES OF BANUELOS-SHULTZ, GREEN SEAL

BANK	A.B.P.	V.FINE	UNC.	★UNC.	BANK	A.B.P.	V.FINE	UNC.	★UNC.
☐ Boston	—	—	45.00	130.00	☐ Chicago	—	—	45.00	130.00
☐ New York	—	—	45.00	130.00	☐ St. Louis	—	—	45.00	130.00
☐ Philadelphia	—	—	45.00	130.00	☐ Minneapolis	—	—	45.00	130.00
☐ Cleveland	—	—	45.00	130.00	☐ Kansas City	—	—	45.00	130.00
☐ Richmond	—	—	45.00	130.00	☐ Dallas	—	—	45.00	130.00
☐ Atlanta	—	—	45.00	130.00	☐ San Francisco	—	—	45.00	130.00

TEN DOLLAR NOTES (1974)
FEDERAL RESERVE NOTES
SERIES OF 1974, SIGNATURES OF NEFF-SIMON, GREEN SEAL

BANK	A.B.P.	V.FINE	UNC.	★UNC.	BANK	A.B.P.	V.FINE	UNC.	★UNC.
☐ Boston	—	—	35.00	120.00	☐ Chicago	—	—	35.00	125.00
☐ New York	—	—	35.00	120.00	☐ St. Louis	—	—	35.00	125.00
☐ Philadelphia	—	—	35.00	120.00	☐ Minneapolis	—	—	35.00	125.00
☐ Cleveland	—	—	35.00	120.00	☐ Kansas City	—	—	35.00	125.00
☐ Richmond	—	—	35.00	120.00	☐ Dallas	—	—	35.00	125.00
☐ Atlanta	—	—	35.00	120.00	☐ San Francisco	—	—	35.00	125.00

TEN DOLLAR NOTES (1977)
FEDERAL RESERVE NOTES
SERIES OF 1977, SIGNATURES OF MORTON-BLUMENTHAL, GREEN SEAL

BANK	A.B.P.	V.FINE	UNC.	★UNC.	BANK	A.B.P.	V.FINE	UNC.	★UNC.
☐ Boston	—	—	35.00	100.00	☐ Chicago	—	—	35.00	100.00
☐ New York	—	—	35.00	100.00	☐ St. Louis	—	—	35.00	100.00
☐ Philadelphia	—	—	35.00	100.00	☐ Minneapolis	—	—	35.00	100.00
☐ Cleveland	—	—	35.00	100.00	☐ Kansas City	—	—	35.00	100.00
☐ Richmond	—	—	35.00	100.00	☐ Dallas	—	—	35.00	100.00
☐ Atlanta	—	—	35.00	100.00	☐ San Francisco	—	—	35.00	100.00

TEN DOLLAR NOTES (1981)
FEDERAL RESERVE NOTES
SERIES OF 1981, SIGNATURES OF BUCHANAN-REGAN, GREEN SEAL
★Notes not issued for all banks

BANK	A.B.P.	V.FINE	UNC.	★UNC.	BANK	A.B.P.	V.FINE	UNC.	★UNC.
☐ Boston	—	—	30.00	90.00	☐ Chicago	—	—	30.00	90.00
☐ New York	—	—	30.00	90.00	☐ St. Louis	—	—	30.00	90.00
☐ Philadelphia	—	—	30.00	90.00	☐ Minneapolis	—	—	30.00	90.00
☐ Cleveland	—	—	30.00	90.00	☐ Kansas City	—	—	30.00	90.00
☐ Richmond	—	—	30.00	90.00	☐ Dallas	—	—	30.00	90.00
☐ Atlanta	—	—	30.00	90.00	☐ San Francisco	—	—	30.00	90.00

SERIES OF 1981A, SIGNATURES OF ORTEGA-REGAN, GREEN SEAL
★Notes not issued for all banks

BANK	A.B.P.	V.FINE	UNC.	★UNC.	BANK	A.B.P.	V.FINE	UNC.	★UNC.
☐ Boston	—	—	30.00	—	☐ Chicago	—	—	30.00	—
☐ New York	—	—	30.00	180.00	☐ St. Louis	—	—	30.00	—
☐ Philadelphia	—	—	30.00	—	☐ Minneapolis	—	—	30.00	—
☐ Cleveland	—	—	30.00	—	☐ Kansas City	—	—	30.00	—
☐ Richmond	—	—	30.00	—	☐ Dallas	—	—	30.00	—
☐ Atlanta	—	—	30.00	100.00	☐ San Francisco	—	—	28.00	—

TEN DOLLAR NOTES (1985)
FEDERAL RESERVE NOTES
SERIES OF 1985, SIGNATURES OF ORTEGA-BAKER, GREEN SEAL
★Notes not issued for all banks

BANK	A.B.P.	V.FINE	UNC.	★UNC.	BANK	A.B.P.	V.FINE	UNC.	★UNC.
☐ Boston	—	—	28.00	90.00	☐ Chicago	—	—	28.00	—
☐ New York	—	—	28.00	90.00	☐ St. Louis	—	—	28.00	90.00
☐ Philadelphia	—	—	28.00	90.00	☐ Minneapolis	—	—	28.00	90.00
☐ Cleveland	—	—	28.00	90.00	☐ Kansas City	—	—	28.00	90.00
☐ Richmond	—	—	28.00	90.00	☐ Dallas	—	—	28.00	90.00
☐ Atlanta	—	—	28.00	90.00	☐ San Francisco	—	—	28.00	90.00

TEN DOLLAR NOTES (1988)
FEDERAL RESERVE NOTES
SERIES OF 1988A, SIGNATURES OF VILLALPANDO-BRADY, GREEN SEAL
★Notes not issued for all banks

BANK	A.B.P.	V.FINE	UNC.	★UNC.	BANK	A.B.P.	V.FINE	UNC.	★UNC.
☐ Boston	—	—	28.00	165.00	☐ Chicago	—	—	28.00	—
☐ New York	—	—	28.00	165.00	☐ St. Louis	—	—	28.00	—
☐ Philadelphia	—	—	28.00	165.00	☐ Minneapolis	—	—	28.00	—
☐ Cleveland	—	—	28.00	165.00	☐ Kansas City	—	—	28.00	—
☐ Richmond	—	—	28.00	—	☐ Dallas	—	—	28.00	—
☐ Atlanta	—	—	28.00	—	☐ San Francisco	—	—	28.00	165.00

TEN DOLLAR NOTES (1990)
FEDERAL RESERVE NOTES
SERIES OF 1990, SIGNATURES OF VILLALPANDO-BRADY, GREEN SEAL

★Notes not issued for all banks

BANK	A.B.P.	V.FINE	UNC.	★UNC.	BANK	A.B.P.	V.FINE	UNC.	★UNC.
☐ Boston	—	—	20.00	—	☐ Chicago	—		20.00	55.00
☐ New York	—	—	20.00	60.00	☐ St. Louis	—	—	20.00	55.00
☐ Philadelphia	—	—	20.00	60.00	☐ Minneapolis	—	—	20.00	—
☐ Cleveland	—	—	20.00	—	☐ Kansas City	—	—	20.00	—
☐ Richmond	—	—	20.00	—	☐ Dallas	—	—	20.00	—
☐ Atlanta	—	—	20.00	—	☐ San Francisco	—	—	20.00	—

TEN DOLLAR NOTES (1993)
FEDERAL RESERVE NOTES
SERIES OF 1993, SIGNATURES OF WITHROW-BENTSEN, GREEN SEAL

★Notes not issued for all banks

BANK	A.B.P.	V.FINE	UNC.	★UNC.	BANK	A.B.P.	V.FINE	UNC.	★UNC.
☐ Boston	—	—	18.00	—	☐ Chicago	—	—	18.00	50.00
☐ New York	—	—	18.00	50.00	☐ St. Louis	—	—	18.00	
☐ Philadelphia	—	—	18.00	50.00					
☐ Cleveland	—	—	18.00	—	☐ Kansas City	—	—	18.00	—
☐ Atlanta	—	—	18.00	—	☐ San Francisco	—	—	18.00	—

TEN DOLLAR NOTES (1995)
FEDERAL RESERVE NOTES
SERIES OF 1995, SIGNATURES OF WITHROW-RUBIN, GREEN SEAL

★Notes not issued for all banks

BANK	A.B.P.	V.FINE	UNC.	★UNC.	BANK	A.B.P.	V.FINE	UNC.	★UNC.
☐ Boston	—	—	20.00	—	☐ Chicago	—	—	20.00	55.00
☐ New York	—	—	20.00	—	☐ St. Louis	—	—	20.00	55.00
☐ Philadelphia	—	—	20.00	—	☐ Minneapolis	—	—	20.00	55.00
☐ Cleveland	—	—	20.00	55.00	☐ Kansas City	—	—	20.00	55.00
☐ Richmond	—	—	20.00	55.00	☐ Dallas	—	—	20.00	55.00
☐ Atlanta	—	—	20.00	58.00	☐ San Francisco	—	—	20.00	55.00

TEN DOLLAR NOTES (1915–1918)
FEDERAL RESERVE BANK NOTES
(Large Size)

Face Design: Portrait of President Jackson to left, bank and city in center, blue seal to the right.

Back Design: Similar to 1914 note.

BANK	SERIES	GOV'T SIGNATURES	BANK SIGNATURES	A.B.P.	GOOD	V.FINE	UNC.
☐New York	1918	Teehee-Burke	Hendricks-Strong	450.00	775.00	2450.00	RARE
☐Atlanta	1915	Teehee-Burke	Bell-Wellborn	720.00	1200.00	3500.00	RARE
☐Atlanta	1918	Elliott-Burke	Bell-Wellborn	450.00	775.00	2450.00	RARE
☐Chicago	1915	Teehee-Burke	McLallen-McDougal	450.00	775.00	2450.00	RARE
☐Chicago	1918	Teehee-Burke	McCloud-McDougal	450.00	775.00	2450.00	RARE
☐St. Louis	1918	Teehee-Burke	Attebery-Wells	450.00	775.00	2450.00	RARE
☐Kansas City	1915	Teehee-Burke	Anderson-Miller	450.00	775.00	2450.00	RARE

BANK	SERIES	GOV'T SIGNATURES	BANK SIGNATURES	A.B.P.	GOOD	V.FINE	UNC.
☐ Kansas City	1915	Teehee-Burke	Cross-Miller	450.00	750.00	2400.00	RARE
☐ Kansas City	1915	Teehee-Burke	Helm-Miller	300.00	500.00	3500.00	RARE
☐ Dallas	1915	Teehee-Burke	Hoopes-Van Zandt	396.00	660.00	2400.00	RARE
☐ Dallas	1915	Teehee-Burke	Gilbert-Van Zandt	600.00	1000.00	3500.00	RARE
☐ Dallas	1918	Teehee-Burke	Talley-Van Zandt	465.00	775.00	3500.00	RARE

TEN DOLLAR NOTES (1929)
FEDERAL RESERVE BANK NOTES
(Small Size)

Face Design: Portrait of Alexander Hamilton.

Back Design: Same as all Small Size $10 notes.
SIGNATURES OF JONES-WOODS, BROWN SEAL

BANK	SEAL	A.B.P.	GOOD	V.FINE	UNC.	★UNC.
☐ Boston	Brown	15.00	25.00	70.00	325.00	RARE
☐ New York	Brown	15.00	25.00	70.00	325.00	3200.00
☐ Philadelphia	Brown	15.00	25.00	70.00	325.00	4000.00
☐ Cleveland	Brown	15.00	25.00	70.00	325.00	4000.00

BANK	SEAL	A.B.P.	GOOD	V.FINE	UNC.	★UNC.
☐Richmond	Brown	15.00	25.00	65.00	400.00	4200.00
☐Atlanta	Brown	15.00	25.00	65.00	310.00	4500.00
☐Chicago	Brown	15.00	25.00	65.00	350.00	3600.00
☐St. Louis	Brown	15.00	25.00	65.00	375.00	3600.00
☐Minneapolis	Brown	15.00	25.00	65.00	375.00	3600.00
☐Kansas City	Brown	15.00	25.00	65.00	375.00	3600.00
☐Dallas	Brown	240.00	400.00	850.00	2280.00	RARE
☐San Francisco	Brown	15.00	25.00	65.00	1320.00	4500.00

TWENTY DOLLAR NOTES

ORDER OF ISSUE

TWENTY DOLLAR NOTES (1861) DEMAND NOTES
(Large Size)

Face Design: Liberty with sword and shield.

Back Design: Intricate design of numerals, "20." Demand Notes have no Treasury Seal.

SERIES	PAYABLE AT	A.B.P.	GOOD	V.GOOD
☐1861	Boston (I)	RARE	RARE	RARE
☐1861	New York (I)	RARE	RARE	RARE
☐1861	Philadelphia (I)	RARE	RARE	RARE
☐1861	Cincinnati (I)	RARE	RARE	RARE
☐1861	St. Louis (I)	(Unknown in any collection)		
☐1861	Boston (II)	RARE	RARE	RARE
☐1861	New York (II)	RARE	RARE	RARE
☐1861	Philadelphia (II)	RARE	RARE	RARE
☐1861	Cincinnati (II)	RARE	RARE	RARE
☐1861	St. Louis (II)	(Unknown in any collection)		

Counterfeits exist. Use caution in buying.

TWENTY DOLLAR NOTES (1862–1863)
UNITED STATES NOTES
(ALSO KNOWN AS LEGAL TENDER NOTES)
(Large Size)

Face Design: Liberty with sword and shield.

Back Design: Second obligation. This note was also issued with first obligation on the back.

SERIES	SIGNATURES	SEAL	A.B.P.	GOOD	V.FINE	UNC.
☐1862	Chittenden-Spinner*	Red	1100.00	1500.00	RARE	RARE
☐1862	Chittenden-Spinner**	Red	1100.00	1500.00	RARE	RARE
☐1863	Chittenden-Spinner**	Red	1100.00	1500.00	RARE	RARE

* First Obligation: Similar to 1875–1907 $5 note.
** Second Obligation: Shown above.

TWENTY DOLLAR NOTES (1869)
UNITED STATES NOTES
(ALSO KNOWN AS LEGAL TENDER NOTES)
(Large Size)

SERIES	SIGNATURES	SEAL	A.B.P.	GOOD	V.FINE	UNC.
☐1869	Allison-Spinner	Red	—	—	—	RARE
Series Back Design: Revised						
☐1875	Allison-New	Red	285.00	475.00	1500.00	RARE
☐1878	Allison-Gilfillan	Red	231.00	385.00	1275.00	RARE
☐1878	Watermark Paper		351.00	585.00	2000.00	RARE
☐1880	Scofield-Gilfillan	Lg. Brown	600.00	1000.00	3375.00	RARE
☐1880	Bruce-Gilfillan	Lg. Brown	276.00	460.00	2775.00	RARE
☐1880	Bruce-Wyman	Lg. Brown	270.00	450.00	2300.00	RARE
☐1880	Bruce-Wyman	Lg. Red	1236.00	2060.00	2275.00	RARE
☐1880	Rosecrans-Jordan	Lg. Red	189.00	315.00	1200.00	RARE
☐1880	Rosecrans-Hyatt	Red Plain	180.00	300.00	1100.00	RARE
☐1880	Rosecrans-Hyatt	Red Spikes	120.00	225.00	875.00	3060.00
☐1880	Rosecrans-Huston	Lg. Red	120.00	225.00	1000.00	3060.00
☐1880	Rosecrans-Huston	Lg. Brown	120.00	225.00	950.00	3315.00
☐1880	Rosecrans-Nebeker	Lg. Brown	120.00	225.00	2400.00	RARE
☐1800	Rosecrans-Nebeker	Sm. Red	120.00	225.00	675.00	2700.00
☐1880	Tillman-Morgan	Sm. Red	120.00	225.00	675.00	2700.00
☐1880	Bruce-Roberts	Sm. Red	120.00	225.00	675.00	2700.00
☐1880	Lyons-Roberts	Sm. Red	120.00	225.00	700.00	2700.00
☐1880	Vernon-Treat	Sm. Red	120.00	225.00	755.00	2700.00
☐1880	Vernon-McClung	Sm. Red	120.00	225.00	700.00	2700.00
☐1880	Teehee-Burke	Sm. Red	120.00	225.00	700.00	2700.00
☐1880	Elliott-White	Sm. Red	120.00	225.00	625.00	2700.00

TWENTY DOLLAR NOTES (1863–1875)
NATIONAL BANK NOTES
FIRST CHARTER PERIOD (Large Size)

Face Design: Battle of Lexington left, name of bank in center. Columbia with flag right.

Back Design: Green border, black center picture of baptism of Pocahontas.

SERIES	SIGNATURES	SEAL	A.B.P.	GOOD	V.FINE	UNC.
☐Original	Chittenden-Spinner	Red	495.00	850.00	3800.00	RARE
☐Original	Colby-Spinner	Red	495.00	850.00	3800.00	RARE
☐Original	Jeffries-Spinner	Red	591.00	850.00	3800.00	RARE
☐Original	Allison-Spinner	Red	495.00	850.00	3800.00	RARE
☐1875	Allison-New	Red	495.00	850.00	3800.00	RARE
☐1875	Allison-Wyman	Red	495.00	850.00	3800.00	RARE
☐1875	Allison-Gilfillan	Red	495.00	850.00	3800.00	RARE
☐1875	Scofield-Gilfillan	Red	495.00	850.00	3800.00	RARE
☐1875	Bruce-Gilfillan	Red	495.00	850.00	3800.00	RARE
☐1875	Bruce-Wyman	Red	495.00	850.00	3800.00	RARE
☐1875	Rosecrans-Huston	Red	495.00	850.00	3800.00	RARE
☐1875	Rosecrans-Nebeker	Red	495.00	850.00	3800.00	RARE
☐1875	Tillman-Morgan	Red	495.00	850.00	3800.00	RARE

TWENTY DOLLAR NOTES (1882)
NATIONAL BANK NOTES
SECOND CHARTER PERIOD (Large Size)

First Issue (Brown seal and brown backs.)
Face Design: Similar to First Charter Period note.
Back Design: Similar to 1882 $5 note. Border is brown, green Charter Number in center.

SERIES	SIGNATURES	SEAL	A.B.P.	GOOD	V.FINE	UNC.
☐1882	Bruce-Gilfillan	Brown	420.00	700.00	1775.00	3780.00
☐1882	Bruce-Wyman	Brown	420.00	700.00	1775.00	3780.00
☐1882	Bruce-Jordan	Brown	420.00	700.00	1775.00	3780.00
☐1882	Rosecrans-Jordan	Brown	420.00	700.00	1775.00	3780.00
☐1882	Rosecrans-Hyatt	Brown	420.00	700.00	1775.00	3780.00
☐1882	Rosecrans-Huston	Brown	420.00	700.00	1775.00	3780.00
☐1882	Rosecrans-Nebeker	Brown	420.00	700.00	1775.00	3780.00
☐1882	Rosecrans-Morgan	Brown	456.00	760.00	1775.00	4500.00
☐1882	Tillman-Morgan	Brown	420.00	700.00	1775.00	3600.00
☐1882	Tillman-Roberts	Brown	420.00	700.00	1775.00	3600.00
☐1882	Bruce-Roberts	Brown	420.00	700.00	1775.00	3600.00
☐1882	Lyons-Roberts	Brown	420.00	700.00	1775.00	3600.00
☐1882	Lyons-Treat	Brown	420.00	700.00	1775.00	4000.00
☐1882	Vernon-Treat	Brown	420.00	700.00	1775.00	4000.00

SECOND CHARTER PERIOD, Second Issue

Face Design: Similar to First Charter Period note.
Back Design: Similar to 1882 $5.00 Second Issue note.

SERIES	SIGNATURES	SEAL	A.B.P.	GOOD	V.FINE	UNC.
☐1882	Rosecrans-Huston	Blue	360.00	600.00	1625.00	3500.00
☐1882	Rosecrans-Nebeker	Blue	360.00	600.00	1625.00	3500.00
☐1882	Rosecrans-Morgan	Blue	459.00	765.00	2000.00	4500.00
☐1882	Tillman-Morgan	Blue	360.00	600.00	1625.00	3500.00
☐1882	Tillman-Roberts	Blue	360.00	600.00	1625.00	3500.00
☐1882	Bruce-Roberts	Blue	360.00	600.00	1625.00	3500.00
☐1882	Lyons-Roberts	Blue	360.00	600.00	1625.00	3500.00
☐1882	Vernon-Treat	Blue	360.00	600.00	1625.00	3500.00
☐1882	Napier-McClung	Blue	360.00	600.00	1625.00	3500.00

SECOND CHARTER PERIOD, Third Issue (Large Size)

Face Design: Similar to First Charter Period note with blue seal.
Back Design: Similar to 1882 Third Issue note, green back, value in block letters.

SERIES	SIGNATURES	SEAL	A.B.P.	GOOD	V.FINE	UNC.
☐1882	Tillman-Morgan	Blue	540.00	900.00	1850.00	RARE
☐1882	Lyons-Roberts	Blue	480.00	800.00	1850.00	RARE
☐1882	Lyons-Treat	Blue	540.00	900.00	1850.00	RARE
☐1882	Vernon-Treat	Blue	540.00	900.00	1850.00	RARE
☐1882	Napier-McClung	Blue	540.00	900.00	1850.00	RARE
☐1882	Teehee-Burke	Blue	540.00	900.00	1850.00	RARE

TWENTY DOLLAR NOTES (1902)
NATIONAL BANK NOTES
THIRD CHARTER PERIOD, First Issue (Large Size)

Face Design: Portrait of McCulloch left, name of bank center, Treasury Seal right.

SERIES	SIGNATURES	SEAL	A.B.P.	GOOD	V.FINE	UNC.
☐1902	Lyons-Roberts	Red	560.00	550.00	1600.00	4200.00
☐1902	Lyons-Treat	Red	560.00	550.00	1600.00	4200.00
☐1902	Vernon-Treat	Red	560.00	550.00	1600.00	4200.00

Second Issue (Date "1902–1908" added on back, Treasury Seal and serial numbers blue)

☐1902	Lyons-Roberts	Blue	75.00	125.00	325.00	950.00
☐1902	Lyons-Treat	Blue	75.00	125.00	325.00	950.00
☐1902	Vernon-Treat	Blue	75.00	125.00	325.00	950.00
☐1902	Vernon-McClung	Blue	75.00	125.00	325.00	950.00
☐1902	Napier-McClung	Blue	75.00	125.00	325.00	950.00
☐1902	Napier-Thompson	Blue	75.00	125.00	325.00	950.00
☐1902	Napier-Burke	Blue	75.00	125.00	325.00	950.00
☐1902	Parker-Burke	Blue	75.00	125.00	325.00	950.00

Third Issue (Date "1902–1908" removed from back, seal and serial numbers blue)

☐1902	Lyons-Roberts	Blue	75.00	125.00	250.00	900.00
☐1902	Lyons-Treat	Blue	75.00	125.00	250.00	900.00
☐1902	Vernon-Treat	Blue	75.00	125.00	250.00	900.00
☐1902	Vernon-McClung	Blue	75.00	125.00	250.00	900.00

SERIES	SIGNATURES	SEAL	A.B.P.	GOOD	V.FINE	UNC.
☐1902	Napier-McClung	Blue	60.00	100.00	275.00	925.00
☐1902	Napier-Thompson	Blue	60.00	100.00	275.00	925.00
☐1902	Napier-Burke	Blue	60.00	100.00	275.00	925.00
☐1902	Parker-Burke	Blue	60.00	100.00	275.00	925.00
☐1902	Teehee-Burke	Blue	60.00	100.00	275.00	925.00
☐1902	Elliott-Burke	Blue	60.00	100.00	275.00	925.00
☐1902	Elliott-White	Blue	60.00	100.00	275.00	925.00
☐1902	Speelman-White	Blue	60.00	100.00	275.00	925.00
☐1902	Woods-White	Blue	60.00	100.00	275.00	925.00
☐1902	Woods-Tate	Blue	60.00	100.00	325.00	1225.00
☐1902	Jones-Woods	Blue	390.00	650.00	1500.00	RARE

TWENTY DOLLAR NOTES (1929)
NATIONAL BANK NOTES

(Small Size)

Face Design, Type I: Portrait of President Jackson in center, name of bank to left, brown seal right. Charter number in black.

Face Design, Type II.

Back Design: The White House, similar to all $20 Small Notes.

SERIES	SIGNATURES	SEAL	A.B.P.	GOOD	V.FINE	UNC.
☐1929, Type I	Jones-Woods	Brown	48.00	80.00	200.00	525.00
☐1929, Type II	Jones-Woods	Brown	48.00	80.00	200.00	525.00

TWENTY DOLLAR NOTES (1880)
SILVER CERTIFICATES

(Large Size)

Face Design: Portrait of Stephen Decatur right. TWENTY SILVER DOLLARS in center.

Back Design: SILVER in large block letters.

SERIES	SIGNATURES	SEAL	A.B.P.	GOOD	V.FINE	UNC.
☐ 1880	Scofield-Gilfillan	Brown	—	—	—	RARE
☐ 1880	Bruce-Gilfillan	Brown	—	—	—	RARE
☐ 1880	Bruce-Wyman	Brown	—	—	—	RARE
☐ 1880	Bruce-Wyman	Sm. Red	—	—	—	RARE

This note was also issued in the Series of 1878. They are very rare.

TWENTY DOLLAR NOTES (1886)
SILVER CERTIFICATES

(Large Size)

Face Design: Portrait of Daniel Manning center, Agriculture left, Industry right.

Back Design: Double-diamond design center.

SERIES	SIGNATURES	SEAL	A.B.P.	GOOD	V.FINE	UNC.
☐ 1886	Rosecrans-Hyatt	Lg. Red	1500.00	2500.00	RARE	RARE
☐ 1886	Rosecrans-Huston	Lg. Brown	1500.00	2500.00	RARE	RARE
☐ 1886	Rosecrans-Nebeker	Lg. Brown	1500.00	2500.00	RARE	RARE
☐ 1886	Rosecrans-Nebeker	Sm. Red	900.00	1500.00	RARE	RARE

TWENTY DOLLAR NOTES (1891)
SILVER CERTIFICATES
(NOT ISSUED IN SMALL SIZE NOTES)
(Large Size)

Face Design: Same as 1886 note.

Back Design: Revised.

SERIES	SIGNATURES	SEAL	A.B.P.	GOOD	V.FINE	UNC.
☐1891	Rosecrans-Nebeker	Red	375.00	625.00	2250.00	RARE
☐1891	Tillman-Morgan	Red	375.00	625.00	2250.00	RARE
☐1891	Bruce-Roberts	Red	375.00	625.00	2250.00	RARE
☐1891	Lyons-Roberts	Red	375.00	625.00	2250.00	RARE
☐1891	Parker-Burke	Blue	375.00	625.00	2250.00	RARE
☐1891	Teehee-Burke	Blue	375.00	625.00	2250.00	RARE

TWENTY DOLLAR NOTES (1882) GOLD CERTIFICATES
(Large Size)

Face Design: Portrait of President Garfield right, TWENTY DOLLARS IN GOLD COIN center.

Back Design: Large "20" left, eagle and arrows center, bright orange color.

SERIES	SIGNATURES	SEAL	A.B.P.	GOOD	V.FINE	UNC.
☐1882*	Bruce-Gilfillan	Brown	—	—	—	RARE
☐1882	Bruce-Gilfillan	Brown	—	—	—	RARE
☐1882	Bruce-Wyman	Brown	1320.00	2200.00	—	RARE
☐1882	Rosecrans-Huston	Brown	1710.00	2850.00	—	RARE
☐1882	Lyons-Roberts	Red	270.00	450.00	2500.00	6000.00

*This note has a countersigned signature.

TWENTY DOLLAR NOTES (1905) GOLD CERTIFICATES
(Large Size)

Face Design: Portrait of President Washington center, "XX"
left, Treasury Seal right.

Back Design: Eagle and shield center, printed in bright
orange color.

SERIES	SIGNATURES	SEAL	A.B.P.	GOOD	V.FINE	UNC.
☐1905	Lyons-Roberts	Red	270.00	450.00	3500.00	RARE
☐1905	Lyons-Treat	Red	270.00	450.00	3500.00	RARE
☐1906	Vernon-Treat	Gold	95.00	160.00	675.00	3215.00
☐1906	Vernon-McClung	Gold	95.00	160.00	675.00	3215.00
☐1906	Napier-McClung	Gold	95.00	160.00	675.00	3215.00
☐1906	Napier-Thompson	Gold	105.00	175.00	800.00	3215.00
☐1906	Parker-Burke	Gold	95.00	160.00	675.00	3215.00
☐1906	Tehee-Burke	Gold	95.00	160.00	675.00	3215.00
☐1922	Speelman-White	Gold	95.00	160.00	675.00	2550.00

TWENTY DOLLAR NOTES (1928) GOLD CERTIFICATES
(Small Size)

Face Design: Portrait of President Jackson center, gold
seal left, gold serial numbers.

Back Design: The White House, printed green, similar to all
Small Size $20 Notes.

SERIES	SIGNATURES	SEAL	A.B.P.	V.FINE	UNC.
☐1928	Woods-Mellon	Gold	180.00	300.00	1150.00

TWENTY DOLLAR NOTES (1890) TREASURY NOTES
(Large Size)

Face Design: Portrait of John Marshall, Supreme Court
Chief Justice, left, "20" center.

Back Design

SERIES	SIGNATURES	SEAL	A.B.P.	GOOD	V.FINE	UNC.
☐1890	Rosecrans-Huston	Brown	1200.00	2000.00	RARE	RARE
☐1890	Rosecrans-Nebeker	Brown	1200.00	2000.00	RARE	RARE
☐1890	Rosecrans-Nebeker	Red	1200.00	2000.00	RARE	RARE

(Large Size)

**Back
Design**

Face Design: Same as previous note.

SERIES	SIGNATURES	SEAL	A.B.P.	GOOD	V.FINE	UNC.
☐1891	Tillman-Morgan	Red	1200.00	2000.00	RARE	RARE
☐1891	Bruce-Roberts	Red	1200.00	2000.00	RARE	RARE

TWENTY DOLLAR NOTES (1914)
FEDERAL RESERVE NOTES

(Large Size)
Face Design: Portrait of President Cleveland center,
Federal Reserve Seal left, Treasury Seal right.

Back Design: Scenes of transportation. Locomotive left, steamship right.

(Small Size)

SERIES OF 1914, SIGNATURES OF BURKE-McADOO, RED TREASURY SEAL

BANK	A.B.P.	V.FINE	UNC.	BANK	A.B.P.	V.FINE	UNC.
☐ Boston	420.00	1000.00	2800.00	☐ Chicago	150.00	1200.00	RARE
☐ New York	420.00	700.00	2550.00	☐ St. Louis	150.00	1200.00	RARE
☐ Philadelphia	870.00	1450.00	RARE	☐ Minneapolis	150.00	1650.00	RARE
☐ Cleveland	870.00	1650.00	RARE	☐ Kansas City	150.00	1650.00	RARE
☐ Richmond	870.00	1650.00	RARE	☐ Dallas	150.00	1650.00	RARE
☐ Atlanta	870.00	1650.00	RARE	☐ San Francisco	150.00	1650.00	RARE

SERIES OF 1914, BLUE TREASURY SEAL AND BLUE SERIAL NUMBERS

(Small Size)

This note was issued with signatures of Burke-McAdoo, Burke-Glass, Burke-Huston, and White-Mellon.

TWENTY DOLLAR NOTES (1914)
FEDERAL RESERVE NOTES
1914, BLUE TREASURY SEAL AND BLUE NUMBERS

DATE	CITY	SIGNATURES	SEAL	A.B.P.	GOOD	V.FINE	UNC.
1914	Boston	Burke-McAdoo	Blue	33.00	55.00	250.00	710.00
1914	Boston	Burke-Glass	Blue	36.00	60.00	250.00	2040.00
1914	Boston	Burke-Huston	Blue	33.00	55.00	250.00	1000.00
1914	Boston	White-Mellon	Blue	33.00	55.00	250.00	1000.00
1914	New York	Burke-McAdoo	Blue	33.00	55.00	250.00	1000.00
1914	New York	Burke-Glass	Blue	33.00	55.00	250.00	1000.00
1914	New York	Burke-Huston	Blue	33.00	55.00	250.00	1000.00
1914	New York	White-Mellon	Blue	33.00	55.00	250.00	710.00
1914	Phila.	Burke-McAdoo	Blue	31.20	52.00	250.00	735.00
1914	Phila.	Burke-Glass	Blue	33.00	55.00	735.00	1685.00
1914	Phila.	Burke-Huston	Blue	33.00	55.00	210.00	640.00
1914	Phila.	White-Mellon	Blue	33.00	55.00	210.00	640.00
1914	Cleveland	Burke-McAdoo	Blue	33.00	55.00	210.00	660.00

DATE	CITY	SIGNATURES	SEAL	A.B.P.	GOOD	V.FINE	UNC.
1914	Cleveland	Burke-Glass	Blue	36.00	60.00	580.00	1300.00
1914	Cleveland	Burke-Huston	Blue	36.00	55.00	360.00	1300.00
1914	Cleveland	White-Mellon	Blue	33.00	55.00	225.00	735.00
1914	Richmond	Burke-McAdoo	Blue	33.00	60.00	500.00	1360.00
1914	Richmond	Burke-Glass	Blue	36.00	60.00	680.00	1360.00
1914	Richmond	Burke-Huston	Blue	34.20	57.00	225.00	1008.00
1914	Richmond	White-Mellon	Blue	33.00	55.00	225.00	580.00
1914	Atlanta	Burke-McAdoo	Blue	33.00	55.00	245.00	1000.00
1914	Atlanta	Burke-Glass	Blue	120.00	200.00	960.00	2040.00
1914	Atlanta	Burke-Huston	Blue	33.00	55.00	200.00	630.00
1914	Atlanta	White-Mellon	Blue	36.00	60.00	580.00	1200.00
1914	Chicago	Burke-McAdoo	Blue	33.00	55.00	175.00	650.00
1914	Chicago	Burke-Glass	Blue	33.00	55.00	200.00	650.00
1914	Chicago	Burke-Huston	Blue	33.00	55.00	250.00	630.00
1914	Chicago	White-Mellon	Blue	33.00	55.00	250.00	630.00
1914	St. Louis	Burke-McAdoo	Blue	33.00	55.00	250.00	630.00
1914	St. Louis	Burke-Glass	Blue	36.00	60.00	580.00	1275.00
1914	St. Louis	Burke-Huston	Blue	33.00	55.00	175.00	650.00
1914	St. Louis	White-Mellon	Blue	33.00	55.00	240.00	650.00
1914	Minneapolis	Burke-McAdoo	Blue	33.00	55.00	210.00	630.00
1914	Minneapolis	Burke-Glass	Blue	45.00	75.00	875.00	2040.00
1914	Minneapolis	Burke-Huston	Blue	36.00	55.00	250.00	625.00
1914	Minneapolis	White-Mellon	Blue	36.00	55.00	210.00	625.00
1914	Kansas City	Burke-McAdoo	Blue	36.00	55.00	340.00	625.00
1914	Kansas City	Burke-Glass	Blue	45.00	75.00	160.00	610.00
1914	Kansas City	Burke-Huston	Blue	33.00	55.00	210.00	615.00
1914	Kansas City	White-Mellon	Blue	36.00	60.00	580.00	1010.00
1914	Dallas	Burke-McAdoo	Blue	33.00	55.00	640.00	1010.00
1914	Dallas	Burke-Glass	Blue	36.00	60.00	725.00	1660.00
1914	Dallas	Burke-Huston	Blue	33.00	55.00	450.00	815.00
1914	Dallas	White-Mellon	Blue	33.00	55.00	210.00	815.00
1914	San Fran.	Burke-McAdoo	Blue	33.00	55.00	365.00	815.00
1914	San Fran.	Burke-Glass	Blue	33.00	55.00	475.00	765.00
1914	San Fran.	Burke-Huston	Blue	33.00	55.00	240.00	695.00
1914	San Fran.	White-Mellon	Blue	33.00	55.00	155.00	615.00

TWENTY DOLLAR NOTES (1928)
FEDERAL RESERVE NOTES
(Small Size)

Face Design: Portrait of President Jackson center, black Federal Reserve Seal with numeral for district in center. City of issuing bank in Seal circle. Green Treasury Seal right.

Back Design: Picture of the White House, similar to all Small Size $20 Notes.
(Small Size)
SERIES OF 1928, SIGNATURES OF TATE-MELLON, GREEN SEAL

BANK	A.B.P.	V.FINE	UNC.	★UNC.	BANK	A.B.P.	V.FINE	UNC.	★UNC.
☐ Boston	33.00	55.00	295.00	2245.00	☐ Chicago	30.00	50.00	325.00	2244.00
☐ New York	27.00	45.00	230.00	1685.00	☐ St. Louis	33.00	55.00	325.00	2910.00
☐ Philadelphia	33.00	55.00	320.00	2040.00	☐ Minneapolis	33.00	55.00	450.00	2910.00
☐ Cleveland	45.00	75.00	310.00	1836.00	☐ Kansas City	51.00	85.00	295.00	2244.00
☐ Richmond	45.00	75.00	320.00	3215.00	☐ Dallas	51.00	85.00	380.00	7500.00
☐ Atlanta	39.00	65.00	380.00	3060.00	☐ San Francisco	51.00	85.00	340.00	2450.00

(Small Size)

SERIES OF 1928A,
SIGNATURES OF WOODS-MELLON, GREEN SEAL

CITY	A.B.P.	V.FINE	UNC.	★UNC.	CITY	A.B.P.	V.FINE	UNC.	★UNC.
☐ Boston	39.00	65.00	400.00	4300.00	☐ Chicago	48.00	80.00	500.00	RARE
☐ New York	39.00	65.00	350.00	4375.00	☐ St. Louis	48.00	80.00	500.00	RARE
☐ Philadelphia	42.00	70.00	350.00	4375.00	☐ Minneapolis		NOT ISSUED		
☐ Cleveland	45.00	75.00	350.00	4375.00	☐ Kansas City	51.00	85.00	700.00	RARE
☐ Richmond	33.00	55.00	340.00	4450.00	☐ Dallas	45.00	75.00	550.00	RARE
☐ Atlanta	39.00	65.00	340.00	4450.00	☐ San Francisco		NOT ISSUED		

TWENTY DOLLAR NOTES (1928)
FEDERAL RESERVE NOTES

(Small Size)

SERIES OF 1928B,
SIGNATURES OF WOODS-MELLON, GREEN SEAL
The face and back design are similar to previous note. Numeral in Federal Reserve Seal is now changed to a letter.

BANK	A.B.P.	V.FINE	UNC.	★UNC.	BANK	A.B.P.	V.FINE	UNC.	★UNC.
☐ Boston	28.80	48.00	240.00	1200.00	☐ Chicago	24.00	40.00	250.00	1500.00
☐ New York	28.80	48.00	240.00	1200.00	☐ St. Louis	31.20	52.00	250.00	1500.00
☐ Philadelphia	28.80	48.00	240.00	1200.00	☐ Minneapolis	31.20	52.00	250.00	1500.00
☐ Cleveland	22.20	32.00	240.00	1200.00	☐ Kansas City	22.20	37.00	250.00	1500.00
☐ Richmond	22.20	37.00	240.00	1200.00	☐ Dallas	42.00	70.00	250.00	1500.00
☐ Atlanta	22.20	22.00	240.00	1200.00	☐ San Francisco	27.50	37.00	250.00	1500.00

SERIES OF 1928C, SIGNATURES OF WOODS-MILLS, GREEN SEAL
Only two banks issued this note.

BANK	A.B.P.	V.FINE	UNC.	★UNC.	BANK	A.B.P.	V.FINE	UNC.	★UNC.
☐ Chicago	495.00	825.00	2000.00	—	☐ San Francisco	840.00	1400.00	RARE	—

TWENTY DOLLAR NOTES (1934)
FEDERAL RESERVE NOTES

(Small Size)

SIGNATURES OF JULIAN-MORGENTHAU, GREEN SEAL
Face and back design are similar to previous note. "Redeemable in Gold" removed from obligation over Federal Reserve Seal.

BANK	A.B.P.	V.FINE	UNC.	★UNC.	BANK	A.B.P.	V.FINE	UNC.	★UNC.
☐ Boston	21.30	35.50	100.00	650.00	☐ St. Louis	23.10	38.50	100.00	700.00
☐ New York	21.30	35.50	100.00	650.00	☐ Minneapolis	23.10	38.50	100.00	700.00
☐ Philadelphia	21.30	35.50	100.00	650.00	☐ Kansas City	23.10	38.50	100.00	700.00
☐ Cleveland	21.30	35.50	100.00	650.00	☐ Dallas	23.10	38.50	100.00	700.00
☐ Richmond	21.30	35.50	100.00	650.00	☐ San Francisco	23.10	38.50	100.00	700.00
☐ Atlanta	21.30	35.50	100.00	650.00	☐ San Francisco*				
☐ Chicago	21.30	35.50	100.00	650.00	(HAWAII)	37.00	150.00	2500.00	12000.00

* The San Francisco Federal Reserve Note with brown seal and brown serial numbers, and overprinted HAWAII on face and back, was a special issue for the armed forces in the Pacific area during World War II.

TWENTY DOLLAR NOTES (1934A)
FEDERAL RESERVE NOTES

(Small Size)

SERIES OF 1934A, SIGNATURES OF JULIAN-MORGENTHAU

BANK	A.B.P.	V.FINE	UNC.	★UNC.	BANK	A.B.P.	V.FINE	UNC.	★UNC.
☐ Boston	22.00	30.00	75.00	550.00	☐ St. Louis	22.80	38.00	70.00	600.00
☐ New York	22.00	30.00	80.00	550.00	☐ Minneapolis	28.50	48.00	75.00	600.00
☐ Philadelphia	22.00	30.00	80.00	550.00	☐ Kansas City	22.80	38.00	75.00	600.00
☐ Cleveland	22.00	30.00	70.00	550.00	☐ Dallas	22.80	38.00	80.00	600.00
☐ Richmond	22.00	30.00	75.00	550.00	☐ San Francisco	22.00	30.00	80.00	600.00
☐ Atlanta	22.00	30.00	70.00	550.00	☐ San Francisco*				
☐ Chicago	22.00	30.00	75.00	550.00	(HAWAII)	28.00	75.00	1500.00	10000.00

* The San Francisco Federal Reserve Note with brown seal and brown serial numbers, and overprinted HAWAII on face and back, was a special issue for the armed forces in the Pacific area during World War II.

(Small Size)

SERIES OF 1934B,
SIGNATURES OF JULIAN-VINSON, GREEN SEAL

BANK	A.B.P.	V.FINE	UNC.	★UNC.	BANK	A.B.P.	V.FINE	UNC.	★UNC.
☐ Boston	25.00	32.50	100.00	1025.00	☐ Chicago	25.00	32.50	100.00	1250.00
☐ New York	25.00	32.50	100.00	1025.00	☐ St. Louis	25.00	32.50	100.00	1250.00
☐ Philadelphia	25.00	32.50	100.00	1025.00	☐ Minneapolis	25.00	32.50	100.00	1250.00
☐ Cleveland	25.00	32.50	100.00	1025.00	☐ Kansas City	25.00	32.50	100.00	1250.00
☐ Richmond	25.00	32.50	100.00	1025.00	☐ Dallas	25.00	32.50	100.00	1250.00
☐ Atlanta	25.00	32.50	100.00	1025.00	☐ San Francisco	25.00	32.50	100.00	1250.00

SERIES OF 1934C,
SIGNATURES OF JULIAN-SNYDER, GREEN SEAL

Back Design: This has been modified with this series, with or without balcony added to the White House.

BANK	A.B.P.	V.FINE	UNC.	★UNC.	BANK	A.B.P.	V.FINE	UNC.	★UNC.
☐ Boston	22.00	32.50	100.00	775.00	☐ Chicago	22.00	32.50	100.00	675.00
☐ New York	22.00	32.50	100.00	775.00	☐ St. Louis	22.00	32.50	100.00	675.00
☐ Philadelphia	22.00	32.50	100.00	775.00	☐ Minneapolis	22.00	32.50	100.00	675.00
☐ Cleveland	22.00	32.50	100.00	775.00	☐ Kansas City	22.00	32.50	100.00	675.00
☐ Richmond	22.00	32.50	100.00	775.00	☐ Dallas	22.00	32.50	100.00	675.00
☐ Atlanta	22.00	32.50	100.00	775.00	☐ San Francisco	22.00	32.50	100.00	675.00

SERIES OF 1934D,
SIGNATURES OF CLARK-SNYDER, GREEN SEAL

BANK	A.B.P.	V.FINE	UNC.	★UNC.	BANK	A.B.P.	V.FINE	UNC.	★UNC.
☐ Boston	22.00	30.00	100.00	850.00	☐ Chicago	22.00	30.00	100.00	775.00
☐ New York	22.00	30.00	100.00	650.00	☐ St. Louis	22.00	30.00	100.00	775.00
☐ Philadelphia	22.00	30.00	100.00	650.00	☐ Minneapolis	22.00	30.00	100.00	925.00
☐ Cleveland	22.00	30.00	100.00	850.00	☐ Kansas City	22.00	30.00	100.00	925.00
☐ Richmond	22.00	30.00	100.00	650.00	☐ Dallas	22.00	30.00	100.00	925.00
☐ Atlanta	22.00	30.00	100.00	850.00	☐ San Francisco	22.00	30.00	100.00	775.00

TWENTY DOLLAR NOTES (1950)
FEDERAL RESERVE NOTES

(Small Size)

SERIES OF 1950,
SIGNATURES OF CLARK-SNYDER, GREEN SEAL

The black Federal Seal and green Treasury Seal are slightly smaller.

BANK	A.B.P.	V.FINE	UNC.	★UNC.	BANK	A.B.P.	V.FINE	UNC.	★UNC.
☐ Boston	22.00	30.00	110.00	550.00	☐ Chicago	22.00	30.00	110.00	550.00
☐ New York	22.00	30.00	110.00	550.00	☐ St. Louis	22.00	30.00	110.00	550.00
☐ Philadelphia	22.00	30.00	110.00	550.00	☐ Minneapolis	22.00	30.00	110.00	550.00
☐ Cleveland	22.00	30.00	110.00	550.00	☐ Kansas City	22.00	30.00	110.00	550.00

BANK	A.B.P.	V.FINE	UNC.	★UNC.	BANK	A.B.P.	V.FINE	UNC.	★UNC.
☐ Richmond	22.00	30.00	110.00	550.00	☐ Dallas	26.00	30.00	110.00	550.00
☐ Atlanta	22.00	30.00	110.00	550.00	☐ San Francisco	26.00	30.00	110.00	550.00

SERIES OF 1950A, SIGNATURES OF PRIEST-HUMPHERY, GREEN SEAL

BANK	A.B.P.	V.FINE	UNC.	★UNC.	BANK	A.B.P.	V.FINE	UNC.	★UNC.
☐ Boston	22.00	25.00	100.00	275.00	☐ Chicago	22.00	25.00	100.00	275.00
☐ New York	22.00	25.00	100.00	275.00	☐ St. Louis	22.00	25.00	100.00	275.00
☐ Philadelphia	22.00	25.00	100.00	275.00	☐ Minneapolis	22.00	25.00	100.00	275.00
☐ Cleveland	22.00	25.00	100.00	275.00	☐ Kansas City	22.00	25.00	100.00	275.00
☐ Richmond	22.00	25.00	100.00	370.00	☐ Dallas	22.00	25.00	100.00	275.00
☐ Atlanta	22.00	25.00	100.00	265.00	☐ San Francisco	22.00	25.00	100.00	275.00

SERIES OF 1950B, SIGNATURES OF PRIEST-ANDERSON, GREEN SEAL

BANK	A.B.P.	V.FINE	UNC.	★UNC.	BANK	A.B.P.	V.FINE	UNC.	★UNC.
☐ Boston	22.00	25.00	85.00	375.00	☐ Chicago	22.00	25.00	85.00	375.00
☐ New York	22.00	25.00	85.00	375.00	☐ St. Louis	22.00	25.00	85.00	375.00
☐ Philadelphia	22.00	25.00	85.00	375.00	☐ Minneapolis	22.00	25.00	85.00	375.00
☐ Cleveland	22.00	25.00	85.00	375.00	☐ Kansas City	22.00	25.00	85.00	375.00
☐ Richmond	22.00	25.00	85.00	375.00	☐ Dallas	22.00	25.00	85.00	375.00
☐ Atlanta	22.00	25.00	85.00	375.00	☐ San Francisco	22.00	25.00	85.00	375.00

SERIES OF 1950C, SIGNATURES OF SMITH-DILLON, GREEN SEAL

BANK	A.B.P.	V.FINE	UNC.	★UNC.	BANK	A.B.P.	V.FINE	UNC.	★UNC.
☐ Boston	22.00	25.00	85.00	475.00	☐ Chicago	22.00	25.00	85.00	475.00
☐ New York	22.00	25.00	85.00	475.00	☐ St. Louis	22.00	25.00	85.00	475.00
☐ Philadelphia	22.00	25.00	85.00	475.00	☐ Minneapolis	22.00	25.00	85.00	475.00
☐ Cleveland	22.00	25.00	85.00	475.00	☐ Kansas City	22.00	25.00	85.00	475.00
☐ Richmond	22.00	25.00	85.00	475.00	☐ Dallas	22.00	25.00	85.00	475.00
☐ Atlanta	22.00	25.00	85.00	475.00	☐ San Francisco	22.00	25.00	85.00	475.00

SERIES OF 1950D, SIGNATURES OF GRANAHAN-DILLON, GREEN SEAL

BANK	A.B.P.	V.FINE	UNC.	★UNC.	BANK	A.B.P.	V.FINE	UNC.	★UNC.
☐ Boston	22.00	28.50	85.00	350.00	☐ Chicago	22.00	28.50	85.00	350.00
☐ New York	22.00	28.50	85.00	350.00	☐ St. Louis	22.00	28.50	85.00	350.00
☐ Philadelphia	22.00	28.50	85.00	350.00	☐ Minneapolis	22.00	28.50	85.00	350.00
☐ Cleveland	22.00	28.50	85.00	350.00	☐ Kansas City	22.00	28.50	85.00	350.00
☐ Richmond	22.00	28.50	85.00	350.00	☐ Dallas	22.00	28.50	85.00	350.00
☐ Atlanta	22.00	28.50	85.00	350.00	☐ San Francisco	22.00	28.50	85.00	350.00

SERIES OF 1950E, SIGNATURES OF GRANAHAN-FOWLER, GREEN SEAL

BANK	A.B.P.	V.FINE	UNC.	★UNC.	BANK	A.B.P.	V.FINE	UNC.	★UNC.
☐ Boston	22.00	30.00	250.00	840.00	☐ Chicago	22.00	25.00	250.00	900.00
					☐ San Francisco	22.00	25.00	250.00	900.00

TWENTY DOLLAR NOTES (1963)
FEDERAL RESERVE NOTES
SERIES OF 1963, SIGNATURES OF GRANAHAN-FOWLER, GREEN SEAL

BANK	A.B.P.	V.FINE	UNC.	★UNC.	BANK	A.B.P.	V.FINE	UNC.	★UNC.
☐ Boston	22.00	25.00	110.00	200.00	☐ Chicago	22.00	25.00	110.00	200.00
☐ New York	22.00	25.00	110.00	200.00	☐ St. Louis	22.00	25.00	110.00	200.00
☐ Cleveland	22.00	25.00	110.00	200.00	☐ Kansas City	22.00	25.00	110.00	200.00
☐ Richmond	22.00	25.00	110.00	200.00	☐ Dallas	22.00	25.00	110.00	200.00
☐ Atlanta	22.00	25.00	110.00	200.00	☐ San Francisco	22.00	25.00	110.00	200.00

SERIES OF 1963A, SIGNATURES OF GRANAHAN-FOWLER, GREEN SEAL

BANK	A.B.P.	V.FINE	UNC.	★UNC.	BANK	A.B.P.	V.FINE	UNC.	★UNC.
☐ Boston	22.00	25.00	85.00	155.00	☐ Chicago	22.00	25.00	85.00	155.00
☐ New York	22.00	25.00	85.00	155.00	☐ St. Louis	22.00	25.00	85.00	155.00
☐ Philadelphia	22.00	25.00	85.00	155.00	☐ Minneapolis	22.00	25.00	85.00	155.00
☐ Cleveland	22.00	25.00	85.00	155.00	☐ Kansas City	22.00	25.00	85.00	155.00
☐ Richmond	22.00	25.00	85.00	155.00	☐ Dallas	22.00	25.00	85.00	155.00
☐ Atlanta	22.00	25.00	85.00	155.00	☐ San Francisco	22.00	25.00	85.00	155.00

TWENTY DOLLAR NOTES (1969)
FEDERAL RESERVE NOTES
SERIES OF 1969, SIGNATURES OF ELSTON-KENNEDY, GREEN SEAL

BANK	A.B.P.	V.FINE	UNC.	★UNC.	BANK	A.B.P.	V.FINE	UNC.	★UNC.
☐ Boston	—	25.00	70.00	150.00	☐ Chicago	—	25.00	70.00	150.00
☐ New York	—	25.00	70.00	150.00	☐ St. Louis	—	25.00	70.00	150.00
☐ Philadelphia	—	25.00	70.00	150.00	☐ Minneapolis	—	25.00	70.00	150.00
☐ Cleveland	—	25.00	70.00	150.00	☐ Kansas City	—	25.00	70.00	150.00
☐ Richmond	—	25.00	70.00	150.00	☐ Dallas	—	25.00	70.00	150.00
☐ Atlanta	—	25.00	70.00	150.00	☐ San Francisco	—	25.00	70.00	150.00

SERIES OF 1969A, SIGNATURES OF KABIS-CONNALLY, GREEN SEAL

BANK	A.B.P.	V.FINE	UNC.	★UNC.	BANK	A.B.P.	V.FINE	UNC.	★UNC.
☐ Boston	—	22.00	85.00	150.00	☐ Chicago	—	22.00	85.00	150.00
☐ New York	—	22.00	85.00	150.00	☐ St. Louis	—	22.00	85.00	150.00
☐ Philadelphia	—	22.00	85.00	150.00	☐ Minneapolis	—	22.00	85.00	150.00
☐ Cleveland	—	22.00	85.00	150.00	☐ Kansas City	—	22.00	85.00	150.00
☐ Richmond	—	22.00	85.00	150.00	☐ Dallas	—	22.00	85.00	150.00
☐ Atlanta	—	22.00	85.00	150.00	☐ San Francisco	—	22.00	85.00	150.00

SERIES OF 1969B, SIGNATURES OF BANUELOS-CONNALLY, GREEN SEAL

BANK	A.B.P.	V.FINE	UNC.	★UNC.	BANK	A.B.P.	V.FINE	UNC.	★UNC.
☐ New York	—	22.00	150.00	600.00	☐ Chicago	—	22.00	225.00	600.00
☐ Cleveland	—	22.00	175.00	600.00	☐ St. Louis	—	22.00	225.00	600.00
☐ Richmond	—	22.00	175.00	600.00	☐ Minneapolis	—	22.00	240.00	600.00
☐ Atlanta	—	22.00	175.00	600.00	☐ Kansas City	—	22.00	240.00	600.00
					☐ Dallas	—	22.00	225.00	600.00
					☐ San Francisco	—	22.00	165.00	600.00

SERIES OF 1969C, SIGNATURES OF BANUELOS-SHULTZ, GREEN SEAL

BANK	A.B.P.	V.FINE	UNC.	★UNC.	BANK	A.B.P.	V.FINE	UNC.	★UNC.
☐ Boston	—	22.00	85.00	175.00	☐ Chicago	—	22.00	85.00	175.00
☐ New York	—	22.00	85.00	175.00	☐ St. Louis	—	22.00	85.00	175.00
☐ Philadelphia	—	22.00	85.00	175.00	☐ Minneapolis	—	22.00	85.00	175.00
☐ Cleveland	—	22.00	85.00	175.00	☐ Kansas City	—	22.00	85.00	175.00
☐ Richmond	—	22.00	85.00	175.00	☐ Dallas	—	22.00	85.00	175.00
☐ Atlanta	—	22.00	85.00	175.00	☐ San Francisco	—	22.00	85.00	175.00

TWENTY DOLLAR NOTES (1974)
FEDERAL RESERVE NOTES
SERIES OF 1974, SIGNATURES OF NEFF-SIMON, GREEN SEAL

BANK	A.B.P.	V.FINE	UNC.	★UNC.	BANK	A.B.P.	V.FINE	UNC.	★UNC.
☐ Boston	—	22.00	85.00	135.00	☐ Chicago	—	22.00	85.00	135.00
☐ New York	—	22.00	85.00	135.00	☐ St. Louis	—	22.00	85.00	135.00
☐ Philadelphia	—	22.00	85.00	135.00	☐ Minneapolis	—	25.00	85.00	135.00
☐ Cleveland	—	22.00	85.00	135.00	☐ Kansas City	—	25.00	85.00	135.00
☐ Richmond	—	22.00	85.00	135.00	☐ Dallas	—	25.00	85.00	135.00
☐ Atlanta	—	22.00	85.00	135.00	☐ San Francisco	—	22.00	85.00	135.00

TWENTY DOLLAR NOTES (1977)
FEDERAL RESERVE NOTES
SERIES OF 1977, SIGNATURES OF MORTON-BLUMENTHAL, GREEN SEAL

BANK	A.B.P.	V.FINE	UNC.	★UNC.	BANK	A.B.P.	V.FINE	UNC.	★UNC.
☐ Boston	—	25.00	70.00	135.00	☐ Chicago	—	25.00	70.00	135.00
☐ New York	—	25.00	70.00	135.00	☐ St. Louis	—	25.00	70.00	135.00
☐ Philadelphia	—	25.00	70.00	135.00	☐ Minneapolis	—	25.00	70.00	135.00
☐ Cleveland	—	25.00	70.00	135.00	☐ Kansas City	—	25.00	70.00	135.00
☐ Richmond	—	25.00	70.00	135.00	☐ Dallas	—	25.00	70.00	135.00
☐ Atlanta	—	25.00	70.00	135.00	☐ San Francisco	—	25.00	70.00	135.00

TWENTY DOLLAR NOTES (1981)
FEDERAL RESERVE NOTES
SERIES OF 1981, SIGNATURES OF BUCHANAN-REGAN, GREEN SEAL

BANK	A.B.P.	V.FINE	UNC.	★UNC.	BANK	A.B.P.	V.FINE	UNC.	★UNC.
☐ Boston	—	25.00	85.00	175.00	☐ Chicago	—	25.00	85.00	175.00
☐ New York	—	25.00	85.00	175.00	☐ St. Louis	—	25.00	85.00	175.00
☐ Philadelphia	—	25.00	85.00	175.00	☐ Minneapolis	—	25.00	85.00	175.00
☐ Cleveland	—	25.00	85.00	175.00	☐ Kansas City	—	25.00	85.00	175.00
☐ Richmond	—	25.00	85.00	175.00	☐ Dallas	—	25.00	85.00	175.00
☐ Atlanta	—	25.00	85.00	175.00	☐ San Francisco	—	25.00	85.00	175.00

SERIES OF 1981A, SIGNATURES OF ORTEGA-REGAN, GREEN SEAL
★Notes not issued for all banks

BANK	A.B.P.	V.FINE	UNC.	★UNC.	BANK	A.B.P.	V.FINE	UNC.	★UNC.
☐ Boston	—	25.00	75.00	—	☐ Chicago	—	25.00	75.00	—
☐ New York	—	25.00	75.00	—	☐ St. Louis	—	25.00	75.00	—
☐ Philadelphia	—	25.00	75.00	—	☐ Minneapolis	—	25.00	75.00	—
☐ Cleveland	—	25.00	75.00	125.00	☐ Kansas City	—	25.00	75.00	—
☐ Richmond	—	25.00	75.00	210.00	☐ Dallas	—	25.00	75.00	—
☐ Atlanta	—	25.00	75.00	150.00	☐ San Francisco	—	25.00	75.00	170.00

TWENTY DOLLAR NOTES (1985)
FEDERAL RESERVE NOTES
SERIES OF 1985, SIGNATURES OF ORTEGA-BAKER, GREEN SEAL
★Notes not issued for all banks

BANK	A.B.P.	V.FINE	UNC.	★UNC.	BANK	A.B.P.	V.FINE	UNC.	★UNC.
☐ Boston	—	22.00	65.00	100.00	☐ Chicago	—	22.00	65.00	100.00
☐ New York	—	22.00	65.00	100.00	☐ St. Louis	—	22.00	65.00	100.00
☐ Philadelphia	—	22.00	65.00	100.00	☐ Minneapolis	—	22.00	65.00	100.00
☐ Cleveland	—	22.00	65.00	100.00	☐ Kansas City	—	22.00	65.00	100.00
☐ Richmond	—	22.00	65.00	100.00	☐ Dallas	—	22.00	65.00	100.00
☐ Atlanta	—	22.00	65.00	100.00	☐ San Francisco	—	22.00	65.00	100.00

TWENTY DOLLAR NOTES (1988)
FEDERAL RESERVE NOTES
SERIES OF 1988A, SIGNATURES OF VILLALPANDO-BRADY, GREEN SEAL

★Notes not issued for all banks

BANK	A.B.P.	V.FINE	UNC.	★UNC.	BANK	A.B.P.	V.FINE	UNC.	★UNC.
☐ Boston	—	22.00	60.00	—	☐ Chicago	—	22.00	60.00	140.00
☐ New York	—	22.00	60.00	140.00	☐ St. Louis	—	22.00	60.00	125.00
☐ Philadelphia	—	22.00	60.00	140.00	☐ Minneapolis	—	22.00	60.00	125.00
☐ Cleveland	—	22.00	60.00	140.00	☐ Kansas City	—	22.00	60.00	125.00
☐ Richmond	—	22.00	60.00	140.00	☐ Dallas	—	22.00	60.00	140.00
☐ Atlanta	—	22.00	60.00	140.00	☐ San Francisco	—	22.00	60.00	—

TWENTY DOLLAR NOTES (1990)
FEDERAL RESERVE NOTES
SERIES OF 1990, SIGNATURES OF VILLALPANDO-BRADY, GREEN SEAL

★Notes not issued for all banks

BANK	A.B.P.	V.FINE	UNC.	★UNC.	BANK	A.B.P.	V.FINE	UNC.	★UNC.
☐ Boston	—	22.00	60.00	95.00	☐ Chicago	—	22.00	60.00	95.00
☐ New York	—	22.00	60.00	95.00	☐ St. Louis	—	22.00	60.00	95.00
☐ Philadelphia	—	22.00	60.00	95.00	☐ Minneapolis	—	22.00	60.00	95.00
☐ Cleveland	—	22.00	60.00	95.00	☐ Kansas City	—	22.00	60.00	—
☐ Richmond	—	22.00	60.00	95.00	☐ Dallas	—	22.00	60.00	—
☐ Atlanta	—	22.00	60.00	95.00	☐ San Francisco	—	22.00	60.00	—

TWENTY DOLLAR NOTES (1993)
FEDERAL RESERVE NOTES
SERIES OF 1993, SIGNATURES OF WITHROW-BENTSEN, GREEN SEAL

★Notes are not issued for all banks

BANK	A.B.P.	V.FINE	UNC.	★UNC.	BANK	A.B.P.	V.FINE	UNC.	★UNC.
☐ Boston	—	22.00	60.00	95.00	☐ Chicago	—	22.00	60.00	—
☐ New York	—	22.00	60.00	95.00	☐ St. Louis	—	22.00	60.00	—
☐ Philadelphia	—	22.00	60.00	95.00	☐ Kansas City	—	22.00	60.00	—
☐ Cleveland	—	22.00	60.00	95.00	☐ Dallas	—	22.00	60.00	—
☐ Richmond	—	22.00	60.00	95.00	☐ San Francisco	—	22.00	60.00	85.00
☐ Atlanta	—	22.00	60.00	95.00					

TWENTY DOLLAR NOTES (1995)
FEDERAL RESERVE NOTES
SERIES OF 1995, SIGNATURES OF WITHROW-RUBIN, GREEN SEAL
★Notes not issued for all banks

BANK	A.B.P.	V.FINE	UNC.	★UNC.	BANK	A.B.P.	V.FINE	UNC.	★UNC.
☐ Boston	—	22.00	50.00	85.00	☐ Chicago	—	22.00	50.00	95.00
☐ New York	—	22.00	50.00	85.00	☐ St. Louis	—	22.00	50.00	95.00
☐ Philadelphia	—	22.00	50.00	85.00	☐ Minneapolis	—	22.00	50.00	85.00
☐ Cleveland	—	22.00	50.00	95.00	☐ Kansas City	—	22.00	50.00	85.00
☐ Richmond	—	22.00	50.00	95.00	☐ Dallas	—	22.00	50.00	95.00
☐ Atlanta	—	22.00	50.00	95.00	☐ San Francisco	—	22.00	50.00	95.00

TWENTY DOLLAR NOTES (1915–1918)
FEDERAL RESERVE BANK NOTES
(ALL HAVE BLUE SEALS)

(Large Size)

Face Design:
Portrait of
President
Cleveland left,
name of bank
and city center,
blue seal right.

Back Design:
Locomotive
and steamship,
similar to
1914 note.

BANK	SERIES	GOV'T SIGNATURES	BANK SIGNATURES	A.B.P.	GOOD	V.FINE	UNC.
☐ Atlanta	1915	Teehee-Burke	Bell-Wellborn	720.00	1200.00	4200.00	RARE
	1915	Teehee-Burke	Pike-McCord	720.00	1200.00	4000.00	RARE
☐ Atlanta	1918	Elliott-Burke	Bell-Wellborn	720.00	1200.00	3500.00	RARE
☐ Chicago	1915	Teehee-Burke	McLallen-McDougal	720.00	1200.00	3500.00	RARE
☐ St. Louis	1918	Teehee-Burke	Attebery-Wells	720.00	1200.00	3500.00	RARE

BANK	SERIES	GOV'T SIGNATURES	BANK SIGNATURES	A.B.P.	GOOD	V.FINE	UNC.
☐ Kansas City	1915	Teehee-Burke	Anderson-Miller				
				1920.00	800.00	3200.00	RARE
☐ Kansas City	1915	Teehee-Burke	Cross-Miller				
				1920.00	800.00	3200.00	RARE
☐ Dallas	1915	Teehee-Burke	Hoopes-Van Zandt				
				1920.00	800.00	3200.00	RARE
☐ Dallas	1915	Teehee-Burke	Gilbert-Van Zandt				
				525.00	875.00	5000.00	RARE
☐ Dallas	1915	Teehee-Burke	Talley-Van Zandt				
				525.00	875.00	4550.00	RARE

TWENTY DOLLAR NOTES (1929)
FEDERAL RESERVE BANK NOTES
(Small Size)

Face Design: Portrait of President Jackson center, name of bank and city left, blue seal right.

Back Design: The White House.

BANK	A.B.P.	V.FINE	UNC.	★UNC.	BANK	A.B.P.	V.FINE	UNC.	★UNC.
☐ Boston	60.00	80.00	270.00	4250.00	☐ Chicago	60.00	80.00	400.00	3850.00
☐ New York	60.00	80.00	260.00	3225.00	☐ St. Louis	60.00	80.00	400.00	3850.00
☐ Philadelphia	60.00	80.00	250.00	3800.00	☐ Minneapolis	60.00	80.00	400.00	4400.00
☐ Cleveland	60.00	80.00	250.00	4250.00	☐ Kansas City	60.00	80.00	1320.00	4400.00
☐ Richmond	60.00	80.00	430.00	3650.00	☐ Dallas	135.00	225.00	1320.00	RARE
☐ Atlanta	60.00	80.00	520.00	4250.00	☐ San Francisco	48.00	80.00	1320.00	RARE

FIFTY DOLLAR NOTES

FIFTY DOLLAR NOTES (1862–1863)
UNITED STATES NOTES
(ALSO KNOWN AS LEGAL TENDER NOTES)
(Large Size)

Face Design: Portrait of Hamilton to left.

Back Design

SERIES	SIGNATURES	SEAL	A.B.P.	GOOD	V.FINE	UNC.
☐1862	Chittenden-Spinner*	Red	—	—	—	RARE
☐1862	Chittenden-Spinner**	Red	—	—	—	RARE
☐1863	Chittenden-Spinner**	Red	—	—	—	RARE

*First Obligation: Similar to 1862 $5 note.
**Second Obligation: Shown above.

FIFTY DOLLAR NOTES (1869) UNITED STATES NOTES
(ALSO KNOWN AS LEGAL TENDER NOTES)
(Large Size)

Face Design: Portrait of Henry Clay to right.

Back Design

SERIES	SIGNATURES	SEAL	A.B.P.	GOOD	V.FINE	UNC.
☐1869	Allison-Spinner	Red	—	—	—	RARE

Only twenty-four pieces of this note remain unredeemed.

FIFTY DOLLAR NOTES (1874–1880)
UNITED STATES NOTES

(Large Size)

Face Design: Franklin to left.

Back Design

SERIES	SIGNATURES	SEAL	A.B.P.	GOOD	V.FINE	UNC.
☐1874	Allison-Spinner	Sm. Red	1980.00	3300.00	RARE	RARE
☐1875	Allison-Wyman	Sm. Red	—	RARE	RARE	RARE
☐1878	Allison-Gilfillan	Sm. Red	1320.00	2200.00	RARE	RARE
☐1880	Bruce-Gilfillan	Lg. Brown	1089.00	1815.00	RARE	RARE
☐1880	Bruce-Wyman	Lg. Brown	2100.00	3520.00	RARE	RARE
☐1880	Rosecrans-Jordan	Lg. Red	2100.00	3520.00	RARE	RARE
☐1880	Rosecrans-Hyatt	Red Plain	VERY RARE			
☐1880	Rosecrans-Hyatt	Red Spike	1452.00	2420.00	RARE	RARE
☐1880	Rosecrans-Huston	Lg. Red	1980.00	3300.00	RARE	RARE
☐1880	Rosecrans-Huston	Lg. Brown	1320.00	2200.00	RARE	RARE
☐1880	Tillman-Morgan	Sm. Red	1440.00	2420.00	RARE	RARE
☐1880	Bruce-Roberts	Sm. Red	—	RARE	RARE	RARE
☐1880	Lyons-Roberts	Sm. Red	1155.00	1925.00	RARE	RARE

FIFTY DOLLAR NOTES (1875) NATIONAL BANK NOTES
FIRST CHARTER PERIOD (Large Size)

Face Design: Washington crossing Delaware left, Washington at Valley Forge, right.

Back Design: Embarkation of the Pilgrims.

SERIES	SIGNATURES	SEAL	A.B.P.	GOOD	V.FINE	UNC.
☐ Original	Chittenden-Spinner	Red w/r	4950.00	8250.00	RARE	RARE
☐ Original	Colby-Spinner	Red w/r	4950.00	8250.00	RARE	RARE
☐ Original	Allison-Spinner	Red w/r	4950.00	8250.00	RARE	RARE
☐ 1875	Allison-New	Red w/s	4950.00	8250.00	RARE	RARE
☐ 1875	Allison-Wyman	Red w/s	4950.00	8250.00	RARE	RARE
☐ 1875	Allison-Gilfillan	Red w/s	4950.00	8250.00	RARE	RARE
☐ 1875	Scofield-Gilfillan	Red w/s	4950.00	8250.00	RARE	RARE
☐ 1875	Bruce-Gilfillan	Red w/s	4950.00	8250.00	RARE	RARE
☐ 1875	Bruce-Wyman	Red w/s	4950.00	8250.00	RARE	RARE
☐ 1875	Rosecrans-Huston	Red w/s	4950.00	8250.00	RARE	RARE
☐ 1875	Rosecrans-Nebeker	Red w/s	4950.00	8250.00	RARE	RARE
☐ 1875	Tillman-Morgan	Red w/s	4950.00	8250.00	RARE	RARE

FIFTY DOLLAR NOTES (1882) NATIONAL BANK NOTES
SECOND CHARTER PERIOD (Large Size)

First Issue (Brown seal and brown back)
Back Design
Face Design: Similar to First Charter Period note.

SERIES	SIGNATURES	SEAL	A.B.P.	GOOD	V.FINE	UNC.
☐1882	Bruce-Gilfillan	Brown	1650.00	2750.00	RARE	RARE
☐1882	Bruce-Wyman	Brown	1650.00	2750.00	RARE	RARE
☐1882	Bruce-Jordan	Brown	1650.00	2750.00	RARE	RARE
☐1882	Rosecrans-Jordan	Brown	1650.00	2750.00	RARE	RARE
☐1882	Rosecrans-Hyatt	Brown	1650.00	2750.00	RARE	RARE
☐1882	Rosecrans-Huston	Brown	1650.00	2750.00	RARE	RARE
☐1882	Rosecrans-Nebeker	Brown	1650.00	2750.00	RARE	RARE
☐1882	Rosecrans-Morgan	Brown	1650.00	2750.00	RARE	RARE
☐1882	Tillman-Morgan	Brown	1650.00	2750.00	RARE	RARE
☐1882	Tillman-Roberts	Brown	1650.00	2750.00	RARE	RARE
☐1882	Bruce-Roberts	Brown	1650.00	2750.00	RARE	RARE
☐1882	Lyons-Roberts	Brown	1650.00	2750.00	RARE	RARE
☐1882	Vernon-Treat	Brown	1650.00	2750.00	RARE	RARE

FIFTY DOLLAR NOTES (1882) NATIONAL BANK NOTES
SECOND CHARTER PERIOD (Large Size)

Second Issue (Blue seal, green back with date "1882–1908".)
Face Design: Washington crossing Delaware left,
Washington at Valley Forge right.

Back Design

SERIES	SIGNATURES	SEAL	A.B.P.	GOOD	V.FINE	UNC.
☐ 1882	Rosecrans-Huston	Blue	1920.00	3200.00	RARE	RARE
☐ 1882	Rosecrans-Nebeker	Blue	1920.00	3200.00	RARE	RARE
☐ 1882	Tillman-Morgan	Blue	1920.00	3200.00	RARE	RARE
☐ 1882	Tillman-Roberts	Blue	1920.00	3200.00	RARE	RARE
☐ 1882	Bruce-Roberts	Blue	1920.00	3200.00	RARE	RARE
☐ 1882	Lyons-Roberts	Blue	1920.00	3200.00	RARE	RARE
☐ 1882	Vernon-Treat	Blue	1920.00	3200.00	RARE	RARE
☐ 1882	Napier-McClung	Blue	1920.00	3200.00	RARE	RARE

Third Issue (As above, "FIFTY DOLLARS" replaces
1882–1908—excessively rare!)

☐ 1882	Lyons-Roberts		RARE	RARE	RARE	RARE

FIFTY DOLLAR NOTES (1902) NATIONAL BANK NOTES
THIRD CHARTER PERIOD (Large Size)

First Issue (Red seal and numbers)
Face Design: Portrait of Sherman left. Name of bank
center. Treasury Seal and numbers.

SERIES	SIGNATURES	SEAL	A.B.P.	GOOD	V.FINE	UNC.
☐1902	Lyons-Roberts	Red	1180.00	1980.00	RARE	RARE
☐1902	Lyons-Treat	Red	1180.00	1980.00	RARE	RARE
☐1902	Vernon-Treat	Red	1180.00	1980.00	RARE	RARE

Second Issue (Treasury Seal)
Numbers remain blue, date "1902–1908" added on back.

☐1902	Lyons-Roberts	Blue	1200.00	2000.00	3500.00	RARE
☐1902	Lyons-Treat	Blue	1200.00	2000.00	3500.00	RARE
☐1902	Vernon-Treat	Blue	1200.00	2000.00	3500.00	RARE
☐1902	Vernon-McClung	Blue	1200.00	2000.00	3500.00	RARE
☐1902	Napier-McClung	Blue	1200.00	2000.00	3500.00	RARE
☐1902	Napier-Thompson	Blue	1200.00	2000.00	3500.00	RARE
☐1902	Napier-Burke	Blue	1200.00	2000.00	3500.00	RARE
☐1902	Parker-Burke	Blue	1200.00	2000.00	3500.00	RARE
☐1902	Teehee-Burke	Blue	1200.00	2000.00	3500.00	RARE

Third Issue (Treasury Seal)
Numbers remain blue, date "1902–1908" removed from back.

☐1902	Lyons-Roberts	Blue	480.00	825.00	2500.00	RARE
☐1902	Lyons-Treat	Blue	480.00	825.00	2500.00	RARE
☐1902	Vernon-Treat	Blue	480.00	825.00	2500.00	RARE
☐1902	Vernon-McClung	Blue	480.00	825.00	2500.00	RARE
☐1902	Napier-McClung	Blue	480.00	825.00	2500.00	RARE
☐1902	Napier-Thompson	Blue	480.00	825.00	2500.00	RARE
☐1902	Napier-Burke	Blue	480.00	825.00	2500.00	RARE
☐1902	Parker-Burke	Blue	480.00	825.00	2500.00	RARE
☐1902	Teehee-Burke	Blue	480.00	825.00	2500.00	RARE
☐1902	Elliott-Burke	Blue	480.00	825.00	2500.00	RARE
☐1902	Elliott-White	Blue	480.00	825.00	2500.00	RARE

SERIES	SIGNATURES	SEAL	A.B.P.	GOOD	V.FINE	UNC.
☐1902	Speelman-White	Blue	225.00	375.00	2500.00	RARE
☐1902	Woods-White	Blue	225.00	375.00	2500.00	RARE

FIFTY DOLLAR NOTES (1929) NATIONAL BANK NOTES
(Small Size)

Face Design: Portrait of President Grant center. Bank left, brown seal right. Brown serial numbers, black Charter Numbers.

Back Design: The Capitol.

SERIES	SIGNATURES	SEAL	A.B.P.	V.FINE	UNC.
☐1929, Type I*	Jones-Wood	Brown	378.00	630.00	1020.00
☐1929, Type II*	Jones-Wood	Brown	378.00	630.00	1428.00

*See Page 92. Type I—Charter Number in black. Type II—Similar. Charter Number added in brown.

FIFTY DOLLAR NOTES (1878–1880)
SILVER CERTIFICATES
(Large Size)

Face Design: Portrait of Edward Everett.

Back Design

SERIES	SIGNATURES	SEAL	A.B.P.	GOOD	V.FINE	UNC.
☐ 1878	Varied	Red	—	—	—	VERY RARE
☐ 1880	Scofield-Gilfillan	Brown	—	—	—	VERY RARE
☐ 1880	Bruce-Gilfillan	Brown	—	—	RARE	UNKNOWN
☐ 1880	Bruce-Wyman	Brown	—	—	—	RARE
☐ 1880	Rosecrans-Huston	Brown	—	—	—	RARE
☐ 1880	Rosecrans-Nebeker	Red	—	—	—	RARE

FIFTY DOLLAR NOTES (1891) SILVER CERTIFICATES
(Large Size)

Face Design: Portrait of Edward Everett.

Back Design

SERIES	SIGNATURES	SEAL	A.B.P.	GOOD	V.FINE	UNC.
☐1891	Rosecrans-Nebeker	Red	—	RARE	RARE	RARE
☐1891	Tillman-Morgan	Red	1000.00	1650.00	RARE	RARE
☐1891	Bruce-Roberts	Red	1000.00	1650.00	RARE	RARE
☐1891	Lyons-Roberts	Red	1000.00	1650.00	RARE	RARE
☐1891	Vernon-Treat	Red	1000.00	1650.00	RARE	RARE
☐1891	Parker-Burke	Blue	1000.00	1650.00	RARE	RARE

FIFTY DOLLAR NOTES (1882) GOLD CERTIFICATES
(Large Size)

Face Design: Portrait of Silas Wright to left.

Back Design: Bright yellow color.

SERIES	SIGNATURES	SEAL	A.B.P.	GOOD	V.FINE	UNC.
☐1882	Bruce-Gilfillan	Brown	2750.00	4500.00	RARE	RARE
☐1882	Bruce-Wyman	Brown	2750.00	4500.00	RARE	RARE
☐1882	Rosecrans-Hyatt	Red	1500.00	2000.00	RARE	RARE
☐1882	Rosecrans-Huston	Brown	6200.00	RARE	RARE	RARE
☐1882	Lyons-Roberts	Red	2650.00	RARE	RARE	RARE
☐1882	Lyons-Treat	Red	720.00	1200.00	2500.00	RARE
☐1882	Vernon-Treat	Red	720.00	1200.00	2500.00	RARE
☐1882	Vernon-McClung	Red	720.00	1200.00	2500.00	RARE
☐1882	Napier-McClung	Red	720.00	1200.00	2500.00	RARE

FIFTY DOLLAR NOTES (1913) GOLD CERTIFICATES
(Large Size)

Face Design: Portrait of President Grant.

Back Design: Bright yellow color.

SERIES	SIGNATURES	SEAL	A.B.P.	GOOD	V.FINE	UNC.
☐1913	Parker-Burke	Gold	600.00	1000.00	1575.00	RARE
☐1913	Teehee-Burke	Gold	650.00	800.00	1575.00	RARE
☐1922	Speelman-White	Gold	650.00	800.00	1575.00	RARE

FIFTY DOLLAR NOTES (1928) GOLD CERTIFICATES
(Small Size)

Back Design: Same as 1929 note.

SERIES	SIGNATURES	SEAL	A.B.P.	GOOD	V.FINE	UNC.
☐1928	Woods-Mellon	Gold	180.00	300.00	RARE	RARE

FIFTY DOLLAR NOTES (1891) TREASURY OR COIN NOTES
(Large Size)

Face Design: Portrait of William H. Seward. Only twenty-five pieces remain unredeemed.
Back Design: Green.

SERIES	SIGNATURES	SEAL	A.B.P.	GOOD	V.FINE	UNC.
☐1891	Rosecrans-Nebeker	Red	—	RARE	—	RARE

FIFTY DOLLAR NOTES (1914)
FEDERAL RESERVE NOTES

(Large Size)

SERIES OF 1914,
SIGNATURES OF BURKE-McADOO, RED SEAL AND RED SERIAL NUMBERS

BANK	A.B.P.	V.FINE	UNC.	CITY	A.B.P.	V.FINE	UNC.
☐ Boston	1950.00	3250.00	RARE	☐ Chicago	1950.00	3250.00	RARE
☐ New York	1950.00	3250.00	RARE	☐ St. Louis	1950.00	3250.00	RARE
☐ Philadelphia	1950.00	3250.00	RARE	☐ Minneapolis	1950.00	3250.00	RARE
☐ Cleveland	1950.00	3250.00	RARE	☐ Kansas City	1950.00	3250.00	RARE
☐ Richmond	1950.00	3250.00	RARE	☐ Dallas	1950.00	3250.00	RARE
☐ Atlanta	1950.00	3250.00	RARE	☐ San Francisco	1950.00	3250.00	RARE

FIFTY DOLLAR NOTES (1914)
FEDERAL RESERVE NOTES
1914, BLUE TREASURY SEAL AND BLUE NUMBERS

DATE	BANK	SIGNATURES	SEAL	A.B.P.	GOOD	V.FINE	UNC.
1914	Boston	Burke-McAdoo	Blue	120.00	200.00	750.00	3050.00
1914	Boston	Burke-Glass	Blue	90.00	150.00	520.00	3050.00
1914	Boston	Burke-Huston	Blue	225.00	375.00	1935.00	RARE
1914	Boston	White-Mellon	Blue	84.00	140.00	575.00	2750.00
1914	New York	Burke-McAdoo	Blue	90.00	150.00	750.00	4200.00
1914	New York	Burke-Glass	Blue	84.00	140.00	1080.00	3775.00
1914	New York	Burke-Huston	Blue	96.00	160.00	750.00	3775.00
1914	New York	White-Mellon	Blue	96.00	160.00	750.00	3775.00

DATE BANK	SIGNATURES	SEAL	A.B.P.	GOOD	V.FINE	UNC.
1914 Philadelphia	Burke-McAdoo	Blue	90.00	150.00	785.00	3600.00
1914 Philadelphia	Burke-Glass	Blue	105.00	175.00	1100.00	3600.00
1914 Philadelphia	Burke-Huston	Blue	90.00	150.00	575.00	2560.00
1914 Philadelphia	White-Mellon	Blue	90.00	150.00	575.00	2560.00
1914 Cleveland	Burke-McAdoo	Blue	90.00	150.00	575.00	2560.00
1914 Cleveland	Burke-Glass	Blue	105.00	175.00	800.00	3360.00
1914 Cleveland	Burke-Huston	Blue	93.00	155.00	785.00	3200.00
1914 Cleveland	White-Mellon	Blue	90.00	150.00	400.00	2800.00
1914 Richmond	Burke-McAdoo	Blue	105.00	175.00	1015.00	3360.00
1914 Richmond	Burke-Glass	Blue	180.00	300.00	900.00	3440.00
1914 Richmond	Burke-Huston	Blue	90.00	150.00	450.00	2560.00
1914 Richmond	White-Mellon	Blue	120.00	200.00	1080.00	2560.00
1914 Atlanta	Burke-McAdoo	Blue	105.00	175.00	900.00	2560.00
1914 Atlanta	Burke-Glass	Blue	165.00	275.00	1500.00	4500.00
1914 Atlanta	Burke-Huston	Blue	81.00	135.00	400.00	2800.00
1914 Atlanta	White-Mellon	Blue	150.00	250.00	700.00	3360.00
1914 Chicago	Burke-McAdoo	Blue	90.00	150.00	575.00	2560.00
1914 Chicago	Burke-Glass	Blue	90.00	150.00	575.00	2560.00
1914 Chicago	Burke-Huston	Blue	120.00	200.00	575.00	2560.00
1914 Chicago	White-Mellon	Blue	120.00	200.00	575.00	2560.00
1914 St. Louis	Burke-McAdoo	Blue	120.00	200.00	1800.00	2560.00
1914 St. Louis	Burke-Glass	Blue	90.00	150.00	1000.00	2560.00
1914 St. Louis	Burke-Huston	Blue	81.00	135.00	540.00	2000.00
1914 St. Louis	White-Mellon	Blue	300.00	500.00	2200.00	RARE
1914 Minneapolis	Burke-McAdoo	Blue	105.00	175.00	720.00	2800.00
1914 Minneapolis	Burke-Glass	Blue	225.00	375.00	1500.00	RARE
1914 Minneapolis	Burke-Huston	Blue	195.00	325.00	2200.00	RARE
1914 Minneapolis	White-Mellon	Blue	213.00	355.00	700.00	2800.00
1914 Kansas City	Burke-McAdoo	Blue	93.00	155.00	900.00	3040.00
1914 Kansas City	White-Mellon	Blue		ONLY 1 KNOWN—RARE		
1914 Dallas	Burke-McAdoo	Blue	105.00	175.00	1080.00	3200.00
1914 Dallas	Burke-Glass	Blue	270.00	450.00	1080.00	RARE
1914 Dallas	Burke-Huston	Blue	270.00	450.00	1080.00	RARE
1914 Dallas	White Mellon	Blue	270.00	450.00	1080.00	3360.00
1914 San Francisco	Burke-McAdoo	Blue	90.00	150.00	500.00	3000.00
1914 San Francisco	Burke-Glass	Blue	240.00	400.00	3200.00	3000.00
1914 San Francisco	Burke-Huston	Blue	90.00	150.00	475.00	3360.00
1914 San Francisco	White-Mellon	Blue	102.00	170.00	575.00	3040.00

FIFTY DOLLAR NOTES (1928)
FEDERAL RESERVE NOTES

(Small Size)

Face Design: Portrait of President Grant center. Black Federal Reserve Seal with number to left. Green Treasury Seal to right.
Back Design: Same as 1929 note.

FIFTY DOLLAR NOTES (1928)
FEDERAL RESERVE NOTES
SERIES OF 1928, SIGNATURES OF WOODS-MELLON, GREEN SEAL

BANK	A.B.P.	V.FINE	UNC.	★UNC.	BANK	A.B.P.	V.FINE	UNC.	★UNC.
☐ Boston	120.00	200.00	1000.00	—	☐ Chicago	100.00	175.00	1020.00	—
☐ New York	120.00	200.00	1000.00	—	☐ St. Louis	120.00	200.00	1020.00	—
☐ Philadelphia	120.00	200.00	1000.00	—	☐ Minneapolis	180.00	300.00	1185.00	—
☐ Cleveland	120.00	200.00	1000.00	—	☐ Kansas City	120.00	200.00	1020.00	—
☐ Richmond	120.00	200.00	1000.00	—	☐ Dallas	120.00	200.00	1185.00	—
☐ Atlanta	120.00	200.00	1000.00	—	☐ San Francisco	120.00	200.00	1020.00	—

SERIES OF 1928A, SIGNATURES OF WOODS-MELLON, GREEN SEAL

BANK	A.B.P.	V.FINE	UNC.	★UNC.	BANK	A.B.P.	V.FINE	UNC.	★UNC.
☐ Boston	75.00	125.00	475.00	—	☐ Chicago	75.00	125.00	480.00	—
☐ New York	75.00	125.00	475.00	—	☐ St. Louis	75.00	125.00	480.00	—
☐ Philadelphia	75.00	125.00	475.00	—	☐ Minneapolis	75.00	125.00	480.00	—
☐ Cleveland	75.00	125.00	475.00	—	☐ Kansas City	75.00	125.00	480.00	—
☐ Richmond	75.00	125.00	475.00	—	☐ Dallas	75.00	125.00	480.00	—
☐ Atlanta	75.00	150.00	475.00	—	☐ San Francisco	75.00	125.00	480.00	—

FIFTY DOLLAR NOTES (1934)
FEDERAL RESERVE NOTES
SERIES OF 1934, SIGNATURES OF JULIAN-MORGENTHAU, GREEN SEAL

BANK	A.B.P.	V.FINE	UNC.	★UNC.	BANK	A.B.P.	V.FINE	UNC.	★UNC.
☐ Boston	60.00	100.00	300.00	975.00	☐ Chicago	60.00	100.00	300.00	975.00
☐ New York	60.00	100.00	300.00	975.00	☐ St. Louis	60.00	100.00	300.00	975.00
☐ Philadelphia	60.00	100.00	300.00	975.00	☐ Minneapolis	60.00	100.00	300.00	975.00
☐ Cleveland	60.00	100.00	300.00	975.00	☐ Kansas City	60.00	100.00	300.00	975.00
☐ Richmond	60.00	100.00	300.00	975.00	☐ Dallas	60.00	100.00	300.00	975.00
☐ Atlanta	60.00	100.00	300.00	975.00	☐ San Francisco	60.00	100.00	300.00	975.00

SERIES OF 1934A, SIGNATURES OF JULIAN-MORGENTHAU, GREEN SEAL

BANK	A.B.P.	V.FINE	UNC.	★UNC.	BANK	A.B.P.	V.FINE	UNC.	★UNC.
☐ Boston	66.00	110.00	475.00	1836.00	☐ Chicago	66.00	110.00	475.00	1530.00
☐ New York	66.00	110.00	350.00	1836.00	☐ St. Louis	66.00	110.00	475.00	1530.00
☐ Philadelphia	66.00	110.00	475.00	1428.00	☐ Minneapolis	72.00	120.00	475.00	1530.00
☐ Cleveland	66.00	110.00	475.00	1428.00	☐ Kansas City	72.00	120.00	475.00	1530.00
☐ Richmond	66.00	110.00	475.00	1428.00	☐ Dallas	72.00	120.00	475.00	1530.00
☐ Atlanta	66.00	110.00	475.00	1428.00	☐ San Francisco	66.00	110.00	475.00	1530.00

SERIES OF 1934B, SIGNATURES OF JULIAN-VINSON, GREEN SEAL

BANK	A.B.P.	V.FINE	UNC.	★UNC.	BANK	A.P.B.	V.FINE	UNC.	★UNC.
					☐ Chicago		75.00	125.00	425.00	—
					☐ St. Louis		75.00	125.00	425.00	—
☐ Philadelphia	63.00	105.00	425.00	4500.00	☐ Minneapolis		120.00	200.00	425.00	—
☐ Cleveland	75.00	125.00	425.00	4500.00	☐ Kansas City		120.00	200.00	425.00	4500.00
☐ Richmond	75.00	125.00	425.00	4500.00	☐ Dallas		135.00	225.00	425.00	—
☐ Atlanta	75.00	125.00	650.00	—	☐ San Francisco		75.00	125.00	425.00	—

SERIES OF 1934C, SIGNATURES OF JULIAN-SNYDER, GREEN SEAL

BANK	A.B.P.	V.FINE	UNC.	★UNC.	BANK	A.B.P.	V.FINE	UNC.	★UNC.
☐ Boston	90.00	150.00	275.00	—	☐ Chicago	66.00	110.00	275.00	2244.00
☐ New York	66.00	110.00	275.00	2244.00	☐ St. Louis	66.00	110.00	275.00	2244.00
☐ Philadelphia	75.00	125.00	275.00	2244.00	☐ Minneapolis	66.00	110.00	275.00	2244.00
☐ Cleveland	63.00	105.00	275.00	2244.00	☐ Kansas City	63.00	105.00	275.00	2244.00
☐ Richmond	63.00	105.00	275.00	2244.00	☐ Dallas	63.00	105.00	275.00	2244.00
☐ Atlanta	90.00	150.00	275.00	—					

SERIES OF 1934D, SIGNATURES OF CLARK-SNYDER, GREEN SEAL

BANK	A.B.P.	V.FINE	UNC.	★UNC.	BANK	A.B.P.	V.FINE	UNC.	★UNC.
☐ Boston	90.00	150.00	375.00	4500.00	☐ Chicago	60.00	100.00	375.00	5000
☐ New York	60.00	100.00	375.00	4500.00					
☐ Philadelphia	60.00	100.00	375.00	4000.00	☐ Minneapolis		120.00	200.00	750.00	—
☐ Richmond	90.00	150.00	375.00	—	☐ Dallas		12 .00	125.00	360.00	
☐ Atlanta	90.00	150.00	375.00	4500.00					

FIFTY DOLLAR NOTES (1950)
FEDERAL RESERVE NOTES
SERIES OF 1950, SIGNATURES OF CLARK-SNYDER, GREEN SEAL

BANK	A.B.P.	V.FINE	UNC.	★UNC.	BANK	A.P.B.	V.FINE	UNC.	★UNC.
☐ Boston	75.00	125.00	300.00	1428.00	☐ Chicago	75.00	125.00	300.00	1224.00
☐ New York	75.00	125.00	300.00	1224.00	☐ St. Louis	75.00	125.00	300.00	1224.00
☐ Philadelphia	75.00	125.00	300.00	1478.00	☐ Minneapolis	75.00	125.00	300.00	1840.00
☐ Cleveland	75.00	125.00	300.00	1224.00	☐ Kansas City	75.00	125.00	300.00	1630.00
☐ Richmond	75.00	125.00	300.00	1224.00	☐ Dallas	75.00	125.00	300.00	1224.00
☐ Atlanta	75.00	125.00	300.00	1224.00	☐ San Francisco	75.00	125.00	300.00	1224.00

SERIES OF 1950A, SIGNATURES OF PRIEST-HUMPHERY, GREEN SEAL

BANK	A.B.P.	V.FINE	UNC.	★UNC.	BANK	A.B.P.	V.FINE	UNC.	★UNC.
☐ Boston	55.00	90.00	225.00	685.00	☐ Chicago	55.00	80.00	220.00	685.00
☐ New York	55.00	90.00	225.00	685.00	☐ St. Louis	55.00	80.00	220.00	685.00
☐ Philadelphia	55.00	90.00	225.00	685.00	☐ Minneapolis	55.00	80.00	220.00	685.00
☐ Cleveland	55.00	90.00	225.00	685.00	☐ Kansas City	55.00	80.00	220.00	685.00
☐ Richmond	55.00	90.00	225.00	685.00	☐ Dallas	55.00	80.00	220.00	685.00
☐ Atlanta	55.00	90.00	225.00	685.00	☐ San Francisco	55.00	80.00	220.00	685.00

SERIES OF 1950B, SIGNATURES OF PRIEST-ANDERSON, GREEN SEAL

BANK	A.B.P.	V.FINE	UNC.	★UNC.	BANK	A.B.P.	V.FINE	UNC.	★UNC.
☐ Boston	—	85.00	230.00	561.00	☐ Chicago	—	85.00	230.00	800.00
☐ New York	—	85.00	230.00	450.00	☐ St. Louis	—	85.00	230.00	800.00
☐ Philadelphia	—	85.00	230.00	561.00	☐ Minneapolis	—	85.00	230.00	800.00
☐ Cleveland	—	85.00	230.00	561.00	☐ Kansas City	—	85.00	230.00	800.00
☐ Richmond	—	85.00	230.00	790.00	☐ Dallas	—	85.00	230.00	800.00
☐ Atlanta	—	85.00	230.00	790.00	☐ San Francisco	—	85.00	230.00	800.00

SERIES OF 1950C, SIGNATURES OF SMITH-DILLON, GREEN SEAL

BANK	A.B.P.	V.FINE	UNC.	★UNC.	BANK	A.B.P.	V.FINE	UNC.	★UNC.
☐ Boston	—	85.00	175.00	800.00	☐ Chicago	—	85.00	175.00	800.00
☐ New York	—	85.00	175.00	800.00	☐ St. Louis	—	85.00	175.00	800.00
☐ Philadelphia	—	85.00	175.00	800.00	☐ Minneapolis	—	85.00	175.00	800.00
☐ Cleveland	—	85.00	175.00	800.00	☐ Kansas City	—	85.00	175.00	800.00
☐ Richmond	—	85.00	175.00	800.00	☐ Dallas	—	85.00	175.00	800.00
☐ Atlanta	—	85.00	175.00	800.00	☐ San Francisco	—	85.00	175.00	800.00

SERIES OF 1950D, SIGNATURES OF GRANAHAN-DILLON, GREEN SEAL

BANK	A.B.P.	V.FINE	UNC.	★UNC.	BANK	A.B.P.	V.FINE	UNC.	★UNC.
☐ Boston	—	85.00	275.00	700.00	☐ Chicago	—	85.00	175.00	580.00
☐ New York	—	85.00	275.00	700.00	☐ St. Louis	—	85.00	175.00	700.00
☐ Philadelphia	—	85.00	275.00	700.00	☐ Minneapolis	—	85.00	200.00	895.00
☐ Cleveland	—	85.00	175.00	700.00	☐ Kansas City	—	85.00	175.00	700.00
☐ Richmond	—	85.00	175.00	700.00	☐ Dallas	—	85.00	275.00	790.00
☐ Atlanta	—	85.00	175.00	700.00	☐ San Francisco	—	85.00	275.00	700.00

SERIES OF 1950E, SIGNATURES OF GRANAHAN-FOWLER, GREEN SEAL

BANK	A.B.P.	V.FINE	UNC.	★UNC.
☐ Chicago	120.00	200.00	500.00	2550.00
☐ New York	120.00	200.00	425.00	1530.00
☐ San Francisco	90.00	150.00	425.00	1530.00

FIFTY DOLLAR NOTES (1963)
FEDERAL RESERVE NOTES
SERIES OF 1963,
(THERE WERE NOT ANY NOTES PRINTED FOR THIS SERIES.)

SERIES OF 1963A, SIGNATURES OF GRANAHAN-FOWLER, GREEN SEAL

BANK	A.B.P.	V.FINE	UNC.	BANK	A.B.P.	V.FINE	UNC.
☐ Boston	—	85.00	225.00	☐ Chicago	—	85.00	225.00
☐ New York	—	85.00	225.00	☐ St. Louis	—	85.00	225.00
☐ Philadelphia	—	85.00	225.00	☐ Minneapolis	—	85.00	225.00
☐ Cleveland	—	85.00	225.00	☐ Kansas City	—	85.00	225.00
☐ Richmond	—	85.00	225.00	☐ Dallas	—	85.00	225.00
☐ Atlanta	—	85.00	225.00	☐ San Francisco	—	85.00	225.00

FIFTY DOLLAR NOTES (1969)
FEDERAL RESERVE NOTES
(WORDING IN GREEN. TREASURY SEAL IS CHANGED FROM LATIN TO ENGLISH)

SERIES OF 1969, SIGNATURES OF ELSTON-KENNEDY, GREEN SEAL

BANK	A.B.P.	V.FINE	UNC.	BANK	A.B.P.	V.FINE	UNC.
☐ Boston	—	85.00	225.00	☐ Chicago	—	85.00	225.00
☐ New York	—	85.00	225.00	☐ St. Louis	—	85.00	225.00
☐ Philadelphia	—	85.00	225.00	☐ Minneapolis	—	85.00	225.00
☐ Cleveland	—	85.00	225.00	☐ Kansas City	—	85.00	225.00
☐ Richmond	—	85.00	225.00	☐ Dallas	—	85.00	225.00
☐ Atlanta	—	85.00	225.00	☐ San Francisco	—	85.00	225.00

SERIES OF 1969A, SIGNATURES OF KABIS-CONNALLY, GREEN SEAL

BANK	A.B.P.	V.FINE	UNC.	BANK	A.B.P.	V.FINE	UNC.
☐ Boston	—	80.00	150.00	☐ Chicago	—	80.00	150.00
☐ New York	—	80.00	150.00	☐ St. Louis	—	80.00	150.00
☐ Philadelphia	—	80.00	150.00	☐ Minneapolis	—	80.00	150.00
☐ Cleveland	—	80.00	150.00	☐ Kansas City	—	80.00	150.00
☐ Richmond	—	80.00	150.00	☐ Dallas	—	80.00	150.00
☐ Atlanta	—	80.00	150.00	☐ San Francisco	—	80.00	150.00

SERIES OF 1969B, SIGNATURES OF BANUELOS-CONNALLY, GREEN SEAL

BANK	A.B.P.	V.FINE	UNC.	BANK	A.B.P.	V.FINE	UNC.
☐ Boston	165.00	275.00	895.00	☐ Chicago	165.00	275.00	895.00
☐ New York	165.00	275.00	895.00				
☐ Richmond	165.00	275.00	895.00	☐ Dallas	165.00	275.00	895.00
☐ Atlanta	165.00	275.00	895.00				

SERIES OF 1969C, SIGNATURES OF BANUELOS-SHULTZ, GREEN SEAL

BANK	A.B.P.	V.FINE	UNC.	BANK	A.B.P.	V.FINE	UNC.
☐ Boston	—	70.00	125.00	☐Chicago	—	70.00	125.00
☐ New York	—	70.00	125.00	☐St. Louis	—	70.00	125.00
☐ Philadelphia	—	70.00	125.00	☐Minneapolis	—	70.00	125.00
☐ Cleveland	—	70.00	125.00	☐Kansas City	—	70.00	125.00
☐ Richmond	—	70.00	125.00	☐Dallas	—	70.00	125.00
☐ Atlanta	—	70.00	125.00	☐San Francisco	—	70.00	125.00

FIFTY DOLLAR NOTES (1974)
FEDERAL RESERVE NOTES
SERIES OF 1974, SIGNATURES OF NEFF-SIMON, GREEN SEAL

BANK	A.B.P.	V.FINE	UNC.	BANK	A.B.P.	V.FINE	UNC.
☐ Boston	—	70.00	125.00	☐Chicago	—	70.00	125.00
☐ New York	—	70.00	125.00	☐St. Louis	—	70.00	125.00
☐ Philadelphia	—	70.00	125.00	☐Minneapolis	—	70.00	125.00
☐ Cleveland	—	70.00	125.00	☐Kansas City	—	70.00	125.00
☐ Richmond	—	70.00	125.00	☐Dallas	—	70.00	125.00
☐ Atlanta	—	70.00	125.00	☐San Francisco	—	70.00	125.00

FIFTY DOLLAR NOTES (1977)
FEDERAL RESERVE NOTES
SERIES OF 1977, SIGNATURES OF MORTON-BLUMENTHAL, GREEN SEAL

BANK	A.B.P.	V.FINE	UNC.	BANK	A.B.P.	V.FINE	UNC.
☐ Boston	—	70.00	125.00	☐ Chicago	—	70.00	125.00
☐ New York	—	70.00	125.00	☐ St. Louis	—	70.00	125.00
☐ Philadelphia	—	70.00	125.00	☐ Minneapolis	—	70.00	125.00
☐ Cleveland	—	70.00	125.00	☐ Kansas City	—	70.00	125.00
☐ Richmond	—	70.00	125.00	☐ Dallas	—	70.00	125.00
☐ Atlanta	—	70.00	125.00	☐ San Francisco	—	70.00	125.00

FIFTY DOLLAR NOTES (1981)
FEDERAL RESERVE NOTES
SERIES OF 1981, SIGNATURES OF BUCHANAN-REGAN, GREEN SEAL

BANK	A.B.P.	V.FINE	UNC.	BANK	A.B.P.	V.FINE	UNC.
☐ Boston	—	70.00	125.00	☐ Chicago	—	70.00	125.00
☐ New York	—	70.00	125.00	☐ St. Louis	—	70.00	125.00
☐ Philadelphia	—	70.00	125.00	☐ Minneapolis	—	70.00	125.00
☐ Cleveland	—	70.00	125.00	☐ Kansas City	—	70.00	125.00
☐ Richmond	—	70.00	125.00	☐ Dallas	—	70.00	125.00
☐ Atlanta	—	70.00	125.00	☐ San Francisco	—	70.00	125.00

SERIES OF 1981A, SIGNATURES OF ORTEGA-REGAN, GREEN SEAL

BANK	A.B.P.	V.FINE	UNC.	BANK	A.B.P.	V.FINE	UNC.
☐ Boston	—	75.00	125.00	☐ Chicago	—	75.00	125.00
☐ New York	—	75.00	125.00	☐ St. Louis	—	75.00	125.00
☐ Philadelphia	—	75.00	125.00	☐ Minneapolis	—	75.00	125.00
☐ Cleveland	—	75.00	125.00	☐ Kansas City	—	75.00	125.00
☐ Richmond	—	75.00	125.00	☐ Dallas	—	75.00	125.00
☐ Atlanta	—	75.00	125.00	☐ San Francisco—		75.00	125.00

FIFTY DOLLAR NOTES (1985)
FEDERAL RESERVE NOTES
SERIES OF 1985, SIGNATURES OF ORTEGA-BAKER, GREEN SEAL

BANK	A.B.P.	V.FINE	UNC.	BANK	A.B.P.	V.FINE	UNC.
☐ Boston	—	75.00	125.00	☐ Chicago	—	75.00	125.00
☐ New York	—	75.00	125.00	☐ St. Louis	—	75.00	125.00
☐ Philadelphia	—	75.00	125.00	☐ Minneapolis	—	75.00	125.00
☐ Cleveland	—	75.00	125.00	☐ Kansas City	—	75.00	125.00
☐ Richmond	—	75.00	125.00	☐ Dallas	—	75.00	125.00
☐ Atlanta	—	75.00	125.00	☐ San Francisco—		75.00	125.00

FIFTY DOLLAR NOTES (1988)
FEDERAL RESERVE NOTES
SERIES OF 1988, SIGNATURES OF ORTEGA-BRADY, GREEN SEAL

BANK	A.B.P.	V.FINE	UNC.	BANK	A.B.P.	V.FINE	UNC.
☐ Boston	—	65.00	110.00	☐ Chicago	—	65.00	110.00
☐ New York	—	65.00	110.00	☐ St. Louis	—	65.00	110.00
☐ Philadelphia	—	65.00	110.00	☐ Minneapolis	—	65.00	110.00
☐ Cleveland	—	65.00	110.00	☐ Kansas City	—	65.00	110.00
☐ Richmond	—	65.00	110.00	☐ Dallas	—	65.00	110.00
☐ Atlanta	—	65.00	110.00	☐ San Francisco—		65.00	110.00

FIFTY DOLLAR NOTES (1990)
FEDERAL RESERVE NOTES
SERIES OF 1990, SIGNATURES OF VILLALPANDO-BRADY,
GREEN SEAL

BANK	A.B.P.	V.FINE	UNC.	BANK	A.B.P.	V.FINE	UNC.
☐ Boston	—	65.00	110.00	☐ Chicago	—	65.00	110.00
☐ New York	—	65.00	110.00	☐ St. Louis	—	65.00	110.00
☐ Philadelphia	—	65.00	110.00	☐ Minneapolis	—	65.00	110.00
☐ Cleveland	—	65.00	110.00	☐ Kansas City	—	65.00	110.00
☐ Richmond	—	65.00	110.00	☐ Dallas	—	65.00	110.00
☐ Atlanta	—	65.00	110.00	☐ San Francisco—		65.00	110.00

FIFTY DOLLAR NOTES (1993)
FEDERAL RESERVE NOTES
SERIES OF 1993, SIGNATURES OF WITHROW-BENTSEN, GREEN SEAL

BANK	A.B.P.	V.FINE	UNC.	BANK	A.B.P.	V.FINE	UNC.
☐ Boston	—	65.00	110.00	☐ Chicago	—	65.00	110.00
☐ New York	—	65.00	110.00	☐ St. Louis	—	65.00	110.00
☐ Philadelphia	—	65.00	110.00	☐ Minneapolis	—	65.00	110.00
☐ Cleveland	—	65.00	110.00	☐ Kansas City	—	65.00	110.00
☐ Richmond	—	65.00	110.00	☐ Dallas	—	65.00	110.00
☐ Atlanta	—	65.00	110.00	☐ San Francisco	—	65.00	110.00

FIFTY DOLLAR NOTES (1996)
FEDERAL RESERVE NOTES
SERIES OF 1995, SIGNATURES OF WITHROW-BENTSEN, GREEN SEAL

BANK	A.B.P.	V.FINE	UNC.	BANK	A.B.P.	V.FINE	UNC.
☐ Boston	—	65.00	110.00	☐ Chicago	—	65.00	110.00
☐ New York	—	65.00	110.00	☐ St. Louis	—	65.00	110.00
☐ Philadelphia	—	65.00	110.00	☐ Minneapolis	—	65.00	110.00
☐ Cleveland	—	65.00	110.00	☐ Kansas City	—	65.00	110.00
☐ Richmond	—	65.00	110.00	☐ Dallas	—	65.00	110.00
☐ Atlanta	—	65.00	110.00	☐ San Francisco	—	65.00	110.00

FIFTY DOLLAR NOTES (1918)

FEDERAL RESERVE BANK NOTES

(Large Size)

Face Design: Portrait of President Grant to left, Federal Reserve Bank in center, blue seal right.

Back Design: Female figure of Panama between merchant ship and battleship. Plates were made for all twelve Federal Reserve Districts. Only St. Louis bank issued. Less than thirty notes are known today.

BANK	SERIES	GOV'T SIGNATURES	BANK SIGNATURES	A.B.P.	V. FINE	UNC.
☐St. Louis	1918	Teehee-Burke	Attebery-Wells	—	RARE	RARE

FIFTY DOLLAR NOTES (1929)
FEDERAL RESERVE BANK NOTES

(Small Size)

Face Design:
Portrait of Grant center, name of bank left, brown serial numbers, black letter for Federal Reserve District.

Back Design:
Same as 1929 $50 note.

BANK	SERIES	SIGNATURES	SEAL	A.B.P.	V.FINE	UNC.	★UNC.
☐ New York	1929	Jones-Woods	Brown	90.00	150.00	400.00	RARE
☐ Cleveland	1929	Jones-Woods	Brown	84.00	140.00	400.00	RARE
☐ Chicago	1929	Jones-Woods	Brown	90.00	150.00	425.00	RARE
☐ Minneapolis	1929	Jones-Woods	Brown	90.00	150.00	525.00	RARE
☐ Kansas City	1929	Jones-Woods	Brown	120.00	200.00	350.00	RARE
☐ Dallas	1929	Jones-Woods	Brown	93.00	155.00	2850.00	RARE
☐ San Francisco	1929	Jones-Woods	Brown	150.00	250.00	350.00	RARE

ONE HUNDRED
DOLLAR NOTES

ORDER OF ISSUE

ONE HUNDRED DOLLAR NOTES (1862–1863)
UNITED STATES NOTES
(ALSO KNOWN AS LEGAL TENDER NOTES)
(Large Size)

Face Design: Eagle with spread wings left, three discs with "100," red seal numbers.

Back Design: Green, two variations of the wording in obligation.

SERIES	SIGNATURES	SEAL	A.B.P.	GOOD	V.FINE	UNC.
☐1862	Chittenden-Spinner*	Red	—	—	—	RARE
☐1862	Chittenden-Spinner**	Red	—	—	—	RARE
☐1863	Chittenden-Spinner**	Red	—	—	—	RARE

*First Obligation: Similar to 1875–1907 $5 note.
**Second Obligation: Shown above.

ONE HUNDRED DOLLAR NOTES (1869–1880)
UNITED STATES NOTES

(Large Size)

Face Design: Portrait of President Lincoln.

Back Design: First Issue

Back Design: Second Issue.

SERIES	SIGNATURES	SEAL	A.B.P.	GOOD	V.FINE	UNC.
☐1869	Allison-Spinner	Red	—	RARE	RARE	RARE

The following notes have a modified back design.
(Small Size)
Second Issue

SERIES	SIGNATURES	SEAL	A.B.P.	GOOD	V.FINE	UNC.
☐1875	Allison-New	Sm. Red	—	RARE	RARE	RARE
☐1875	Allison-Wyman	Sm. Red	—	RARE	RARE	RARE
☐1878	Allison-Gilfillan	Sm. Red	—	RARE	RARE	RARE
☐1880	Bruce-Gilfillan	Lg. Brown	—	RARE	RARE	RARE
☐1880	Bruce-Wyman	Lg. Brown	—	RARE	RARE	RARE
☐1880	Rosecrans-Jordan	Lg. Red	—	RARE	RARE	RARE
☐1880	Rosecrans-Hyatt	Red Plain	—	RARE	RARE	RARE
☐1880	Rosecrans-Hyatt	Red Spike	—	RARE	RARE	RARE
☐1880	Rosecrans-Huston	Lg. Red	—	RARE	RARE	RARE
☐1880	Rosecrans-Huston	Lg. Brown	—	RARE	RARE	RARE
☐1880	Tillman-Morgan	Sm. Red	—	RARE	RARE	RARE
☐1880	Bruce-Roberts	Sm. Red	—	RARE	RARE	RARE
☐1880	Lyons-Roberts	Sm. Red	—	RARE	RARE	RARE

ONE HUNDRED DOLLAR NOTES (1966) U.S. NOTES
(ALSO KNOWN AS LEGAL TENDER NOTES)
(Small Size)

Face Design: Portrait of Franklin, red seal, red serial numbers.

Back Design: Independence Hall.

SERIES	SIGNATURES	SEAL	A.B.P.	V.FINE	UNC.	*UNC
☐1966*	Granahan-Fowler	Red	120.00	200.00	800.00	2000.00
☐1966A	Elston-Kennedy	Red	165.00	275.00	1280.00	—

*This is the first note to be issued with the new Treasury Seal with wording in English instead of Latin.

ONE HUNDRED DOLLAR NOTES (1875)
NATIONAL BANK NOTES

FIRST CHARTER PERIOD (Large Size)

Face Design: Perry leaving the Saint Lawrence, left.

Back Design: Border green, center black, signing of the Declaration of Independence.

SERIES	SIGNATURES	SEAL	A.B.P.	GOOD	V FINE	UNC.
☐ Original	Chittenden-Spinner	Red	—	RARE	RARE	RARE
☐ Original	Colby-Spinner	Red	—	RARE	RARE	RARE
☐ Original	Allison-Spinner	Red	—	RARE	RARE	RARE
☐ 1875	Allison-New	Red	—	RARE	RARE	RARE
☐ 1875	Allison-Wyman	Red	—	RARE	RARE	RARE
☐ 1875	Allison-Gilfillan	Red	—	RARE	RARE	RARE
☐ 1875	Scofield-Gilfillan	Red	—	RARE	RARE	RARE
☐ 1875	Bruce-Gilfillan	Red	—	RARE	RARE	RARE
☐ 1875	Bruce-Wyman	Red	—	RARE	RARE	RARE
☐ 1875	Rosecrans-Huston	Red	—	RARE	RARE	RARE
☐ 1875	Tillman-Morgan	Red	—	RARE	RARE	RARE

ONE HUNDRED DOLLAR NOTES (1882)
NATIONAL BANK NOTES
SECOND CHARTER PERIOD (Large Size)
First Issue (Brown seal and brown backs.)

SERIES	SIGNATURES	SEAL	A.B.P.	GOOD	V.FINE	UNC.
☐1882	Bruce-Gilfillan	Brown	2500.00	3850.00	RARE	RARE
☐1882	Bruce-Wyman	Brown	2500.00	3850.00	RARE	RARE
☐1882	Bruce-Jordan	Brown	2500.00	3850.00	RARE	RARE
☐1882	Rosecrans-Jordan	Brown	2500.00	3850.00	RARE	RARE
☐1882	Rosecrans-Hyatt	Brown	2500.00	3850.00	RARE	RARE
☐1882	Rosecrans-Huston	Brown	2500.00	3850.00	RARE	RARE
☐1882	Rosecrans-Nebeker	Brown	2500.00	3850.00	RARE	RARE
☐1882	Rosecrans-Morgan	Brown	2500.00	3850.00	RARE	RARE
☐1882	Tillman-Morgan	Brown	2500.00	3850.00	RARE	RARE
☐1882	Tillman-Roberts	Brown	2500.00	3850.00	RARE	RARE
☐1882	Bruce-Roberts	Brown	2500.00	3850.00	RARE	RARE
☐1882	Lyons-Roberts	Brown	2500.00	3850.00	RARE	RARE

SECOND CHARTER PERIOD (Large Size)

Second Issue (Blue seal, green back with date "1882–1908")

Back Design: Green with date "1882–1908" center.

SERIES	SIGNATURES	SEAL	A.B.P.	GOOD	V.FINE	UNC.
☐1882	Rosecrans-Huston	Blue	1800.00	3000.00	RARE	RARE
☐1882	Rosecrans-Nebeker	Blue	1800.00	3000.00	RARE	RARE
☐1882	Tillman-Morgan	Blue	1800.00	3000.00	RARE	RARE
☐1882	Tillman-Roberts	Blue	1800.00	3000.00	RARE	RARE
☐1882	Bruce-Roberts	Blue	1800.00	3000.00	RARE	RARE
☐1882	Lyons-Roberts	Blue	1800.00	3000.00	RARE	RARE
☐1882	Vernon-Treat	Blue	1800.00	3000.00	RARE	RARE
☐1882	Napier-McClung	Blue	1800.00	3000.00	RARE	RARE

This note was also issued with (value) ONE HUNDRED DOLLARS
on the back. Very rare.   —

ONE HUNDRED DOLLAR NOTES (1902)
NATIONAL BANK NOTES
THIRD CHARTER PERIOD (Large Size)

Face Design: Portrait of John J. Knox left.

Back Design: Male figures with shield and flags.
First Issue (Red seal)

SERIES	SIGNATURES	SEAL	A.B.P.	GOOD	V.FINE	UNC.
☐1902	Lyons-Roberts	Red	1800.00	3000.00	RARE	RARE
☐1902	Lyons-Treat	Red	1800.00	3000.00	RARE	RARE
☐1902	Vernon-Treat	Red	1800.00	3000.00	RARE	RARE

Second Issue*
Design is similar to previous note. Seal and serial numbers are now blue; back of note has date "1902–1908" added.

SERIES	SIGNATURES	SEAL	A.B.P.	GOOD	V.FINE	UNC.
		Blue	600.00	1000.00	3000.00	RARE

Third Issue*
Design continues as previous notes. Seal and serial numbers remain blue, date "1902–1908" removed from back.

SERIES	SIGNATURES	SEAL	A.B.P.	GOOD	V.FINE	UNC.
		Blue	570.00	850.00	3200.00	RARE

* The notes of the **Second and Third Issue** appeared with various signatures: Lyons-Roberts, Lyons-Treat, Vernon-Treat, Vernon-McClung, Napier-McClung, Parker-Burke, Teehee-Burke, Elliott-Burke, Elliott-White, Speelman-White, Woods-White.

ONE HUNDRED DOLLAR NOTES (1929)
NATIONAL BANK NOTES
(Small Size)

Face Design: Portrait of Franklin center. Name of bank and city left. Brown seal right.

SERIES SIGNATURES	SEAL	A.B.P.	V.FINE	UNC.
☐ 1929 Type I Jones-Woods	Brown	270.00	500.00	1350.00
☐ 1929 Type II Jones-Woods	Brown	375.00	675.00	1850.00

ONE HUNDRED DOLLAR NOTES (1878)
SILVER CERTIFICATES

SERIES SIGNATURES	SEAL	A.B.P.	V.FINE	UNC.
☐ 1878 Scofield-Gilfillan-White	Red			UNIQUE
☐ 1878 Scofield-Gilfillan-Hopper	Red	NO SPECIMENS KNOWN		
☐ 1878 Scofield-Gilfillan-Hillhouse	Red	NO SPECIMENS KNOWN		
☐ 1878 Scofield-Gilfillan-Anthony	Red			UNIQUE
☐ 1878 Scofield-Gilfillan-Wyman (printed signature of Wyman)	Red	NO SPECIMENS KNOWN		
☐ 1878 Scofield-Gilfillan	Red			VERY RARE
☐ 1880 Scofield-Gilfillan	Brown	EXTREMELY RARE		
☐ 1880 Bruce-Gilfillan	Brown	RARE	RARE	RARE
☐ 1880 Bruce-Wyman	Brown	RARE	RARE	RARE
☐ 1880 Rosecrans-Huston	Brown	RARE	RARE	RARE
☐ 1880 Rosecrans-Nebeker	Brown	RARE	RARE	RARE

ONE HUNDRED DOLLAR NOTES (1891)
SILVER CERTIFICATES

(Large Size)

Face Design: Portrait of President Monroe.

SERIES	SIGNATURES	SEAL	A.B.P.	GOOD	V.FINE	UNC.
☐1891	Rosecrans-Nebeker	Red	—	RARE	RARE	RARE
☐1891	Tillman-Morgan	Red	—	RARE	RARE	RARE

This note was also issued in the Series of 1878 and 1880. They are very rare.

ONE HUNDRED DOLLAR NOTES (1882–1922)
GOLD CERTIFICATES

(Large Size)

Face Design: Portrait of Thomas H. Benton.

SERIES	SIGNATURES	SEAL	A.B.P.	GOOD	V.FINE	UNC.
☐1882	Bruce-Gilfillan	Brown	—	RARE	RARE	RARE
☐1882	Bruce-Wyman	Brown	—	RARE	RARE	RARE
☐1882	Rosecrans-Hyatt	Lg. Red	—	RARE	RARE	RARE
☐1882	Rosecrans-Huston	Lg. Brown	—	RARE	RARE	RARE
☐1882	Lyons-Roberts	Sm. Red	198.00	330.00	2800.00	RARE
☐1882	Lyons-Treat	Sm. Red	324.00	540.00	4500.00	RARE
☐1882	Vernon-Treat	Sm. Red	258.00	430.00	2800.00	RARE
☐1882	Vernon-McClung	Sm. Red	258.00	430.00	2575.00	RARE
☐1882	Napier-McClung	Sm. Red	207.00	345.00	2800.00	RARE
☐1882	Napier-Thompson	Sm. Red	270.00	450.00	2600.00	RARE
☐1882	Napier-Burke	Sm. Red	255.00	425.00	2600.00	RARE
☐1882	Parker-Burke	Sm. Red	255.00	425.00	2600.00	RARE
☐1882	Teehee-Burke	Sm. Red	255.00	425.00	2600.00	RARE
☐1922	Speelman-White	Sm. Red	255.00	425.00	2600.00	RARE

ONE HUNDRED DOLLAR NOTES (1928)
GOLD CERTIFICATES
(Small Size)

Face Design: Portrait of Franklin center. Yellow seal to left. Yellow numbers.

SERIES	SIGNATURES	SEAL	A.B.P.	GOOD	V.FINE	UNC.
☐1928	Woods-Mellon	Gold	210.00	350.00	1100.00	4650.00

ONE HUNDRED DOLLAR NOTES (1890–1891)
TREASURY OR COIN NOTES
(Large Size)

Face Design: Portrait of Commodore Farragut to right.

Back Design: Large "100," called "Watermelon Note."

Back Design: ONE HUNDRED in scalloped medallion.

SERIES	SIGNATURES	SEAL	A.B.P.	GOOD	V.FINE	UNC.
☐1890	Rosecrans-Huston	Brown	—	RARE	RARE	RARE
☐1890	Rosecrans-Nebeker	Red	—	RARE	RARE	RARE

ONE HUNDRED DOLLAR NOTES (1914)
FEDERAL RESERVE NOTES

(Large Size)

Face Design: Portrait of Franklin in center.
Back Design: Group of five allegorical figures.

SERIES OF 1914,
SIGNATURES OF BURKE-McADOO, RED SEAL
AND RED SERIAL NUMBERS

BANK	A.B.P.	GOOD	V.FINE	UNC.	BANK	A.B.P.	GOOD	V.FINE	UNC.
☐ Boston	780.00	1320.00	RARE	RARE	☐ Chicago	780.00	1320.00	RARE	RARE
☐ New York	780.00	1320.00	RARE	RARE	☐ St. Louis	780.00	1320.00	RARE	RARE
☐ Philadelphia	780.00	1320.00	RARE	RARE	☐ Minneapolis	780.00	1320.00	RARE	RARE
☐ Cleveland	780.00	1320.00	RARE	RARE	☐ Kansas City	780.00	1320.00	RARE	RARE
☐ Richmond	780.00	1320.00	RARE	RARE	☐ Dallas	780.00	1320.00	RARE	RARE
☐ Atlanta	780.00	1320.00	RARE	RARE	☐ San Francisco	780.00	1320.00	RARE	RARE

SERIES OF 1914, DESIGN CONTINUES AS PREVIOUS NOTE,
BLUE SEAL AND BLUE SERIAL NUMBERS

This note was issued with various signatures for each bank (Burke-McAdoo, Burke-Glass, Burke-Huston, White-Mellon).

BANK	A.B.P.	V.FINE	UNC.	BANK	A.B.P.	V.FINE	UNC.
☐ Boston	720.00	1200.00	2860.00	☐ Chicago	720.00	1200.00	2860.00
☐ New York	720.00	1200.00	2860.00	☐ St. Louis	720.00	1200.00	2860.00
☐ Philadelphia	720.00	1200.00	2860.00	☐ Minneapolis	720.00	1200.00	2860.00
☐ Cleveland	840.00	1400.00	2860.00	☐ Kansas City	720.00	1200.00	2860.00
☐ Richmond	720.00	1200.00	2860.00	☐ Dallas	720.00	1200.00	2860.00
☐ Atlanta	840.00	1400.00	2860.00	☐ San Francisco	720.00	1200.00	2860.00

ONE HUNDRED DOLLAR NOTES (1928)
FEDERAL RESERVE NOTES
(Small Size)

Face Design: Portrait of Franklin, black Federal Reserve Seal left with number, green Treasury Seal right.

SERIES OF 1928,
SIGNATURES OF WOODS-MELLON, GREEN SEAL

BANK	A.B.P.	V.FINE	UNC.	BANK	A.B.P.	V.FINE	UNC.
☐ Boston	150.00	275.00	725.00	☐ Chicago	150.00	275.00	725.00
☐ New York	150.00	275.00	725.00	☐ St. Louis	150.00	275.00	725.00
☐ Philadelphia	150.00	275.00	725.00	☐ Minneapolis	150.00	275.00	725.00
☐ Cleveland	150.00	275.00	725.00	☐ Kansas City	150.00	275.00	725.00
☐ Richmond	150.00	275.00	725.00	☐ Dallas	150.00	275.00	725.00
☐ Atlanta	150.00	275.00	725.00	☐ San Francisco	150.00	275.00	725.00

SERIES OF 1928A,
SIGNATURES OF WOODS-MELLON, GREEN SEAL

The number is in black and the Federal Reserve Seal is changed to a letter.
(Small Size)

BANK	A.B.P.	V.FINE	UNC.	BANK	A.B.P.	V.FINE	UNC.
☐ Boston	135.00	250.00	450.00	☐ Chicago	135.00	250.00	450.00
☐ New York	135.00	250.00	450.00	☐ St. Louis	135.00	250.00	450.00
☐ Philadelphia	135.00	250.00	450.00	☐ Minneapolis	135.00	250.00	450.00
☐ Cleveland	135.00	250.00	450.00	☐ Kansas City	135.00	250.00	450.00
☐ Richmond	135.00	250.00	450.00	☐ Dallas	135.00	250.00	450.00
☐ Atlanta	135.00	250.00	450.00	☐ San Francisco	135.00	250.00	450.00

ONE HUNDRED DOLLAR NOTES (1934)
FEDERAL RESERVE NOTES
SERIES OF 1934, SIGNATURES OF JULIAN-MORGENTHAU, GREEN SEAL

BANK	A.B.P.	V.FINE	UNC.	BANK	A.B.P.	V.FINE	UNC.
☐ Boston	—	175.00	325.00	☐ Chicago	—	175.00	325.00
☐ New York	—	175.00	325.00	☐ St. Louis	—	175.00	325.00

BANK	A.B.P.	V.FINE	UNC.	BANK	A.B.P.	V.FINE	UNC.
☐ Philadelphia	—	160.00	325.00	☐ Minneapolis	—	160.00	325.00
☐ Cleveland	—	160.00	325.00	☐ Kansas City	—	160.00	325.00
☐ Richmond	—	160.00	325.00	☐ Dallas	—	160.00	325.00
☐ Atlanta	—	160.00	325.00	☐ San Francisco	—	160.00	325.00

SERIES OF 1934A, SIGNATURES OF JULIAN-MORGENTHAU, GREEN SEAL

BANK	A.B.P.	V.FINE	UNC.	BANK	A.B.P.	V.FINE	UNC.
☐ Boston	—	160.00	325.00	☐ Chicago	—	160.00	325.00
☐ New York	—	160.00	325.00	☐ St. Louis	—	160.00	325.00
☐ Philadelphia	—	160.00	325.00	☐ Minneapolis	—	160.00	325.00
☐ Cleveland	—	160.00	325.00	☐ Kansas City	—	160.00	325.00
☐ Richmond	—	160.00	325.00	☐ Dallas	—	160.00	325.00
☐ Atlanta	—	160.00	325.00	☐ San Francisco	—	160.00	325.00

SERIES OF 1934B, SIGNATURES OF JULIAN-VINSON, GREEN SEAL

BANK	A.B.P.	V.FINE	UNC.	BANK	A.B.P.	V.FINE	UNC.
☐ Boston	—	190.00	380.00	☐ Chicago	—	190.00	380.00
☐ New York	—	190.00	380.00	☐ St. Louis	—	190.00	380.00
☐ Philadelphia	—	190.00	380.00	☐ Minneapolis	—	190.00	380.00
☐ Cleveland	—	190.00	380.00	☐ Kansas City	—	190.00	380.00
☐ Richmond	—	190.00	380.00	☐ Dallas	—	190.00	380.00
☐ Atlanta	—	190.00	380.00	☐ San Francisco	—	190.00	380.00

SERIES OF 1934C, SIGNATURES OF JULIAN-SNYDER, GREEN SEAL

BANK	A.B.P.	V.FINE	UNC.	BANK	A.B.P.	V.FINE	UNC.
☐ Boston	—	190.00	380.00	☐ Chicago	—	190.00	380.00
☐ New York	—	190.00	380.00	☐ St. Louis	—	190.00	380.00
☐ Philadelphia	—	190.00	380.00	☐ Minneapolis	—	190.00	380.00
☐ Cleveland	—	190.00	380.00	☐ Kansas City	—	190.00	380.00
☐ Richmond	—	190.00	380.00	☐ Dallas	—	190.00	380.00
☐ Atlanta	—	190.00	380.00	☐ San Francisco	—	190.00	380.00

SERIES OF 1934D, SIGNATURES OF JULIAN-SNYDER, GREEN SEAL

BANK	A.B.P.	V.FINE	UNC.	BANK	A.B.P.	V.FINE	UNC.
☐ New York	—	RARE	RARE	☐ St. Louis	195.00	350.00	925.00
☐ Philadelphia	195.00	350.00	925.00	☐ Dallas	195.00	350.00	925.00
☐ Atlanta	195.00	350.00	925.00				
☐ Chicago	195.00	350.00	925.00				

ONE HUNDRED DOLLAR NOTES (1950)
FEDERAL RESERVE NOTES
SERIES OF 1950, SIGNATURES OF CLARK-SNYDER, GREEN SEAL

BANK	A.B.P.	V.FINE	UNC.	UNC.★	BANK	A.B.P.	V.FINE	UNC.	UNC.★
☐ Boston	—	175.00	360.00	1840.00	☐ Chicago	—	175.00	360.00	1840.00
☐ New York	—	175.00	360.00	1840.00	☐ St. Louis	—	175.00	360.00	1840.00
☐ Philadelphia	—	175.00	360.00	1840.00	☐ Minneapolis	—	175.00	360.00	1840.00
☐ Cleveland	—	175.00	360.00	1840.00	☐ Kansas City	—	175.00	360.00	1840.00
☐ Richmond	—	175.00	360.00	1840.00	☐ Dallas	—	175.00	360.00	1840.00
☐ Atlanta	—	175.00	360.00	1840.00	☐ San Francisco	—	175.00	360.00	1840.00

SERIES OF 1950A, SIGNATURES OF PRIEST-HUMPHERY, GREEN SEAL

BANK	A.B.P.	V.FINE	UNC.	UNC.★	BANK	A.B.P.	V.FINE	UNC.	UNC.★
☐ Boston	—	130.00	310.00	870.00	☐ Chicago	—	130.00	310.00	870.00
☐ New York	—	130.00	310.00	870.00	☐ St. Louis	—	130.00	310.00	870.00
☐ Philadelphia	—	130.00	310.00	870.00	☐ Minneapolis	—	130.00	310.00	870.00
☐ Cleveland	—	130.00	310.00	870.00	☐ Kansas City	—	130.00	310.00	870.00
☐ Richmond	—	130.00	310.00	870.00	☐ Dallas	—	130.00	310.00	870.00
☐ Atlanta	—	130.00	310.00	870.00	☐ San Francisco	—	130.00	310.00	870.00

SERIES OF 1950B, SIGNATURES OF PRIEST-ANDERSON, GREEN SEAL

BANK	A.B.P.	V.FINE	UNC.	UNC.★	BANK	A.B.P.	V.FINE	UNC.	UNC.★
☐ Boston	—	130.00	210.00	895.00	☐ Chicago	—	130.00	210.00	895.00
☐ New York	—	130.00	210.00	895.00	☐ St. Louis	—	130.00	210.00	895.00
☐ Philadelphia	—	130.00	210.00	895.00	☐ Minneapolis	—	130.00	210.00	895.00
☐ Cleveland	—	130.00	210.00	895.00	☐ Kansas City	—	130.00	210.00	895.00
☐ Richmond	—	130.00	210.00	895.00	☐ Dallas	—	130.00	210.00	895.00
☐ Atlanta	—	130.00	210.00	895.00	☐ San Francisco	—	130.00	210.00	895.00

SERIES OF 1950C, SIGNATURES OF SMITH-DILLON, GREEN SEAL

BANK	A.B.P.	V.FINE	UNC.	UNC.★	BANK	A.B.P.	V.FINE	UNC.	UNC.★
☐ Boston	—	130.00	210.00	790.00	☐ Chicago	—	130.00	210.00	790.00
☐ New York	—	130.00	210.00	790.00	☐ St. Louis	—	130.00	210.00	790.00
☐ Philadelphia	—	130.00	210.00	790.00	☐ Minneapolis	—	130.00	210.00	790.00
☐ Cleveland	—	130.00	210.00	790.00	☐ Kansas City	—	130.00	210.00	790.00
☐ Richmond	—	130.00	210.00	790.00	☐ Dallas	—	130.00	210.00	790.00
☐ Atlanta	—	130.00	210.00	790.00	☐ San Francisco	—	130.00	210.00	790.00

SERIES OF 1950D, SIGNATURES OF GRANAHAN-DILLON, GREEN SEAL

BANK	A.B.P.	V.FINE	UNC.	UNC.★	BANK	A.B.P.	V.FINE	UNC.	UNC.★
☐ Boston	—	130.00	260.00	1230.00	☐ Chicago	—	130.00	260.00	1230.00
☐ New York	—	130.00	260.00	1230.00	☐ St. Louis	—	130.00	260.00	1230.00
☐ Philadelphia	—	130.00	260.00	1230.00	☐ Minneapolis	—	130.00	260.00	1230.00
☐ Cleveland	—	130.00	260.00	1230.00	☐ Kansas City	—	130.00	260.00	1230.00
☐ Richmond	—	130.00	260.00	1230.00	☐ Dallas	—	130.00	260.00	1230.00
☐ Atlanta	—	130.00	260.00	1230.00	☐ San Francisco	—	130.00	260.00	1230.00

SERIES OF 1950E, SIGNATURES OF GRANAHAN-FOWLER, GREEN SEAL

BANK	A.B.P.	V.FINE	UNC.
☐ Chicago	120.00	200.00	1200.00
☐ New York	141.00	235.00	1200.00
☐ San Francisco	141.00	235.00	1200.00

ONE HUNDRED DOLLAR NOTES (1963)
FEDERAL RESERVE NOTES
SERIES OF 1963, (THERE WERE NOT ANY NOTES PRINTED FOR THIS SERIES.)

SERIES OF 1963A, SIGNATURES OF GRANAHAN-FOWLER, GREEN SEAL

BANK	A.B.P.	V.FINE	UNC.	UNC.★	BANK	A.B.P.	V.FINE	UNC.	UNC.★
☐ Boston	—	120.00	235.00	735.00	☐ Chicago	—	120.00	130.00	735.00
☐ New York	—	120.00	235.00	735.00	☐ St. Louis	—	120.00	130.00	735.00
☐ Philadelphia	—	120.00	235.00	735.00	☐ Minneapolis	—	120.00	130.00	735.00
☐ Cleveland	—	120.00	235.00	735.00	☐ Kansas City	—	120.00	130.00	735.00
☐ Richmond	—	120.00	235.00	735.00	☐ Dallas	—	120.00	130.00	735.00
☐ Atlanta	—	120.00	235.00	735.00	☐ San Francisco	—	120.00	130.00	735.00

ONE HUNDRED DOLLAR NOTES (1969)
FEDERAL RESERVE NOTES
SERIES OF 1969, SIGNATURES OF ELSTON-KENNEDY, GREEN SEAL

BANK	A.B.P.	V.FINE	UNC.	UNC.★	BANK	A.B.P.	V.FINE	UNC.	UNC.★
☐ Boston	—	120.00	225.00	475.00	☐ Chicago	—	120.00	225.00	475.00
☐ New York	—	120.00	225.00	475.00	☐ St. Louis	—	120.00	225.00	475.00
☐ Philadelphia	—	120.00	225.00	475.00	☐ Minneapolis	—	120.00	225.00	475.00
☐ Cleveland	—	120.00	225.00	475.00	☐ Kansas City	—	120.00	225.00	475.00
☐ Richmond	—	120.00	225.00	475.00	☐ Dallas	—	120.00	225.00	475.00
☐ Atlanta	—	120.00	225.00	475.00	☐ San Francisco	—	120.00	225.00	475.00

SERIES OF 1969A, SIGNATURES OF KABIS-CONNALLY, GREEN SEAL

BANK	A.B.P.	V.FINE	UNC.	UNC.★	BANK	A.B.P.	V.FINE	UNC.	UNC.★
☐ Boston	—	120.00	225.00	475.00	☐ Chicago	—	120.00	225.00	475.00
☐ New York	—	120.00	225.00	475.00	☐ St. Louis	—	120.00	225.00	475.00
☐ Philadelphia	—	120.00	225.00	475.00	☐ Minneapolis	—	120.00	225.00	475.00
☐ Cleveland	—	120.00	225.00	475.00	☐ Kansas City	—	120.00	225.00	475.00
☐ Richmond	—	120.00	225.00	475.00	☐ Dallas	—	120.00	225.00	475.00
☐ Atlanta	—	120.00	225.00	475.00	☐ San Francisco	—	120.00	225.00	475.00

SERIES OF 1969B (THERE WERE NO NOTES PRINTED FOR THIS SERIES.)

SERIES OF 1969C, SIGNATURES OF BANUELOS-SHULTZ, GREEN SEAL

BANK	A.B.P.	V.FINE	UNC.	UNC.★	BANK	A.B.P.	V.FINE	UNC.	UNC.★
☐ Boston	—	120.00	225.00	450.00	☐ Chicago	—	120.00	225.00	450.00
☐ New York	—	120.00	225.00	450.00	☐ St. Louis	—	120.00	225.00	450.00
☐ Philadelphia	—	120.00	225.00	450.00	☐ Minneapolis	—	120.00	225.00	450.00
☐ Cleveland	—	120.00	225.00	450.00	☐ Kansas City	—	120.00	225.00	450.00
☐ Richmond	—	120.00	225.00	450.00	☐ Dallas	—	120.00	225.00	450.00
☐ Atlanta	—	120.00	225.00	450.00	☐ San Francisco	—	120.00	225.00	450.00

ONE HUNDRED DOLLAR NOTES (1974)
FEDERAL RESERVE NOTES
SERIES OF 1974, SIGNATURES OF NEFF-SIMON, GREEN SEAL

BANK	A.B.P.	V.FINE	UNC.	UNC.★	BANK	A.B.P.	V.FINE	UNC.	UNC.★
☐ Boston	—	120.00	200.00	430.00	☐ Chicago	—	120.00	200.00	420.00
☐ New York	—	120.00	200.00	430.00	☐ St. Louis	—	120.00	200.00	420.00
☐ Philadelphia	—	120.00	200.00	430.00	☐ Minneapolis	—	120.00	200.00	420.00
☐ Cleveland	—	120.00	200.00	430.00	☐ Kansas City	—	120.00	200.00	420.00
☐ Richmond	—	120.00	200.00	430.00	☐ Dallas	—	120.00	200.00	420.00
☐ Atlanta	—	120.00	200.00	430.00	☐ San Francisco	—	120.00	200.00	420.00

ONE HUNDRED DOLLAR NOTES (1977)
FEDERAL RESERVE NOTES
SERIES OF 1977, SIGNATURES OF MORTON-BLUMENTHAL, GREEN SEAL

BANK	A.B.P.	V.FINE	UNC.	UNC.★	BANK	A.B.P.	V.FINE	UNC.	UNC.★
☐ Boston	—	120.00	200.00	395.00	☐ Chicago	—	120.00	200.00	395.00
☐ New York	—	120.00	200.00	395.00	☐ St. Louis	—	120.00	200.00	395.00
☐ Philadelphia	—	120.00	200.00	395.00	☐ Minneapolis	—	120.00	200.00	395.00
☐ Cleveland	—	120.00	200.00	395.00	☐ Kansas City	—	120.00	200.00	395.00
☐ Richmond	—	120.00	200.00	395.00	☐ Dallas	—	120.00	200.00	395.00
☐ Atlanta	—	120.00	200.00	395.00	☐ San Francisco	—	120.00	200.00	395.00

ONE HUNDRED DOLLAR NOTES (1981)
FEDERAL RESERVE NOTES
SERIES OF 1981, SIGNATURES OF BUCHANAN-REGAN, GREEN SEAL

BANK	A.B.P.	V.FINE	UNC.	BANK	A.B.P.	V.FINE	UNC.
☐ Boston	—	120.00	200.00	☐ Chicago	—	120.00	200.00
☐ New York	—	120.00	200.00	☐ St. Louis	—	120.00	200.00
☐ Philadelphia	—	120.00	200.00	☐ Minneapolis	—	120.00	200.00
☐ Cleveland	—	120.00	200.00	☐ Kansas City	—	120.00	200.00
☐ Richmond	—	120.00	200.00	☐ Dallas	—	120.00	200.00
☐ Atlanta	—	120.00	200.00	☐ San Francisco	—	120.00	200.00

SERIES OF 1981A, SIGNATURES OF ORTEGA-REGAN, GREEN SEAL

BANK	A.B.P.	V.FINE	UNC.	BANK	A.B.P.	V.FINE	UNC.
☐ Boston	—	120.00	200.00	☐ Chicago	—	120.00	200.00
☐ New York	—	120.00	200.00	☐ St. Louis	—	120.00	200.00
☐ Philadelphia	—	120.00	200.00	☐ Minneapolis	—	120.00	200.00
☐ Cleveland	—	120.00	200.00	☐ Kansas City	—	120.00	200.00
☐ Richmond	—	120.00	200.00	☐ Dallas	—	120.00	200.00
☐ Atlanta	—	120.00	200.00	☐ San Francisco	—	120.00	200.00

ONE HUNDRED DOLLAR NOTES (1985)
FEDERAL RESERVE NOTES
SERIES OF 1985, SIGNATURES OF ORTEGA-REGAN, GREEN SEAL

BANK	A.B.P.	V.FINE	UNC.	BANK	A.B.P.	V.FINE	UNC.
☐ Boston	—	120.00	200.00	☐ Chicago	—	120.00	200.00
☐ New York	—	120.00	200.00	☐ St. Louis	—	120.00	200.00
☐ Philadelphia	—	120.00	200.00	☐ Minneapolis	—	120.00	200.00
☐ Cleveland	—	120.00	200.00	☐ Kansas City	—	120.00	200.00
☐ Richmond	—	120.00	200.00	☐ Dallas	—	120.00	200.00
☐ Atlanta	—	120.00	200.00	☐ San Francisco	—	120.00	200.00

ONE HUNDRED DOLLAR NOTES (1988)
FEDERAL RESERVE NOTES
SERIES OF 1988, SIGNATURES OF ORTEGA-BRADY, GREEN SEAL

BANK	A.B.P.	V.FINE	UNC.	BANK	A.B.P.	V.FINE	UNC.
☐ Boston	—	120.00	200.00	☐ Chicago	—	120.00	200.00
☐ New York	—	120.00	200.00	☐ St. Louis	—	120.00	200.00
☐ Philadelphia	—	120.00	200.00	☐ Minneapolis	—	120.00	200.00
☐ Cleveland	—	120.00	200.00	☐ Kansas City	—	120.00	200.00
☐ Richmond	—	120.00	200.00	☐ Dallas	—	120.00	200.00
☐ Atlanta	—	120.00	200.00	☐ San Francisco	—	120.00	200.00

ONE HUNDRED DOLLAR NOTES (1990)
FEDERAL RESERVE NOTES
SERIES OF 1990, SIGNATURES OF VILLALPANDO-BRADY, GREEN SEAL

BANK	A.B.P.	V.FINE	UNC.	BANK	A.B.P.	V.FINE	UNC.
☐ Boston	—	—	170.00	☐ Chicago	—	—	170.00
☐ New York	—	—	170.00	☐ St. Louis	—	—	170.00
☐ Philadelphia	—	—	170.00	☐ Minneapolis	—	—	170.00
☐ Cleveland	—	—	170.00	☐ Kansas City	—	—	170.00
☐ Richmond	—	—	170.00	☐ Dallas	—	—	170.00
☐ Atlanta	—	—	170.00	☐ San Francisco	—	—	170.00

ONE HUNDRED DOLLAR NOTES (1993)
FEDERAL RESERVE NOTES
SERIES OF 1993, SIGNATURES OF WITHROW-BENTSEN, GREEN SEAL

BANK	A.B.P.	V.FINE	UNC.	BANK	A.B.P.	V.FINE	UNC.
☐ Boston	—	—	160.00	☐ Chicago	—	—	160.00
☐ New York	—	—	160.00	☐ St. Louis	—	—	160.00
☐ Philadelphia	—	—	160.00	☐ Minneapolis	—	—	160.00
☐ Cleveland	—	—	160.00	☐ Kansas City	—	—	160.00
☐ Richmond	—	—	160.00	☐ Dallas	—	—	160.00
☐ Atlanta	—	—	160.00	☐ San Francisco	—	—	160.00

ONE HUNDRED DOLLAR NOTES (1996)
FEDERAL RESERVE NOTES
SERIES OF 1996, SIGNATURES OF WITHROW-RUBIN, GREEN SEAL

BANK	A.B.P.	V.FINE	UNC.	BANK	A.B.P.	V.FINE	UNC.
☐ Boston	—	—	160.00	☐ Chicago	—	—	160.00
☐ New York	—	—	160.00	☐ St. Louis	—	—	160.00
☐ Philadelphia	—	—	160.00	☐ Minneapolis	—	—	160.00
☐ Cleveland	—	—	160.00	☐ Kansas City	—	—	160.00
☐ Richmond	—	—	160.00	☐ Dallas	—	—	160.00
☐ Atlanta	—	—	160.00	☐ San Francisco	—	—	160.00

ONE HUNDRED DOLLAR NOTES (1929)
FEDERAL RESERVE BANK NOTES
(ISSUED ONLY IN SERIES OF 1929)

(Small Size)

Face Design: Portrait of Franklin, brown seal and numbers.

Back Design

BANK & CITY	SIGNATURES	SEAL	A.B.P.	V.FINE	UNC.
☐New York	Jones-Woods	Brown	150.00	275.00	575.00
☐Cleveland	Jones-Woods	Brown	150.00	275.00	575.00
☐Richmond	Jones-Woods	Brown	120.00	225.00	575.00
☐Chicago	Jones-Woods	Brown	150.00	275.00	575.00
☐Minneapolis	Jones-Woods	Brown	150.00	275.00	575.00
☐Kansas City	Jones-Woods	Brown	120.00	225.00	575.00
☐Dallas	Jones-Woods	Brown	126.00	225.00	2244.00

FIVE HUNDRED, ONE THOUSAND, FIVE THOUSAND, AND TEN THOUSAND DOLLAR NOTES

(Production of notes in denominations above one hundred dollars was discontinued in 1969.)

FEDERAL RESERVE
FIVE HUNDRED DOLLAR NOTES

	A.B.P.	V.FINE	UNC.	BANK
☐ 1928	720.00	1200.00	3750.00	ALL BANKS
☐ 1934	720.00	1200.00	3750.00	ALL BANKS
☐ 1934A	720.00	1200.00	2750.00	ALL BANKS EXCEPT BOSTON/ATLANTA
☐ 1934B	—	RARE	RARE	ATLANTA ONLY
☐ 1934C	—	RARE	RARE	BOSTON ONLY
▼ Gold Certs.				
☐ 1928	—	RARE	RARE	

ONE THOUSAND DOLLAR NOTES

	A.B.P.	V.FINE	UNC.
☐ 1928	1500.00	2500.00	RARE
☐ 1934	1500.00	2500.00	RARE
☐ 1934A	1500.00	2500.00	RARE
▼ Gold:			
☐ 1928	—	RARE	RARE
☐ 1934	—	RARE	RARE

FIVE THOUSAND DOLLAR NOTES

	A.B.P.	V.FINE	UNC.	BANK
☐ 1928	—	RARE	RARE	
☐ 1934	—		RARE	
☐ 1934A	—	RARE		ST. LOUIS ONLY
☐ 1934B	—	RARE		NEW YORK
☐ Gold Certs.	—		RARE	

TEN THOUSAND DOLLAR NOTES

	A.B.P.	V.FINE	UNC.	BANK
☐ 1928	—	RARE	RARE	
☐ 1934	—	RARE	RARE	
☐ 1934A	—	RARE	RARE	CHICAGO ONLY
☐ Gold Certs.	—	RARE	RARE	

WESTERN SCRIP & OBSOLETES

By W.R. "Bill" Rindoné

First a word regarding these western notes. Paper was generally despised in the West where gold was the main source of exchange. However, certain realities dictated the use of paper currency. Notes listed here fall into nine categories:

1) SUTLER NOTES (S); Forts in the military west needed a traceable form of barter payable between paydays.

2) PRIVATE BANK NOTES (B); Western banks isolated from the eastern monetary sources couldn't wait months for gold delivery when their daily existence was tenable at best.

3) MERCHANT SCRIP (M); Businesses needed a means to pay their workers and issue credits to customers. Companies also used scrip to ensure that wages were spent at their company store.

4) BUSINESS COLLEGE NOTES (C); These were printed for use within the classes to facilitate the handling of currency. A large number of these notes were readily accepted in city commerce.

5) WARRANTS (W); These are notes issued by government authority. They may be Federal, State, County, City, and have been issued for Postmasters, School, Roads, Juror pay, or a wide variety of other reasons. City, County, and State governments needed a medium to pay for services where non-existent funds still required the continuance of local government. They were notes with the "promise" of money.

6) COMMUNAL SCRIP (CS); Civic Groups and rural areas needed a way to trade or barter labor, necessities or agriculture goods. Storehouses were maintained and deposits made which were exchanged for notes that could be returned later for items needed as they became available. Includes U.S. Government.

7) ADVERTISING NOTES (A); These represented promises to the holder and either had a face value or were printed on other notes such as Private Bank or CSA notes. Some were printed as close copies of U.S. Federal Currency.

8) PANIC or DEPRESSION SCRIP (D); Widespread runs on banks (1907) or the closing of all banks (1933) necessitated a form of currency that could keep commerce operating while Federal notes were in short supply. It should be noted that the Federal Gov't welcomed these notes and ignored currency laws banning them.

9) CERTIFICATE OF DEPOSIT (CD); Negotiable Deposits were placed in Banks and Certificates issued that could be used in lieu of cash. These were bearer items. Some are quite valuable today.

Comments or information regarding existing unlisted or listed issues is encouraged and should be sent to Bill Rindone, P.O. Box 790, Aurora, OR 97002 or emailed to bnnw@bnnw.net. Scans and data may be submitted for the states/territories listed. This listing of Western Scrip is part of an ongoing research project.

Prices listed are for the most common of the denominations shown and for the condition most frequently found. A short glossary of terms can be found after the listings.

ALASKA

1920 $100 Valdez Igloo of Pioneers of Alaska

DENOMINATION	PRICE
1820 Russian-America - 50K Russian-American Company. "Seal Skin" money.	$6000
1954 Alaska Terr. - $100 Black Diamond Certificate (A)	$05
1916 Alaska - $1, $5, $10, $50 Klondyke Koin Scrip.	$350
1847–52 Aleutians, AT-10 Kopeks 1 Rouble, etc. Russian-America Sealskin Money (M)	$6500
1922c Anchorage, AT - $5 Finley Shoes. Poll Parrot (M)	$175
1950 Anchorage, AT - $1, 5, 10, 20, Bi-Lo Grocery Alaska (M)	$11
1954 Anchorage - $100 Black Diamond Certificate, Territorial.	$50
1923c Chichagoff - 5¢, 10¢, 25¢, 50¢ Chicagoff Development (Chichagoff Gold Mine) Scrip (M)	$125
19-- Dillingham 5¢, 10¢, 25¢, 50¢ Fisherman's Co-Op Trading Post and Roadhouse (M)	Set $22
1900c Eagle - 5c, 10c, 25c Eagle Trading Company, founded 1897.	$125
1908 Fairbanks, AT - $1 United States Construction Co.	$375

DENOMINATION	PRICE
1915 Fairbanks, AT - $1 Fraternal Order of Eagles, March 26, 1915.	$850
1907c Fairbanks, AT - 25¢, 50¢ Salchaket Trading Co. Scrip (M)	$8500
19-- ND Fairbanks - 1 share Alaska-Colonial Currency (A)	$42
1910 Iditarod - Miners and Merchants Bank Certificate of Deposit.	$175
1900 Juneau - $800 Var.$ First Nat'l Bank of Juneau Cert. of Deposit (B)	$550
19-- Juneau - 5¢, 10¢, 25¢, 50¢ Juneau Hotel Scrip (M)	$20
1939 Ketchikan - $20 Tongass Trading Co. (M)	$425
1939 Ketchikan - $20 Cordell Transfer Co. (M)	$400
1894 Kodiak - 2¢. U.S. Postal Note. Alaska was a U.S. district in 1894 (US)	$9775
1960 Kodiak - $1 Snowflake Certificate (A)	$30
1894 Sitka - 2¢ U.S. Postal note. One of only three Alaska known. (US)	$10000
1907 Nome, AT - $1, $2, $5, $10, $20, $50, $100 Nome Clearing House (D)	$9000
1916 Skagway - 50 Bunk Money reads, "50 - W.P.A.C."	$240
1920–33 Skagway, AT - $5, $10, $20, $50 White Pass Dance Hall (Issue #1 pictoral) (A)	$450
1920–33 Skagway, AT - $5, $10, $20, $50 White Pass Dance Hall (#2 Black on color paper) (A)	$250
1920–33 Skagway, AT - $5, $10, $20, $50 White Pass Dance Hall (#3 Colored Ink) (A)	$250
1902–43 - Skagway - 1 Meal Ticket round card, Pullen House. Famous hotel that burned in 1943	$45
1916c Thane - 5c Gastineau Mining Co. Scrip chits (M)	$85
1920 Valdez, AT - $10, $20, $50, $100 Valdez Igloo, Pioneers of Alaska (A)	$105
1954 Anchorage - $100 Black Diamond Certificate, Territorial.	$45

ARIZONA

1902 $4 Fiege & Company, Arizona Territory

DENOMINATION	PRICE
1933 Arizona - 50¢, $1.00 Arizona Grocery Co. (no city shown) (D)	$725
1924–?? ND Arizona - 1¢, 5¢, 10¢, 25¢, 50¢ Arizona State Hospital Script (M)	$50
1907 Benson - $1 Bank of Benson (D)	$1750
1907 Bisbee, AT - $1 Miner's and Merchants Bank (D)	$1650

DENOMINATION	PRICE
1913 Bisbee - 25¢ Bank of Bisbee/Mercantile Bank of Cananea (B)	$780
1913 Bisbee - $50, $100 Miner's and Merchants Bank CD (B)	$1400
1933 Buckeye - 5¢, 10¢, 25¢, 50¢ Buckeye Merchants (D)	$1250
1880s Clifton - 10c Longfellow Mining Co. store (M)	$1800
1880s Clifton - 25c Arizona Copper Co. at the Clifton Store	$1250
1913 Douglas - 25c Bank of Bisbee, for the Moctezuma Copper Co. (M)	$600
1933 Flagstaff - 50¢ Arizona State Teachers College (D)	$265
1880s Evans Point - 50c Evans-Van Hecke Mining Co. Cardboard R7 (M)	$4025
1907 Globe, AT - $1 Old Dominion Commercial Company (D)	$600
1879 Hackberry AT - $2.50 Hackberry Mill & Mining Co. (M)	$5500
1880c Hampden, AT - 25¢, 50¢, $1, $2 Territorial Script of F S Collins & Co. (M)	$7200
1904 Harshaw, AT - $3, $7 Var.$ Mowry Mines, American Industrial Development Co. (M)	$1000
1904 Holbrook - $10 Arizona Co-Operative Mercantile Institution (M)	$200
1933c - 25¢/25¢ Ritz Theatre. for Civilian Conservation Corp. (D)	$105
1900–04 Johnson City, AT - $1, $2, $3, $4 Fiege & Co. Commisary & Meat Market. (M)	$850
1862c Mesilla - 50c William D. Skillman "Redeemable in Confederate" (M)	RARE
1933 Nogales - $1 Nogales Herald Newspaper (D)	$525
1933 Phoenix - $1, $5, $10, $20, $50, $100 Phoenix Clearing House Certificate (D)	$600
1933 Phoenix - $1 Arizona Republic and Phoenix Gazette Newspapers (D)	$700
1933 Phoenix - 50¢, $1 Arizona Grocery Co. (D)	$700
1887 Pima Cnty - $150 Pima County Bank Certificate of Deposit	$500
1880s Pinal - $1 Pinal Gold & Silver Mining Co., Office in SF & Arizona. (M)	$6500
1900–03 Russellville, AT - $1, $2, $3, $4 Fiege Co. Commisary & Meat Market (M)	$1000
1878 Smith's Mill - 25c A. T. Smith's Mill Store. (M)	$3000
1901 Snowflake - $4.50 Arizona Co-Op Mercantile (M)	$1200
1881 Tombstone - $1000 Agency Pima County (CD)	$140
1883 Tucson - 1¢. U.S. Postal Note uncancelled. (US)	$2185
1890c Tucson, AT - 25¢, 50¢ L. Zeckendorf & Co. (M)	$9500
1870–81c Tucson, AT - 5c, 25c, 50c, $1, $5 Lord & Williams, Arizona Terr (M)	$12000
1895c Tucson, AT - 5¢ Lord & Williams, Arizona Territory (M)	$9500
1907 Tucson, AT - $1 Arizona Nat'l Bank (D)	$625
1933 Tucson - $20 Consolidated National Bank (D)	$525
1933 Tucson - $1 Arizona Daily Star Newspaper (D)	$500
1940 Tucson - 10¢, 25¢, 50¢ Old Tucson issued during filming of "ARIZONA" (A)	$85
1880c Tucson, AT - $10, $20 Safford, Hudson & Co. Bankers Scrip (B)	$135
1890s Tucson, AT - 50c L. Zeckendorf & Co. (M)	$6500
1905c Twin Buttes, AT - $2.50, $5, $10 Twin Buttes Mining and Smelting Scrip (M)	$140
1933 Tucson - 1 Bit, Wolfeville - Tucson Lodge 385, B.P.O.E.	$475

CALIFORNIA

1880 Stockton - 50¢ E.E. Washburn Commission Scrip

DENOMINATION	PRICE
19-- ND State of California - $1 Colonization of Sanguine People. (A)	$105
1933 State - Var.$ State of California Warrant (W)	$135
1933 Alameda - 25¢ Unemployed Relief Assoc. (D)	$495
1922 Anaheim - $500, $1000 Chamber of Comm. Valencia Orange Show (W)	$375
1933 Anaheim - $1 Anaheim Emergency Voucher (D)	$225
1933 Anaheim - $1 Emergency Plan Voucher (D)	$170
1933 Anderson-Cottonwood - $1 A-C Irrigation District (D)	$25
1929 Angels Camp - $10, $25 Gold, Jumping Frog Jubilee (A)	$100
1948 Angels Camp - 5 Skins, Calaveras County Fair - Jumping Frog Jubilee (A)	$30
1865–85 Contra Costa County - 5¢, 10¢ Black Diamond Mining Co. (M)	$650
1869–76 Bakersfield - $25 Kernville Stage, Valley Express Co. (M)	$800
1880's Bakersfield - Var.$ Board of Supervisors of Kern County (W)	$60
1933 Barstow - 25¢, 50¢, $1 Barstow Printer Scrip (D)	$175
1907 Berkeley - $5, $10 The First National Bank (D)	$2000
1933 Berkeley - $1 Chamber of Commerce clear envelope (D)	$30
1879 Bodie - $55 The Bodie Bank. Cert. of Deposit (CD)	$175
1933 Burlingame - $1, $2.50 City of Burlingame (D)	$185
1933 Carmel - $1 Carmel-by-the Sea Business Assoc. (D)	$85
1933 Chico - $1 Chico Chamber of Commerce (D)	$100
1932 Chula Vista - $1 Emergency Relief Voucher (D)	$190
1865 Colusa - Var.$ $35 Treasurer of Colusa County (W)	$125
1933 Compton - Time Barter, Unemployed Co-Operative Relief (D)	$40
1933 Crescent City - 25¢ Clamshell, B & A Steamship Co. (D)	$500
1933 Crescent City - 10¢, 25¢ Clamshell, Chamber of Commerce	$500
1933 Crescent City - 50¢ Clamshell, Cleanatorium Odorless Cleaners (D)	$550
1933 Crescent City - 25¢ Clamshell, Electric Shop (D)	$475
1933 Crescent City - 10¢ Clamshell, Public Utilities Office (D)	$475
1933 Crescent City - 50¢ (paper), Davis' Associated Service Station (D)	$765
1870s Darwin - $20 The Defiance Mining Co at Office in Darwin, Inyo	$5000
1870s Darwin - 25c New Coso Mining Company at Office in Darwin, Inyo	$725
18-- Downieville - Var.$ Banking House of PA Lamping & Co. Cert of Deposit. (B)	$130
1876 Eureka District, Tulare County, - $3 Settlers' Ditch Script (W)	$50

DENOMINATION	PRICE
1860c Fort Jones - 25¢ Adam B. Carlock Store (M)	$1800
1907 Fresno - $1 Fresno Clearing House (D)	$1500
1880c Fresno - $3 Kutner, Goldstein & Co. General Merchandise & Grain (A)	$125
191_ Greenville - $10 C.E. Young, payable at Indian Valley Bank. (M)	$100
1933 Hollywood - Var.$ Hollywood Cooperative Exchange (D)	$100
1965 Hollywood - Advertising film Major Dundee on back of 1862 U.S. $5 (A)	$22
1880s Humboldt Cty - $100 Humboldt County School Bank (W)	$40
1900c Jackson - 2¢ Redlick's Standard Goods (A)	$25
1933–34 Lancaster - 50¢, $1, $5 Lancaster Chamber of Commerce (D)	$150
1878 Los Angeles - $25 Silver. LA County Bank. Depression bearer note. (B)	$160
1880s Los Angeles - $1000 Woodbury's College Bank R-7 (C)	$625
1890 Los Angeles - First Nat'l Bank of Los Angeles ABNCo Specimen (CD)	$275
1908 Los Angeles - Wm. H. Carlson $5 July 1, 1908 (M)	$265
1914 Los Angeles - $1000 Los Angeles Clearing House (B)	$2800
1933 Los Angeles - $1, $5, $10, $20, $50, $100 Los Angeles Clearing House Certificate (D)	$90
1933 Los Angeles - Var.$, $5 L.A Cooperative Exchange (D)	$45
1933 Los Angeles - 10¢ U.C.L.A. Associated Students (C)	$60
1933 Los Angeles - 5¢ U.S.C. Book Store and Cafe (D)	$45
1933 Los Angeles - $1 U.S. Spring & Bumper Co. (D)	$60
ND Maltermoro - $5 St. George Vineyard at Stores, (Fresno County)	$850
1852 Marysville - Var.$ Treasurer of Yuba County Warrant (W)	$445
1860–70s Marysville - Var.$ George North & Company Due Bill (W)	$150
1880c Marysville - $3 Eastman & Wright, watchmaker and engraver (A)	$65
1932 Merced - $1 Merced Merchants Trade-At-Home Scrip (D)	$85
1933 Merced - 50¢ City of Merced Depression Scrip (D)	$45
1935 Merced - Var.$ Merced Sun-Star Scrip (D)	$80
1910 Modesto - 1¢, 2¢, 3¢, 50¢ Lewis Shoe Co., The Stork System of Savings (M)	$100
1910 Modesto - 1¢, 2¢, 3¢, 4¢ Latz's, Trustee, Stork Savings (M)	$105
1910 Modesto - 1¢, 2¢, 3¢, 4¢ The Osvald Hardware Co. Stork Savings (M)	$150
1932 Modesto - 1c, 2c Modesto Bank of America - Stork Savings (D)	$145
1933 Monterey - Monterey Peninsula Convention, Tourist & Publicity Bureau (D)	$90
1933 Monterey-Pacific Grove - 50¢, $1 Trade Warrant (D)	$125
1860c Napa - $1000 Napa Collegiate Institute R-7 (C)	$1050
1886–90's Oakland - $10 DePue & Aydelotte Business College (C)	$1050
1871–80 Oakland - 50¢ Golden Gate Academy Commerical College Bank (A)	$875
1877 Oakland - $5 Oakland Business College (C)	$400
1880's Oakland - $5 W. Wilson Commission scrip (M)	$150
1894 Oakland - 2¢ U.S. Postal note dated May 12, 1894. (US)	$740
1899 Oakland - Central Cyclery, reverse of CSA facsimile. (A)	$160
1933 Oakland - 5¢, 10¢, 25¢, 50¢, $1 Natural Development Assoc. (Chits) (D)	$30
1933 Oakland - $1, $5, $10, $20 Oakland Clearing House Assoc. (D)	$250
1880c Oroville - C.A. Parlin, watchmaker and jeweler Ad Note (A)	$150
1933 Oxnard - 25¢ City of Oxnard Depression (D)	$100
1932 Pacific Grove - $1 Pacific Grove Tribune RARE (D)	$300
1870s Panamint - 50c Surprise Valley Mill & Water Co., Inyo Co. (M)	$1200
1933 Pasadena - 25¢, 50¢, $1, $5 Hunting Hotel Company (D)	$125
1933 Petaluma - 10¢ Cochrane Lumber Co. RARE (D)	$250

DENOMINATION	PRICE
19-- ND Perris - Perris Market, M.A. Wolcott, Proprietor (A)	$25
1933 Pismo Beach - $1 Clamshell, Beach Camp (D)	$500
1933 Pismo Beach - 25¢, 50¢, $1 Clamshell, Beach Store AA Erhart (D)	$545
1933 Pismo Beach - 25¢, 50¢, $1 Clamshell, California Market (D)	$525
1933 Pismo Beach - $1 Clamshell, Pismo Beach Chamber of Commerce (D)	$625
1933 Pismo Beach - 25¢, 50¢ Clamshell, Harter Drug Co. (D)	$550
1933 Pismo Beach - 25¢, 50¢, $1 Clamshell, Henderson's Drug Store (D)	$525
1933 Pismo Beach - 25¢, 50¢, $1 Clamshell, Hi-way Cigar Store (D)	$575
1933 Pismo Beach - 25¢, 50¢, $1 Clamshell, Leiter's Pharmacy (D)	$550
1933 Pismo Beach - 25¢, 50¢, $1 Clamshell, Philipps' Tidewater Service Stn (D)	$800
1933 Pismo Beach - 25¢, 50¢, $1 Clamshell, Restwell Cabins (D)	$675
1933 Pismo Beach - $1, $5, $10 Clamshell, Wolverton Sign Company (D)	$900
1897 Portersville - $2 Labor Exchange Branch No. 136.	$475
1907 Riverside - $5 Associated Banks of Riverside, CA, (D)	$200
1933 Riverside - $1, $,5 $10, $20 Associated Banks of Riverside Clearing House (D)	$100
1933 Riverside - $1 Sherman Institute, American Indian school. (D)	$450
1863 Sacramento - $50 California and Salt Lake Mail Line (M)	RARE
1865 Sacramento - Var.$ Controller's Office - Soldiers Relief (W)	$220
1852 Sacramento - $100 Rhodes & Lusk Banking & Express (B)	$450
1877 Sacramento - $3 A.M. Smith June, 1st Ad Note (A)	$350
1880c Sacramento - $10 Elite Theater Ad Note (A)	$125
1880 Sacramento - Var.$ Treasurer of State, Controllers Warrant (W)	$70
1880c Sacramento - $1, $5 Business College Bank - (C)	$275
1883 Sacramento - Store at N.W. Corner 9th and J Sts. One Dollar Gold Note. (M)	$1500
1887c Sacramento - Sacramento Shirt Factory baseball Ad Note (A)	$1700
1887 Sacramento - $3 R.E. Gogings, apothecary Ad Note (A)	$150
19-- ND Sacramento - Reliance Lithograph Company (A)	$20
1887 Sacramento - Fred. Mason 1887 Ad Note (A)	$4100
1877 Sacramento - $3 A.M. Smith June, 1st (A)	$295
1887 Sacramento - $5 California School Bank (C)	$850
1887c San Diego - 5% K.C. Naylor, Jewelers, baseball Ad Note (A) %	$1400
1893 San Diego - $1 San Diego and Phoenix Railroad Co. (M)	$1275
1933 San Diego - $1, $5, $10, $20 San Diego Clearing House (D)	$85
1935 San Diego - 1, 5 Nuggets Gold Gulch, San Diego Exposition (A)	$30
1935 San Diego - 1, 5, 10, 20 Jardin de Plaisir, San Diego Expo (A)	$30
1849 San Francisco - $1, $5 The Miner's Bank, One Dollar on Demand. (B)	$18,000
1850 St. Francisco - 25¢, 50¢, $1 Miner's Bank of Savings of Alta California (N)	$2200
1850 San Francisco - $1000 Banking House of F. Argenti & Co., (B)	$19,000
1850s San Francisco - 25c, $20 Burgoyne & Co., San Francisco (B)	$3,750
1853 San Francisco - $50 California, N.Y. & European Steamship Co. (C)	$7500
1854 San Francisco - Var.$ Bacon & Page Duplicate of Exchange (B)	$450
1859 San Francisco - $100 Pacific Loan & Security Bank. Cert. of Deposit. (CD)	$650
1867 San Francisco - $1, $3, $5, $10, $50, $100, $500, $1000 Pacific Business College (D)	$275
18-- ND San Francisco, - H. Van Valkenburgh (The San Francisco Gold Dust Office) (M)	$1380
18-- San Francisco - $10, $20 Manly & Orr Style Unissued Scrip (M)	$300

DENOMINATION	PRICE
1867 San Francisco - $1, $5, $100, $1000 Union Business College (C)	$300
1860s–80s SF - $5, $10 Black Diamond Mining Company.	$400
1870 San Francisco - 10¢ Bank of Lower California pay in Gold Coin (CB)	$550
1870s San Francisco - $1 Gold, Amador Canal & Mining Company. (M)	$5000
1873 San Francisco. - $5 Thalia Verein. Liberty, eagle and shield. German text. (A)	$850
1874 San Francisco - $1 Bradley & Rulofson Advertising Note (A)	$880
1876 San Franciso - 50 cents, $5 Imperial Government of NORTON I. (A)	$8825
ND San Francisco - $2 Ivanpah Consolidated Mill & Mining Company (M)	$1600
ND San Francisco - $1 Pinal Gold & Silver Mining Co., Offices SF & Ariz. (M)	$6500
ND San Francisco - $10 Bank of New York	$12,650
ND San Francisco - 50c R. H. Taylor & Co., Upper California. (M)	$550
1877 San Francisco - $5 Thalia Verein April 3, 1877 (M)	$100
1880s San Francisco, - $500 St. Mary's College (C)	$1250
1880s San Francisco, - Josiah J. Lecount Ad Note (A)	$400
1880s San Francisco. $100 Crane & Brigham. Perry's special corn & bunion cure. (A)	$650
1880s San Francisco - $5 Davis & Son. San Francisco Loan Office. (A)	$350
1880s San Francisco - $10/$3 O'Meara & Painter. Eagle flanked by Xs.	$375
1880c San Francisco - $5 Brooks & Capp. The Golden Era. (A)	$345
1886 San Francisco. - $4.20 June 12, 1886. A rare cashed note. (US)	$720
1890s San Francisco - $20 William G. Badger, Commission Scrip. (M)	$650
1893 San Francisco, - $125,000 Pacific Bank, Feb. 23, 1893 (A)	$345
1894 San Francisco - $10 Dr. L. C. Harmon. Savings bond look alike. (A)	$100
1890s San Francisco, - Rosenstock, Price & Co. Ad Note (A)	$460
1898 San Francisco - Labor Exchange 1 Unit 1898 (W)	$300
1900c San Francisco - $1, $5, $10, $20, $50, $1000 Heald's Business College (C)	$275
1907 San Francisco - $1, $5, $10, $20 San Francisco Clearing House Certificate (D)	$45
1907 San Francisco - $1 Northern Electric Company (D)	$750
1907 San Francisco - $5, $10, $20 Northern Electric Company (D)	$1250
1915 San Francisco - $10, $50 Panama Pacific Exposition, 49 Camp (A)	$165
1915 San Francisco - $1, Native Sons & Native Daughters of the Golden West (A)	$165
1922 San Francisco - $1 The Johnson Studio (A)	$150
1931 San Francisco - One Meal. Depression Scrip "The Kitchen" good for one meal. (D)	$85
1933 San Francisco - $1, $5, $10 Standard Oil Company of California (D)	$175
1933 San Francisco - $1 San Francisco Clearing House Certificate (D)	$650
1907 San Francisco, - $50 Ocean Shore Railway Company (D)	$700
1865 San Joaquin - Var.$ San Joaquin County Warrant (W)	$165
18-- San Jose - $1, $5, $10, $20, $50, $100 San Jose High School Bank (C)	$185
1870, 80's San Jose - Var.$ Treasurer for Santa Clara County (W)	$90
1880c ND San Jose - Wilcox Silver Tipped Shoes. Knight on horse. (A)	$250
1928 San Jose - 2 ½¢ The Bit House, yellow chit. (A)	$90
1937 San Jose - Var.$ American Revolving Finance Co. (D)	$90
1937 San Jose - 5¢, 10¢, 25¢, 50¢ American Revolving Finance Co. (D)	$135
1934–36 San Jose - 25¢, 50¢, $1 California Market (D)	$165
1934–36 San Jose - $5, $10, $20, $50, $100, $500, $1000 California Market (D)	$85
1933 San Jose - 5¢ Ralph Mitchell, Wood flat. (A)	$18
1880c San Jose - B McIlriach, Grocer - Tiffany Commission Scrip (M)	$300

DENOMINATION	PRICE
1770s San Joaquin - $500 San Joaquin Valley College Bank (C)	$195
1907 San Luis Obispo - $5 San Luis Obispo County Bankers (D)	$450
1939 San Luis Obispo - $1 American Revolving Finance Co. (D)	$160
1887c Santa Barbara - 5 IXL Store baseball Ad Note (A)	$1450
1884 Santa Cruz - 25¢, 50¢, $1, $20, $100 Chestnutwood's College Bank (C)	$250
1933 Santa Cruz - $1 Santa Cruz Trade Warrant (D)	$50
1897 Santa Maria - 5¢ Labor Exchange Branch 177 (W)	$350
1933 Santa Monica - 50¢ Santa Monica Bureau of Relief (D)	$90
1907 Santa Rosa, - $1, $10, $20, $1000 Sonoma County Clearing House (D)	$1500
1880c Stockton - $2 Stockton Business College (C)	$750
1880c Stockton - 50¢ E.E. Washburn Commission Scrip (A)	$475
1887c Stockton - J. Glick Reliable Jeweler and Watchmaker	$1250
1907 Stockton - $5, $10, $20, $500, $1000 Stocking Clearing House (D)	$500
1933 Stockton - $1 "Pefferbill" reprint (D)	$30
1866 Taylorsville - $5 Sincerity Lodge. (M)	$250
1866 Taylorsville - $10 C.E. Young, General Merchandise. (M)	$85
1933 Truckee - 50¢, $1 Truckee Chamber of Commerce (D)	$350
1933 Tulare - 50¢, $1 City of Tular Relief Certificate (D)	$200
1907 Ventura $1, $2, $5, $10, $20 San Luis Obispo County Bankers (D)	$400
1932 Watsonville - $2.50 Pajaro Valley National Bank (4 known) (D)	$3200
1907c Weed - 30¢ Weed Lumber Co. good for one 30¢ meal. (D)	$80
1885 Woodbridge - $500 San Joaquin Valley College Bank (C)	$800
1850s Steamship Brother Jonathan 2nd Cabin Ticket. Homeward. Ca. (M)	$3500
1880s American Exchange in Europe, Limited, London. $10 or One Share.	$185
1854 Calif. - 25c Adams & Co's Express. Cardboard Chit. Ca. 1845 Mint.	$165
1860c Arapahoe, CT - $5 Oregon State Bank at Arapahoe (B)	$3500

COLORADO

DENOMINATION	PRICE
1896 Aspen - 5/100 1/4 $5 Labor Exchange Aspen Colorado (W)	$800
1863 Black Hawk Pt, CT - 15c Gov's Tobacco & Cigar Store (M)	$19,000
1909 ND Boyero - 1¢, 5¢ HF Davis, General Merchandise (M)	$650
1933 Castle Rock - Var.$ Douglas County Treasurer's Warrant (D)	$170
1930c Canon City - 25¢ Batchelor Dairy (Orange) (A)	$50
1933 Castle Rock - Var.$ Douglas County Treasurer's (W)	$195
1863 Central City - 20c Central City Bakery, Colo. Territory. (M)	$8500
1880s Cerro - 5c Arizona Mining Co. Office or Store (M)	$15,000
1911 Cokedale - 5c, 10c Gottlieb Mercantile. (M)	$775
1880c Colorado Springs - $3 Geo. Fechter Advertising Note (A)	$950

DENOMINATION	PRICE
1883 Colorado Spgs. - 5c U.S. Postal Note. Sept 4, 1883. (US)	$3200
19-- ND Colorado Springs - Pelta's Department Store Premium Scrip (A)	$85
1907 Colorado Springs - $2, $5, $10, $20 Commercial Bank & Trust (Clearing House) (D)	$180
1907 Colorado Springs - $1, $5, $10 First Nat'l Bank (Clearing House) (D)	$200
1933 Crede - 50¢, $1 Town of Crede (D)	$135
1933 Delta - Var.$ - Natural Development Assoc. (D)	$150
1859 Denver - $5, $25 Treas. of the Territory of Jefferson, Denver (G)	$19,000
1859c Denver - $5 Clark, Gruber & Co. with Bison (B)	$130,000
1860 Denver - 50¢ Woolworth & Co. (M)	$1950
1860 Denver - $5 Clark, Gruber & Co, Terr. of Jefferson. Pikes Peak Gold. (B)	$950
1861–63 Denver, CT - 10c, 20c, 25c, 50c, $1 Banking House CA Cook & Co. (B)	$10,000
1867 Denver - One Sack of Flour or $10, First Nat'l Bank of Denver. (B)	$1500
1877 Denver - $2, $5, $100 Business College Bank of Colorado (C)	$1200
1887 Denver - $5 J. Thorrington, Boots & Shoes baseball Ad Note (A)	$3000
1890 Denver - 5c Colorado Telephone Co.	$795
1897 Denver - 1/10, 1/4, 1/2, 1, 2 Labor Exchange #158. Good for hours of labor (W)	$185
1899 Denver - $1 Colorado Supply Co. (M)	$1500
1900c Denver - 25c Hindman Mercantile (M)	$750
1900 Denver $1 Western Trading & Supply Co., Denver, Colorado. (M)	$800
1900 Denver - 25c State Mercantile Company. Existence Not Confirmed	
1901 Denver - 10¢, 25¢ The Miner's Trading Company (M)	$1600
1901–05 Denver 5¢, 10¢, 25¢ Colorado Supply Co. (M)	$175
1901–10 Denver $1, $2, $5 Colorado Supply Co. (M)	$375
1904 Denver - 5c Hensley Supply Co. (M)	$650
1905 Denver 5¢ Rocky Mountain Supply Co. (M)	$750
1905–07 Denver - 5¢, 25¢ Western Stores Co. (M)	$550
1905c Denver - 50¢, $1 Western Trading & Supply (M)	$450
1905 Denver - 25c South Canon Supply Co. Red "25" center (M)	$1250
1905 Denver - $1 Sunnyside Coal Mining Co. (M)	$1550
1907 Denver - $5, $10 Colorado Nat'l Bank (D)	$250
1907 Denver - $5 Denver Nat'l Bank Panic of '07 cashiers check (D)	$500
1907 Denver - $5, $10, $20 Capitol Nat'l Bank of Denver (D)	$225
1907 Denver - $5, $10, $20 First Nat'l Bank of Denver (D)	$225
1907 Denver - $5, $10, $20 Nat'l Bank of Commerce (D)	$250
1907 Denver - $5, $10 United States Nat'l Bank (D)	$225
1910 Denver. - $5 Colorado Supply Co. Red FIVE (M)	$6800
1910 Denver - $5, $10 Gem City Business College R7 Discovery notes	$1250
1921 Denver - $1 Askin & Marine Company, Green and Gold (A)	$385
1933 Denver - $5, $10, $20 The International Trust Company (D)	$175
1933 Denver - $2.50 trade scrip booklet from the State Theatre (M)	$85
1933 (ND) Durango - 5¢, 10¢, 25¢ Community Council Scrip (D)	$225
1922 Elizabeth - $1 Elizabeth Mercantile Co. $1 or 100 pds wheat. (G)	$375
1907 Fort Collins - $2, $5, $10 Ft. Collins Clearing House (D)	$120
1907 Fort Collins - $2, $5 Commercial Bank & Trust (D)	$130
1907 Fort Collins - $5, $10 Poudre Valley Nat'l Bank of Ft. Collins (D)	$250
1907 Fort Collins - $5, $10 First Nat'l Bank of Ft. Collins (D)	$230

DENOMINATION	PRICE
1912 Fort Collins - 1c, 2c, 3c, 4c, 5c, 10c Edmonds Dry Goods, Stork (M)	$135
1912 Fort Collins - 1c, 2c, 3c, 4c, 5c, 10c Collins Cash Clothing, Stork (M)	$135
1912 Fort Collins - 1c, 2c, 3c, 4c, 5c, 10c Lowell-Moore Hardware, Stork (M)	$150
1933 Fort Collins - 1¢, 2¢, 3¢, 4¢, 5¢, 10¢ Edmonds Dry Goods, Stork Savings (D)	$165
1933 Fort Collins - 1¢, 2¢, 3¢, 4¢, 5¢, 10¢ Collins Cash Clothing Co., Stork (D)	$150
1933 Fort Collins - 1¢, 2¢, 3¢, 4¢, 5¢, 10¢ Lowell-Moore Hardware Co., Stork (D)	$150
1860s Fort Lyon - 10c, 50c, $1, $2 Sutler's Check, Fort Lyon, Col. Ter. (S)	$6500
1897 Fruita - 1/10, 1/4, 1/2, 1, 2 Labor Exchange. Good for hours of labor (W)	$550
1896 Garrison - 5/100 Labor Exchange # 153.	$550
1884 Georgetown - 7¢ U.S. Postal note. Only nine Colorado notes known (US)	$2250
1906 Gold Boulder - $1.50 Gold Boulder Mining Co, Punch card. (M)	$1000
1933 Golden - $1 Golden Welfare Association (D)	$160
1915 Goldfield - $2, $50 Var.$ City of Goldfield Colorado (W)	$70
1896 Hotchkiss - 1/10, 1/2 Labor Exchange #156. (CS)	$450
1933 Hot Sulphur Springs - $5 First State Bank (D)	$300
1933 Julesburg - $1 Town of Julesburg (D)	$175
1933 Kremmling - $1 Bank of Kremmling (D)	$185
1924 Leadville - $50 Days of '79. Leadville Lodge B.P.O.E. (A)	$170
1907 Loveland - $1, $20 Loveland National Bank (D)	$525
1907 Loveland - $1, $5 Larimer County Bank (D)	$440
1900c Ludlow - 5c Woodward Brothers, Merchandise (M)	$1625
1860s Missouri City, CT - Treas. of Consolidated Ditch Co. (M)	$16,000
1899 Pueblo - 25c, 50c, $1 Colorado Supply Co. (M)	$650
1900c Pueblo - 5¢ Herman & Shloss, General Merchandise (M)	$600
1910 Pueblo - 5c, 10c, 25c, 50c The Union Trading Company. (M)	$850
1933 Pueblo - Depression Scrip, existence unconfirmed (D)	
1907 Rocky Ford - $1, $5, $10, $20 State Bank of Rocky Ford (D)	$450
19?? Rocky Ford - 50c, $1 Clarks Corner (A)	$21
1949 Rocky Ford - 5¢ Watermelon Day - Cloth Watermelon (A)	$40
1885c Ruby City - Var.$ The Bank of Ruby City. ABNCo. (CD)	$350
1859 St. Vrain - $5.67 St. Vrain, Golden City & Colo. Wagon-Road Co (W)	$750
1880c Salida - $3 New York Clothing House Adv. Note (A)	$600
1933 Springfield - Var.$ Baca County Treasurer's Warrant (D)	$350
1933 Sterling - $1, $5, $10 Commercial Savings Bank (D)	$150
1933 Sterling - $1 Sterling, City of, Scrip Certificate (D)	$150
1933 Sterling - $1 Sterling Lions Club (D)	$250
1933 Sterling - $1, $5 Sterling Security State Bank (D)	$135
1935 Sterling - 10¢, 25¢ Logan County Fair (A)	$35
1892 Trinidad - $1 Trinidad Fuel Co	$650
1894 Trinidad - 5c Victor Coal & Coke Co. (M)	$1050
1905 Trinidad - 10c Chicosa Mercantile Co.	$700
1912 Trinidad - $1 The Aiello Mercantile Company (M)	$1000
1933 Trinidad - Depression Scrip, existence unconfirmed (D)	
18-- Walsenburg - 5¢ Pinion Supply Co. (M)	$800

DAKOTA TERRITORY

1868 $50 First Empire City Outfitting Store

DENOMINATION	PRICE
1868 Territory - US Treasury payroll for Territorial civil servants (W)	$475
1888 Canton, DT - Var.$ Town Treasurer Canton D.T. (W)	$135
1870s Central City, DT, Black Hills - $1 Dorr Heffleman, First Central Bank.	$17,500
1868 Cheyenne, DT - $50 First Empire City Outfitting Store (A)	$16,500
1888c Deadwood, DT - Chase's Clothing, Boots, Shoes baseball Ad Note (A)	$4500
1888 Deadwood, DT - I.H. Chase 1888 Baseball Adv. Note (A)	$11,000
1888 Devil's Lake, DT - 1¢ US Postal note. Only 5 recorded DT. (G)	$9500
1871 Ft. Rice, DT - $55 U.S. Infantry Pay Voucher (W)	$500
1861–64 Fort Abercrombie, D. T. - 5c J.M. Stone & Co, Proprietor Sutler's Store. (S)	$16,000
19-- ND Holabird - Var.$ County of Hyde, Holabird School Township (W)	$195
1880s–90s Watertown DT - $5 Chalmers Bonded Investment Co., (A)	$16,500
1889 ND Holabird - Var.$ County of Hyde, Holabird School Township (W)	$200
1885–89 Watertown - $5 Chalmers Bonded Investment Co., Watertown N B (A)	$3500

HAWAII

1933 $1 Honolulu Clearing House Certificate, Hawaii Territory

DENOMINATION	PRICE
1879 Hawaiian Islands - $50 Department of Finance. Certificate of Deposit	$1500
192- Honokaa - Var.$ The Bank of Hawaii, Certificate of Deposit	$1250
1874 Honolulu - $100 Hawaiian Treasury Certificate of Deposit	$7000
1887 Honolulu - $10, $20, $50, $100 Bank of Claus Spreckels (B)	$8500
18-- Hawaiian Islands $10, $20, $50, $100 Certificate of Deposit. (B)	$12,500

DENOMINATION	PRICE
1922c Honolulu - 5c Orange Lantern Ball Room. 1st at A st. (M)	$350
1933 Honolulu - $1 Honolulu Clearing House Certificate, Hawaii (D)	$135
1933 Honolulu - $5 Honolulu Clearing House Certificate, Hawaii (D)	$350
1933 Honolulu - $10 Honolulu Clearing House Certificate, Hawaii (D)	$575
1974 Honolulu - $2 Windjammer Cruises	$20
1942 Kahuilui, Maui - $3 Naval Air Station NASKA (S)	$150
1835 Kaua'i - Hapawalu (12.5c), Hapaha (25c) Hapalua (50c) Sm chits $	$7200
1839 Kaua'i - $3, $5 Ladd & Company scrip ($3) Whaling ($5) Ships $	RARE
1911 Kona - $3 Kona & Kau Railway Company Coupon (W)	$75
1840c Lahaina - 50c Lahainaluna Seminary Business College. (C)	$9900
1843 Maui - 3c to $1 Rev. Lorrin Andrews of the Lahainaluna Seminary.	$25,000
1844 Wailuku - 6 1/4c Edward Bailey for Wailuku Female Seminary.	$14,000

IDAHO

1885 $5 Coeur D'Alene Water Supply Company Territorial

DENOMINATION	PRICE
1888 Alturas County, IT - Idaho Territorial School Warrant. Green (W)	$350
1867 Boise City, IT - $10, $20, $50, $100 Du Rell & Moore, First Nat'l Bank of Idaho (B)	$3700
1883 Boise City, IT - Treasurer of Idaho Territory Warrant (W)	$295
1928 Boise - 100 Boldts Restaurants - Battleship US$ Idaho at Bremerton (A)	$275
1907 Boise - $1, $20, $10 First Nat'l Bank of Idaho (D)	$400
1933 Boise - 5¢, 10¢ Farmer-Labor Exchange (D)	$750
1933 Boise - $5, $20 Chamber of Commerce - Nat'l Grange Harvest Festival (D)	$500
1933 Boise - $5 Ida-Ha Cafe Scrip card for meals (M)	$85
1943 Boise - 1¢ Retail Merchants Bureau. Minute Man in "V". Blue (M)	$8
1932 Caldwell - $1, $5 Dairymen's Co-Operative. Blue/Gold (D)	$50
1933 Caldwell - $5 Dairymen's Co-Operative. Gold (D)	$60
1935 Caldwell - $1, $5 Dairymen's Co-Operative. Plum (D)	$60
1937 Caldwell - $5 Dairymen's Co-Operative. Green (D)	$60
1885 Coeur D'Alene - $5 Coeur D'Alene Water Supply Company (M)	$950
1907 Coeur D'Alene - $5, $10, $20, $50 American Trust Company (D)	$1250
1860s Devil's Gate - 12 1/2¢, 50c Devil's Gate Toll Road. Yellow cardboard (M)	$675
1935 Elk River - $1 Civilian Conservation Corp. 590th Co. (D)	$375
1892 Franklin - 5¢, 10¢ Oneida Mercantile Union (M)	$6500
1894 Franklin - 10¢, 25¢ Lowe & Company (M)	$3700
1874 Granite Creek, IT - 25c Alex. Danskin Dealer in Genl Merch. (M)	$7500

DENOMINATION	PRICE
1867 Idaho City - $10, $20, $50, $100 Du Rell & Moore FNB of Idaho (B)	$3950
1895 Idaho Falls - 1/20 1 Labor Exchange (W)	$1500
1936 Lapwai - 25¢ Idaho Spaulding Centennial. Wood (D)	$135
1864 Laramie, I.T. - Var.$ Asst. Treasurer of the United States (W)	$350
1866c Lewiston - Lewsiton Road, (good for) _ Head of Cattle, Mules or Horses	$765
1933 Malad City - 10¢, 25¢, 50¢ Unbankable Certificate, Malad City, ID (D)	$900
1907 Milner - $1 Twin Falls North-Side Land & Water (W)	$1750
1894 Moscow - 2¢ U.S. Postal note. Only six (6) Idaho notes recorded (US)	$1900
1915 Moscow - Var.$ Latah County Warrant (W)	$135
1890c Preston - 5¢, 10¢, 50¢ W.C. Parkinson & Co. (M)	$3000
1868 Rocky Bar - Alturas County Territorial Warrant (W)	$365
1867 Silver City - $10, $20, $50, $100 Du Rell & Moore First Nat'l Bank of Idaho (B)	$3950
1876–89 Silver City - Var.$ Owyhee County Territorial Warrant (W)	$265
1890 Silver City - Var.$ Owyhee County Warrant (W)	$135
1863 Virginia City - $1 Tutt & Donnell, !$ Gold Dust. Indian/bison (M)	$17,500

KANSAS

1871 $1 City of Leavenworth, Kansas Territory

DENOMINATION	PRICE
1860's 1st Kansas Cavalry 25c Sutler note (S)	$13,800
1907 Atchison - $1000 Clearing House (D)	$900
1907 Atchison - $1, $2, $5 Atchison State Bank (D)	$475
1907 Atchison - $1, $2, $5 Exchange Nat'l Bank (D)	$260
1907 Atchison - $1, $2, $5, $10 First Nat'l Bank of Atchison (D)	$250
1900c Baileyville - Bailey and Co. Due bill Green (M)	$125
1899 Beauville - 5¢ Beauville mercantile (M)	$500
1890c ND Broken Bow - $10 Broken Bow Business College (B)	$1000
1884 Burlington - 1¢ U.S. Postal note. (US)	$750
1857c Chetopa, KT - $2 City of Chetopa (B)	$675
1933 Clay Center - 5¢, 50¢ Chamber of Commerce (D)	$19
1854 Delaware, KT - $1, $2 Delaware City Bank (B)	$425
1890s Dodge City - $1 W. F. DEAN'S GROCERIES and QUEENSWARE (M)	$500
1855 Easton - $1 Easton Bank Train. (D)	$650
1890s Florence - $10 "For use in public schools Florence" Ks (C)	$115
1854 Fort Leavenworth KT - $2, $3, $5, $10 Merchants Bank (B)	$175
1856 Fort Leavenworth, KT - $1, $5, $10 Drovers Bank (B)	$5000

DENOMINATION	PRICE
1880 Fort Scott - 5¢, $50 Kansas Normal College Bank (B)	$950
1898 Freedom - 1/10 Labor Exchange #199. (CS)	$325
1933 Garden City - United States Sugar & Land Co. (D)	$600
1933 Gardner - City of Gardner, KS (D)	$140
1880s Garnett - $1 M. D. Calkins & Co's. $1. Silver Tipped Boots and Shoes (A)	$250
1880c Greenwood - A.W. Sanders Groceries Ad Note ($100 CSA) (A)	$165
1800c Hiawatha - L.S. McNamar Ad Note (A)	$180
1882 Holton - $1, $5, $10 Commercial Institute Bank (B)	$100
1889 Hutchinson - 5 Star Clothiers baseball advertising note (A)	$1495
1907c Independence - $1, $5, $10 Citizen's Nat'l Bank (D)	$385
1907c Independence - $1, $5, $10, $20 Commercial Nat'l Bank (D)	$385
1907c Independence - $1 First Nat'l Bank (D)	$385
1863 Junction City - 25¢ Streeter & Strickler (M)	$1375
1933 Kansas City - Var.$ Goodwill Barter and Exchange Centers (D)	$120
1869 Larned - J.H. Dow, General Merchandise, Adv. Note (A)	$325
1880s Lawrence - 50¢ E. A. Skinner, Durfee House "$2 per Day." (A)	$325
18-- Lawrence - $2, $3 The Bank of Wm. H.R. Lykins (B)	$1400
18-- Lawrence - $3 The Lawrence Bank (B)	$3300
1857 Lawrence, KT - $2, $3 Redwing Bank (B)	$1000
1861 Lawrence - Var.$ Nat'l Bank of Lawrence Cert. of Deposit (B)	$110
1856 Leavenworth City, KT - $3, $5, $10 Drovers Bank. Ormsby (B)	$1200
1870s Lawrence - $20 Western Business College Bank (C)	$275
187- Lawrence - $3 Macauley's Commercial Institute (C)	$275
1880's Lawrence - 50c E. A. Skinner. Durfee House. "$2 per Day." (A)	$300
18-- Lawrence - $2, $3 The Bank of Wm. H. R. Lykins (B)	$950
18-- Lawrence $1, $3, $5 The Lawrence Bank (B)	$3220
18-- Lawrence - 10c The Business College Bank, Lawrence Ks (C)	$280
1861 Lawrence - Var.$ Nat'l Bank of Lawrence Cert. of Deposit (CD)	$110
1856 Leavenworth City, KT - $2, $3 Drovers Bank. Ormsby (B)	$750
1856 Leavenworth City, KT - $1 The City Bank (B)	$375
1856 Leavenworth City, KT - $2, $3 The City Bank (B)	$900
1871 Leavenworth - $1, $2, $3 City of Leavenworth (B)	$385
1862 Leavenworth - $1 Scott, Kerr & Co. (B)	$700
18-- ND Leavenworth - Var.$ Western Business College (C)	$285
1856 Lecompton, KT - $1, $3, $5 The State Bank (B)	$1300
1861 Manhattan - $1 John Pipher & Co. Eagle + ship.	$1500
1933 McPherson - $1, $5 City of McPherson, Kansas, (D)	$415
1933 Neodesha - 5¢ ,10¢, 25¢, 50¢, $1, $5 Chamber of Commerce (D)	$60
1898 Osage City - 1/10 labor Exchange #223. (CS)	$325
1933 Oswego - $5 First Nat'l Bank of Oswego (D)	$135
1933 Parsons - $5 Parson's Commercial Bank (D)	$225
1890s Pittsburg - 10¢, $375, $5 Note Rogers Coal Co. (M)	$1300
1894 Pittsburg - 10¢ The Wear Coal Co. (M)	$375
1901 Pittsburg, etc. - $1 A Hood & Sons Implement Co. (M)	$185
1907 Pittsburg - $1, $2, $5, $10 Associated Banks of Pittsburg (D)	$270
1905 Rook County - Var.$ State of Kansas Warrant (W)	$70
1933 Russell - 50¢ City of Russell (D)	$65

DENOMINATION	PRICE
1933 Sedan - 25¢ Sedan Depression Scrip (D)	$135
18-- ND Seneca - 50¢ Lappin & Scrafford (M)	$650
1880s Topeka - $5 Kansas Pacific Railway. Steer (A)	$1150
1880c Topeka - 10¢ C.C. Andrews and Company (M)	$135
1880s Topeka - 50¢ Karp & Turnbull (M)	$75
1880s Topeka - 10¢ Kore & Hackman (M)	$100
1855 Topeka, KT - $20 The State of Kansas (W)	$750
1867 Topeka - $1, $10, $20 Union Military Scrip. Bare-breasted maid (W)	$225
1867 Topeka - Var.$ Union Military Scrip. Penned amts-Plain (G)	$325
1867 Topeka - $100 Union Military Scrip. Lincoln vignette. (W)	$825
1907 Topeka - $2, $5 Associated Banks of Topeka (D)	$400
1933 Trego - $1 County of Trego. Yellow and very ornate. (D)	$375
1915c - 25¢, 50¢, $1, $5 Albert H. Shuler / Citizens State Bank (M)	$50
1880s Wichita - $2, $50 Southwestern Business College (C)	$175
1880s Wichita - 1¢, 3¢, 15¢, Southwestern Business College (C)	$30
1914 Wichita - Wichita Clearing House Assoc. (D)	$125
1933 Wichita - 5¢ Unemployed Trading Post (D)	$250
1933 Wichita - $1 Howard W. Shroeder / Farmers State Bank (M)	$170
1934 Wilmore - $1 Jack, Merchants of Wilmore (D)	$15
18-- Wyandott - $1, $2 Kansas State Savings Bank. Green/black (B)	$230
18-- Wyandott - $3 Kansas State Savings Bank. Green/black (B)	$850
1857c ND 1057c Wyandott - $2 The City of Wyandott (M)	$350
18-- Wyandott - $1, $3 Kansas City Savings Bank. Green overprint. (B)	$500

MISSOURI

DENOMINATION	PRICE
1862 State Issue - $1, $2, $3, $5, $10, $20 STATE OF MISSOURI White or Blue paper (W)	$130
18-- ND State Issue- $1, $2, $3, $5, $50, $100 MISSOURI DEFENCE BOND (W)	$115
1874 State Issue - Var.$ STATE OF MISSOURI Civil War settlements (W)	$60
1859 Arrow Rock - $20 Bank of the State of Missouri. (Ctf)	$640
18-- ND Carrollton - 50c Henry Myers. Indian chief, left. (M)	$4300
1890 Chillicothe - $5, $10 Chil. Normal School & Business Institute (C)	$200
1907 Doe Run - $1, $2, $5 Doe Run Lead Co. (D)	$25

DENOMINATION	PRICE
1874 Gads Hill - $1 Clear Water Lumber Co. Washington, lower left. (M)	$190
1857 Fayette - $20 Bank of the State of Missouri. Two women seated (Ctf)	$230
1858 Fayetteville - Bank of the State of Missouri. (B)	$350
1862 Granby $1 Leads Mine Scrip. Present at Fort Smith to Major Geo W. Clark (M)	$210
1862 Hannibal - 10c City of Hannibal. RECEIVABLE FOR ALL CITY DUES (W)	$460
1872 Iron Mountain - 10c, $2 American Iron Mountain. U.S. Fractional lookalike. (M)	$315
1933 Jackson - $15, $25, $45, $100, $125 Treas. of Jackson County. Sig Harry Truman (D)	$115
1862 Jefferson - $10 State of Missouri Defence Warrant. seal Girl (B)	$125
1907 Joplin - $1, $2, $5 Joplin State Bank (D)	$110
1907 Joplin - $1, $5 Miner's Bank of Joplin (D)	$225
1870 Kansas City - $1, $2 City of Kansas (W)	$210
1872 Kansas City - $50 First Nat'l Bank - Spaldings Commercial College. (C)	$200
1880c Kansas City - $2, $10 Student's Bank - Spalding's Comm'l College (C)	$190
1891 Kansas City - 1¢ U.S. Postal note. Aug. 5, 1891. (US)	$550
1898 Kansas City - 5/100 Labor Exchange #199. (CS)	$350
1907 Kansas City - $1, $2, $5, $10 Commerce Trust Company (D)	$50
1907 Kansas City - $2, $5, $10 Kansas City Clearing House (D)	$75
1907 Kansas City - $1, $2 Union National Bank of Kansas City (D)	$200
1907 Kansas City - $5 Missouri Savings Bank (D)	$300
1897 Marshall - 1/2 Labor Exchange # 183. (W)	$115
18-- LeGendre Mines - $2 Chas. Le Gendre & Co. (M)	$100
1862 Lexington - $1 Farmers Bank of Missouri	$325
1961 Liberty - $1 Farmers Bank of Missouri. Slaves in cornfield. (B)	$805
1869 Maramec - 5c Maramec Iron Works, Steer ctr. (M)	$250
1862 Neosho - 50c Roberts & Eppem. Redeemable in CSA Money. (M)	$315
1853 Palmyra - $20 Bank of the State of Missouri. Male portraits in corners. (Ctf)	$325
1880's Paris - W.S. Moore, Shoes, Adv. Note (A)	$75
1871 Pilot Knob - 10c Pilot Knob Iron Company. Train. (M)	$800
1876 Pleasant Hill - 5 W. C. Davis. Clay Bros. Cook stoves. (A)	$130
1818 St. Genevieve - $3, 10 Bank of Missouri (B)	$750
1865c St. Joseph - $20, $100 First Nat'l Bank - Nat'l Business Colleges	$175
1907 St. Joseph - $1, $2, $5, $10 St. Joseph Clearing House (D)	$225
1907 St. Joseph - $1, $5 Drovers and Merchants Bank (D)	$125
1907 St. Joseph - $1, $2 Merchants Bank (D)	$100
1907 St. Joseph - $1 First National Bank of Saint Joseph (D)	$150
1907 St. Joseph - $2, $5 Burnes National Bank of Saint Joseph (D)	$180
1860 St. Joseph & Hannibal - 50¢ Missouri. Woolworth & Co. (M)	$400
1838 $20 Bank of the State of Missouri. Payable at B of A, N.Y. (B)	RARE
1862 Sarcoxie - $2 Dixon & Nichols Confederate Note. Plow, etc. Pay in CSA notes (M)	$9000
18-- St. Louis - Page, Bacon & Co. Orig Bill of Exch. Danforth proof (B)	$1000
18-- St. Louis - $2 Bank of St. Louis. Horses frightened by storm. (B)	$525
1817 St. Louis - $2 Bank of St. Louis (B)	$3000
1819 St. Louis - $20 Bank of Missouri. Statue of Jefferson, ships beyond. (B)	$1200
18-- St. Louis - $10 Exchange Bank of St. Louis. Girl with scythe. (B)	$1150
1819 St. Louis - $5 Missouri Exchange Bank. (B)	$1900

DENOMINATION	PRICE
1819 St. Louis - 37 1/2¢ Bank of St. Louis. Ornate end panels. (B)	$4025
1820 St. Louis - Bank of Missouri. $1, $5, $10. April 1, 1820. (B)	$230
1829 St. Louis - $5 Bank of the United States (B)	$450
1839 St. Louis - 50c, 75c A. T. Crane, Postmaster, "POST OFFICE CHANGE"	$430
1837 St. Louis - 50c, 75c Epperand and Hawken. Famous gunmaker. (M)	$460
1859 St. Louis - $10 Merchants Bank of St. Louis (B)	$650
1859 St. Louis - $5 Southern Bank of St. Louis (B) unk.	
1859 St. Louis - $5 Terre Haute, Alton & St. Louis RR Co. (M)	$85
1859 St. Louis - $10, $50 Mechanic's Bank. Three maids/Wash./Ship (B)	$185
1860s St. Louis - $40, $50 North Missouri Railroad Adv. Note (A)	$250
1861 St. Louis - $1, $20 Union Bank of Missouri. (B)	$920
1860s St. Louis - $10, $20, $50 Rohrer's Business College (C)	$385
1869 St. Louis - $1 Public School Library Society of St. Louis (G)	$350
1873 St. Louis - $1, $2, $3 City of St. Louis (B)	$135
1874 St. Louis - $20 St. Louis & Southeastern Railroad (M)	$175
1870s St. Louis - $1 Dr. J.J. McLean. Adv. note (A)	$160
1880 St. Louis - $100 Butcher's and Drover's Bank (B)	$180
18-- St. Louis - $5 Bank of St. Louis (B)	$400
1880s St. Louis - $10,000 St. Louis Mutual Life Ins. Adv note. (A)	$270
1880s St. Louis - $3 A. B. Mayer. "Dry Buffalo Bones." on $3 Defense Bond.	$375
1887c St. Louis - Nat'l Baseball Assoc. baseball Ad Note (A)	$1250
1887c St. Louis - Thom. Wand, Livery and Boarding Stable baseball Ad Note (A)	$3450
1907 St. Louis - $1 Central Nat'l Bank of St. Louis (D)	$225
1907 St. Louis - $1, $2, $5, $10, $20 Commerce Trust Co. Treasurers (D)	$150
1907 St. Louis - $1, $5, $10 Mechanics-American Nat'l Bank of St. Louis (D)	$170
1907 St. Louis - $1, $5, $10 Nat'l Bank of Commerce in St. Louis (D)	$110
1907 St. Louis - $1, $5, $10 Third Nat'l Bank of St. Louis (D)	$115
1912 St. Louis - 50¢ American Women's League (A)	$25
1880s Savannah - $5 Savannah Business College Bank (C)	$250
1880s Savannah - $10,000 Savannah Business College Bank (C)	$750
1890s Sedalia - $500 Central Business College, on CSA replica (C)	$140
1907 Sedalia - $1, $2, $5, $10 Citizen's Nat'l Bank (D)	$375
1907 Sedalia - $1, $2, $5, $10 Sedalia Trust Co. (D)	$275
1840 Steelville - 10c Steelville. Printed at the Herald. Wheat/scythe ctr (M)	$150

MONTANA

$20 Peoples Nat'l Bank of Helena

DENOMINATION	PRICE
1865 Beaver Head County, MT - Var.$ Territorial Warrant	$150
1868 Territory - $100 Interest Bearing Note issued by Territory of Montana (W)	$750
1898 Belt - $1 Labor Exchange #289 (CS)	$1950
1890c Billings - Montana Mining and Business College (C)	$850
1900–07 Butte - 25¢, 50¢, $1 Montana Mining Loan & Investment Co.	$95
1964 Butte - $20 Century of Mining (A)	$20
1933 Conrad - $1 Farmers State Bank of Conrad (D)	$500
1933 Forsyth - 25c, 50c, $1 Forsyth Mercantile (D)	$250
1889 Fort Keogh, M.T. - 25c MacQueen & Young, Post Traders. (S)	$3500
1880c Fort Shaw, MT - $3 J.H. McKnight & Co., Indian Post Trader, (S)	$2400
1905–14 Great Falls - Var.$ City of Great Falls, Cascade County (W)	$18
1894 Great Falls - 2c United States Postal Notes, Uncut Pair	$9775
1933 Great Falls - $1 Black Eagle Commandery, Conrad Nat'l Bank on Leather (D)	$1450
1890s Havre - 5c, $1 F.A. Buttrey Company Notes. (M)	$475
1864 Helena - Stebbins&Co. has deposited one purse 54.6 ozs DWT (Gold) CD	$235
1866 Helena, MT - Var.$ First Nat'l Bank of Helena (B)	$125
1867 Helena - $50 Var.$ Banking House of L.H. Hershfield (B)	$295
1873 Helena, MT - $50 First Nat'l Bank Helena, Territorial CD (B)	$135
18-- ND Helena - $5, $10, $20, $50 Peoples Nat'l Bank of Helena (B)	$1000 to $1600
1870s Helena - $50 "Queen City of the Rockies." Covered wagon Green (A)	$750
1887 Helena, MT - Var.$ Territory of Montana Warrant (Liberty/shield) (W)	$40
1887 Helena - Var.$ Holter Hardware Interest bearing Cert. of Deposit. (M)	$95
1893 Helena - Var.$ State of Montana Warrant (Liberty/shield) (W)	$40
1901 Helena - $1000 Helena Business College / Jackman Commercial	$950
1869 Helena - Var.$ First NB of Helena, MTerr. Orig Bill of Exch.(B)	$1900
1901 Helena - Var.$ State of Montana Warrant (State Capitol) (W)	$55
1919 Helena - $10, $20, $100 Helena Commercial Club "Pay Dirt" (A)	$100
1869 Jefferson County, MT - Var.$ Treasurer of Jefferson County (W)	$100
1915c Lewistown - $25 Elk's Fair. Green/stag/brown (A)	$65
1920c Lewistown - Elks Monte Carlo. Blue w/Dog (A)	$45
1920c Lewistown - $10, $20, $25 Days of '49 BPOE Brown/blue (A)	$40
1909 Miles City - $5, $10 Bank of Elkville. Heart of the Yellowstone (B)	$360
1910c Missoula - 1c to 50c, $5 to $500 Garden City Commercial College (C)	$350
1910c Missoula - $500, $1000 Garden City Business College (C)	$500
1910c Missoula - $50, $100 Garden City Commercial College (C)	$350
1915c Missoula - $5 Missoula Stampede (A)	$160
1933 Missoula - 5¢, 10¢, 25¢, 50¢, $1, $5, $10 Missoula County Peoples Exchange (D)	$185
1933 Montana - $1 Montana Trade Certificate (D)	$750
1934 Montana - $1 H. A. Stephens - One Dollar for 50 minutes work.	$250
1933 Scobey, Poplar & Glascow - 25¢, $1 St. Pauls Rural Parish (D)	$260
1890s Sheridan 25c, 50c R. P. Bateman, Sheridan, Montana. (M)	$2600
1868 Smith River - $10 Holographic scrip (M)	$160
1897 Stevensville - $20 Labor Exchange #207 (CS)	$1500
1860c Virginia - Holladay Overland Mail and Express Co. Unissued (M)	$75
1869 Virginia City, MT - $600 Territorial Revenue, Treasurer's Office MT	$250

NEBRASKA

1857 $5 Brownville Bank & Land Co., Nebraska Territory

DENOMINATION	PRICE
1862 Territory - US Treasury pay for Territorial Governor A. Saunders (W)	$175
1933 Aurora - $1 Aurora Scrip Money, Republican-Register Newspaper (D)	$110
1980s Beatrice - $1, $5, $10, $50 Beatrice College Bank R7 (C)	$325
1933 Beatrice - $1, $5 American Legion/Chamber of Commerce (D)	$90
1856 Bellevue, NT - $1, $2, $3, $5, $10 Fontenelle Bank (B)	$200
1885c Blair - 50¢ Haller Proprietary Co. "Haller's Remedies" on CSA (A)	$275
1930s Boy's Town - 5¢, 10¢, 25¢, 50¢, $1 & $5 Boy's Town Currency (M)	$20
1907 Bradshaw - $5, $10, $15, $20, $25, $35, $45 Bradshaw First Nat'l Bank (D)	$42
1900c Broken Bow - $10 Broken Bow Business College rev of CSA (C)	$175
1856 Brownville, NT - $1, $2, $3, $5, $10 Brownville Bank	$325
1856 Brownville, NT - $1, $2, $3, $5, $10 Nemaha Valley Bank (B)	$155
1856 Brownville, NT - $3, $10 Nemaha Valley Bank	$300
1857 Brownville, NT - $1 Nemaha Valley Bk. June 8, Lazy One R7 (B)	$2700
1857 Brownville, NT - $2 Nemaha Valley Bk. June 8, Lazy Two (B)	$975
1859 Dakota City, NT - $1, $2, $5 Bank of Dakota (B)	$2500
1885 Dakota City - Var.$ Dakota County Cert. of Account (W)	$70
1857 DeSoto, NT - $1, $2, $3, $5 The Waubeek Bank (B)	$225
1857 DeSoto, NT - $1 Western Land & Exchange Co. (ABNCo) (B)	$1950
1857-63 DeSoto, NT - $1, $2, $3, $5 Bank of DeSoto (Green) (B)	$140
1860 DeSoto, NT - $1 Bank of Desoto (Red) (R)	$425
1860 DeSoto, NT - $2, $3, $5 Bank of Desoto (Red) (B)	$550
1860 DeSoto, NT - $1, $2, $3, $5 Corn Exchange Bank (B)	$550
1933 Douglas County - $10 Douglas County Employee's Committee (D)	$400
1856 Florence, NT - $1, $2, $3, $5, $10 The Bank of Florence (B)	$100
1933 Fremont - 5¢, 25¢, $1 Retail Merchants Association (D)	$150
1933 Grand Island - $1 S N Wolbach Sons (D)	$100
1933 Hastings - Var.$ Hastings Clearing House (D)	$125
1933 Holdrege - 5¢ Chamber of Commerce (D)	$150
1933 Lexington - $1 City of Lexington (D)	$100
1878 Lincoln - $1, $2 The City of Lincoln	$260
1890s Lincoln - $1, $5, $10 College Currency, Business Dept. (C)	$100
1900c Lincoln - $1, $5, $10 Lincoln Business College Currency (C)	$75
1907 Lincoln - $1, $2, $5, $10 City Nat'l Bank of Lincoln (D)	$250
1907 Lincoln - $1, $2, $5, $10 Farmer's and Merchant's Bank (D)	$250
1907 Lincoln - $1, $2, $5, $10, $20 First NB of Lincoln (D)	$250

DENOMINATION	PRICE
1907 Lincoln - $10 Nat'l Bank of Commerce (D)	$400
1902 Madison - Var.$ Madison County Warrant (W)	$40
1858 Nebraska City, NT - $1, $2, $5, $10 Platte Valley Bank (B)	$2350
1870 Nelson - $5 Nelson's College Currency First International Bank (B)	$140
1933 Nelson - 25¢ Moratoriun Shin Plaster (D)	$50
1933 Norfolk - $1 City of Norfolk (D)	$135
1933 Norfolk - $1 Norfolk Cereal & Flour Mills (D)	$140
1880s Omaha - 233 Iler & Co. American Life Bitters. Indians (A)	$300
1880c Omaha - Iler & Company American Life Bitters (A)	$200
18-- Omaha City - $2, $5 Omaha & Chicago Bank (proof $600) reg issue (B)	$1500
1880c Omaha - $3 F. Johnson Dry Goods. (M)	$375
1856 Omaha, NT - $1, $2, $5, $10 Bank of Nebraska (B)	$250
1856 Omaha, NT - $1, $2, $3, $5, $10, $20 Western Exchange Fire & Marine (B)	$90
1856 Omaha City - $10, $20 Western Exchange Fire & Marine Insurance Co. (B)	$550
1857 Omaha, NT - $3, $5, $10 Brownville Bank & I and Co. (D)	$275
1857 Omaha, NT - $1, $3, $5 City of Omaha (D)	$125
1858 Omaha City, NT - $25 Territorial Warrant. Female Riding Deer (G)	$50+
1861 Omaha City, NT - Var.$ Territorial Warrant	$70
1857 Omaha, NT - $1, $2 Nebraska Land & Banking (B)	$2350
1857 Omaha, NT - $1, $2, $5, $10 Omaha Bank & Land Co. (B)	$140
1857c Omaha, NT - $1, $5, $10 Western Exchange and Land Co. (B)	$2300
1933 Omaha - 5¢, 25¢, 50¢, $1, $5 Married Men's Council of Omaha (D)	$130
1885 Omaha - 10c Rathbun's Business College (C)	$225
1890's Omaha - $10 Johnson & Flodman, "The legal Tender Store" Dry Goods. (M)	$345
1907 Omaha - $1000, $5000, $10,000 Omaha Clearing House (D)	$500
1907 Omaha - $1, $5 First Nat'l Bank of Omaha (D)	$325
1907 Omaha - $2 Merchants Nat'l Bank of Omaha (D)	$440
1907 Omaha - $1, $2, $5, $10 Nat'l Bank of Commerce, Omaha (D)	$200
1907 Omaha - $2, $5, $10, $20 Nebraska Nat'l Bank of Omaha (D)	$475
1907 Omaha - $1, $5 Omaha Nat'l Bank, Omaha (D)	$375
19-- ND Omaha - 10,000 Omaha Athletic Club, probably club money for events.	$80
1933 Omaha - 5¢, 25¢, 50¢, $1, $5 Married Men's Council of Omaha	$130
1933 Roseland - 10¢, 25¢, 50¢, $1 Snyder's Shop (D)	$60
1907 South Omaha - $1, $2, $5, $10 South Omaha Nat'l Bank of South Omaha	$260
1907 South Omaha - $1, $5, $10, $20 Union Stock Yards Nat'l Bank	$250
1869 Superior - $3 Padden, Ebert & Padden. Hardware & Cutlery (A)	$200
1857 Tekama, NT - $1, $2, $5 Bank of Tekama (B)	$160
1908 Wausa - $5, $10 Commercial Bank (D)	$50
1900c York - 50¢ York College of Commerce (C)	$225
1933 York County - 5¢ York County Scrip (D)	$180

NEVADA

1872c $50 Manhattan Silver Mining Co.

DENOMINATION	PRICE
1917c Aurora - $20 (CSA) Esmeralda Hotel Ad Note. (A)	$700
1872c Austin - $1, $5, $10, $20 Manhattan Silver Mining Co. (M)	$130
1872c Austin - $1, $3, $5, $10, $20, $50, $100 Manhattan Silver Mining Co. (M)	$1610
1872c Austin - $3, $50, $100 Manhattan Silver Mining Co. (M)	$375
1870–80c Bristol - 25c Store of J. N. Curtis. (M)	$5500
1870–81 Carson City - Var.$, State Controller's Warrant Legislature Fund. (W)	$80
1877 Carson - $20 Carson City Savings Bank, Cert. of Deposit (CD)	$90
1886 Carson City - Var.$ State Controller's Warrant General Fund. (W)	$90
1900c Carson City - Var.$ State Controller's Warrant Orphans Home Fund. (W)	$85
1881 Carson City - Var.$ Carson City Savings Bank (B)	$125
1886 Carson City - Var.$ State Controller's Warrant (W)	$80
1876 Carson City - Var.$ Carson City Savings Bank (B)	$125
1913–28 Carson City - $1000 Slippery Gulch Currency (A)	$650
18-- Consolidated Mines - 5 Exploitation Mercantile Co. (M)	$650
19-- ND Elko - Dodson & Dodson Chiropracters, Cardboard (M)	$50
1925 Ely - $500, $1000, $2000, $4000 First Nat'l Bank of Ely (CD)	$1000
187- Eureka - $2, $3, $5, $10 Butter Cup Silver Mining Co. (M)	$5500
18-- ND Eureka - Wm. Joannes advertising note on Confederate $500. (S)	$950
1915 Eureka - $5 Lincoln Hotel Cafe punch card (M)	$150
1915 Eureka - Var.$ Eureka County Warrant (G)	$15
1880–90s Fay - 10c, 25c, 50c Shawmut and Nevada Mining & Milling Co. (M)	$4300
1861–64 Goldhill, NT - Var.$ Wells Fargo & Co., Nevada Territory CD (B)	$245
1907c Goldfield - 10c, 25c, $1 Consolidated Mines Co. (M)	$1050
1881 Gold Hill - $120 Town of Gold Hill warrant (W)	$85
1930–50 Lovelock - 12 1/2c Davin's Rendevous (G)	$75
1918c Luning - Luning Hotel advertising note (A)	$900
1906 Palisade - One Trip "Scrip" "Issued by Eureka, Hmltn & Ely Stage Line" (M)	$750
1914 Pioche - Var.$ Bank of Pioche - Certificate of Deposit (CD)	$125
1908 Rawhide - 25¢, 50¢ The Northern (Saloon) (M)	$130
1890s Reno - $5, $10 The Reno Savings Bank. Dollars in Gold.	$7500
1907 Reno - $1 Reno Clearing House (D)	$2000
1907 Rhyolite - $1, $5, $10, $20 Rhyolite Clearing House (D)	$3000
1950 South Tahoe - South Tahoe Casino. Good for $2 (M)	$22

DENOMINATION	PRICE
1870 Storey - Var.$ County of Storey Warrant (G/W)	$80
18-- ND -5c Southern Nevada Mercantile Co. (M)	$1200
1900 Tonopah - Var.$ Midway Milling Co. warrant (W)	$40
1862 Virginia City, NT - $39 White & Murphy Gold & Silver Mining (W)	$285
1870 Virginia - Var.$ Storey, County of (plum color) (W)	$150
1877 Virginia - $5, $10, $20 Society of Pacific Coast Pioneers (M)	$350
1878 Virginia - $3 C. P. Babcock. Advertiser signed on back. (M)	$1250
1878c Virginia - $3 M. Friedmann advertiser (A)	$1300
1886 Virginia - County of Storey Warrant (W)	$45
1880s Virginia - $5 H. S. Beck. Furniture and household decorations. (A)	$550
1918–19 Winnemucca - Var.$ Humboldt County warrant	$12
19-- ND State of Nevada - 100 grams of silver, Houston Duo-Monetary System.	$35

NEW MEXICO

1900c 5¢ Southwestern Mercantile. Jarilla, NM Territory

DENOMINATION	PRICE
1864 Albuquerque - $600 James Murphy Holygraph in Spanish (M)	$450
1890 ND El Capitan, NMT - 5¢ El Capitan Store Blue/Yellow (M)	$2300
1909 Cimarron - $5 Continental Tie & Lumber. February 1, 1909. (M)	$1275
1933 ND 1933 Gallup - 5¢, 10¢, 25¢, 50¢, $1, $5, $10 Gallup American Coal Co. (M,D)	$600
1899c Havre - $5 Southwestern Mercantile. (M)	$725
1900c Jarilla, NMT - 5¢ Southwestern Mercantile. Jarilla became Orogrande in 1905 (M)	$2500
1862–64 Las Cruces, NMT - J.L. May "Good For Two Drinks" Ptd on cloth. (M)	$5750
1895 Las Cruces, NMT - $5 Bounty for Mountain Lion (W)	$175
1907 Las Vegas - $1, $5, $10, $20 Las Vegas Clearing House Assn. (D)	$1750
1898 Lincoln County, NMT - Blue/Stag Territory of New Mexico warrant (W)	$200
1904 Lincoln County, NMT - Territory of New Mexico warrant (W)	$180
1890s North Capitan - 5¢ Southwestern Mercantile Company of New Mexico (M)	$2250
1914 Obar - $5 New Mexico Land & Immigration Co. (M)	$230
1860c Pinos Altos, NMT - $3 Buckhorn Furnace Store (M)	$4200
1904 Raton - Blossburg Mercantile Company. 10¢, 25¢, 50¢. (M)	$1250
1863 Santa Fe, Nuevo Mejico - 12 1/2¢. Spiegelberg Hermanos (M)	$12,500

DENOMINATION	PRICE
1863 Sante Fe, Nuevo Mejico - 50c Spiegelberg Hermanos. All red/Small eagle. (M)	$8000
1863 Sante Fe - 12 1/2c A. & L. Zeckendorf. Possibly Unique (M)	$12,000
1863 Sante Fe - Var.$ Territorial Treasurer's warrant. (M)	$300
1869 Sante Fe - $125 Territory of New Mexico Treasurer's warrant.	$350
1925 Sante Fe - 1/4c Fidel Bros - Nat'l Cert Corp Green (M)	$160
1925 Sante Fe - 1¢ Fidel Bros - Nat'l Cert Corp Brown (M)	$135
1899 Santa Rita - 25c Gilchrist & Dawson, Inc., Santa Rita, N.M.T. (M)	$1000
1959 Tatum - 5c Lovington National Bank. Green or Black on wood (A)	$25

NORTH DAKOTA

DENOMINATION	PRICE
1893c Fargo - $5, $10, $50, $100, $200, $500 Fargo Business College (Bliss) (B)	$105
1907 Fargo - $5, $10, $100 Fargo Clearing House Assoc. (D)	$750
1933 State - $1, $5 (Two issues of each) State of North Dakota (D)	$195
1910c ND Plaza - 1/2¢, 1¢, 2¢, 4¢ First Nat'l Bank of Plaza, NW Bankers & Merchants (B)	$35

OKLAHOMA STATE, INDIAN TERRITORY, BAD LANDS

1894 Eufala—Foley and Tully, Indian Territory

DENOMINATION	PRICE
1862 Baptist Mission, Choctaw Nation - 25c C. N. William A. Musgrove.	$5000
1897 Blue County - Var.$ Blue County Warrant	$140
1862 Boggy Depot, Choctaw Nation IT - 75c Franke & Eastburn.	$7200
1900c Buck, Indian Territory - 10¢, 25c, $1 McAlester Coal Mining Co.	$700
1903 Canadian County - 50c Okla. Terr. Treasurer's District School Warrant	$135
1850 Cherokee Nation - $75 Exec. Dep't. Signed Chief John Ross. (G)	$4500
1864 Choctaw City - Var.$ Choctaw Nation Auditor's Warrant	$2600
1863 Choctaw Nation - $1 Choctaw Treasury Warrant	$1500
1864 Choctaw Nation - 25c, 50c, $1 B.H.Epperson, pay ain TX. (M)	$8500
1862 Choctaw City - $1 Nat'l Treas. Choctaw Nation, Armstrong Acad. (M)	$5000
1892 Choctaw Railway Line - 25c, $1 Grady Trading Co. (M)	$600
1933 Enid - $1 Enid Retail Merchants Assoc.	$140
1894 Eufala - 25c Foley & Tully. (M)	$500
1898 Eufaula, IT - $2 C. H. Tully, $2 on Demand in Merchandise. (M)	$285
1898 Eufala, IT - $5 Tully Mercantile Co. (M)	$450
1903 Eufala - 10c, 50c, $1 Tully Mercantile Co.	$500
1862 Fort Gibson, C.N. - 25c, 50c F.H. Nash.	$4000
1862 Ft McCulloch, C.N. - $1, $3 Major Wm. Quesenbury (G)	$25,000
1893 Grady - 25c, $1 Grady Trading Co. Choctaw Coal & Railway (M)	$535
1902–08 Guthrie - $1, $2 Guthrie Savings Bank	$85
1909 Hailey - 5c, 10c, 25c, 50c Hailey Coal & Mining Co. (M)	$100
1900–08 Haileyville, IT - 5c, 10c, 25c, 50c, $1 Hailey-Ola Coal Co. (M)	$80
1890c Heliswa, IT - 15c C.C. Bruner & Son, Heliswa Store, Seminole Nation	$1840
1900 Hillabee, IT - 10c Porter Bros' General Merchant. 10c in Goods. (M)	$525
1890c Kingfisher City - $1, $2, $5 Treasurer of the Village of Kingfisher City.	$1500
1898 Krebs, IT - $1 Osage Trade Company, One Dollar in Merchandise. (M)	$225
1888 Lehigh, IT - 10c A.N. Garland Co. Train vignette/red reverse (M)	$1500
1933 Luther - $1, $5, $10 Morgan and Hayes	$140
1895–07 Lutie, IT - 5c, 10c, 25c, 50c, $1, Hailey Coal Co.	$175
1895–07 McAlester, IT - 5c, 10c, 25c, 50c, $1, $2 JJ McAlester Trade Note	$50
1890s Midway, IT - $2, $5 Midway Store (M)	$1400
1895 Muskogee Nation - $3 Court House, Stag. "Court Scrip" at end. (G)	$950
1869c North Fork, Creek Nation - 25c, 50c Robt. Sanger	$35,000
1933 Okla. City - $1, $5, $10 Cash Relief Trust (D)	$150
1933 Okla. City - 5c, 10c, 25c, 50c, $1 Self Help Exchange	$90
1933 Okla. City - $1 The Shirtsleeve Exchange	$60
1933 Okla. starewide - $1 Oklahoma Independents Thrift Currency (D)	$150
1896 Okmulgee - $1, $2, $5, $10, Parkinson Store due bill for merchandise	$225
1933 Okmulgee - $1 City of Okmulgee Trade Script (D)	$60
1896 Osage - $1 Osage Trading Company (M)	$225
1894–96 Perry, IT - 50c, $1, $5 Treasurer of "P" County (W)	$125
1924 Ponca City - $1, $5, $10, $20 Miller 101 Ranch	$60
1933 Ponca City - $1, $5, $10, Kay County Clearing House	$95
1933 Ponca City - $1, $5 Ponca City News	$100
1933 Sapulpa - 25c, 50c, $1, $5, $10 Sapulpa Chamber of Commerce	$50
1903 Sasakwa, IT - 50c, $1.50, $2.50, Jno. F. Brown & Sons. Seminole	$2600
189- South McAlester - 25c Indian Trading Co. issued remainder.	$350
1862 Tahlequah - 50c, $1 Cherokee Nation	$8500

| 1933 Wellston - $1, $5 Morgan & Hayes | $175 |
| 1890s Wewoka, IT - 5c, $1, $5 Wewoka Trading Company (M) | $1750 |

OREGON

1897 1/10 Toledo Labor Exchange. Pay in hours

DENOMINATION	PRICE
1933 Albany - 25¢, 50¢, $1, $5 Albany Scrip Assoc. City of Albany (D)	$110
1933 Albany - $1 Thrift Currency, merchant scrip (D)	$195
1933 Albany - 10¢ Sternberg Saddlery/Albany Tanning Co. Scallop Leather (D)	$200
1933 Albany - 25¢, $1 Sternberg Saddlery/Albany Tanning Co. Rectangle Leather (D)	$235
1933 Albany - 50¢ Valley Bottling Co. (D)	$165
1948 Albany - 5c Albany Centennial Wood (A)	$18
1933 Astoria - $1 Astoria Budget Newspaper scrip. Blue (D)	$175
1933 Astoria - 10¢ Guardsman's Scrip; Oregon Nat'l Guard. Pink (D)	$80
1934 Astoria - 10¢ Guardsman's Scrip; Oregon Nat'l Guard (D)	$95
1890c Baker - $1, $2, $5, $19, $20, $50, $100, $500 Business College (C)	$300
1986 Baker - $3 State of Eastern Oregon Yellow/Brown (A)	$15
1959 Bend - $1 Bend Buck printed on Deerskin (A)	$15
1915c ND Canyon City - $10 Whiskey Gulch Gang (A)	$35
1933c Cascade Locks - Five Dam Bucks - Merrill's BBQ (D)	$250
1907 Clatskanie - $1, $2, $5 Columbia County Clearing House (D)	$400
1933 Clatskanie - 50¢, $2, $5 Merchant's "Windmill" Scrip (D)	$185
1897 Corvallis - 1/2 Labor Exchange (W)	$750
1933 Enterprise - 50¢, $1 Chamber of Commerce, Series A, Buckskin Currency (D)	$180
1933 Enterprise - 50¢, $1 C of C, Series B, Buckskin Currency (Deer Hide) (D)	$500
1933 Enterprise - 25¢ C of C, Series C (paper) (D)	$100
1933 Enterprise - 50¢, $1 C of C, Series D Black, Buckskin Currency (Deer Hide) (D)	$165
1907 Eugene - $1, $2, $5, $10 Eugene Clearing House (D)	$500
1933 Eugene - 50¢ Townsend Recovery Certificate (D)	$700
1850–66 Ft. Dalles - 1 2 3 5 10 20 Loaves of Bread signed Post Treas. Steel (S)	$450
1933 Grant's Pass - 25¢, 50¢, $1 The Oregon Caveman, Inc. (D)	$175
1933 Heppner - 5¢, 25¢, 50¢, $1, $5 Heppner Sheepskin Scrip on paper (D)	$10
1933 Heppner - 25¢ ,50¢, $1, $5 Heppner Sheepskin Scrip on Leather (D)	$115
1959 Hermiston - 100th Anniversary of Oregon, Green on Yellow (M)	$25
1933 Hillsboro - 25¢, 50¢, $1, $5, $10 Washington County Scrip (D)	$10
1959 Independence - 100th Anniversary of Oregon on Leather (M)	$15
1933 Klamath Falls - 25¢ Capt. O.C. Applegate/American Legion Wood/round (D)	$15
1896 La Grande - 1/10 hour Labor Exchange, Branch 122 (W)	$400

DENOMINATION	PRICE
1933 LaGrande - 5¢, 20¢ LaGrande Emergency Wage (D)	$125
1940 Lake County - 5¢ Lake County Centennial, silver cardboard (M)	$25
1959 Lake County - $1 Lake County Buck printed on Cowhide (M)	$14
Lincoln Cnty - 25¢, 50¢, $1, $5, $10 Lincoln County School Scrip (D)	$175
1997 Marshfield - $1/4 Marshfield Labor Exchange (W)	$600
1918 Marshfield - $5, $10, $20 Homeguard WW1 Scrip (M)	$145
1910c Marshfield - $1 Marshfield Fuel & Supply Co. (M)	$100
1933 Medford - 10¢, 50¢, $1, $5 Association Labor Agreement (D)	$245
1933 Medford - $1 Colonial Bakery (D)	$375
1933 Medford - $1 Medford Chamber of Commerce (D)	$285
1933 Medford - $1 The Toggery	$400
1933 Multnomah - 25¢, 50¢, $1, $5 Mulnomah County Scrip (D)	$12
1859 Myrtle Creek - State Centennial (G)	$15
1860 Napolean - Var.$ Treasurer of Josephine County (W)	$250
1858 New Clackamas, OT - New Clackamas Banking House, Territorial (B)	$2200
1933 Newport - Newport Relief Committee Script (D)	$23
1933 North Bend - 50¢, $1, $2 1/2, $5, $10 City of North Bend (1st series wood) (D)	$40
1933 North Bend - 25¢, 50¢, $1, $5, $10 City of North Bend. (2nd series wood) (D)	$25
1959 North Bend - 25¢, 50¢ City of North Bend, Oregon Centennial (wood) (M)	$15
1925 Oakridge - $20 End of Steel (continental railroad) Green Goes 201 form (M)	$45
1925 Oakridge - $20 End of Steel Celebration, Green, Buffaloes (M)	$50
1847 Oregon City, OT - $5.00 Circulating Order Bond for 6% Int.	$4200
1848 Oregon City, OT - American Soc. for Encouraging Settlement of OR Terr. (M)	$5500
1855 Oregon City, OT - $10 John B. Preston, Surveyor General. Due Bill	$750
1881 Oswego - 5c Oswego Iron Companys (M)	$4750
1882 Oswego - $3 Oswego Iron & Steel Companys (M)	$4750
1907c Parkdale - $5 Mount Hood Lodge (M)	$350
1873 ND Pendleton - 25¢ Boston Store (M)	$900
1890s Pendleton - $500 Pendleton Business College MAV-350 overprint (C)	$210
1933 Pendleton - 25¢, 50¢, $1 City of Pendleton (D)	$90
1933 Pendleton - $5 City of Pendleton (D)	$225
1915 Pendleton - $10 Pendleton Round-up (negotiable) (A)	$80
1920–39 Pendleton - $10 Pendleton Round-up (negotiable). (A)	$22
1950s Pendleton - $10 Pendleton Round-up (A)	$10
1933 Pilot Rock - 25¢, 50¢, $1 Pilot Rock Wheat Scrip (D)	$100
1866 Portland - $1, $2, $5, $10, $20, $50, $100, $500 Portland Business College (M)	$135
1873 Portland - $20 A.F. Smith Pianos and Organs. Tiffany Scrip (M)	$1000
1880c Portland - $1, $2, $5, $10, $20, $50, $100, $500 Portland Business College (M)	$100
1881c Portland - $1 Portland Business College. Ship left, man ctr. (C) R7	$650
1882 Portland - $1 Portland Business College (M)	$250
1887 Portland - $5 Eastman Printing, Engraving, Photography (A)	$450
1888c Portland - $1, $10, $20, $50 Portland Business College. scroll ctr(C)	$185
1900c Portland - $1, $2, $5, $10, $20, $50, $100, $500 Port Bus College. lamp (C)	$100
1905c Portland - $1 Portland Business College Fancy/ornate R7 (C)	$250
1907 Portland - $1, $5 Portland Clearing House. Large/Plain (D)	$325
1907 Portland - $1, $2, $5, $10, $20 Portland Clearing House. Lion (D)	$235

DENOMINATION	PRICE
1933 Portland - $1, $5, $10, $20 Portland Clearing House. Eagle (D)	$18
1933 Portland - $2 Pacific Savings Bank (D)	$450
19-- ND Portland - 50¢ Unemployed Citizens League Montavilla Local (D)	$250
1933 Portland - $1 Western Industrial Pioneers, Inc. (D)	$200
18-- ND (1870–1910) Portland - Oregon Coal & Navigation Co. Due Bill (M)	$100
1926–34 ND (1926–34) Portland - $1 Anne Louise Millinery, Hollywood Theatre Bldg. (M)	$165
1959 Prineville - $1 Crook County Centennial Buck printed on deerskin	$12
1933 Reedsport - 25¢, $1 Reedsport Emergency Scrip (D)	$100
1933 Reedsport - $2.50 Reedsport Emergency Scrip (not issued) (D)	$250
1936 Roseburg - 25c Roseburg Golf and Country Club (M)	$25
1937 Roseburg - 75c Bridgeway Golf Course (M)	$30
1933 St.Helens - $1, $2, $5 St. Helen's Chamber of Commerce (D)	$95
1933 St.Helens - 50¢, $1, $2, $5 Sentinel-Mist Publishing (D)	$300
1880c Salem - #3 Adolph Mayer, Dry Goods, Fancy Goods. Advertiser	$550
1896 Salem - 1/2, 1, 2 Labor Exchange (W)	$450
1880c Salem - $1, $2 Capital Business College (M)	$295
1900 Salem - Var.$ Treasurer of Marion County Warrant (W)	$27
1913 Salem - 5 Kopecks Salem Bing Cherry Festival (M)	$375
1922 Salem - 25 Kopecks Salem Bing Cherry Festival (M)	$375
1925 Salem - $100 American Legion Armistice Day. Blu/Yel, (W)	$80
1932–33 Salem - 5c Capitol Press. Good for 5c (D)	$25
1933 Salem - 25¢, 50¢ Local Exchange/Premium Currency (D)	$90
1933 Sherman County - 25¢ Sherman County Scrip Association (D)	$600
1933 Silverton - $1 Appeal Tribune issued on Coolidge-McClaine Bank (D)	$750
1933 Silverton - 25¢, 50¢, $1 Silverton American Legion Scrip (D)	$30
1897 Toledo - 1/10 Labor Exchange (CS)	$750
1933 Union County - 5¢, 25¢ ,50¢, $1 Union County Emergency Wage (D)	$125
1933 Union County - 5¢, 10¢, 25¢, 50¢, $1, $5 Labor Exchange Certificate (D)	$135
1985 Wallowa - 50¢, $2 Wallowa County centennial scrip printed on buckskin. (A)	$15
1933 Woodburn - 5¢ Woodburn Clearing House (D)	$800

SOUTH DAKOTA

1932 $1 The City of Elk Point, SD

DENOMINATION	PRICE
1880s–90s Watertown DT - $5 Chalmers Bonded Investment Co. (A)	$9500
1948 Bonesteel - 5c Gregory County Jubilee. Wood flat (A)	$15
1888 Deadwood, DT - I.H. Chase 1888 Baseball Adv. Note (A)	$7200
1895c A Deadwood - Var.$ State of South Dakota, Lawrence County (W)	$65
1899 Deadwood - $5 or 1 Sh. Carbonate Flume Co. Uncancelled (M)	$55
1932 Elk Point - $1 The City of Elk Point (D)	$115
1900c Flandreau - Var.$ Flandreau State Bank. Cert. of Deposit (CD)	$25
1933 Huron - Var.$ Huron College Warrant (D)	$550
1933 Madison - $1 The City of Madison (D)	$525
1933 Marion - $1 The City of Marion (D)	$600
1910 Newell - 10c Greene Clothing Company/NW State Bank Stork (A)	$750
1948 Rapid City - $5 KOTA Radio, c/s Bean Bag Market (M)	$30
1948 Rapid City - $10 KOTA Radio, c/s Rapid City Clothing (M)	$25
1895 Tyndall - $1 County of Bon Homme warrant (W)	$125

TEXAS

DENOMINATION	PRICE
186– Anderson - $3 Treasurer of Grimes County	$565
1863 Austin - 25c Chief Justice of Travis County	$395
1839 Austin - $1, $5, $10, $20, $50 REPUBLIC OF TEXAS. Cut Cancelled.	$300
1839 Austin - $1, $5, $10, $20, $50 REPUBLIC OF TEXAS. Not Cancelled.	$500
1841 Austin - $25, $50 City of Austin, For Men of Texian Navy	$130
1862 Austin - $1, $2.50, $3, $5, $10, $20, $50, $100 Treasury Warrant State	$50
1878 Austin - Var.$ City of Austin, City Warrant	$130
1863 Beaumont - $1 Treasurer of Jefferson County. Beaumont	$700
1862 Bend - $10 County of Fort Bend	$450
1933 Borger - 25c Borger Clearing House	$230
1933 Borger - $2 Borger Daily Herald	$225
1862 Brazos - $2 Treasurer of Brazo County	$325
1862 Brenham - $5 Brenham, Payable in CSA notes.	$225
1862 Brenham - 50c, $1, $2, $3, $5 Washington County Scrip	$120
1862 Caldwell - 50c Burleson County Scrip	$295
18-- Columbia - $1 Commercial & Agricultural Bank of Texas	$360
18-- Columbia - $2, $3 Comm'l & Agricultural Bank of Texas (B)	$2400
1863 Corpus Christi - 25c Nueces County Court note	$190
1908 Ft. Bend - Var.$ Treas. of Fort Bend County	$20
1862 Goliad - 25c Goliad County, Goliad Supply Warrant	$700
1862 Hill Cnty - 25c, $2.50 Treasurer of Hill County	$330

DENOMINATION	PRICE
1837 Houston - $100, $500 Consolidated Funds, Houston	$135
1837 Houston - $1, $3, $5, $10, $20, $50 THE GOVERNMENT OF TEXAS	$300
1837 Houston - $100 THE TREASURER OF THE REPUBLIC OF TEXAS	$90
1838 Houston - $1, $3, $5, $10, $20, $50, $100 GOVERNMENT OF TEXAS	$180
1863–4 Houston - $1 W.H. Fliot "Redeemable in CSA notes" (M)	$350
1865 Jefferson - 5c, 10c C.D. Cosner	$300
1933 Kristenstad - $1, $2.50, $5, $10, $50, $100 John Kristensen	$30
1862 Lamar - $2, Treasurer of Lamar County	$525
1863 Madisonville - $1 Madison County, Jan. 1, 1863	$350
1862 Marion - 10c County Court of Marion County	$200
1862 Matagorda - 50c, $2 The County of Matagorda	$450
1862 Nacogdoches - $5 Treasurer of Nacogdoches County	$690
18- Nacogdoches - $2, $3, $5, Kelsey Douglas	$315
1862 New Braunfels - 10c City of New Braunfels Oct. 29, 1862	$1100
1863 Newton Cnty - $1 Treasurer of Newton County	$900
1931 San Antonio - $1 First National Bank of San Antonio, Junior Thrift	$130
1933 San Antonio - $1 San Antonio Panic Scrip	$450
1863 Springfield - 25c, $1 Treasurer of Limestone County	$300
1865 Titus - $5 County of Titus	$150
1890c Tyler, Texas - $1000 College National Bank (C)	$135
1938 Waco - $5, $10 Mt. Carmel Trade Currency	$18
1862 Walker - $1.50 Walker County Warrant	$85
1844 Wash. on Brazos - Var.$ TREASURER OF THE REPUBLIC OF TEX., Texian Print,	$100
186- Wharton Cnty - $2 Treasurer of Wharton County	$200
1862 - $2, $5 R. W. Rodgers, Train/Ship, Green Rev. AU	$70

UTAH

1903 25¢ Boden & Grahl, Meats and Groceries, Brigham City

DENOMINATION	PRICE
1878 Bingham Canyon - $10. Issued by Frisco Anne Mine. (M)	$3500
1876c Brigham City - 10¢ Brigham City Co-Operative (M)	$1400
1903 Brigham City - 25¢ Boden & Grahl, Meats and Groceries (M)	$750
1890s Fairview - 10¢, 50¢ Fairview Co-Op. Mercantile Co. (G)	$1750
1890s Fairview - 10¢, 25¢ Swen & Lars Neilson. Store (M)	$1100
1868 Fort Bridger, UT - $1 to $10 Utah Territory; W.A. Carter Post Trader (S)	$1000

DENOMINATION	PRICE
1890's Goshen - 15¢ Ercanbrack & Sons (M)	$5500
1877 Grantsville - 5c Grantsville Co-Operative Store. (G)	$2500
1880c Koosharem - $? J.B. Sorenson Co. Unissued, amt blank (M)	$380
1890s Lehi - 5¢, 15¢ Peoples Co-Op Institution (W)	$5750
1875 Logan - 25¢, 50c Logan Branch, Z.C.M.I. (CS)	$7500
1880s Logan - 5c, 25c United Order Manufacturing & Building Co. (CS)	$7475
1890s Logan - 10¢ Cache Valley Mercantile Co. (M)	$1700
1890s Logan - 5¢ ,10¢, 50¢ Equitable Co-Op. Association, Limited (G)	$4900
1890s Logan - 5¢, 10¢, 25¢, $1 Fourth Ward Co-Op (G)	$750
1890s Logan - 5¢ Fifth Ward Co-Op (G)	$650
1890s Logan - 10¢, 25¢, $1, $2 Goodwin Brothers (M)	$5000
1890s Logan - 10¢, 25¢, 50¢, $1 Logan Branch Z.C.M.I. (G)	$565
1890s Logan - 10¢, 25¢ Logan Meat Market (M)	$4550
1890s Logan - 5¢ Logan Meat Market Co. (M)	$4600
1890s Logan - 5¢, 15¢ Second Ward Store (G)	$4600
1895–97 Logan - 5¢ Cache Stake Tithing Store House (G)	$7000
1901 Logan - 5¢, 25¢ - Logan Store House (G)	$2250
1890s Magna - Louis Falvo & Son's (M)	$3750
1890s Manti City - 5¢ Sanpete Tithing Store House (G)	$5000
1890s Mount Pleasant - 5c, 10c Sanpete Co-Op. (G)	$6000
1890s Murray - 10¢ Workingmen's Store (M)	$4750
1933 Mutual - 2¢, 5¢, 10¢, 25¢, Mutual Store (M)	$165
1907 Ogden - $1, $2, $5, $10 Ogden Clearing House (D)	$375
1907 Ogden - $1, $2, $5, $10, $20 First Nat'l Bank of Ogden (D)	$225
1900c ND Park City - 10¢ The Cozy (M)	$65
1890s Payson - 5¢ Payson Co-Operative Store (M)	$4500
18-- Pleasant Grove - 5¢ Pleasant Grove, Utah Store (G)	$5000
1878 Provo - 10c, 50c Sup't Provo Co-operative Mercantile Inst., charge Provo woolen (G)	$2750
1890s Provo - $75 Provo Tithing Office/Deseret Dramatic Association. 3" x 1 1/2" G)	$2000
1890s Provo - 10¢, 25¢ Co-Operative Institution West Branch (G)	$800
1890s Provo - 25¢, $5 Sup't Provo Co-Operative Institution (G)	$3800
1890s Provo - 25¢, $5 W.H. Freshwater "in merchandise at retail" (G)	$3800
1893 Provo - 10c Provo Woolen Mills Company (M)	$3800
1899 Provo - 15c Provo Store. Woman w/ sword balancing scale. Red (M)	$1250
1864 Rush Valley - Tooele Cnty. 200' of ore. Rush Valley Mining Dist. (M)	$600
1890s Scipio - 5¢, 10¢, 15¢, 25¢, 50¢, $1, $2, $5 Co-Op. Mercantile Institution (G)	$400
1908 Richfield - $1, $2, $5, $10 Gold Mountain Consolidated Mining Co. (D)	$260
1933 Roosevelt City - $1 Roosevelt City Scrip (D)	$150
1901 St. George - 5¢, 10¢ St. George StoreHouse (M)	$4200
1849 Salt Lake, UT - 50¢, $1, $2, $3 Valley Notes w/ "B Young" sig. (M)	$2750
1849 Salt Lake, UT - 25¢ Valley Note unsigned remainder. (G)	$395
1849 SLC, UT - $1, $2, $3, $5, $10 Reissued Kirtland Safety Society Bank. (G)	$14,000
1856 Salt Lake, UT - $1, $2, $3 The Drover's Bank (B)	$1450
1858 Salt Lake, UT - $1, $2, $3, $5 Deseret Currency Association (M)	$11,000
1858–61 Salt Lake, UT - $3 Utah Territory Mercantile Currency (M)	RARE
1858–61 SLC, UT - Mercantile Currency, Great SLC copper plate.	$24,000

DENOMINATION	PRICE
1858 Salt Lake, UT - $10, $50 California & Salt Lake Mail Line (M)	$30,000
1862 Salt Lake, UT - $625 Due Bill, United States to Gov. of Utah Terr. (G)	$165
1863 Salt Lake City, UT - 50¢, $3 Walker Brothers (Bankers) (M)	$6000
1865 Salt Lake City, UT - $50 Holladay & Halsey (Bankers) (M)	$6500
1867 Salt Lake, UT - Var.$ First Nat'l Bank of Utah (B)	$3800
1866 Salt Lake, UT - 25¢, 50¢, $1, $2 Great Salt Lake City Corporation (B)	$1200
1868 Salt Lake, UT - 5¢, $1, $5, $10, $50 Deseret University Bank (B)	$4100
1869 Salt Lake City - $1 James Townsend/SLC Theatre. Holygraphic (W)	$400
1870 Salt Lake, UT - 25¢, 50¢, $1, $2, $5, $10 Zion's Co-Operative Mercantile Institution (M)	$2750
1870 Salt Lake, UT - $1, $2, $5 Series A Zion's Co-Operative Mercantile Institution (M)	$3750
1870s Salt Lake, UT - $1 Salt Lake City, Utah Territory "workmen" (M)	$2550
1874 Salt Lake, UT - $1, $2, $3, $5, $10 WB Welles, Salt Lake City Nat'l Bank (B)	$3000
1890s ND Salt Lake - $10 Mill Creek Commercial Bank (B)	$2500
1890s Salt Lake City - 5¢ Deseret Meat Market (M)	$2200
1890–95 Salt Lake, UT - Elk Liquor Co. Advertiser (A)	$435
1887–96 Salt Lake, UT - 5¢, 10¢, 25¢, 50¢ - General Tithing Store House (G)	$250
1896–1897 Salt Lake - 5¢, 10¢ ,25¢, 50¢ State - General Tithing Store House (G)	$225
18-- ND Salt Lake - 5¢, 10¢, 25¢ Bishop's Office Coupon. Brn/blk Gen'l Store Hse (G)	$375
1896 -97 Salt Lake - 5¢, 10¢, 25¢, 50¢, $1, $10 Bishop's General Store House (G)	$175
1898–1906 Salt Lake - 5¢, 10¢, 25¢, 50¢ Bishop's General Store House (G)	$90
1890s ND Salt Lake City - 25¢, $5, $10 Beaver Wool Manufacturing & Milling Co. (M)	$1700
1890c ND Salt Lake, UT - $1000 LDS Business College (C)	$1275
1893 Salt Lake City - 5¢ Gen'l Tithing Store House. "For Meat" overprinted "Produce" (M)	$5000
1900c Salt Lake - 10¢ United Order of Tailors (M)	$750
1907 Salt Lake - $1 Deseret Nat'l Bank (Cashiers Checks) (D)	$450
1907 Salt Lake - $1 McCormick Bank (D)	$450
1907 Salt Lake - $1 Utah-Idaho Sugar Co. (D)	$550
1907 Salt Lake - $100 Salt Lake City Clearing House (D)	$385
1933 Salt Lake - $1 Church of Jesus Christ of Latter-Day Saints (D)	$1250
1933 Salt Lake - 5¢ ,10¢, 25¢, 50¢, $1 Natural Development Association (D)	$275
1933 Salt Lake - $1 Trade Stimulus Certificate (D)	$175
1936 Salt Lake - $1 United National Prosperity - ESSAY (D)	$475
1937 Salt Lake - $1 Pension Prosperity (D)	$200
1890s Spanish Fork - 25¢ Spanish Fork Co-Op. (M)	$5000
1890s Spanish Fork - 10¢ Young Men's Co-Op. Institution (M)	$5000
1903 Tooele City - Var.$ Treasurer of the 43rd Quorum (G)	$65

WASHINGTON

1933 25¢ Everett, WA Sockeye Trade Note

DENOMINATION	PRICE
1906 Aberdeen - $5 Palace Restaurant Meal Card (M)	$50
1933 Aberdeen - 25¢ Old Ironsides/Samuel Benn Wood/round (D)	$16
1933 Almira - 5¢ Almira Grand Coulee Dam Scrip (D)	RARE
1907 Anacortes - $1 Bank of Commerce (D)	$775
1910c Avon - 5c, 25c Small 3 x 1 1/2" Cardboard Chit (M)	$18
1893 Bellingham - $1 Fair Department Store (M)	$400
1907 Bellingham - $1, $2, $5, $10, $20 Bellingham Clearing House (D)	$150
1933 Bellingham - $1, $5, $10, $20 Bellingham Clearing House (D)	$175
1933 Bellingham - 5¢ Henry Roeder Round/wood (D)	$40
1933 Blaine - 5¢, 10¢, 25¢, 50¢, $1 Blaine Relief Assoc. (D)	$22
1933 Blaine - 5c, 10c, 25c, 50c, $1 Blaine Relief Assoc. (no # or initials) (D)	$12
1933 Bremerton - 25¢ Old Ironsides/American Legion Wood/round (D)	$15
1933 Brewster - $1 Townsend Test Fund - 1st Nat'l Bank (D)	$650
1933c Bridgeport - $5, $10 Columbia Trading Co. Pay at FNB Brewster (D)	$375
1895 Buckley - 1/20 Labor Exchange #61 Green. (CS)	$650
1933 Camas - $10 American Legion - 50th Anniv. of Camas (D)	$600
1933 Centralia - 1c, 5c SW Washington Pioneer. Wood (D)	$70
1933 Centralia - 25¢, 50¢, $1, $5 Centralia Daily Chronicle (D) (4 known)	$450
1935 Centralia - Emergency Tax Token (Orange cardboard) (US)	$30
1933 Chelan - 10¢, 25¢, 50¢, $1 Townsend Test Fund - Miners & Merchants Bank (D)	$525
1933 Callam County - $1 Angeles Co-Operative Creamery (D)	$170
1907 Chehalis County - $1 Associated Banks of Chehalis County (D)	$600
1907c Chehalis - 5c The Olympia, popular early watering hole. Cardboard (M)	$22
1937 Chelan - 50c Townsend Test Fund - provide $200@ month pensions. (M)	$500
1933 Clallam County - 1c, 25c Bloedel-Donovan (D)	$12
1911–19 Coupeville - Var.$ County of Island Warrants (W)	RARE
1932–3 Cowlitz County - 5c, 15c, 25c, $1 Liberty Service Token (D)	$150
1932–3 Cowlitz County (Port Angeles) - 5¢ (other denoms may exist) Liberty Service Token (D)	$250
1934 Cowlitz County - 1c Co-Operative Exchange (D)	$100
1933 Deer Park - $1, $2, $5 Deer Park Lumber Co. (D)	$225
1907 Ellensburg - $1 Associated Banks of Ellensburg (D)	$425
1910c Ephrata - 25c The Ephrata Pool Hall. (M) Cardboard	$15
1933 Everett - 25¢ Sockeye (Salmon shaped). Convention Committee (D)	$500
1933 Everett - $1 City of Everett Trade Extension Warrant (D)	$400
1991 Fairhaven - Var.$ Fairhaven Street Warrants.	RARE
1933 Friday Harbor - 25¢, 50¢, $1 Haxkett-Larson American Legion Post (D)	$50
1933 Grand Coulee - 25¢ Grand Coulee Dam Quarter (concrete) (D)	$35

DENOMINATION	PRICE
1933 Grays Harbor - $1, $5, $10, $20 Grays Harbor Associated Banks (D)	$140
1910c Harrington - The Magnet. Cardboard 1x2" Scrip (M)	$15
1912 Hoquiam - 10c Rychard Bros & Cox, Stork System (M)	$375
1933 Hoquiam - $1 Olde Ironsides (Round wood) (D)	$135
1912 Hoquiam - 1¢, 2¢ ,3¢, 4¢, 5¢, 10¢, 25¢, 50¢ Stork System Savings 1912 (D)	$37
1933 Hoquiam - 1¢, 2¢, 3¢, 4¢, 5¢, 10¢ Stork System Savings @ 1917 (D)	$20
1939 Hoquiam - 25¢ Hoquiam Jubilee Assoc. 3" round wood (A)	$18
1933 Ilwaco - 5¢, 25¢, 50¢, $1 Ilwaco Salmon Currency (D)	$125
1933 Issaquah - 25¢ Farmer's Trade Note (D) (6 known)	RARE
1933 Kalama - Port of Kalama Scrip (D)	$130
1933 Kelso - $3, $10, $15 County Dairymen's Assocation (D)	$200
1913 Kennewick - 10 Bones Columbia River Valley Grape Festival (A)	$85
1897 LaCenter - 5/100, 1/4, 1, 2, 10 Labor Exchange #259. (G)	$500
1933 Linden - $1 City of Linden (D)	$500
1933 Longview - 25¢ Longview Chamber of Commerce (D)	$17
1935 Longview - Retail Merchants Emergency Tax Token (Green)	$19
1949 Longview - 5c Silver Jubilee of Longview (G)	$15
1896 Marysville - 1/4 1 Labor Exchange #62 by Cole/Fisher Lumber (CS)	$750
1933 Montesano - 5¢, 10¢ United Producer's Money (D)	$150
1933 Mt. Rainier - $10 Mt. Ranier Clearing House (D)	$500
1893 Mount Vernon - $1 Mount Vernon Red Shingle Scrip. None known	
1893 New Whatcom - 5c, 15c, 25c, 50¢, $1, $5 Cissna Dept. Store. (M)	$800
1894 New Whatcom - 50¢ U.S. Postal note April 24, 1894 (M)	$1150
1933 Okanogan - $1 Okanogan Commercial Club "WineSap" (D)	$170
1888 Okanogan County - $40 Okanogan County Territorial Warrant (W)	$325
1898 Olympia - $5, $10 Commissioners Scrip Treas. State of Washington. (W)	$750
1907 Olympia - $1 Associated Banks of Olympia (D)	$250
1933 Olympia - 25¢, $1, $2, $5 Community Service Bureau (D)	$50
1933 Olympia - 25¢ Olympia Oyster Money, Chamber of Commerce (D)	$350
1933 Omak - $1, $5, $10 Bile-Coleman Lumber Co. (D)	$175
1933 Pasco - 50¢, $1 Pasco Relief Scrip (D)	$225
1935 Pasco-Kennewick - Emergency Tax Token (Red) (US)	$30
1933 Peshastin - 25¢, 50¢, $1 Peshastin Ponderosa Scrip (D)	$185
1887 Port Angeles, W1 - 5c, 10c, 25c, 50c, $1 Puget Sound Co-Op Colony (D)	$2200
1893 Port Angeles - 50c G.M. Lauridsen. Yellow tint, diagonal title. (D)	$1500
1894 Port Angeles - Var.$ City of Port Angeles - City Council (D)	$600
1933c Port Ludlow - 5c, 10c, 25c Puget Mill Co. Scrip (M)	$25
1933 Port Townsend - $1, $5, $10 First American Bank (D)	$40
1910c Pullman - City Club, Small cardboard Chit (M)	$14
1910c Pullman - Smoke House, Small cardboard Chit (M)	$14
1933 Raymond - 25¢, 50¢, $1, $5 Raymond Oyster Money (D)	$85
1933 Rock Island - 25¢ Rock Island Dam Scrip (D)	$130
1907 Seattle - $1000 The Seattle Clearing House Assoc. (D)	$1400
1907 Seattle - $1, $2, $5, $10, $20 Seattle Clearing House Assoc. (D)	$175
1907 Seattle - $500, $1000, $5000, $10000 Seattle Clearing House Assoc. (B)	RARE
1931 Seattle - 1 vote Citizens of the City of Seattle (A)	$40
1932 Seattle - 10¢ Theatre Scrip for Unemployed (D)	$135
1933 Seattle - $1, $5, $10, $20 Seattle Clearing House Assoc. (D)	$150

DENOMINATION	PRICE
1933 Seattle - 25¢, $1 Community Service Bureau (D)	$80
1935 Seattle - 1/5 mil Five Points Cafes Tax Chit cardboard (M)	$20
1935 Seattle - 1/5 mil Neuperts Grocery Tax Chit cardboard (M)	$27
1915c ND 1915c Sequim - $1 Chas. Fenwick Rifles (A)	$37
1907 Skagit County - $1, $5 Skagit County Clearing House (D)	$450
1933 Skagit County - $1 Skagit Community Scrip (D)	$230
1907 Snohomish - $1, $2, $5, $10, $20 Snohomish County Associated Bank (D)	$350
1933 South Bend - 25¢, 50¢, $1, $5, $10 Willapa Harbor Currency (wood) (D)	$100
1933 South Bend - 25¢, 50¢, $1, $5, $10 Willapa Harbor Currency (paper) (D)	$130
1894 Spokane - 2¢ U.S. Postal note May 14, 1894. (US)	$750
1907 Spokane - $1, $2, $5, $10, $20 Clearing House Association (D)	$100
1910c Spokane - 25¢ Imperial Pool Room. Red Cardboard 1 x 2" (M)	$18
1929 Spokane - Exchange Lumber Co. Description of new 1929 notes (A)	$50
1933 Spokane - 50¢, $1, $5 Baird-Naundorf Lumber Co. (D)	$130
1933 Spokane - $1 Commercial Creamery (D)	$150
1933 Spokane - 25¢ ,50¢, $1 Davenport Hotel (D)	$130
1933 Spokane - 25¢, 50¢, $1, $5 Dessert Hotel (D)	$130
1933 Spokane - $2, $5 Federated Exchange Cert. McClintock-Turnkey Co. (D)	$95
1933 Spokane - $1 John W. Graham Co. (D)	$225
1933 Spokane - $1, $5 Long Lake Lumber Co. (D)	$80
1933 Spokane - 50¢, $1, $5 Spokesman-Review Newspaper (D)	$175
1933 Spokane - $1 Tull & Gibbs (D)	$300
1935 Spokane - City of Spokane Emergency Tax Scrip cardboard (G)	$18
1939 Spokane - 5¢ Columbia Cavalcade Golden Jubilee (A)	$18
1910c Sprague - 25c Ludtke & Whiteside cardboard Chit	$28
1880c Tacoma, W.T. - $5 W.H. Fife Advertising Note (A)	$1800
1880c Tacoma, WT - $3 George J. Turrell Shoe Dealer, Wash. Territory (A)	$1600
1907 Tacoma - $1, $2, $5, $10, $20 Tacoma Clearing House Assoc. (D)	$165
1907 Tacoma - $500, $1000, $5000 Tacoma Clearing House Assoc. (B)	$1200
1933 Tacoma - 25¢, $1, $2, $5, $10 Community Service Bureau (D)	$40
1933 Tacoma - 5¢, 10¢, 25¢, 50¢ Natural Development Assoc. Centi/Vallars (D)	$450
1933 Tacoma - 1 Units, 5 Units, New Commonwealth (D)	$130
1931–32 Tenino - 25¢, $1, $5, $10 (Paper) Chamber of Commerce (D)	$130
1932–33 Tenino - 25¢, 50¢, $1 (Wood) Chamber of Commerce (D)	$100
1932 Tenino - 25¢, 50¢ (Wood) Chamber of Commerce Double Denomination (D)	$9000
1933c Tenino - 5¢ Jiffy Lunch, small/wood (D)	$125
1933c Tenino - 5¢ D.M. Major, small/wood (D)	$130
1933c Tenino - 5¢ Tenino Chamber of Commerce, small/wood (D)	$90
1933c Tenino - 1¢, 2¢, 3¢ Thurston County Independent, small/wood with postal stamp (D)	$4000
1933–35 Tenino - A series of 1/5¢ wooden sales tax "chits" approximately 1" square were issued by several firms and are sought after. They include: Campbell & Campbell, Drug Store, Jack Horner, Jiffy Lunch, L.A. McLain, Mecca Cafes, Paramount Service Station, Penny's Garage, Tenino Cash Market, Thurston County Independent, E.E. Walker, and White Front Garage. Most are valued in the range of	$40
1939 Tenino - 25¢ Lions Club, Lion Money (A)	$65
1971 Tenino - 25c, 50c, $1 Tenino Centennial on Wood (A)	$8

DENOMINATION	PRICE
1933 Toppenish - $10 The Traders Bank (Unique) (D)	$800
1933 Toppenish - $1 Toppenish Commercial Club "Toppenish Wampum" (D)	$750
1933 Waitsburg - $1 Waitsburg Civic Relief Committee (D)	$350
1883 Walla Walla, WT - 50¢ U.S. Postal note, Sept. 3, 1883. (US)	$11,000
1894 Walla Walla - 1¢ U.S. Postal note June 28, 1894. (US)	$775
1910c Walla Walla - 5c, 10c The Maze. Blue cardboard 2x1" (M)	$15
1936 Walla Walla - 10c Whitman Centennial numbered. (G)	$10
1937 Walla Walla - 10c Southeastern Washington Fair cow. (M)	$38
1933 Wapato - 25¢ Community Service Bureau (D) RARE	$300
1933 Wenatchee - $1 Wenatchee Chamber of Commerce - Apple Jack (D)	$225
1933 Wenatchee - 25¢, 50¢, $1 Wenatchee Daily World Publishing Co. (D)	$22
1933 Woodland - 5¢, 10¢, 25¢, 50¢ City of Woodland - Welfare Scrip (D)	$125
1933 Yakima - 10c City Creamery (M)	$100

WYOMING

1870 $8 Post Trader, Fort Bridger, Wyoming Territory

DENOMINATION	PRICE
1908 Cambria - $1 Cambria Trading Company. Blue print. Miner on front (M)	$175
1897 Cambria - $5 Kirkpatrick Brothers & Collins. Gray print. Miner	$195
1867 Cheyenne, WT - $3000 Morton E Post Banking House Wyoming Terr.	$500
1869c ND Cheyenne, WT - Wyoming Territory - Gray & Pearse Advertising Note	$4200
1869c ND Cheyenne, WT - 50¢ Central House, C.W. Tappan (A)	$2250
1931 Cheyenne - $1 Cheyenne Frontier Night Show (blue)	$395
1907 Cheyenne - $1, $5, $10 Cheyenne Clearing House (D)	$450
1907 Cheyenne - $1, $5, $10 First Nat'l Bank of Cheyenne (D)	$500
1907 Cheyenne - $1, $5, $10 Stock Grower's NB of Cheyenne (D)	$550
1907 Cheyenne - $1, $5, $10 Citizen's Nat'l Bank of Cheyenne (D)	$550
1910 Cheyenne - 1¢, 2¢, 3¢, 4¢, 5¢, 10¢ A E Roedel Druggist, Citizen's Nat'l bank (M)	$300
1910 Cheyenne - 1¢, 2¢, 3¢, 4¢, 5¢, 10¢ The Bon Company, Citizen's Nat'l Bank, Stork (M)	$350
1910 Cheyenne - 1¢, 2¢, 3¢, 4¢, 5¢, 10¢ Cheyenne Creamery Co. Stock Grower's NB (M)	$325
1933 Cheyenne - $50 City of Cheyenne - The Scrip Commission (D)	$275
1933–34 Cheyenne - $1 Cheyenne Frontier Days (D)	$275
1933 Cheyenne - Natural Development Assoc. Centi/Vallars SENC (D)	RARE
1964 Cheyenne - $1 Cheyenne Autumn Trail Dedication "Cheyenne Wampum" (W)	$30
1877 Evanston, WT - Var.$ Territory of Wyoming, County of Uinta warrant (W)	$125
1870 Ft. Bridger. WT - $1 to $8 Sutler note; WA Carter Post Trader, Wyo. Territory (S)	$4500
1882 Laramie City, WT - $10 A.M. Watkins. "Hats, Caps, Boots, Shoes, NOTIONS, ETC." (A)	$3800

DENOMINATION	PRICE
1912 Laramie - 3¢, 25¢ A E Roedel Druggist, Citizen's Nat'l Bank, Stork (1910 Copyright) (D)	$425
1912 Laramie - 50¢ Gem City Grocery, First State Bank, Stork (1910 Copyright) (D)	$325
1933 Laramie - 50¢ City of Laramie Scrip - Scrip Commission (D)	$350
1912 Laramie - 10c Woodford Clothing. First State Bank, Stork	$450
1912 Laramie - 10c Laramie Drug Store, First State Bank, Stork	$350
1933 Laramie - 50c County of Albany (G)	$600
1933–34 Riverton - 5¢, 10¢, 25¢, 50¢, $1 Riverton Lion's Club. Paper (D)	$200
1933–34 Riverton - 50¢ Riverton Lion's Club. Paper (D)	$200
1933 Riverton - 50¢ Riverton Lions Club. Scrip printed on buckskin (D)	$250

Glossary: Adv.=Advertising; c(following date)=circa; CD=Certificate of Deposit; CS=Communal Scrip, ND=No Printed Date; Var.$=Various amounts, Ctf=Counterfeit, G=Government, U.S., State., Local or Communal

MISC WARRANTS, BILLS of EXCHANGE, BOUNTIES, FORMS

CALIFORNIA

DENOMINATION	PRICE
1859 Hensley & Morrill, Sacramento, Ca Engraved Bill of Exchange, Fine.	$120
1851 RF Hastings & Co. Bankers, Sacramento, Ca Bill of Exchange, Fine.	$120
1855 D. O. Mills & Co, Sacramento, Ca, Second Bill of Exchange. Fine	$575
1852 Page, Bacon & Co, Sacramento Ca, Vignetted 2nd Exch, F-VF.	$300
1852 Burgoyne & Co., San Fran, Cal, Bank Check Fine with cancels.	$165
1851 Burgoyne & Co., San Francisco, Ca, Bill of Exchange, Fine.	$325
1851 Drexel, Sather & Church, San Fran, Cal Duplicate Bill of Exch. Whaling VF.	$2185
1856 Drexel, Sather & Church, San Fran, Cal. Second Bill of Exchange. Bldg Fine.	$400
1859 Nathan Mayer de Rothschild & Co, San Fran, Second Bill of Exchange. Fine	$2300
1858 Auditor's Office Warrant, Santa Clara County, California. County Treasurer	$320
1869 Alexander Cohen, San Fran, First Bill of Exchange. $106.00 Dog/steamer Fine.	$320
1863 Hentsch & Berton. Second Bill of Exchange. sailing vignette. Fine	$375
1869 Hickox & Spear. Original Bill of Exchange. By Lecount & Mansour. VG	$350
1861 Tallant & Wilde. Second Bill of Exchange. $125.00. July 10, 1861. Fine	$300
1867 Knox & Beans, San Jose. Second Bill of Exchange. $300.00. Sailor Fine.	$400
1880s Pacific Bank, San Fran, Cal. Cert of Deposit Form VF by A. Gast & Co.	$175
1859 Pacific Loan & Security Bank, San Fran, Cal. Cert of Deposit. VF	$550
1853 Cal Water Co Bearer Draft. Tuolumne Hydraulic Assoc, Sonora. Fine	$275
1853 Republican Water Company, Algiers, Ca. Bearer Draft $15.00. Mar	$300
1858 Langton's Pioneer Express. Package receipt for transit gold dust	$1400
1869 Hentsch & Berton, San Fran, Cal, Bank Checks. (#) Fine.	$1100
18-- Miner's Exchange & Savings Bank, San Fran First Bill of Exchange. Fine.	$950
18-- First Bill of Exch. by Britton & Rey, San Fr. Vignette of Banking House, Fine	$900
18-- S. Molitor & Co, Assayers, San Fr, Cal. Three Cents Red Postal Envelope with Marysvill Freeman & Co red advertising banner Fine	$550

HAWAII

1907 Honolulu —$100 First of Exch on Bishop & Co. (B)	$750

MONTANA

1862 Wright & Co. NY. Sight Draft - Two sailors taking Columbia out to sea	$700
1867 L.H. Hershfield, Banking House, Helena, Mont Terr. miner/dog.	$220
1869 First NB of Helena, Montana Terr. Orig Bill of Exch. Fine.	$1900
1853 American Express Co. Wells, Butterfield & Co., NY Sight Draft. Fine.	$1800
1863 Territorial Warrant, $8 "bounty for killing one bear" Helena, Montana Terr.	$500

NEBRASKA

1863 Office of Territorial Auditor, Omaha, Territory of Nebraska. Pay Warrant	$750

TEXAS

1974 Joseph Metcalf & Co. Original Bill of Exchange VF	$235

SPECIAL REPORT: UNCUT SHEETS

As very few notes exist in the form of full uncut sheets, this is a limited area for the collector. Also, the prices are high, well out of range for most hobbyists.

Uncut sheets available on the market are of Small Size Notes exclusively. In most instances it is not known precisely how they reached public hands. Some were undoubtedly presented as souvenir gifts to Treasury Department officials. In any event, uncut sheets have never been illegal to own, since the notes they comprise are precisely the same as those released into general circulation.

The sheets differ in the number of notes, from a low of six in National Currency sheets to a high of eighteen for some sheets of United States (Legal Tender) Notes and Silver Certificates. Others have twelve notes. These differences are due entirely to the printing method being used at their time of manufacture. Any given note was always printed in sheets of the same size, with the same number of specimens per sheet. If you have an uncut sheet with twelve notes, it means that all notes from the series were printed twelve to a sheet.

The condition standards for uncut sheets are the same as those for single notes. Obviously, an uncut sheet did not circulate as money, but some specimens became worn or damaged as a result of careless storage, accident, or other causes. These impaired sheets do turn up in the market, but there is not much demand for them. Almost every buyer of uncut sheets wants Uncirculated condition. Quite often an uncut sheet will be framed when you buy it. This should be considered a plus, as the frame has probably kept the sheet in immaculate condition. Just to be entirely safe, however, it is wise to examine the reverse side of the sheet for possible staining or other problems.

The following prices were current for uncut sheets in Uncirculated grade at publication time. Gem Uncirculated sheets in absolutely pristine condition command higher prices than those shown.

SILVER CERTIFICATES

DENOMINATION	SERIES	NO. OF NOTES PER SHEET	CURRENT PRICE RANGE IN UNC. CONDITION
$1	1928	12	2000.00–4000.00
$1	1934	12	3000.00–4000.00
$5	1934	12	2000.00–3060.00
$10	1934	12	3000.00–5500.00
$1	1935	12	1200.00–1840.00
$5	1953	18	1500.00–2040.00
$10	1953	18	RARE

UNITED STATES NOTES (LEGAL TENDER NOTES)

DENOMINATION	SERIES	NO. OF NOTES PER SHEET	CURRENT PRICE RANGE IN UNC. CONDITION
$1	1928	12	RARE
$2	1928	12	RARE
$5	1928	12	2000.00–3060.00
$2	1953	18	1000.00–2040.00
$5	1953	18	1800.00–3260.00

NATIONAL CURRENCY

DENOMINATION	SERIES	NO. OF NOTES PER SHEET	CURRENT PRICE RANGE IN UNC. CONDITION
$5	1929	6	2000.00–4000.00
$10	1929	6	2000.00–3060.00
$20	1929	6	1000.00–3060.00
$50	1929	6	RARE
$100	1929	6	RARE
EMERGENCY NOTES:			
Hawaii $1	1935A		RARE
No. Africa $1	1935A		RARE

MULES
(MIXED PLATE NUMBERS)

All U.S. currency has plate numbers on the face and back. These plate numbers are in the lower right corner somewhat close to the fine scroll design. They refer to the number of the engraved plate used to print the sheet of notes. Each plate can be used for about 100,000 impressions. It is then destroyed and a new plate with the next number in sequence is put into use.

During the term of Treasury officials Julian and Morgenthau, the plate numbers were changed from almost a microscopic to a larger size, far easier to read. Due to this improvement the series designation then in use was an advance on United States Notes, Silver Certificates, and Federal Reserve Notes. The signatures remained Julian-Morgenthau. National Currency and Gold Certificates were not affected, as these were discontinued earlier.

During the changeover period in printing, plates were sometimes mixed up, producing a note with a large number on one side and a small number on the other side. Notes of this variety are called "mules," or "mule notes." This is from a term applied to coins struck with the obverse or reverse die of one year and the opposite side from a die of another year.

Many collectors are eager to add one or more of these mule notes to their collection. Some of the most common mule notes are:

$2 UNITED STATES NOTES
1928-C, 1928-D

$1 SILVER CERTIFICATES
1935, 1935-A

$5 UNITED STATES NOTES
1928-B, 1928-C, 1928-D, 1928-E

$5 SILVER CERTIFICATES
1934, 1934-A, 1934-B, 1934-C

$10 SILVER CERTIFICATES
1934, 1934A

Mules were also issued in the Federal Reserve Note Series. However, these are not as popular with collectors as the United States Notes and Silver Certificates because of the higher denominations and the twelve districts involved.

The schedule below shows some of the most common mule notes and their values in new condition. The combination of the prefix and suffix letters of the serial numbers on notes is known as "Blocks." For instance: A—A Block, B—A Block.

			UNC.
$2 UNITED STATES NOTE	1928-D	B—A	655.00
		C—A	260.00
		*—A	260.00
$5 UNITED STATES NOTE	1928-B	E—A	260.00
		*—A	680.00
	1928-C	E—A	260.00
		*—A	260.00
$1 SILVER CERTIFICATE	1935	N—A	
		Thru	260.00
		P—A	
	1935-A	M—A	
		Thru	230.00
		V—A	
		C—B	230.00
$5 SILVER CERTIFICATE	1934-A	D—A	
		Thru	230.00
		G—A	
		*—A	220.00
$10 SILVER CERTIFICATE	1934	A—A	210.00
		*—A	210.00
	1934-A	A—A	350.00

Front   **SIZES DIFFERENT**   **Back**

INTRODUCTION TO
UNITED STATES
FRACTIONAL CURRENCY

Events following the outbreak of the Civil War resulted in a shortage of circulating coinage. Trade was hampered as many merchants, especially in large cities, were unable to make change and only customers presenting the exact amount for a purchase could buy—but they were generally as short on coins as the shop proprietors. Various attempts were made to solve this problem by issuing credit slips (which most customers didn't care for), tokens (which they also didn't care for), and using postage stamps as money. Finally, in 1862, the government stepped in, recognizing that the economy was being seriously hurt, and issued a series of small paper notes as equivalents of coinage denominations. They carried designs adapted from the current postage stamps of the day and were known as Postage Currency or Postal Currency. The more popular title is now Fractional Currency. There were five separate issues of Fractional Currency, three of which occurred during the Civil War and two thereafter, the final one as late as 1874. That a need existed for coin substitutes as late as the 1870s demonstrates the drain placed upon coinage during the war and the long period of recovery. A total of six denominations were issued, from 3¢ to 50¢, comprising 23 designs and more than 100 varieties. Because of its small size and lack of visual impact, Fractional Currency was long shunned by collectors. In recent years it has enjoyed an unprecedented surge of popularity, which, if continued, promises to drive prices beyond present levels. All told, more than $360,000,000 worth of Fractional Currency was circulated. It would be extremely plentiful today but for the fact that most notes were redeemed, leaving only about $2,000,000 outstanding. This is what collectors have to work with, and a good deal of these are badly preserved.

FIRST ISSUE—Postage Currency August 21st, 1862
5-10-25-50
SECOND ISSUE—Fractional Currency October 10th, 1863
5-10-25-50
THIRD ISSUE—Fractional Currency December 5th, 1864
3-5-10-15-25-50
FOURTH ISSUE—Fractional Currency July 14th, 1869
10-15-25-50
FIFTH ISSUE—Fractional Currency February 26th, 1874
10-25-50

THE FRACTIONAL CURRENCY SHIELD

Fractional currency shields were sold by the Treasury Department for $4.50 each, unframed, from June 1867 through June 1868. Specimen notes printed only on one side were used. Very Good–condition shields are valued at $2500 to $5000. Choice condition shields in contemporary frames can sell for $7000. Shields with pink or green are more valuable.

FRACTIONAL CURRENCY NOTES

The following notes may be collected by issue or by denomination. We list them here by denomination for convenience. Also, since most of these notes were hastily cut from large sheets, the margin size can vary. Specimens are narrow margined while proofs have wide margins. Prices listed are for Nice "well centered" Uncirculated notes.

THREE-CENT NOTES

THIRD ISSUE

Face Design:	SPECIMEN	FACE		REVERSE
Portrait of President	Light Port.	175.00		150.00
Washington.	Dark Port.	110.00		110.00
	PROOF			
	Light Port	625.00		350.00
	Dark Port	350.00		350.00

Back Design:
Large "3"
green.

REGULAR ISSUES	A.B.P.	GOOD	V.FINE	UNC.
☐ With Light Portrait	15.00	25.00	40.00	275.00
☐ With Dark Portrait	15.00	25.00	50.00	400.00

FIVE-CENT NOTES

FIRST ISSUE	SPECIMEN	FACE	150.00	REVERSE	75.00
	PROOF	FACE	420.00	REVERSE	310.00

Face Design:
Portrait of
President
Jefferson,
brown.

Back Design:
"5" black.

REGULAR ISSUES	A.B.P.	GOOD	V.FINE	UNC.
☐ Perforated edges, monogram ABNCO on back	10.80	18.00	35.00	475.00
☐ Perforated edges, without monogram on back	9.00	15.00	60.00	700.00
☐ Straight edges, monogram ABNCO on back	12.00	20.00	35.00	280.00
☐ Straight edges, without monogram on back	12.00	20.00	35.00	700.00

FIVE-CENT NOTES

SECOND ISSUE	SPECIMEN	FACE	100.00	REVERSE	75.00
	PROOF	FACE	275.00	REVERSE	250.00

Face Design:
Portrait of
President
Washington.

Back Design:
Shield and
brown, "5"s.

REGULAR ISSUES	A.B.P.	GOOD	V.FINE	UNC.
☐ Value only in bronze on back	7.20	12.00	30.00	250.00
☐ Surcharges 18-63 on back	7.20	12.00	30.00	295.00
☐ Surcharges S-18-63 on back	10.80	18.00	30.00	390.00
☐ Surcharges R-1-18-63 on back, fiber paper	10.80	18.00	65.00	1000.00

FIVE-CENT NOTES

THIRD ISSUE	SPECIMEN	FACE	100.00	REVERSE	75.00
	PROOF	FACE	275.00	REVERSE	235.00

Face Design:
Portrait of
Spencer M.
Clark.

Back Design:
Green or
red.

REGULAR ISSUES	A.B.P.	GOOD	V.FINE	UNC.
☐ Without letter "A" on face, red back	7.20	12.00	35.00	525.00
☐ With letter "A" on face, red back	7.20	12.00	36.00	700.00
☐ Without letter "A" on face, green back	6.00	10.00	32.00	200.00
☐ With letter "A" on face, green back	6.00	10.00	32.00	325.00

This note was authorized to have the portraits of the explorers Lewis and Clark on the face. Mr. Spencer M. Clark, who was then head of the Bureau of Currency, flagrantly placed his own portrait on this note. This caused Congress to pass legislation forbidding the likeness of any living person on U.S. currency.

TEN-CENT NOTES

FIRST ISSUE	SPECIMEN	FACE	125.00	REVERSE	110.00
	PROOF	FACE	425.00	REVERSE	335.00

Face Design:
Portrait of
President
Washington.

Back Design:
"10,"
black.

REGULAR ISSUES	A.B.P.	GOOD	V.FINE	UNC.
☐Perforated edges, monogram ABNCO on back	6.00	10.00	42.00	495.00
☐Perforated edges, without monogram on back	6.00	10.00	42.00	510.00
☐Plain edges, monogram ABNCO on back	7.20	12.00	30.00	415.00
☐Plain edges, without monogram on back	7.20	12.00	48.00	1132.00

TEN-CENT NOTES

SECOND ISSUE	SPECIMEN	FACE	125.00	REVERSE	115.00
	PROOF	FACE	325.00	REVERSE	315.00

Face Design:
Portrait of
President
Washington.

Back Design: "10," green.

REGULAR ISSUE	A.B.P.	GOOD	V.FINE	UNC.
☐Value only surcharge on back	6.00	10.00	40.00	295.00
☐Surcharge 18-63 on back	6.00	10.00	40.00	295.00
☐Surcharge S-18-63 on back	4.80	8.00	32.00	295.00
☐Surcharge I-18-63 on back	12.00	20.00	55.00	475.00
☐Surcharge O-63 on back	240.00	400.00	1110.00	2660.00
☐Surcharge T-1-18 63 on back, fiber paper	15.00	25.00	140.00	975.00

TEN-CENT NOTES

THIRD ISSUE	SPECIMEN	FACE	110.00	REVERSE	175.00
	PROOF	FACE	300.00	REVERSE	275.00

Face Design:
Portrait of
President
Washington.

Back Design: "10," green or red.

REGULAR ISSUES	A.B.P.	GOOD	V.FINE	UNC.
☐Printed signatures Colby-Spinner, green back	6.00	10.00	60.00	225.00
☐As above, figure "1" near left margin on face	6.00	10.00	60.00	225.00
☐Printed signatures Colby-Spinner, red back	6.00	10.00	38.00	415.00
☐As above, figure "1" near left margin, red back	8.40	14.00	47.00	475.00
☐Autographed signatures Colby-Spinner, red back	9.60	16.00	140.00	775.00
☐Autographed signatures Jeffries-Spinner, red back	9.60	16.00	140.00	705.00

TEN-CENT NOTES

FOURTH ISSUE	SPECIMEN	FACE	335.00	REVERSE	RARE
	PROOF	FACE	335.00	REVERSE	RARE

Face Design:
Bust of
Liberty.

Back Design:
Green with TEN and "10."

REGULAR ISSUES	A.B.P.	GOOD	V.FINE	UNC.
☐ Large red seal, watermarked paper	7.20	12.00	38.00	175.00
☐ Large red seal, pink fibers in paper	7.20	12.00	38.00	175.00
☐ Large seal, pink fibers in paper, right end blue	7.20	12.00	38.00	175.00
☐ Small red seal, pink fibers, right end blue	7.20	12.00	42.00	206.00

TEN-CENT NOTES

FIFTH ISSUE	PROOF	FACE	RARE	REVERSE	$400.00

Face Design:
William
Meredith.

Back Design:
Green.

REGULAR ISSUES	A.B.P.	GOOD	V.FINE	UNC.
☐ Green seal, long narrow key	6.00	10.00	25.00	185.00
☐ Red seal, long narrow key	6.00	10.00	25.00	115.00
☐ Red seal, short stubby key	6.00	10.00	25.00	115.00

FIFTEEN-CENT NOTES
FACES AND BACKS PRINTED SEPARATELY
THIRD ISSUE ALL ARE SPECIMENS AND UNISSUED.

Face Design:
Sherman and
President
Grant.

Back Design:
Green or red.

	SPECIMEN UNC.	PROOF UNC.
☐ With printed signatures Colby-Spinner	300.00	788.00
☐ With autographed signatures Colby-Spinner	2200.00	RARE
☐ With autographed signatures Jeffries-Spinner	300.00	775.00
☐ With autographed signatures Allison-Spinner	300.00	775.00
☐ Green back	180.00	365.00
☐ Red back	175.00	365.00

FIFTEEN-CENT NOTES

FOURTH ISSUE PROOF FACE RARE REVERSE 500.00

Face Design:
Bust
of Columbia.

Back Design:
Green
with "15"s.

REGULAR ISSUES	A.B.P.	GOOD	V.FINE	UNC.
☐Large seal, watermarked paper	21.00	35.00	85.00	445.00
☐Large seal, pink fibers in paper	21.00	35.00	85.00	445.00
☐Large seal, pink fibers in paper, right end blue				
	21.00	35.00	85.00	445.00
☐Smaller red seal, pink fibers, right end blue	21.00	35.00	85.00	445.00

TWENTY-FIVE-CENT NOTES

FIRST ISSUE	SPECIMEN	FACE	110.00	REVERSE	110.00
	PROOF	FACE	300.00	REVERSE	225.00

Face Design:
Five 5¢
Jefferson
Stamps.

Back Design:
Black,
large "25."

REGULAR ISSUES	A.B.P.	GOOD	V.FINE	UNC.
☐Perforated edges, monogram ABNCO on back	7.20	12.00	37.00	700.00
☐Perforated edges, without monogram on back	8.40	14.00	65.00	800.00
☐Straight edges, monogram ABNCO on back	6.00	10.00	28.00	280.00
☐Straight edges, without monogram on back	9.00	15.00	75.00	900.00

TWENTY-FIVE-CENT NOTES

SECOND ISSUE	SPECIMEN	FACE	120.00	REVERSE	120.00
	PROOF	FACE	275.00	REVERSE	225.00

Time and climatic condition have changed the purple color on the back of this note into many variations.

Face Design:
Portrait of
President
Washington.

Back Design:
Purple with
"25."

REGULAR ISSUES

	A.B.P.	GOOD	V.FINE	UNC.
☐Value only surcharge on back	7.20	12.00	40.00	290.00
☐Surcharge 18-63 on back	8.40	14.00	40.00	450.00
☐Surcharge A-18-63 on back	7.20	12.00	40.00	325.00
☐Surcharge 1-18-63 on back	24.00	40.00	218.00	725.00
☐Surcharge 2-18-63 on back	7.20	12.00	40.00	400.00
☐Surcharge S-18-63 on back	9.60	16.00	40.00	400.00
☐Surcharge T-1-18-63 on back, fiber paper	15.00	25.00	108.00	900.00
☐Surcharge T-2-18-63 on back, fiber paper	15.00	25.00	108.00	700.00

TWENTY-FIVE-CENT NOTES

THIRD ISSUE	SPECIMEN	FACE	165.00	REVERSE	100.00
	PROOF	FACE	325.00	REVERSE	200.00

All notes have printed signatures of Colby-Spinner.

Face Design:
Portrait of
Fessenden.

Back Design:
Green or
red with "25"
CENTS."

	A.B.P.	GOOD	V.FINE	UNC.
☐Face—bust of Fessenden between solid bronze surcharges, fiber paper, back—green, surcharge M-2-6-5 in corners	135.00	225.00	910.00	3000.00
☐As above, with letter "A" in lower left corner of face	180.00	300.00	2000.00	7000.00
☐Face—Fessenden, open scroll bronze surcharges, fiber paper, back—green, surcharges M-2-6-5 in corners	12.00	20.00	136.00	650.00
☐As above with letter "A" in lower left corner of face	11.40	19.00	180.00	900.00
☐Face—Fessenden, open scroll surcharges, plain paper, back—green, value surcharges only	9.00	15.00	52.00	225.00
☐As before, letter "A" in lower left corner of face, back—green, plain paper	10.80	18.00	52.00	225.00
☐Face—Fessenden, red back, value surcharge only	15.00	25.00	80.00	350.00
☐As above, letter "A" in lower left corner of face	12.00	20.00	80.00	700.00

TWENTY-FIVE-CENT NOTES
FOURTH ISSUE SPECIMENS AND PROOFS RARE

Face Design:
Portrait of
President
Washington
and Treasury Seal.

Back Design:
Green.

REGULAR ISSUES	A.B.P.	GOOD	V.FINE	UNC.
☐Large seal, plain watermarked paper	6.00	10.00	28.00	175.00
☐Large seal, pink silk fiber in paper	6.00	10.00	28.00	225.00
☐Large seal, pink fibers in paper, right end blue	5.10	8.50	25.00	300.00
☐Smaller red seal, right end blue	6.00	10.00	25.00	300.00

TWENTY-FIVE-CENT NOTES
FIFTH ISSUE SPECIMENS AND PROOFS RARE

Face Design:
Portrait of
Walker and red
seal.

Back Design:
Black.

A.B.P.		REGULAR ISSUES		
	GOOD	V.FINE	UNC.	
☐With long narrow key in Treasury Seal	6.00	10.00	24.00	145.00
☐With short stubby key in Treasury Seal	6.00	10.00	24.00	145.00

FIFTY-CENT NOTES

FIRST ISSUE	SPECIMEN	FACE	150.00	REVERSE	125.00
	PROOF	FACE	760.00	REVERSE	550.00

Face Design:
Five 10¢
Washington
stamps.

Back Design:
Green.

REGULAR ISSUES	A.B.P.	GOOD	V.FINE	UNC.
☐Perforated edges, monogram ABNCO on back	9.00	15.00	120.00	900.00
☐Perforated edges, without monogram on back	12.00	20.00	82.00	1000.00
☐Straight edges, monogram ABNCO on back	6.00	10.00	53.00	300.00
☐Straight edges, without monogram	12.00	20.00	108.00	1800.00

FIFTY-CENT NOTES

SECOND ISSUE	SPECIMEN	FACE	150.00	REVERSE	175.00
	PROOF	FACE	350.00	REVERSE	270.00

Face Design:
Portrait of
President
Washington.

Back Design:
Red.

REGULAR ISSUES	A.B.P.	GOOD	V.FINE	UNC.
☐Surcharge 18-63 on back	9.00	15.00	45.00	400.00
☐Surcharge A-18-63 on back	9.00	15.00	22.00	400.00
☐Surcharge O-1-18-63, fiber paper	15.00	25.00	105.00	650.00
☐Surcharge R-2-18-63, fiber paper	10.80	18.00	65.00	700.00
☐Surcharge T-1-18-63, fiber paper	9.00	15.00	65.00	650.00

FIFTY-CENT NOTES

THIRD ISSUE	SPECIMENS	FACE	175.00	REVERSE	175.00
	PROOFS	FACE	330.00	REVERSE	280.00

Face Design:
Justice with
sword,
shield,
scales.

Back Design:
Green
or red.

The following notes have printed signatures of Colby-Spinner and have *green backs*.

REGULAR ISSUES	A.B.P.	GOOD	V.FINE	UNC.
☐Value surcharge and A-2-6-5 on back, fiber paper				
	18.00	30.00	130.00	1540.00
☐As above with "1" and letter "A" on face, A-2-6-5 on back				
	51.00	85.00	825.00	3850.00
☐As above with "1" only on face, A-2-6-5 on back				
	19.20	32.00	115.00	910.00
☐As above with letter "A" only on face, A-2-6-5 on back				
	21.60	36.00	115.00	910.00
☐A-2-6-5 on back, *narrowly spaced,* plain paper				
	7.20	12.00	118.00	760.00
☐As above, numeral "1" and letter "A" on face				
	12.00	20.00	85.00	690.00

	A.B.P.	GOOD	V.FINE	UNC.
☐As above, numeral "1" only on face	7.20	12.00	70.00	690.00
☐As above, letter "A" only on face	10.80	18.00	140.00	575.00
☐A-2-6-5 on back, *widely spaced*, plain paper				
	10.80	18.00	140.00	600.00
☐As above, numeral "1" and letter "A" on face				
	27.00	45.00	380.00	1650.00
☐As above, numeral "1" only on face	7.20	12.00	95.00	800.00
☐As above, letter "A" only on face	7.20	12.00	95.00	800.00
☐Without position letters or back surcharges	7.20	12.00	95.00	575.00
☐As above with numeral "1" and letter "A" on face				
	15.00	25.00	162.00	1650.00
☐As above with numeral "1" only on face	7.20	12.00	95.00	700.00
☐As above with letter "A" only on face	7.50	12.50	95.00	700.00

The following notes have printed signatures of Colby-Spinner and *red backs*.

	A.B.P.	GOOD	V.FINE	UNC.
☐Value surcharge and S-2-6-4 on back, fiber				
	—	—	7000.00	RARE
☐As above, numeral "1" and letter "A"	—	—	50,000.00	RARE
☐As above, numeral "1" only on face	—	—	10,000.00	RARE
☐As above, letter "A" only on face	—	—	12,000.00	RARE
☐Value surcharge and A-2-6-5 on back, plain				
	12.00	20.00	108.00	875.00
☐As above, numeral "1" and letter "A"	46.20	77.00	550.00	2420.00
☐As above, numeral "1" only on face	12.00	20.00	165.00	795.00
☐As above, letter "A" only on face	12.00	20.00	165.00	795.00
☐No surcharge on back, plain paper	12.00	20.00	125.00	795.00
☐As above, numeral "1" and letter "A" on face				
	30.00	50.00	290.00	2420.00
☐As above, numeral "1" only on face	14.40	24.00	210.00	1100.00
☐As above, letter "A" only on face	18.00	30.00	210.00	850.00

The following notes have autographed signatures of Colby-Spinner and *red backs*.

	A.B.P.	GOOD	V.FINE	UNC.
☐Value surcharge and S-2-6-4 on back, fiber	60.00	100.00	380.00	2000.00
☐Value surcharge and A-2-6-5 on back, fiber	45.00	75.00	220.00	1650.00
☐Value surcharge only on back, plain paper	18.00	30.00	150.00	1320.00

FIFTY-CENT NOTES

THIRD ISSUE	SPECIMEN	FACE	165.00	REVERSE	140.00
	PROOF	FACE	400.00	REVERSE	325.00

Face Design: Bust of Spinner with surcharges.
Back Design: Green or red.

The following notes have printed signatures of Colby-Spinner, and *green backs.*

REGULAR ISSUES	A.B.P.	GOOD	V.FINE	UNC.
☐Value surcharge and A-2-6-5 on back	16.20	27.00	130.00	425.00
☐As above, numeral "1" and letter "A" on face	24.65	41.00	250.00	825.00
☐As above, numeral "1" only on face	12.00	20.00	825.00	465.00
☐As above, letter "A" only on face	10.80	18.00	110.00	550.00
☐Value surcharge only on back	7.20	12.00	95.00	525.00
☐As above, numeral "1" and letter "A" on face	16.50	28.00	95.00	525.00
☐As above, numeral "1" only on face	9.00	15.00	95.00	525.00
☐As above, letter "A" only on face	9.00	15.00	95.00	525.00

TYPE II BACK DESIGN

	A.B.P.	GOOD	V.FINE	UNC.
☐No back surcharge	10.80	18.00	165.00	475.00
☐Numeral "1" and letter "A" on face	22.20	37.00	205.00	1200.00
☐Numeral "1" only on face	10.20	17.00	165.00	700.00
☐Letter "A" only on face	13.20	22.00	180.00	750.00

The following notes have a portrait of Spinner, printed signatures of Colby-Spinner, *red backs,* and are Type I.

REGULAR ISSUES	A.B.P.	GOOD	V.FINE	UNC.
☐Value surcharge and A-2-6-5 on back	30.00	50.00	65.00	465.00
☐As above with numeral "1" and letter "A"	30.00	50.00	155.00	1100.00
☐As above with numeral "1" only on face	10.20	17.00	82.00	550.00
☐As above with letter "A" only on face	15.00	25.00	140.00	550.00

The following notes have autographed signatures, *red backs,* and are Type I.

	A.B.P.	GOOD	V.FINE	UNC.
☐Autographed signatures COLBY-SPINNER, back surcharged value and A-2-6-5	30.00	50.00	155.00	650.00
☐Autographed signatures ALLISON-SPINNER, back surcharged value and A-2-6-5	24.00	40.00	155.00	690.00
☐Autographed signatures ALLISON-NEW, back surcharged value and A-2-6-5	405.00	675.00	2200.00	3600.00

FIFTY-CENT NOTES
FOURTH ISSUE SPECIMENS AND PROOFS RARE

Face Design:
Bust
of Lincoln.

**Back
Design:**
Green.

	A.B.P.	GOOD	V.FINE	UNC.
☐Plain paper	18.00	30.00	65.00	1200.00

FIFTY-CENT NOTES
FOURTH ISSUE SPECIMENS AND PROOFS RARE

Face Design:
Bust
of Stanton.

**Back
Design:**
Green
with "50."

	A.B.P.	GOOD	V.FINE	UNC.
☐Red seal and signatures ALLISON-SPINNER, paper with pink fibers, blue ends	12.00	20.00	75.00	465.00

FIFTY-CENT NOTES
FOURTH ISSUE SPECIMENS AND PROOFS RARE

Face Design:
Bust of
Samuel
Dexter.

**Back
Design:**
Green with
"50."

	A.B.P.	GOOD	V.FINE	UNC.
☐Green seal, pink fibers, blue ends	7.20	12.00	48.00	455.00

FIFTY-CENT NOTES
FIFTH ISSUE SPECIMENS AND PROOFS RARE

Face Design:
Bust
of Crawford.

**Back
Design:**
Green with
"50."

	A.B.P.	GOOD	V.FINE	UNC.
☐Signatures ALLISON-NEW, paper with pink fibers, blue ends	6.00	10.00	45.00	250.00

ERROR OR FREAK NOTES
by Doris A. and Fredrick J. Bart

Notes have been misprinted since the earliest days of currency. The BEP utilizes fully automatic, high-speed, sheet-fed-currency presses that produce nearly 10,000 sheets per hour. During this process the paper undergoes multiple separate printing and cutting operations before release as individual notes.

Errors, misprints, oddities, freaks, or curiosities—regardless of the label—demonstrate a deviation from the intended finished product. Whether human or mechanical causes, errors on paper money possess an appearance and appeal dissimilar to correctly printed notes. Errors may arise at, or between, any point in the production process. As currency designs continue to evolve and anti-counterfeiting measures continue to expand, there will likely be some variablilty to the printing process explained below.

First (back) printing; each sheet from a thirty-two subject printing plate bearing the back design.

Second (face) printing; this consists of the black portion of the face of the note. Includes the portrait, intricate outer border design, series, signatures and titles of the Treasurer of the United States and the Secretary of the Treasury.

Third (over)printing; the final stage. This includes the serial numbers and seals. The condition of the note, to a certain extent, will affect the desirability and consequently the value of the error. A "common" error such as an ink smear or gutter fold carries minimal premium above face. On the other hand, rarer varieties such as multiple printings or major printed folds will retain much of its premium even if the note is no longer new. Double denominations still reign as the king of errors with the face being of one denomination and the back another.

In this chapter we have provided you information on the different types of errors that have occurred along with estimates. Estimates are provided in Very Fine and Uncirculated. The values, while not perfect, reflect the current market. Prices, however, change with the passing of time and supply and demand.

MISMATCHED SERIAL NUMBERS

Mismatched numbers can occur several different ways. The lower left serial number different from the upper right. Most numbering irregularities stem from a press operator failing to set the same sequence of numbers on the two different numbering wheels prior to printing. Mismatches can also happen when one numbering mating sticks while the other continues to advance.

MISMATCH LAST 2 DIGITS

	ABP	VF	CU
$1 FRN 1963 MISMATCH B57476979A/78A	$200.00	$300.00	$500.00

MISMATCH PREFIX

	ABP	VF	CU
$2 FRN 1976 MISMATCH H/B45432860A	$200.00	$300.00	$500.00

MISMATCH 2ND DIGIT

	ABP	VF	CU
$5 FRN 1974 MISMATCH J36/35139551B	$200.00	$350.00	$550.00

INVERTED THIRD PRINT

Inverted overprints are also known as inverted third printing. The third printing consists of the serial numbers, seals, and district numbers. On the early small size notes, from 1935 till 1963-A the signatures were part of the third printing. These dramatic errors result from uncut half sheets being inserted into the overprinting presses 180 degrees from the correct orientation. However, when the sheet becomes inverted, the overprint appears to shift toward the bottom of the note. When the upside down sheets enter subsequent cutting stages for separation unto individual notes the resulting product contains either a segment of the adjacent note or the upper margin from the sheet at the top. This appearance typifies every inverted overprint beginning with the series 1981. Robert Azpiazu coined the term Type II invert. The inverted overprint generated nationwide interest in the field of paper money errors in 1976-78 after the unprecedented numbers escaped the Bureau of Engraving and Printing (BEP). As plentiful as the $2 1976 inverted overprints were when they were released, they appear today to be just as scarce.

	ABP	VF	CU

$1 FRN 1974 INVERTED
3RD PRINTING $200.00 $400.00 $700.00

	ABP	VF	CU

$10 FRN 1950A INVERTED
3RD PRINTING $250.00 $500.00 $1250.00

	ABP	VF	CU

$100 FRN 1974 TYPE II INVERTED
3RD PRINTING $5.00 $1000.00 $1750.00

OFFSET PRINTING COMPLETE

Offset printing are impressive currency errors. They look like one side of the note "bled through" to the other.

A brief review of the printing process will permit the reader to better understand how the error occurred. Under normal operating conditions, a sheet of currency passes between the inked printing plate and the impression cylinder.

The impression cylinder forces the paper into the intaglio recesses in the printing press. When the paper fails to enter the press the plate contacts the impression cylinder. As the next sheets enter the press they receive not only the intended printing on the correct side but on the opposite side a transfer or offset printing as well. This transferred image becomes lighter with each sheet and disappears entirely after ten to twelve sheets. The rich, bold offset impressions from the first couple of sheets bring the highest prices.

MINOR

	ABP	VF	CU
$10 FRN 1988A FULL OFFSET	$15.00	$25.00	$100.00

MODERATE

	ABP	VF	CU
$1 FRN 1988 FULL OFFSET	$25.00	$65.00	$125.00

MAJOR

	ABP	VF	CU
$10 FRN 1985 FULL OFFSET	$50.00	$100.00	$250.00

PARTIAL OFFSETS

Partial or incomplete offset printings arise in much the same fashion as the complete offsets described above. However, as the name indicates, partial offsets involve merely a portion of the design. An incomplete offset develops when the impression cylinder becomes exposed to part of the inked printing plate through a fold, tear, or defect in a sheet of currency stock.

MINOR

	ABP	VF	CU
$20 FRN 1985 PARTIAL OFFSET	$25.00	$25.00	$45.00

MODERATE

	ABP	VF	CU
$1 FRN 1993 PARTIAL OFFSET	$15.00	$35.00	$75.00

MAJOR

	ABP	VF	CU
$1 FRN 1974 FULL OFFSET	$15.00	$25.00	$50.00

PRINTED FOLD

Printed or exterior folds demonstrate a portion of the design intended for one side printed on the opposite side of the note. Currency paper is subject to being folded along the entire route from blank sheet to finished product. Whenever a section of the sheet folds over onto itself prior to or during contact with a printing plate, a printed fold error ensues. The sheet may remain folded after the printing or open prior to subsequent, if any, printing operations and the cutting knives. The ultimate shape of the note depends upon whether the sheet unfolds before being cut.

MINOR

	ABP	VF	CU
$5 FRN 1977 PRINTED FOLD	$260.00	$350.00	$550.00

MODERATE

	ABP	VF	CU
$1 FRN 1963-A PRINTED FOLD	$300.00	$450.00	$600.00

MAJOR

	ABP	VF	CU
$1 FRN 2001 PRINTED FOLD	$500.00	$1500.00	$2500.00

THIRD PRINT ON REVERSE

Not surprisingly, the overprint on the back error demonstrates the third printing elements on the back of the note. The serial numbers, Treasury seal, and if applicable, the Federal Reserve bank or universal seal and corresponding district numerals appear on the wrong side. The error develops when an uncut half sheet enters the overprinting press with the back—instead of the face—closest to the printing head. This produces a note which appears to have a mistake on both sides.

	ABP	VF	CU
$20 FRN 1993 INVERTED 3RD PRINTING ON BACK	$750.00	$1500.00	$3000.00

BOARD BREAKS

The designation "board break" refers to the error resulting from a partially broken impression cylinder. An impression cylinder, or rigging, carries a wooden external wrapper; rigid enough to ideally sustain the workload yet pliable enough to squeeze the currency sheet into the plate.

During the production of United States paper money, the currency sheet passes between the plate cylinder and the impression cylinder. Because the impression cylinder must endure such extreme pressure the area becomes fatigued. The end result of such fatigue is failure as segments either compress into the cylinder or fall away. This produces a white unprinted area on the finished piece of paper money. Consequently, every note printed using the imperfect impression cylinder will exhibit the identical error matching in size and shape, and location, unless the defect expands and/or until the rigging is replaced.

	ABP	VF	CU
$2 FRN 1976 BOARD BREAK	$15.00	$35.00	$75.00

MISSING PRINTINGS

The missing printing error reaches circulation devoid of an entire impression. Technically, the first, second or third printing design elements might be absent.

To properly qualify as a missing printing error the note must have completely failed to receive any portion of the intended design at the skipped printing stage. Notes which demonstrate even the tiniest portion of the design originate from an alternate etiology and are not classified as missing printings.

When the error occurs in the first printing the results are a blank back. With the second printing the note is missing the black printing. If it occurs in the third printing, the seals, serial numbers, and district numbers are affected.

	ABP	VF	CU
$2 FRN 1976 MISSING FIRST PRINTING	$1500.00	$3000.00	$7500.00

	ABP	VF	CU
$1 FRN 19XX MISSING SECOND PRINTING	$350.00	$650.00	$950.00

	ABP	VF	CU
$1 FRN 1985 MISSING THIRD PRINTING	$200.00	$350.00	$550.00

FAULTY ALIGNMENT

The faulty alignment error results from an improper relationship between the printed design on one side of the note relative to the other. The currency sheet accepts the printing of one side off-register in comparison to the other side, which bears a correctly positioned image.

Faulty alignment errors are correctly centered on one side. This criterion differentiates a faulty alignment mistake from a cutting error.

MINOR

	ABP	VF	CU
$1 FRN 2003 FAULTY ALIGNMENT	$15.00	$30.00	$75.00

MODERATE

	ABP	VF	CU
$20 FRN 1988-A FAULTY ALIGNMENT	$35.00	$75.00	$200.00

MAJOR

	ABP	VF	CU
$1 FRN 1988-A FAULTY ALIGNMENT	$50.00	$150.00	$300.00

INSUFFICIENT INKING

The insufficient inking error develops when the ink fountain fails to fully charge or fill the printing plate with ink. The ink fountain stores the ink alongside the press. When the reservoir runs low, pressure weakens, or a partial obstruction in the supply tube occurs, inadequate amounts of ink flood the intaglio design in the plate. The net result is a printed image which is faint or incomplete.

The insufficient inking may affect all or part of the design, depending upon the area affected on the printing plate. Typically, the error involves a significant portion of, if not the entire design. However, isolated segments of insufficient ink are not uncommon. Predictably the larger the insufficiently inked area the greater the premium.

Most insufficient inking mistakes appear on the first or second printing. The overprint is occasionally affected. The typical presentation of insufficient ink on the third print involves a single digit in the serial number which in whole or part is absent.

MINOR

	ABP	VF	CU
$1 FRN 1988A INSUFFICIENT INKING	$50.00	$100.00	$250.00

MODERATE

	ABP	VF	CU
$5 FRN 1988A INSUFFICIENT INKING	$75.00	$150.00	$350.00

MAJOR

	ABP	VF	CU
$1 FRN 1988 INSUFFICIENT INKING	$150.00	$250.00	$500.00

MULTIPLE PRINTINGS

The multiple printing error bears the normal impression of the first, second, and third printing operations plus a complete or partial extra impression of one of the printings. The error can result from several causes. The most common origin involves a stack of imprinted sheets being re-fed through the press for a printing it has already received. This produces the sheet of notes with two complete images that are separated, as the sheet does not contact the printing plate in the identical location.

Multiple printings can also occur when a currency sheet enters the press and the press operator stops the machinery. The sheet subsequently returns to the beginning of the press and receives the complete impression of the design on the second pass through. In this instance, the head portion of the sheet will demonstrate a multiple printing, whereas the tail segment will posses a single impression only.

MINOR

	ABP	VF	CU
$10 FRN 1985 MULTIPLE PRINTING SERIAL NUMBERS	$250.00	$500.00	$1500.00

MODERATE

	ABP	VF	CU
$10 FRN 1977 MULTIPLE PRINTING 2ND PRINTING	$250.00	$650.00	$1500.00

MAJOR

	ABP	VF	CU
$2 FRN 1976 MULTIPLE 3RD PRINTING	$5000.00	$10,000.00	$19,500.00

MISALIGNED OVERPRINTS

Misaligned overprint errors are readily recognized by the eccentric placement of the final printing element. Typically, this involves the serial numbers and seals. The overprint may assume a skewed or shifted orientation.

The apparent shift in the overprint on the completed note usually results from the improper feeding of the currency sheet into the overprint press. The sheet enters the final printing operation at a angle or with unequal amounts of paper on the right and left sides. The overprint shift may also arise from an existing fold in the currency paper that affects the dimensions of the uncut half sheet and consequently alters the relative position of the notes receiving the final printing.

MINOR

	ABP	VF	CU
$5 FRN 1977 INSUFFICIENT INKING	$25.00	$50.00	$150.00

MODERATE

	ABP	VF	CU
$20 NTL 1929 MISALIGNED OVERPRINT	$750.00	$1750.00	$3500.00

MAJOR

	ABP	VF	CU
$1 FRN 2003 MISALIGNED OVERPRINT	$250.00	$750.00	$2500.00

INK SMEAR

Ink smears result from inadequately cleaned printing plates. The amount of residual ink left on the surface of the plate determines the size and shape of the smear, which may range from a fine line or small spot to a broad band covering the entire face or back design. The extra ink either obliterates a portion of the intended design or covers areas normally left blank. The value or premium commanded by an ink smear relates directly to the size of the excess ink.

MINOR

	ABP	VF	CU
$1 FRN 1969 INK SMEAR	$25.00	$50.00	$75.00

MODERATE

	ABP	VF	CU
$5 FRN 1969C INK SMEAR	$100.00	$250.00	$500.00

MAJOR

	ABP	VF	CU
$1 FRN 1988A INK SMEAR	$100.00	$250.00	$500.00

GUTTER OR INTERIOR FOLDS

Gutter or interior folds demonstrate a blank, unprinted, white channel interrupting the back face, or over printing. Gutter folds develop when a double wrinkle occurs in the currency paper as it receives a printed image. The pleated area remains protected and continues devoid of an impression. With the pleat or fold intact and undisturbed from its position at the time of printing, no error is apparent. The design appears complete and the note seems to conform to appropriate dimension. However, when the crease is opened, the characteristic white gutter disturbing the design becomes exposed.

Single gutter or interior folds involve an overlap of paper caused by the wrinkle. Not too infrequently, numerous wrinkles occur yielding a note with multiple gutters that open accordion style. Single and multiple gutters may affect only the face or back or both surfaces of a note. Gutter folds are the second most abundant error, lagging behind the ink smear mistakes.

MINOR

	ABP	VF	CU
$1 FRN 1963 GUTTER (INTERIOR FOLD)			
SINGLE	$10.00	$25.00	$40.00

MODERATE

	ABP	VF	CU
$1 SC 1935D GUTTER (INTERIOR FOLD)			
MULTIPLE	$25.00	$50.00	$100.00

MAJOR

	ABP	VF	CU
$5 FRN1977-A GUTTER (INTERIOR FOLD)			
SINGLE	$50.00	$150.00	$300.00

OBSTRUCTED PRINTINGS

Whenever stray material comes between the currency paper and the printing plate during a printing operation, an obstructed printing error occurs. Typically, a scrap of paper lies atop the unfinished sheet of currency stock as it passes through the press. However, other miscellaneous foreign items (such as tissue paper, cellophane, fiber thread, adhesive bandage backings, masking tape, clot, and cardboard, etc) may be responsible for a blank area on the bill. The design void on the completed note corresponds to the dimensions of the obstructing material.

In typical scenario, the scrap falls from the currency paper during the subsequent printing, cutting, and packaging stages. If the resulting white space on the note is not detected, the piece enters circulation, while the foreign scrap remains within the BEP. On rare occasions, the scrap adheres on the note throughout subsequent printing stages. With the errant material in place, no error may be apparent; however, upon removal the void becomes obvious. By possessing both portions, one is able to recreate and explain the occurrence. The obstructed print error retaining the foreign material ranks among the rarest and most valuable paper money mistakes.

MINOR

	ABP	VF	CU
$20 FRN 1969C OBSTRUCTED PRINTING	$50.00	$150.00	$300.00

MODERATE

	ABP	VF	CU
$5 FRN 1977 OBSTRUCTED PRINTING	$75.00	$200.00	$400.00

MAJOR

	ABP	VF	CU
$1 FRN 19XX OBSTRUCTED PRINTING	$100.00	$200.00	$500.00

MINOR

	ABP	VF	CU
$1 FRN 1977A OBSTRUCTED PRINTING WITH RETAINED FRAGMENT	$250.00	$500.00	$2500.00

MODERATE

	ABP	VF	CU
$5 FRN 1977 OBSTRUCTED PRINTING WITH RETAINED FRAGMENT	$250.00	$500.00	$2500.00

MAJOR

	ABP	VF	CU
$1 FRN 1988 OBSTRUCTED PRINTING WITH RETAINED FRAGMENT	$500.00	$1500.00	$3500.00

DOUBLE DENOMINATIONS

The double denomination reigns supreme among paper money errors. No other mistake conjures the romance, mystique, and fascination of the double denomination. In fact, across the entire spectrum of paper money collecting, very few notes equal the allure of the two-value oddity. More publicity is showered upon the double denomination than any other misprint.

The double denomination note —with the face and back each representing a different value—happens in a rather simple manner. After a currency sheet receives the back printing of one denomination, the sheet enters the face and overprinting operations for another denomination. The confusion presumably arises during the transportation of the currency stock to the second printing stage, after a storage period subsequent to the first printing.

Depending on the orientation of the note, the error is either blatantly obvious or totally obscure to the viewer.

When both sides of the notes are visible, as in turning a page in a book, the disparity in denominations is readily apparent. However, when either side is viewed independently no error shows, as each side is perfect unto itself.

	ABP	VF	CU
$10/$5 1928-A DOUBLE DENOMINATION	$10,000.00	$20,000.00	$35,000.00

INVERTED BACKS

In actuality, the so-called "inverted back" error is an inverted face. Although the verso appears upside down when viewing both sides of the note from the front, as in turning a page in a book, the traditional designation "inverted back" contradicts the printing sequence. At the BEP, the back of the note accepts the first printing operations and rightfully should serve as the reference to judge the alignment of subsequent printings.

The inverted back error arises when a stack of currency sheets, after receiving the first (or back) printing, rotates 180 degrees and enters the presses upside down for the face and overprinting stages. This type of mistake exists on virtually every category of United States paper money from colonial currency through fractional currency and military payment certificates to modern size Federal Reserve Notes.

	ABP	VF	CU
$1 SC 1923 INVERTED BACK	$300.00	$750.00	$2500.00

	ABP	VF	CU
$2 USN 1928 INVERTED BACK	$300.00	$750.00	$2500.00

CUTTING ERRORS

Cutting errors come in two distinct varieties. Both the precipitating cause and the resultant appearance are distinctly different. However, in both scenarios the mistake occurs after the currency stock correctly accepts the first, second, and third printings. The miscut arises during the terminal stages of production when the sixteen subject half-sheets are separated into two subject blocks and then into individual notes.

A cutting error generated by misalignment of the uncut sheets upon meeting the knives produces a batch of notes with identical mistakes. Typically, such an error contains most of a dominant primary note and varying degrees of a secondary note nestled within the confines of the dimensions prescribed for the class of paper money. The division can range from the finished product exhibiting equal parts of the primary and secondary notes (and consequently possessing two different serial numbers) to a primary note with an abnormally wide margin or simply the design border of the secondary note. The cutting error, unlike the faulty alignment mistake, demonstrates an equal amount of poor centering on both sides of the note. Not surprisingly, the value of this type of cutting error rests directly upon the amount of the secondary note present.

MINOR

	ABP	VF	CU
$20 FRN 1993 CUTTING ERROR	$25.00	$50.00	$100.00

MODERATE

	ABP	VF	CU
$20 FRN 1990 CUTTING ERROR	$200.00	$500.00	$1000.00

MAJOR

	ABP	VF	CU
$1 FRN 2006 CUTTING ERROR	$250.00	$500.00	$1500.00

CONFEDERATE MONEY

The Civil War Centennial of 1961–65 has generally been credited with sparking an interest in the collecting and study of Confederate or C.S.A. Notes. This, however, is not totally borne out by facts, as C.S.A. currency had advanced steadily in value since the 1940s. It rides a crest of popularity today surpassing that of the early 1960s. This is due in part to the exhaustive research carried out since that time and numerous books and articles published. Even today, some C.S.A. Notes would still appear to be undervalued based on their availability vs. regular U.S. issues.

History. It became apparent upon the outbreak of the Civil War that both sides would experience extreme coinage shortages, and each took to the printing of notes that could be exchanged in lieu of specie or "real money" (which always meant coined money until the 1860s). The South suffered more serious difficulties than the North as it never had a sufficient number of metal plate printing presses at its command. Also, with the war being fought on its territory rather than the North's, there was an ever-present danger of sabotage to plants printing money or engaging in related activities. The Confederacy tried by all available means to satisfy the currency demand and succeeded in distributing quite a large quantity of notes. Its shortage was taken up by notes issued by private banks, individual states, counties, cities and railroads. Merchant script, to take the place of rapidly disappearing small change, poured forth in abundance during this period. All told, the Confederate Congress authorized the printing of about one and a half billion dollars' worth of paper currency. It is impossible to determine the total actually produced, but it would appear that this figure was far surpassed. At the war's conclusion, these notes were worthless, as the C.S.A. no longer existed and the federal government refused to redeem them. Many were discarded as scrap, but a surprising number were held faithfully by their owners who believed "the South will rise again." The South did indeed rise, industrially and economically, and those old C.S.A. Notes rose, too. They still aren't spendable, but many are worth sums in excess of face value as collectors' pieces. Until about 1900, however, practically no value was placed on Confederate currency—even by collectors.

Designs. Some surprising designs will be observed, including mythological gods and goddesses that seem to relate very little to the Southern artistic or cultural climate of the 1860s. Many scholarly efforts have been made to explain away the use of such motifs, but the simple fact is that they appeared not so much by choice as by necessity. Southern printers, not having the facilities of their Northern counterparts, were compelled to make do with whatever engravings or "stock cuts" were already on hand, as inappropriate as they might have proved. However, a number of original designs were created reflecting unmistakably regional themes and at times picturing heroes or leaders of the Confederacy. Slaves at labor, used as a symbol of the South's economic strength and its supposed advantage over the North, where labor was hired, was a frequent motif. Sailors were also depicted, as well as railroad trains and anything else that appeared symbolic of Southern industry. Probably the most notable single design, not intended to carry the satirical overtones it now possesses, is "General Francis Marion's Sweet Potato Breakfast" on the $10 1861 issue note.

In general, the C.S.A. Notes are not so badly designed a group as might be anticipated in light of conditions. The designing was, in fact, several leagues improved over the printing, which often left much to be desired. George Washington is depicted—not for being the first U.S. President but as a native son of Virginia. Jefferson Davis, President of the C.S.A., is among the more common portraits. He became even more disliked in the North than he otherwise might have been because of his picture turning up on currency. But after the war he took a moderate stand and erased the old ill feelings; he even had words of praise for Lincoln. Other individuals whose portraits (not necessarily very faithful) will be encountered are:

- John C. Calhoun, U.S. Senator who led the battle for slavery and Southern Rights (later called "states rights")
- Alexander H. Stephen, Davis' Vice-President of the C.S.A.
- Judah P. Benjamin, Secretary of State and holder of various official titles in the Southern government
- C.G. Memminger, Secretary of the Treasury
- Lucy Pickens, "Queen of the South," was the wife of South Carolina's Governor. She is the only woman (aside from mythological types) shown on C.S.A. currency
- John E. Ward
- R.M.T. Hunter

Printers. The study of printers of C.S.A. notes is complex, made no less so by the fact that a few contractors only engraved plates and/or produced the transfers for others to print with, while a few firms had the ability to do both. Some notes were printed entirely from metal plates (intaglio), some entirely from stone plates (lithography) and some were printed by utilizing both techniques. National Bank Note Company in NYC printed the first notes. American Bank Note Company at New Orleans printed six Types after changing their imprint to Southern Bank Note Company for political reasons. Jules Manouvrier in New Orleans printed only one issue. Hoyer & Ludwig, the first strictly Southern printing firm, were soon followed by Keatinge & Ball, Blanton Duncan and Archer & Daly with print firms in Richmond. The move to Columbia in May of 1862 was made by Keatinge & Ball and Col. Duncan for security reasons. J.T. Paterson set up shop at the same time with Evans & Cogswell following about seven months later.

Cancellations. Several varieties of cancels are commonly found on C.S.A. notes. Most common of these is the Cut Cancel (CC), in which a sharp knife, razor or bank hammer was used to make piercings in a design or pattern. Unless roughly executed, such cuts do not reduce a specimen's value by much more than 10% to 15%. In the case of some notes, examples without cancellation are almost impossible to find. The COC, or Cut-Out Cancel, instead of leaving slits, a portion of the paper has been removed in the signature blocks along the bottom border. The reduction of value for a COC is about 30%. The HOC, or Hole-Out Cancel, is most objectionable because a large hole was made in the center of the note removing part of the design. The reduction of value for a HOC is 50% or more. Considered a "space filler" if the issue is fairly common, a scarce or rare note with HOC may be very desirable to some collectors. POC, or Punch-Out Cancel, is typically found on Types 1-11. These holes are very small and reduce the value of a note only about 20%. IC, or Ink Cancel, is where *Cancelled* is written across the face of the note in brown or red ink. Seldom encountered on CSA notes, it has little bearing on value. Whenever a note is being sold, presence of a cancel, of whatever type, should be plainly spelled out. Some collectors are not interested in canceled specimens. In time, as the scarce issues become even scarcer, they will probably have to be accepted as a fact of life.

Signatures. The first six notes issued, the four from Montgomery and T5 & 6 from Richmond, were hand-signed by the Register and Treasurer themselves. Thereafter, because the Treasury Secretary felt hand signatures helped prevent counterfeiting, and because of the quantities of notes spewing forth, clerks were hired to sign "for Register" and "for Treasurer." There were about 200 different people who signed for each Treasury official, making for thousands of signature combinations. Mostly the clerks were women, many the wives or daughters of soldiers who had been killed in action. Since the notes were signed in Richmond through April of 1864 (when all operations were removed to Columbia, South Carolina), most of the signers were from there. Some moved to Columbia, and others were hired there.

It is most interesting to many people to find that they had relatives who signed Confederate money, and many people search for such notes. A complete listing of all the names from the Confederate Records appears in Colonel Criswell's extensive book, *Confederate and Southern States Currency.*

Condition Grades. While condition standards are basically the same for Confederate currency as other notes of their age, some allowance must be made for paper quality and deficiencies in printing and cutting. These matters have nothing to do with the preservation or wear and can be observed just as frequently in Uncirculated specimens as in those in average condition. Without a source of good paper, printers were obliged to use whatever was most easily and quickly obtainable. Often the paper was thin, or stiff, or contained networks of minute wrinkles which interfered with printing. Cutting was generally not done by machine, as in the North, but by hand with a pair of scissors—workers actually took the sheets and cut apart notes individually. When paper-cutting devices were employed, they were apparently not of the best quality. In any case, regular edges on C.S.A. Notes are uncommon, and their absence does not constitute grounds for classifying an otherwise perfect specimen in a condition grade below Uncirculated. When the occasional gem is located—a well-printed, well-preserved note on good paper, decently cut—its value is sure to be higher than those listed. The collector is not advised to confine himself to such specimens, as his activities would become seriously limited.

Uncirculated—UNC. An Uncirculated note shows no evidence of handling and is as close to "new condition" as possible. An Uncirculated specimen may, however, have pinholes or a finger smudge, which should be mentioned in a sales offering. If these are readily noticeable, the note deserves to be classified as "Almost Uncirculated." Crispness is hardly a criterion of uncirculation as this quality is expected in notes graded as low as Very Fine.

Almost Uncirculated—A.U. Similar to the above grade, but not quite as good as an Uncirculated specimen. The note bears no indication of having actually circulated other than minor handling such as counting smudges and bent corners.

Extremely Fine—X.F. An X.F. note is on the borderline between Uncirculated and Circulated. It has not been heavily handled but may reveal several imperfections: a pinhole, finger smudge, counting crinkles, or a light wallet fold. The fold is not so heavy as to be termed a crease.

Very Fine—V.F. Has been in circulation but is not worn or seriously creased. It must still be clean and crisp, without stains or tears. Average Circulated for most CSA Type Notes is a split grade of Fine to Very Fine by today's standards.

Fine—F. A note that has been in circulation and shows it, but has no physical injuries or just slight ones.

Very Good—V.G. A well-circulated note bearing evidence of numerous foldings. It may possibly have creased corners and wrinkles as well as light staining, smudging, or pinholes, but major defects (such as a missing corner) would place it into an even lower category.

Good—G. Good notes have been heavily circulated, worn, possibly stained or scribbled on edges, could be frayed or "dog-eared." There may be holes larger than pin punctures, but not on the central portion of design. This is the lowest grade of condition acceptable to a collector, and only when nothing better is available. Unless very rare, such specimens are considered space-fillers only.

Average Buying Prices—A.B.P. The Average Buying Prices given here are the approximate sums paid by retail dealers for specimens in Good condition. As selling prices vary, so do buying prices, and in fact they usually vary more. A dealer who is overstocked on a certain note is sure to offer less than one who has no specimens on hand. The dealer's location, size of operation, and other circumstances will also influence the buying price. We present these figures merely as approximate guides to what sellers should expect.

Type Numbers. Each Confederate note pictured in this book has a Criswell "Type" number next to the image. The variety numbers for each Criswell Type are listed at the beginning of each of the price listings.

FOR MORE INFORMATION

Considered to have been the foremost authority on Confederate currency in his day, the late Col. Grover C. Criswell published a wide variety of books and pamphlets from 1957-1996. His last release, *Confederate Paper*

Money (5th Edition, 1996), covers in depth all the major varieties for each Confederate Type Note illustrated in this book as well as most of the known counterfeits. His previous edition, *Confederate and Southern States Currency* (4th Edition—1992), which was his first to introduce counterfeits, covered all the currency issued by the Confederate States Central Government, the Southern States, the Indian Territories, the Florida Republic and Territory, and the Republic of Texas. His works provided both casual readers and serious students with historical background and indepth information for over 40 years. The one book that covers it all and is still considered the most comprehensive reference tool in use today is his 4th Edition. New and used copies may still be purchased from numismatic dealers and book retailers priced from $25 to $50.

Crutch Williams:

A full time Numismatist since 1968, Crutch Williams is now semi-retired. He has held consulting positions with several numismatic firms over the years. He started his online business, *Crutchfield's Currency*, in February of 1994. Crutch is always happy to assist any collector, dealer, student or museum with any type project and/or answer questions regarding any aspect of paper money.

Dealer & Numismatic Associations

- American Numismatic Association (ANA LM-1543) *Since 1968*
- Professional Currency Dealers Association
- Society of Paper Money Collectors (SPMC LM-0025)
- International Bank Note Society (IBNS LM-128)
- Professional Currency Grading Service (PCGS #689)
- Numismatic Guaranty Corporation (NGC #465)
- Also <u>Life Member:</u> TNA, ANS, CSNA, FUN

<u>ANA</u> MEMBER
LM-1543

SOCIETY OF PAPER MONEY COLLECTORS INC.
LM-0025

LM-128

Pcda PROFESSIONAL CURRENCY DEALERS ASSOCIATION

WM. "CRUTCH" WILLIAMS II

Founder: CSA Trainmen   www.CSATrainmen.com

CONFEDERATE STATES OF AMERICA—
1861 ISSUE, MONTGOMERY, ALABAMA
$1,000,000 authorized by "Act of March 9th."
Written dates "1861."
"NATIONAL BANK NOTE CO., NY"

TYPE
1

Face Design: Green and black, bears "Interest Ten Cents Per Day,"
607 issued. John C. Calhoun left, Andrew Jackson right.

CRISWELL	NOTE	A.B.P.	GOOD	UNC.
☐1	$1000	7000.00	10,000.00	RARE

"NATIONAL BANK NOTE CO., NY"

TYPE
2

Face Design: Green and black, bears "Interest Five Cents Per Day,"
607 issued. Cattle crossing a brook.

CRISWELL	NOTE	A.B.P.	GOOD	UNC.
☐2	$500	9000.00	12,500.00	RARE

CONFEDERATE STATES OF AMERICA—
1861 ISSUE
"NATIONAL BANK NOTE CO., NY"

TYPE
3

Face Design: Green and black, bears "Interest One Cent Per Day."
Railway train, Minerva left.

CRISWELL	NOTE	A.B.P.	GOOD	UNC.
☐3	$100	4000.00	6500.00	VERY SCARCE

"NATIONAL BANK NOTE CO., NY"

TYPE
4

Face Design: Green and black, bears "Interest Half A Cent Per Day."
Negroes hoeing cotton.

CRISWELL	NOTE	A.B.P.	GOOD	UNC.
☐4	$50	3500.00	6000.00	VERY SCARCE

CONFEDERATE STATES OF AMERICA—1861 ISSUE
"AMERICAN BANK NOTE CO., NY"
(Though ostensibly by the "SOUTHERN BANK NOTE CO.")

TYPE
5

Face Design: Green and black, red fibre paper, bears "Interest One Cent Per
Day." Railway train, Justice left and Minerva right.

CRISWELL	NOTE	A.B.P.	GOOD	UNC.
☐5	$100	550.00	900.00	3000.00

TYPE
6

Face Design: Green and black, red fibre paper, bears "Interest Half A Cent
Per Day." Pallas and Ceres seated on bale of cotton, Washington at right.

CRISWELL	NOTE	A.B.P.	GOOD	UNC.
☐6	$50	500.00	850.00	2750.00

CONFEDERATE STATES OF AMERICA—1861 ISSUE
$20,000,000 authorized by "Act of May 16th, 1861"
(All lithographic date "July 25th, 1861")
"HOYER & LUDWIG, RICHMOND, VA"

TYPE
7

Face Design: Ceres and Proserpina flying, Washington left.

CRISWELL	NOTE	A.B.P.	GOOD	UNC.
☐7-13	$100	450.00	750.00	3000.00

TYPE
8

Face Design: Washington, Tellus left.

CRISWELL	NOTE	A.B.P.	GOOD	UNC.
☐14-22	$50	100.00	150.00	600.00

CONFEDERATE STATES OF AMERICA—1861 ISSUE

TYPE
XXI

Face Design: Female Riding Deer, Indian Smoking Pipe, red-orange tint.

CRISWELL	NOTE	A.B.P.	GOOD	UNC.
☐XXI	$20 Original	150.00	200.00	500.00
☐XXI	$20 Reprint	75.00	125.00	250.00

Samuel Upham of Philadelphia is known to have printed examples of this note in 1863 to sell as souvenirs of the War of the Rebellion. He claimed no credit for the satirical design and no proof has ever surfaced as to where the design originated. It has been written that a few early collectors thought it might have been a crude Confederate issue because it existed during the War, but that theory was already being discarded by 1877. Classified as a bogus fantasy note for well over 135 years, the fact it was never a real note has never dampened collector interest. In fact, collector demand was so great that reprints were made to satisfy that demand well into the 1930s. The originals have a straight back leg on the R in Richmond and are blank on the back. On the reprints, the back leg looks like a fish hook or a J. Many of the reprints also have reverse designs. All examples are collectible and "*No collection of Confederate Notes is complete without one!*"

TYPE
9

CRISWELL	NOTE	A.B.P.	GOOD	UNC.
☐23-33	$20	75.00	110.00	550.00

CONFEDERATE STATES OF AMERICA—1861 ISSUE

TYPE
10

Face Design: Liberty seated by eagle, with shield and flag.

There are at least forty-two minor varieties of this note, including a supposed ten or eleven stars on shield. Usually the stars are so indistinct that a note may show from six to fifteen stars. The other differences are minute changes in the size of the "10" in the upper corners. We list only the major type.

CRISWELL	NOTE	A.B.P.	GOOD	UNC.
☐34-41	$10	150.00	225.00	RARE

TYPE
11

Face Design: Liberty seated by eagle, sailor left.

CRISWELL	NOTE	A.B.P.	GOOD	UNC.
☐42-45	$5	750.00	1250.00	VERY RARE

CONFEDERATE STATES OF AMERICA—1861 ISSUE
(Written date "July 25th, 1861")
"J. MANOUVRIER, NEW ORLEANS"

TYPE
12

Back Design: CONFEDERATE STATES OF AMERICA and two large V in blue ink.
This is the only 1861 note that has a reverse design.

CRISWELL	NOTE	A.B.P.	GOOD	UNC.
☐46-49	$5	900.00	1500.00	RARE

$100,000,000 authorized by "Act of Aug. 19th, 1861."
$50,000,000 authorized by "Act of Dec. 24th, 1861."
"HOYER & LUDWIG, RICHMOND, VA"

TYPE
13

(Lithographic date "September 2nd, 2d, & s, 1861")
Face Design: Negroes loading cotton, sailor left.

CRISWELL	NOTE	A.B.P.	GOOD	UNC.
☐50-58	$100	60.00	100.00	400.00

CONFEDERATE STATES OF AMERICA—1861 ISSUE

TYPE 14

Face Design: Moneta seated by treasure chests, sailor left.

CRISWELL	NOTE	A.B.P.	GOOD	UNC.
☐59-78	$50	45.00	75.00	375.00

"SOUTHERN BANK NOTE CO., NEW ORLEANS"

TYPE 15

Face Design: Black and red on red fibre paper. Railway train, Justice right, Hope with anchor left.

CRISWELL	NOTE	A.B.P.	GOOD	UNC.
☐79	$50	1300.00	1800.00	RARE

CONFEDERATE STATES OF AMERICA—1861 ISSUE
"KEATINGE & BALL, RICHMOND, VA"

TYPE
16

Face Design: Black and green, red fibre paper. Portrait of Jefferson Davis.

CRISWELL	NOTE	A.B.P.	GOOD	UNC.
☐80-98	$50	100.00	150.00	1500.00

"HOYER & LUDWIG, RICHMOND, VA"

TYPE
17

Face Design: Black with green ornamentation, plain paper. Ceres seated
between Commerce and Navigation, Liberty left.

CRISWELL	NOTE	A.B.P.	GOOD	UNC.
☐99-100	$20	400.00	600.00	3500.00

CONFEDERATE STATES OF AMERICA—1861 ISSUE
"HOYER & LUDWIG, RICHMOND, VA"

TYPE
18

Face Design: Large sailing vessel, sailor at capstan left.

CRISWELL	NOTE	A.B.P.	GOOD	UNC.
☐101-136	$20	15.00	35.00	200.00

"SOUTHERN BANK NOTE CO., NEW ORLEANS"

TYPE
19

Face Design: Black and red on red fibre paper. Navigator seated by charts, Minerva left, blacksmith right.

CRISWELL	NOTE	A.B.P.	GOOD	UNC.
☐137	$20	1200.00	1700.00	RARE

CONFEDERATE STATES OF AMERICA—1861 ISSUE
"B. DUNCAN, COLUMBIA, SC"

TYPE
20

Face Design: Industry seated between cupid and beehive, bust of A. H.
Stephens left.

CRISWELL	NOTE	A.B.P.	GOOD	UNC.
☐139-143	$20	20.00	35.00	275.00

"KEATINGE & BALL, COLUMBIA, SC"

TYPE
21

Face Design: Portrait of Alexander H. Stephens.

CRISWELL	NOTE	A.B.P.	GOOD	UNC.
☐144-149	$20	125.00	250.00	2500.00

CONFEDERATE STATES OF AMERICA—1861 ISSUE
"SOUTHERN BANK NOTE CO., NEW ORLEANS"

TYPE
22

Face Design: Black and red, red fibre paper. Group of Indians, Thetis left, maiden with "X" at right.

CRISWELL	NOTE	A.B.P.	GOOD	UNC.
☐150-152	$10	250.00	350.00	SCARCE

"LEGGETT, KEATINGE & BALL, RICHMOND, VA"

TYPE
23

Face Design: Black and orange/red. Wagonload of cotton, harvesting sugar cane right. John E. Ward left.

CRISWELL	NOTE	A.B.P.	GOOD	UNC.
☐153-155	$10	500.00	750.00	VERY SCARCE

CONFEDERATE STATES OF AMERICA—1861 ISSUE
"LEGGETT, KEATINGE & BALL, RICHMOND, VA"

TYPE
24

Face Design: Black and orange/red. R.M.T. Hunter left, vignette of child right.

CRISWELL	NOTE	A.B.P.	GOOD	UNC.
☐156-167	$10	100.00	150.00	2000.00

"KEATINGE & BALL, RICHMOND, VA"

TYPE
25

Face Design: Hope with anchor, R.M.T. Hunter left, C. G. Memminger right.

CRISWELL	NOTE	A.B.P.	GOOD	UNC.
☐168-171	$10	150.00	225.00	1250.00

CONFEDERATE STATES OF AMERICA—1861 ISSUE
"KEATINGE & BALL, RICHMOND, VA"

TYPE 26

Face Design: Hope with anchor, R.M.T. Hunter left, C.G. Memminger right.

Face Design: *Solid red "X" and "X" overprint.

CRISWELL	NOTE	A.B.P.	GOOD	UNC.
☐173-214	$10	40.00	70.00	2000.00

*There are three types of red "X" and "X" overprints. That section of the note on which the overprints appear is illustrated in double size.

Face Design: *Coarse lace "X" and "X" red overprint.

Face Dosign: Fine lace "X" and "X" red overprint.*

Face Design: Liberty seated by shield and eagle.

TYPE
27

CRISWELL	NOTE	A.B.P.	GOOD	UNC.
☐221-229	$10	5000.00	7500.00	EXTREMELY RARE

CONFEDERATE STATES OF AMERICA—1861 ISSUE
"HOYER & LUDWIG, RICHMOND, VA"

Face Design: Ceres and Commerce with an urn.

TYPE
28

CRISWELL	NOTE	A.B.P.	GOOD	UNC.
☐230-236	$10	25.00	40.00	1100.00

"B. DUNCAN, RICHMOND, VA"

TYPE 29

Face Design: Negro picking cotton.

CRISWELL	NOTE	A.B.P.	GOOD	UNC.
☐237	$10	100.00	150.00	SCARCE

CONFEDERATE STATES OF AMERICA—1861 ISSUE
"B. DUNCAN, COLUMBIA, SC"

TYPE 30

Face Design: Gen. Francis Marion's "Sweet Potato Dinner." R. M. T. Hunter left, Minerva right.

CCRISWELL	NOTE	A.B.P.	GOOD	UNC.
☐238-241	$10	20.00	40.00	900.00

"SOUTHERN BANK NOTE CO., NEW ORLEANS"

**TYPE
31**

Face Design: Black and red on red fibre paper. Minerva left; Agriculture, Commerce, Industry, Justice, and Liberty seated at center; statue of Washington right.

CRISWELL	NOTE	A.B.P.	GOOD	UNC.
☐243-245	$5	200.00	275.00	SCARCE

CONFEDERATE STATES OF AMERICA—1861 ISSUE
"LEGGETT, KEATINGE & BALL, RICHMOND, VA"

**TYPE
32**

Face Design: Black and orange/red. Machinist with hammer, boy in oval left.

CRISWELL	NOTE	A.B.P.	GOOD	UNC.
☐246-249	$5	450.00	700.00	SCARCE

"LEGGETT, KEATINGE & BALL, RICHMOND, VA"

TYPE
33

Face Design: Black and white note with blue-green ornamentation.
C.G. Memminger, Minerva right.

CRISWELL	NOTE	A.B.P.	GOOD	UNC.
☐250-256	$5	150.00	250.00	SCARCE

CONFEDERATE STATES OF AMERICA—1861 ISSUE
"KEATINGE & BALL, RICHMOND, VA"

TYPE
34

Face Design: C.G. Memminger, Minerva right.

CRISWELL	NOTE	A.B.P.	GOOD	UNC.
☐262-270	$5	65.00	95.00	1500.00

"HOYER & LUDWIG, RICHMOND, VA"

TYPE 35

Face Design: Loading cotton left, Indian princess right.

CRISWELL	NOTE	A.B.P.	GOOD	UNC.
☐271	$5	6000.00	8500.00	EXTREMELY RARE

CONFEDERATE STATES OF AMERICA—1861 ISSUE
"HOYER & LUDWIG, RICHMOND, VA"

TYPE 36

Face Design: Ceres seated on bale of cotton, sailor left.

CRISWELL	NOTE	A.B.P.	GOOD	UNC.
☐272-282	$5	15.00	35.00	350.00

CONFEDERATE STATES OF AMERICA—1861 ISSUE
"B. DUNCAN, RICHMOND, VA"

TYPE 37

Face Design: Sailor seated beside bales of cotton, C.G. Memminger left, Justice and Ceres right.

CRISWELL	NOTE	A.B.P.	GOOD	UNC.
□284-285	$5	30.00	50.00	1000.00

"B. DUNCAN, COLUMBIA, SC"

TYPE 38

Face Design: Personification of South striking down Union, J.P. Benjamin left. Dated "September 2, 1861" through an error. No Confederate Note less than $5 was authorized in 1861.

CRISWELL	NOTE	A.B.P.	GOOD	UNC.
□286	$2	250.00	350.00	VERY SCARCE

CONFEDERATE STATES OF AMERICA—1862 ISSUE
$165,000,000 Authorized by "Act of April 17th."
"HOYER & LUDWIG, RICHMOND, VA."

TYPE
39

Face Design: Railway train, straight steam from locomotive, milkmaid left.
Bears "Interest at Two Cents Per Day."

CRISWELL	NOTE	A.B.P.	GOOD	UNC.
☐287-289	$100	40.00	65.00	350.00

Dated May 5 to May 9, 1862

J.T. PATERSON, COLUMBIA, S.C. (At Lower Left)

☐290-293	$100	30.00	45.00	175.00

VARIOUS WRITTEN DATES, JUNE 4th–JULY 28th, 1862

J.T. PATERSON, COLUMBIA, S.C. (At Lower Right)

☐294-296	$100	30.00	45.00	150.00

VARIOUS WRITTEN DATES, JULY 24th–SEPTEMBER 12th, 1862

TYPE
40

"J.T. PATERSON, COLUMBIA, S.C."
Face Design: Railway train, diffused steam from locomotive, milkmaid left.
Bears "Interest at Two Cents Per Day."

CRISWELL	NOTE	A.B.P.	GOOD	UNC.
☐298-309	$100	30.00	45.00	180.00

VARIOUS WRITTEN DATES, AUGUST 9th–JANUARY 16th, 1862

CONFEDERATE STATES OF AMERICA—1862 ISSUE
"KEATINGE & BALL, COLUMBIA, S.C."
On the following notes there are two types of ornamental scrolls in the upper right corners.

TYPE 41

Face Design: "HUNDRED" red-orange underprint. Bears "Interest at Two Cents Per Day." Negroes hoeing cotton, J.C. Calhoun left, Columbia right.

CRISWELL	NOTE	A.B.P.	GOOD	UNC.
☐310-314	$100	80.00	120.00	375.00

Completely Handwritten Date: Aug 26th or Aug 30th, 1862 (Scroll No. 1)

☐315-324	$100	45.00	55.00	225.00

Written dates, AUG. to DEC. "1862." ("186" of date is engraved.)

☐325-331	$100	55.00	75.00	275.00

Dated January 1st–January 6th, 1863.

C.S.A. Trainmen
The CSA Trainmen study Confederate Treasury history and research these 1862 Interest Hundreds, also known as 730 Notes. These notes were issued from many different locations and interest was paid by both civil and military Agents. For more information on the People, Places and Stamps found on these notes, visit:

www.CSATrainmen.com

CONFEDERATE STATES OF AMERICA—1862 ISSUE
$5,000,000 authorized by "Act of April 18th, 1862"
$5,000,000 authorized by "Act of September 23rd, 1862"
"B. DUNCAN, COLUMBIA, S.C."

TYPE 42

Face Design: Personification of South striking down Union, J.P. Benjamin left.

CRISWELL	NOTE	A.B.P.	GOOD	UNC.
☐334-337	$2	15.00	25.00	300.00

TYPE 43

Face Design: "2" and "Two" green underprint. Personification of South striking down Union, J.P. Benjamin left.

CRISWELL	NOTE	A.B.P.	GOOD	UNC.
☐338	$2	35.00	55.00	RARE

CONFEDERATE STATES OF AMERICA—1862 ISSUE

TYPE
44

Face Design: Steamship at sea. Lucy Holcombe Pickens right. Liberty left.

CRISWELL	NOTE	A.B.P.	GOOD	UNC.
☐339-341	$1	20.00	35.00	400.00

TYPE
45

Face Design: "1" and "One" green underprint. Steamship at sea. Lucy Holcombe Pickens right. Liberty left.

CRISWELL	NOTE	A.B.P.	GOOD	UNC.
☐342-342A	$1	35.00	55.00	2000.00

CONFEDERATE STATES OF AMERICA—1862 ISSUE

"September 2, 1862." No engraver name.

TYPE
46

Face Design: Ceres reclining on cotton bales. R.M.T. Hunter at right.

CRISWELL	NOTE	A.B.P.	GOOD	UNC.
☐343-344	$10	45.00	75.00	750.00

Essay Notes
September 2, 1862
"KEATINGE & BALL, COLUMBUS, S.C."
Printed Signatures

TYPE
47

Please note that it is **COLUMBIA** and not Liberty seated on cotton bale!
Face Design: Columbia seated on bale of cotton. R.M.T. Hunter right.

CRISWELL	NOTE	A.B.P.	GOOD	UNC.
☐345	$20		EXTREMELY RARE	

CONFEDERATE STATES OF AMERICA—1862 ISSUE

TYPE 48

Face Design: Ceres holding sheaf of wheat. R.M.T. Hunter right.

CRISWELL	NOTE	A.B.P.	GOOD	UNC.
☐346	$10		EXTREMELY RARE	

ESSAY NOTES

The Essay Notes (T47 & T48) are not regular issues. They are Model Notes that the Treasury Note Division at Columbia used for the experiment of adding signatures printed facsimile. Printing signatures, instead of the notes being hand signed, was a practice adopted in the North early in 1862 to save time. This practice was never adopted in the South. Evidence does exist that some of these notes were paid out and/or passed to Confederate soldiers by paymasters, railroad conductors and merchants between January and June of 1863. How and why these notes reached circulation and who introduced them are questions we may never have answers to. While Essay Notes are a desirable and ambitious addition to anyone's collection, they are not necessary for the completion of a regular Issue C. S. A. Type Set!

CONFEDERATE STATES OF AMERICA—1862 ISSUE
$90,000,000 authorized by "Act of Oct. 13th, 1862"
"KEATINGE & BALL, COLUMBIA S.C."
December 2nd, 1862

Face Design: Fancy green reverse. Lucy Holcombe Pickens. George W. Randolph right.

TYPE 49

CRISWELL	NOTE	A.B.P.	GOOD	UNC.
☐347-349	$100	75.00	150.00	950.00

CONFEDERATE STATES OF AMERICA—1862 ISSUE
"KEATINGE & BALL, RICHMOND, VA." (THIRD SERIES)

TYPE
50

Face Design: Black and green. Ornate green reverse. Jefferson Davis.

CRISWELL	NOTE	A.B.P.	GOOD	UNC.
☐350-362	$50	100.00	175.00	1250.00

CONFEDERATE STATES OF AMERICA—1862 ISSUE
"KEATINGE & BALL, COLUMBIA, S.C."

TYPE
51

Face Design: Fancy blue reverse. State Capitol at Nashville, Tennessee.
A.H. Stephens.

CRISWELL	NOTE	A.B.P.	GOOD	UNC.
☐363-368	$20	25.00	45.00	550.00

CONFEDERATE STATES OF AMERICA—1862 ISSUE

TYPE
52

Face Design: Fancy blue reverse. State Capitol at Columbia S.C., R.M.T. Hunter. Printed on pink paper.

CRISWELL	NOTE	A.B.P.	GOOD	UNC.
☐369-378	$10	15.00	30.00	225.00

TYPE
53

Face Design: Fancy blue reverse. State Capitol at Richmond, VA., C.G. Memminger. Printed on pink paper.

There are many varieties of printers names on notes of this issue, though all have the same engraver's names. In general, the only valuable ones are those with two "Printers" names.

CRISWELL	NOTE	A.B.P.	GOOD	UNC.
☐379-390	$5	15.00	30.00	235.00

TYPE 54

Face Design: Judah P. Benjamin. Printed on pink paper.

CRISWELL	NOTE		A.B.P.	GOOD	UNC.
☐391-396	$2		30.00	50.00	225.00

TYPE 55

Face Design: Clement C. Clay. Printed on pink paper.

CRISWELL	NOTE		A.B.P.	GOOD	UNC.
☐397-401	$1		25.00	40.00	275.00

CONFEDERATE STATES OF AMERICA—1863

$50,000,000 authorized monthly, from April 1863 to January 1864, "By Act of March 23rd, 1863."

All notes of this year are dated April 6th, 1863, but a red overprinted date appears on all the $5, $10, $20, $50, and $100 denominations showing the year and month of issue.

"KEATINGE & BALL, COLUMBIA, S.C."

TYPE 56

Face Design: Green reverse. Lucy H. Pickens. Two soldiers left. George W. Randolph right.

CRISWELL	NOTE		A.B.P.	GOOD	UNC.
☐402-404	$100		60.00	125.00	350.00

"KEATINGE & BALL, RICHMOND, VA."

TYPE 57

Face Design: Green and black, ornate green reverse, Jefferson Davis.

CRISWELL	NOTE	A.B.P.	GOOD	UNC.
☐406-417	$50	45.00	75.00	325.00

CONFEDERATE STATES OF AMERICA—1863

TYPE 58

Face Design: Fancy blue reverse. State Capitol at Nashville, TN., A.H. Stephens.

CRISWELL	NOTE	A.B.P.	GOOD	UNC.
☐418-428	$20	20.00	35.00	325.00

**TYPE
59**

Face Design: Blue back. State Capitol at Columbia, S.C., R.M.T. Hunter.

CRISWELL	NOTE	A.B.P.	GOOD	UNC.
☐429-447	$10	15.00	25.00	225.00

Engravers' names on lower margin.

**TYPE
60**

Face Design: Fancy blue reverse. State Capitol at Richmond, VA.
C.G. Memminger.

CRISWELL	NOTE	A.B.P.	GOOD	UNC.
☐448-469	$5	15.00	25.00	200.00

Pink Paper.

**TYPE
61**

Face Design: Judah P. Benjamin.

CRISWELL	NOTE	A.B.P.	GOOD	UNC.
☐470-473	$2	30.00	45.00	750.00

**TYPE
62**

Face Design: Clement C. Clay. Pink Paper.

CRISWELL	NOTE	A.B.P.	GOOD	UNC.
☐474-484	$1	20.00	35.00	200.00

"ARCHER & DALY, RICHMOND, VA."

**TYPE
63**

Face Design: Bust of Jefferson Davis. Pink Paper.

CRISWELL	NOTE	A.B.P.	GOOD	UNC.
☐485-488	50 Cents	10.00	25.00	65.00

CONFEDERATE STATES OF AMERICA—1864

$200,000,000 was authorized by "Act of February 17th, 1864."
All notes of this year are dated "Feb. 17th, 1864."

The actual amount issued was probably ten times the figure given above and the amount printed even greater. Thus, there are many minor varieties of each type including color variations, flourishes, and more signature combinations than any other year. The authors list only the **important** types. The most common Confederate Notes appear in this year.

"KEATINGE & BALL, COLUMBIA, S.C."

TYPE
64

Face Design: Reddish horizontal line background. Equestrian statue of Washington and Confederate flag at left. Gen. T.J. "Stonewall" Jackson right.

CRISWELL	NOTE	A.B.P.	GOOD	UNC.
☐489-489B	$500	150.00	250.00	875.00

Criswell's famous so-called "HAVANA COUNTERFEIT."

Same as $100 Note illustrated on the next page, but
1/4 inch narrower, and 1/4 inch shorter.
This note only exists in Serial Letter "D."

CRISWELL	NOTE	A.B.P.	GOOD	UNC.
☐ 492	$100	40.00	60.00	125.00

Although labeled a counterfeit since 1957, this note was listed in Bradbeer, Chase and Fuller as genuine, and evidence exists proving that it was accepted as such in the Confederacy. It is an excellent copy, in some ways better engraved than the normal notes, but is easily distinguishable by its slightly smaller size. It is listed separately from the regular issues in this book because few collectors desire to be without one. It is by far the most popular of the *so-called* counterfeit Confederate Type Notes.

TYPE 65

Face Design: Reddish network background. Intricate blue reverse with "Hundred" in large letters. Lucy Pickens. Two soldiers left. George W. Randolph right.

CRISWELL	NOTE	A.B.P.	GOOD	UNC.
☐490-494	$100	25.00	45.00	180.00

TYPE 66

Face Design: Reddish network background. Intricate blue reverse with "Fifty" in large letters. Jefferson Davis.

CRISWELL	NOTE	A.B.P.	GOOD	UNC.
☐495-503	$50	25.00	40.00	110.00

TYPE 67

Face Design: Reddish network background. Intricate blue reverse with "Twenty" in large letters. State Capitol at Nashville, TN. A.H. Stephens right.

CRISWELL	NOTE	A.B.P.	GOOD	UNC.
☐504-539	$20	15.00	25.00	75.00

"KEATINGE & BALL, COLUMBIA, S.C."
("PTD. BY EVANS & COGSWELL" On left end)

**TYPE
68**

Face Design: Reddish network background. Intricate blue reverse with "Ten" in large letters. Horses pulling cannon. R.M.T. Hunter at right.

CRISWELL	NOTE	A.B.P.	GOOD	UNC.
☐540-553	$10	15.00	25.00	55.00

"KEATINGE & BALL, COLUMBIA, S.C."

**TYPE
69**

Face Design: Reddish network background. Intricate blue reverse with "Five" in large letters. State Capitol at Richmond, VA. C.G. Memminger at right.

CRISWELL	NOTE	A.B.P.	GOOD	UNC.
☐558-565	$5	15.00	25.00	65.00

TYPE 70

Face Design: Reddish network background. Judah P. Benjamin.

CRISWELL	NOTE	A.B.P.	GOOD	UNC.
☐566-571	$2	25.00	40.00	95.00

TYPE 71

Face Design: Reddish network background. Clement C. Clay.

CRISWELL	NOTE	A.B.P.	GOOD	UNC.
☐572-577	$1	35.00	50.00	195.00

"ENGRAVED BY ARCHER & HALPIN, RICHMOND, VA."

TYPE 72

Face Design: Bust of Jefferson Davis. Pink Paper.

CRISWELL	NOTE	A.B.P.	GOOD	UNC.
☐578-579	50 Cents	15.00	25.00	65.00

The Blackbooks!